The FLOWER EXPERT

Dr. D. G. Hessayon

All Editions & Reprints: 2,695,000 copies

First published 1999
This edition 1999
Reprinted 2003

Published by Expert Books
a division of Transworld Publishers

TRANSWORLD PUBLISHERS
61-63 Uxbridge Road, London W5 5SA
a division of the Random House Group Ltd

 Distributed in the United States
by Sterling Publishing Co. Inc.,
387 Park Avenue South,
New York,
NY 10016-8810

EXPERT BOOKS

Contents

Reproduction by Spot On Digital Imaging Ltd., Gomm Road, High Wycombe, Bucks.,HP13 7DJ
Printed and bound by Mohn Media Mohndruck GmbH

ISBN 0 903505 52 5
© D.G.HESSAYON 2003

CHAPTER 1

INTRODUCTION

The world around us has seen many changes since The Flower Expert first appeared in 1984. There is now a mobile phone in our pocket or handbag and a personal computer on the desk. Internet and digital, BSE and EMU — to get away from all this change it is comforting to be able to look over the neighbour's fence and see that at least the world of garden flowers has stayed the same.

As always Snowdrops herald in the New Year and shortly afterwards Daffodils and Crocuses provide splashes of yellow, mauve, white and blue in the grass and under trees. As the days get longer the flower beds begin to display their spring colours — yellow and orange Wallflowers, blue Forget-me-nots and the multicolours of Tulips and Pansies. Alongside the colourful beds is the rockery which is lit up in April by sheets of Aubrieta, Arabis and Alyssum saxatile.

This is the bright scene we have seen in each spring since our childhood, but as usual early summer is a rather barren time for garden flowers. That changes in midsummer when we see the flower garden in its full glory. In the herbaceous and mixed border are the perennials — Delphinium, Achillea, Phlox, Geum, Pinks, Lupin and all the rest. In the beds now cleared of Wallflowers and Tulips are the bedding plants — Geraniums, Lobelia, Alyssum, Salvia, Tagetes, Antirrhinum and so on. Then the days shorten and as always the late-flowering types take over. This is the time when year after year the autumn favourites appear — plants like large-flowered Chrysanthemum, Dahlia, Fuchsia, Sedum spectabile and Michaelmas Daisy.

Nothing may seemed to have changed in the traditional floral year and in the world of garden flowers since the first edition of The Flower Expert, but we see a different picture if we look a little more closely. Growing plants in containers is now much more widely practised, and the range of bedding plants to fill them has widened.

There are new names in the catalogues — Scaevola, Bidens, Bacopa, Eustoma, Laurentia, Diascia, Cuphea, Mina etc. Even old names like Petunia and Verbena have been enriched by the introduction of the Surfinia and Tapien ranges. Take another look over your neighbour's fence — these days you may find a bed or container filled with winter-flowering bedding plants such as Polyanthus 'Crescendo' and Universal Pansies rather than Wallflowers waiting for the spring. There have been changes, then —in this book several thousand varieties of garden flowers are described and hundreds of them are introductions of the 1980s and 1990s. Changes have not been restricted to new genera, species and varieties — the idea of buying seedlings and plugs and then growing them on before planting out has become more popular and the range of plants on offer in this form has increased.

New plants, new ways of buying some of them .... and new names. Here and there in the A-Z guide you will find that some plants have been given new Latin names since the previous edition. The most outstanding example is the genus Chrysanthemum which has been split up all over the place. The showy Mums are now Dendranthema and the old favourite Shasta Daisy is Leucanthemum.

So things have not stood still in the garden flower world. The wider range of border perennials, rockery perennials, bulbs and bedding plants which is available these days means that you can be more adventurous. Every garden can be made more interesting by introducing uncommon plants to go alongside established favourites. There are Chionodoxas and Winter Aconites as well as Snowdrops to herald in the year and there are Nerines and Cyclamens as well as Michaelmas Daisies to bid it goodbye. But do not be foolhardy. It is folly to buy a pot-grown perennial or packet of seed of some unusual variety just because the picture or description appeals to you. You must first find out if it is right for your garden.

And that is the main purpose of this book. In Chapter 2 you will find the likes and dislikes for all sorts of out-of-the-way plants as well as for the established favourites — garden flowers old and new to light up your garden all year round.

THE RANGE OF GARDEN FLOWERS

ROCKERY PERENNIALS

A rockery perennial is a hardy plant which does not produce woody shoots — the leaves and stems usually die down as winter approaches and new shoots appear in spring, but a few are evergreen. Because of its short height, small leaves etc it is associated with the rock garden but these plants are also used at the front of herbaceous and mixed borders. The rockery perennial is one of the permanent features of the garden although this description can be deceptive — some last for only a few years.

The dividing line between rockery and border perennials is an indistinct one. A hardy perennial which grows less than 1 ft (30 cm) high is generally classed as a rockery perennial and those which grow over 1 ft (30 cm) high are border perennials, but there are exceptions.

ANNUALS and BIENNIALS

An annual is a temporary resident in the garden — it grows from seed and then flowers and dies all in a single round of the seasons. A hardy annual (HA) can withstand frost and so the seeds may be sown outdoors whenever the soil is suitable in spring or in some cases in the previous autumn. This is not the only way of growing hardy annuals — most people prefer to raise or buy them as bedding plants (see page 5) for setting out in May.

A half-hardy annual (HHA) cannot withstand frost and having to wait until the danger has passed before sowing outdoors means that the period of flowering is seriously curtailed. For this reason half-hardy annuals are generally treated as bedding plants — seedlings are raised under glass in spring and then planted out in late May-early June.

A hardy biennial (HB) is grown from summer-sown seed, producing stems and leaves in the first season and flowering the next. After flowering it dies. This temporary resident is used for spring-flowering bedding in borders, beds and containers.

The dividing line between biennials and border perennials is not quite as clear-cut as you might suppose. For example Hollyhocks are listed as border perennials but they decline quite quickly if grown as permanent residents in the border — it is much better to grow them as biennials.

BORDER PERENNIALS

A border perennial is a hardy plant which does not produce woody shoots — the leaves and stems generally die as winter arrives and new shoots appear in spring, but a few are evergreen. Because of its height, size of leaf etc it is associated with the herbaceous border rather than the rock garden, but these plants are also widely used in mixed borders. The border perennial is one of the permanent features of the garden, although this description can be deceptive — some last for only a few years and many of the long-lasting ones have to be lifted and divided every few years.

Some border perennials can tolerate a few degrees of frost but are killed if frosts are long and severe. Avoid these borderline types if you live in a frost-prone area — elsewhere the crowns should be covered with a mulch in winter.

Several border perennials form bulbs or bulb-like storage organs below ground — Agapanthus and Kaffir Lily are examples. These plants, however, are not described as bulbs in the A-Z guide because they are generally sold as growing plants and not as dormant bulbs.

TENDER PERENNIALS

A tender perennial is a half-hardy plant (HHP) which cannot withstand frost. Because of this lack of hardiness it has to spend winter indoors and then return to the garden once the danger of frost has passed. The way the plants are overwintered varies — Pelargoniums are kept under glass as green plants, Dahlias are stored as tubers and Chrysanthemums as roots. In the garden they are grown in beds, borders or containers — many gardeners treat Pelargoniums and half-hardy Fuchsias as bedding plants which are dumped in autumn.

BULBS

A bulb (more correctly a bulbous plant) produces an underground fleshy storage organ which is offered for sale in the dormant state for planting in the garden. Included here are the true bulbs, which consist of fleshy or scale-like leaves, together with corms (flattened and thickened stem bases), tubers (swollen roots and stems) and some rhizomes (fleshy creeping stems).

Some bulbs are permanent residents. These are left in the ground to flower each year, spreading in some cases to form large clumps. Lifting and dividing is only necessary when overcrowding threatens other plants or is affecting the quality of the display. Examples of these permanent residents are Crocus, Snowdrop and Narcissus — do not remove the leaves after flowering as this is the stage when food is produced for next year's bulbs.

The remaining bulbs are grown in the garden for part of the year. When flowering is over they are lifted and rested indoors as dormant bulbs until planting times comes round again. Examples include Gladiolus, Tuberous Begonia and Tulip.

BEDDING PLANTS

A bedding plant is a species or variety which is transplanted at the leafy stage to its place in the garden or in a container where it provides a display for a limited period. It is usually but not always grown for its floral rather than its foliage display. This definition describes a use for and not a type of plant. A Pelargonium kept indoors is a 'flowering house plant' or a 'greenhouse plant' — the same specimen planted outdoors in summer is a 'bedding plant'.

Bedding out has traditionally been the main use for these plants — the standard procedure was to fill the flower bed with annuals planted in lines, circles and geometric blocks, but this formality has declined. Flower beds tend to be much more irregular these days, and many bedding plants are now used to fill pockets in a mixed border or rockery. In addition the boom in container growing has led to an increase in interest in bedding plants.

All the plant types apart from bulbs set out on page 4 are used as bedding plants. Half-hardy annuals raised from seed sown under glass in spring dominate the picture — most of the popular ones belong here, including Impatiens, Tagetes, Lobelia, Petunia, Begonia and Salvia. Hardy annuals can be sown directly where they are to flower, but a number are grown as bedding plants — examples are Alyssum, Clarkia, Centaurea, Godetia and Nigella. Biennials are represented by Bellis, Myosotis, Cheiranthus and Dianthus barbatus. A few rockery perennials such as dwarf Viola and Diascia are offered as bedding plants, and border perennials which are used for bedding include Polyanthus and hardy Fuchsia. Tender perennials have an important part to play — Pelargonium and half-hardy Fuchsia varieties have been favourite bedding plants for a long time, but these days you will find many more such as Eustoma, Canna, Kalanchoe, Cuphea and Abutilon at the garden centre.

BOG PLANTS

A bog plant is defined as a species or variety which requires damp humus-rich soil which is never allowed to dry out, but cannot be expected to survive in permanently waterlogged ground. Some experts prefer the term 'poolside plant' as the usual home for these plants is in the swampy soil around a pond, although many bog plants will grow quite happily in a humus-rich border which is kept watered in dry weather.

The dividing line between bog plants and some other perennials is vague because the definition depends on the habitat rather than any distinct property of the plant. You will find Astilbe and Hemerocallis described as border perennials in this book, but in a water gardening guide you will find them listed as bog plants. On the other hand Lysichiton, Zantedeschia and several others are listed as bog plants in the A-Z guide even though they will grow happily in the shallow water margin inside the pond.

THE PLACE FOR GARDEN FLOWERS

PATIO or PATHWAY

A pathway is a hard-surface strip which leads somewhere. A patio doesn't — it is basically an outdoor extension of a room. Cracks between the stones in these areas can be filled with various mat-forming rockery perennials. Some (e.g Acaena and Thyme) can withstand foot traffic.

MIXED BORDER

The mixed border has taken over from the herbaceous border as the most popular way of growing border perennials. Gone are most of the slavish rules about colour, height etc, and the flowering season has been extended by including other types of plants. Like all borders it is designed to be viewed from two or three sides and not from all angles. The shape is often irregular and no longer strictly rectangular. The usual pattern is a framework of flowering shrubs, roses and decorative evergreens. Border perennials form large and colourful patches and close to the front a number of pockets are left to be filled with bulbs and bedding plants.

FLOWER BED

A bed is a planted area which is designed to be viewed from all sides — a flower bed is the traditional home for annuals, biennials and bulbs. The occupants are usually planted in autumn for a spring display and in late spring for a summer show.

RAISED BED

The sides of a raised bed are made of a retaining wall and the space within is filled with free-draining soil. The raised bed is particularly useful where the drainage of the garden soil is poor or where age or infirmity makes stooping by the gardener difficult.

HERBACEOUS BORDER

In the early years of the 20th century the herbaceous border was an essential feature of the larger garden. It was long and narrow with a backcloth of a wall or clipped hedge. Border perennials were used in tiers, with tall-growing varieties at the back and clumps of low-growing plants at the front. It is a lot of work and is lifeless in winter, and so its popularity has declined. These days the constant slope from back to front is often broken by including an occasional tall plant near the front.

ISLAND BED

The island bed is a modern variation of the traditional herbaceous border — like its predecessor it is designed for border perennials, with the tallest in the centre and the shortest around the edge. The shape is often irregular.

PEAT BED

A peat bed is a variation of the raised bed. The retaining wall is made up of peat blocks and the in-fill is a lime-free compost plus soil in which the peat compost is greater than the soil fraction. An excellent home for lime-haters — grow alpines and ferns in the cracks.

ROCKERY

A rockery or rock garden is a planted area devoted to rockery perennials, dwarf conifers and bulbs. Low-growing annuals are frequently used to fill gaps and to supplement the summer and autumn display. Ideally the rockery should imitate a natural stone outcrop.

SCREEN

Shrubby climbers such as Honeysuckle, Clematis and Ivy are usually chosen for screening, but there are several flowering annuals which can be used for clambering up arches and trellis-work. Nasturtium and Sweet Pea are the big two, but there are also Cobaea, Ipomoea and Thunbergia.

FOCAL POINT

A focal point can be created by using a specimen plant — this is a perennial grown to be admired on its own as distinct from being grouped with other plants. Obviously great care must be taken over its selection and maintenance, and the usual choice is a shrub or tree. Several border perennials make excellent specimen plants — examples include Cortaderia, Agapanthus and Paeonia.

HANGING BASKET

A hanging basket is a container which is suspended from a hook or bracket. In nearly all cases it is filled with compost rather than soil and carries bedding plants rather than perennials. Most of the ones which are bought are ready-filled wire baskets — these open containers will need watering daily if a water-retaining liner is missing. Consider a closed basket made of plastic or fibre to cut down the watering chore — self-watering baskets are available.

COTTAGE GARDEN

The picture on page 99 illustrates the lack of design and formality in the cottage garden — annuals and perennials rub shoulders with roses, vegetables, herbs, shrubs and pots. Once an essential feature of the rural scene but becoming rarer every year.

SINK GARDEN

A sink garden is made from an old stone or glazed sink in which the drainage hole has been covered with crocks or rubble and then filled with a free-draining compost to 2 in. (5 cm) below the rim. The outer surface can be covered with a cement/sand/peat mixture to give a more natural appearance. Use the sink garden for miniature rockery perennials, dwarf conifers and miniature bulbs. Place some small rocks between the plants and cover the surface with stone chippings.

WILDFLOWER GARDEN

A wildflower meadow is a grassy area into which native plants are introduced and allowed to flower. Mowing takes place once the flowering season is over. Several suitable flowers (e.g Bugle, Star of Bethlehem, Knapweed and Ragged Robin) are listed in the A-Z guide but the best plan is to buy a wildflower seed mixture at the garden centre and sow in spring.

GRASSLAND

Grassland may seem an odd place for garden flowers, but the photograph on page 55 shows how attractive naturalised bulbs can look. A word of warning. The leaves cannot be mown for several weeks after the flowers have faded — choose a semi-wild area at the back of the lawn or a circle of uncut grass around a tree for Narcissus, Scilla, Colchicum, Muscari, Fritillaria etc.

CONTAINER

Tubs, troughs, pots and window boxes differ from hanging baskets by virtually always having closed sides and by standing on a firm base or being attached to a firm vertical surface. A useful way of growing showy annuals or bulbs close to the house and for displaying specimen plants.

CHAPTER 2
GARDEN FLOWERS A-Z

In the introduction on page 3 the traditional floral round was described, starting with the Snowdrops in early spring and ending with the Chrysanthemums and Michaelmas Daisies of late autumn. But this is not the whole story — you will see other blooms when you look over your neighbour's fence. There will be blossom on the Ornamental Cherries in spring and flowers on the Floribunda Roses until the first frosts arrive. Garden flowers are the main part of the floral story and are dealt with in this book, but there are also roses, climbers, flowering shrubs and flowering trees which are dealt with in other Expert titles.

Garden flowers range in size from tiny alpines peeping through the soil to man-sized giants in the border, but they all share three basic features. Firstly, they can all be grown outdoors during their flowering season. A few are also quite at home in the living room or conservatory and some are too delicate to survive the frosts of winter, but all are sold for growing in the garden for all or part of the year.

Secondly, garden flowers do not have permanent woody stems. Some border and tender perennials have stems with woody bases, but these stems do not form a permanent woody framework. The borderline plants between perennials and shrubs are the subshrubs — low-growing plants with green stems which are not killed by frost. Depending on the book you read Vinca is either a garden flower or a dwarf shrub.

Finally, garden flowers produce sufficient bloom to provide a significant display. Nearly all the examples in this chapter qualify quite easily but there are the borderline ones. As an example Stachys byzantina (Lamb's Ears) is grown for its ground-covering grey leaves but earns a place in this book as it bears spikes of pale purple flowers in June. Ballota acetabulosa is another grey-leaved ground cover but it is not included as the floral display is insignificant. Among the grasses only Cortaderia with its large silky plumes is

included. Many other ornamental grasses have interesting inflorescences but the plants cannot be considered as garden flowers.

Garden flowers are divided into a number of major groups and these are defined on pages 4-5. Annuals and biennials are mainly employed as bedding plants although a few annuals are sown where they are to grow and flower as they resent transplanting. Bulbs make up another large group of garden flowers and it is a pity that so many gardeners restrict themselves to a handful of types such as Crocus, Narcissus, Tulip, Gladiolus and Lily. There are so many interesting and unusual bulbs listed in this A-Z guide — remember that no other group can match them for their ability to provide floral colour in the garden all the year round. Plant at the recommended depth — the figures given in this book refer to the distance between the soil surface and the bottom of the bulb.

An enormous number of plants are classified as hardy perennials, and depending on their height are called border or rockery perennials. To see border perennials at their best look at a well-planned herbaceous border in midsummer. When starting from scratch make sure you get rid of perennial weeds before planting and choose the smaller and sturdier modern varieties to reduce the need for staking. Plant in groups of three or five.

Rockery perennials are dwarf hardy perennials which are suitable for growing in a rock garden — it is impossible to be more precise. Alpines were originally collected from the Alps, Andes, Rocky Mountains and other highland areas but not all rockery perennials are alpines — some come from lowland areas such as deserts and the seashore. Finally there are the tender perennials which bloom outdoors in summer or autumn but need protection indoors during winter as potted plants or dormant bulbs or roots.

With each genus you will find the group or groups to which it belongs. Sometimes it is simple with just a single group involved, but it can be more complex — a Mimulus species or variety can be a bedding plant, border perennial, rockery perennial or bog plant.

ABUTILON Flowering Maple

Bedding plant: tender perennial

There are shrubby Abutilons such as A. suntense which are hardy enough to be grown as perennials against a sunny wall. For the flower bed it is more usual to grow it from seed as a bedding plant for use as a focal point in the middle or at the back of the display. The large bell-shaped blooms appear from the end of June to late September — the plants grow about 2 ft (60 cm) high.

VARIETIES: The Bedding Abutilons are varieties of **A. hybridum**. In the seed catalogues you will find **A. 'Large-flowered Mixed'** — a selection of white, yellow, orange, pink and red types. In specialist seed catalogues and on the bench of large garden centres in spring you will find named varieties — look for **'Canary Bird'** (yellow), **'Boule de Neige'** (white), **'Kentish Belle'** (apricot) and **'Ashford Red'** (red).

SITE & SOIL: Well-drained soil and full sun are necessary.

PROPAGATION: Sow seeds in February in gentle heat. Plant out in early June.

A. hybridum 'Canary Bird'

Abutilon hybridum 'Ashford Red'

ACAENA New Zealand Burr

Rockery perennial

A carpeting perennial with a number of uses — covering cracks between paving stones, providing ground cover between plants and forming a blanket over bulbs. It is low-growing (1-3 in./2.5-7.5 cm) but it spreads rapidly and can swamp nearby plants. The tiny flowers are insignificant, but they are followed in late summer by burr-like seed heads which are often showy.

VARIETIES: The most popular species is **A. microphylla** — height 2 in. (5 cm), spread 2 ft (60 cm), flowering period July-September with burrs appearing from August onwards. The leaves are bronzy-green and the burrs are bright red. For more restrained growth choose the variety **'Copper Carpet'**. Not all have bronzy leaves — **A. 'Blue Haze'** has blue-grey foliage and dark red burrs.

SITE & SOIL: Well-drained soil is essential — thrives in full sun or light shade.

PROPAGATION: Divide clumps in autumn or spring.

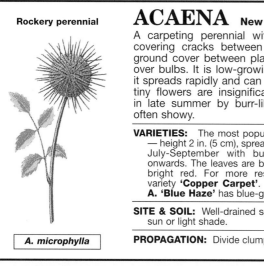

A. microphylla

Acaena microphylla

ACANTHUS Bear's Breeches

Border perennial

Acanthus is a handsome plant grown for both its foliage and floral display. The deeply-divided arching leaves clothe the bases of the tall spires of tubular purple and white flowers which appear in midsummer. A long-lived plant which tolerates drought better than most, but it dislikes disturbance and heavy soil. Cut back to near ground level once flowering has finished.

VARIETIES: **A. spinosus** is the one to choose. It is the hardiest one and has the largest leaves, but it also has sharp spines. The flower heads bear white-lipped blooms and can be used indoors, both fresh and dried. Height 4 ft (1.2 m), spread 2$\frac{1}{2}$ ft (75 cm), flowering period July-September. **A. mollis** is taller with soft spines but less attractive leaves and flowers.

SITE & SOIL: Any well-drained soil will do — light land is preferred. Thrives in sun or light shade.

PROPAGATION: Divide overcrowded clumps in early autumn.

A. spinosus

Acanthus spinosus

ACHILLEA Yarrow, Milfoil

The flat plates of tiny flowers are a familiar summer sight in herbaceous borders everywhere and in many rockeries. These flower heads are excellent for cutting and can be dried for winter decoration. Yellow is the usual colour but you can also find white, cream, pink and red. These blooms are not the only attractive feature — the green or silvery foliage is nearly always fern-like and provides a welcome contrast to the large leaves of so many herbaceous border plants. All are easy to grow with no special soil requirements and they have above-average drought tolerance, but the taller varieties may need staking on exposed sites. Cut down to ground level in autumn. The Alpine Yarrows are useful for covering areas of dry sandy soil or crevices between rocks and the plants are easily propagated in spring.

VARIETIES: **A. filipendulina** is a stately Achillea for the back of the border and its variety **'Gold Plate'** is the most popular tall Yarrow. It grows about 4 ft (1.2 m) high and should be planted at 2 ft (60 cm) intervals — the flat-topped 6 in. (15 cm) wide flower heads appear between June and September. **'Cloth of Gold'** is similar but rather more compact. For the middle of the border there are a couple of excellent yellow-flowered hybrids with grey-green foliage — **A. 'Coronation Gold'** and **A. 'Moonshine'**. As a change from yellow choose one of the colourful **A. millefolium** varieties which grow 2-3 ft (60-90 cm) high — look for **'Cerise Queen'** (crimson), **'Paprika'** (deep orange) and **'Lilac Beauty'** (mauve). **A. 'Lachsschonheit'** is salmon-pink. **A. ptarmica** and its varieties have narrow leaves and white flowers. For the front of the border and the rockery there are the 6-12 in. (15-30 cm) dwarf **A. tomentosa** and its varieties with 3 in. (7.5 cm) yellow flower heads and ferny grey leaves. For a white-flowered dwarf choose **A. argentea**.

SITE & SOIL: Any well-drained soil will do — thrives best in full sun.

PROPAGATION: Sow seeds in the open in late spring or divide clumps in autumn or spring.

Border perennial
•
Rockery perennial

Achillea filipendulina
'Gold Plate'

Achillea millefolium
'Cerise Queen'

Achillea argentea

A. 'Coronation Gold'

A. tomentosa

ACIDANTHERA Abyssinian Gladiolus

Bulb

This Gladiolus-like plant produces its attractive fragrant blooms in autumn when most bulbous plants have passed their flowering season, but it is not for everyone. It is not hardy, so the corms must be lifted before the onset of frost and then replanted in spring. In addition it needs a sunny site in a mild area of the country.

VARIETIES: You will find it listed as **A. bicolor murieliae** or **A. 'Murieliae'** in the bulb catalogues but in most textbooks it is called **Gladiolus callianthus**. The 2-3 in. (5-7.5 cm) wide star-shaped flowers are borne on 3 ft (90 cm) stalks above the sword-like leaves — at the base of each petal there is a prominent purple blotch. Overwinter corms in a dry and reasonably warm place.

SITE & SOIL: Any well-drained soil will do — a warm and sunny site is necessary.

PROPAGATION: Dig up cormlets in October and replant in April. Flowering may take several years.

A. bicolor murieliae

Acidanthera bicolor
murieliae

Border perennial

A. 'Spark's Variety'

ACONITUM Monkshood

Monkshood was an old favourite for the back of the border and for growing under trees, but it is no longer popular. The problem is that all parts are poisonous, so care is needed. All have deeply-cut leaves and the helmet-shaped flowers are borne on tall spikes. Blue is the usual colour, July-August is the usual flowering season and 4 ft (1.2 m) is the usual height, but there are variations.

VARIETIES: **A. 'Spark's Variety'** (blue-purple) and **A. 'Bressingham Blue'** (violet-blue) are popular and typical varieties which bloom in summer. For a brighter display choose **A. cammarum 'Bicolor'** for its spikes of white/violet-blue flowers. **A. 'Ivorine'** is a pale yellow, early-flowering compact hybrid. Grow **A. carmichaelii 'Arendsii'** (blue) or **'Barker's Variety'** (lavender-blue) for autumn flowers.

SITE & SOIL: Well-drained, moisture-retentive soil is necessary — thrives best in light shade.

PROPAGATION: Divide clumps in autumn.

Aconitum carmichaelii 'Arendsii'

Border perennial

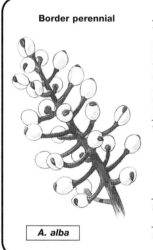

A. alba

ACTAEA Baneberry

This uncommon member of the buttercup family makes an eye-catching addition to the woodland, moist border or poolside garden. The large ferny or toothed leaves are not the main feature and the clusters of small white flowers in early summer will not attract much attention. Actaea is grown for its display of berries in autumn — large, colourful but very poisonous.

VARIETIES: The White Baneberry (listed as **A. alba** or **A. pachypoda**) is the one to choose. It grows about 3 ft (90 cm) high and from late summer produces showy spikes of pea-sized white berries on bright red stalks. There are other species, such as **A. rubra** (red berries) and **A. spicata** (large black berries), but they are much less likely to attract attention.

SITE & SOIL: Moisture-retentive soil is necessary — thrives best in partial shade.

PROPAGATION: Divide clumps in spring.

Actaea alba

Border perennial
•
**Bedding plant:
hardy annual**

A. amurensis 'Flore Pleno'

ADONIS Adonis

Adonis is not a popular plant and you will have to hunt to find a supplier of the perennial species for the rockery or front of the border. It is worth looking for — bright yellow flowers appear above feathery foliage in February. The annual species is also hard to find, although it is no more difficult to grow than its close relatives Larkspur and Love-in-the-mist.

VARIETIES: The Border Adonis is **A. amurensis** — 1 ft (30 cm) high with 1½ in. (3.5 cm) bowl-shaped yellow flowers. The variety **'Flore Pleno'** has green-centred double flowers. These types thrive best in acid soil and a shady site, but the Annual Adonis **A. annua** (Pheasant's Eye) prefers non-acid soil and full sun. This bedding plant bears cupped 1 in. (2.5 cm) scarlet, dark-eyed flowers.

SITE & SOIL: Depends on type — see above.

PROPAGATION: Divide clumps in late summer — sow seeds of Annual Adonis in the garden in early spring.

Adonis annua

AETHIONEMA Aethionema

Rockery perennial

This shrubby evergreen or semi-evergreen covers the ground with a mat of fleshy grey leaves and for many weeks in summer there is a tightly packed covering of flower heads. Each head is a cluster of tiny 4-petalled flowers in colours ranging from palest pink to deepest rose. Alkaline soil is best, but the popular types do well in neutral or slightly acid soil.

VARIETIES: The one you are most likely to find is **A. 'Warley Rose'** — rosy red, height 6 in. (15 cm), spread 1 ft (30 cm). For a deeper shade of rose choose **A. 'Warley Ruber'**. The tallest Aethionema is **A. grandiflorum** reaching 1 ft (30 cm) with pale pink flowers from May to August. At the other end of the scale there is the 2 in. (5 cm) dwarf **A. oppositifolium**.

SITE & SOIL: Any well-drained soil — full sun is necessary.

PROPAGATION: Easily raised from seeds. With named varieties plant cuttings in a cold frame in early summer.

A. 'Warley Rose'

Aethionema grandiflorum

AGAPANTHUS African Lily

Border perennial

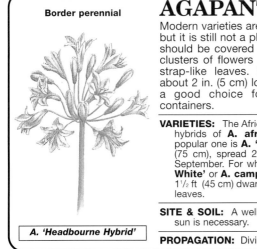

Modern varieties are hardier than the original species, but it is still not a plant for cold areas and the crowns should be covered with peat over winter. In summer clusters of flowers appear on long stems above the strap-like leaves. Each trumpet-shaped bloom is about 2 in. (5 cm) long and is nearly always blue. It is a good choice for cutting and for planting in containers.

VARIETIES: The African Lilies you are most likely to find are hybrids of **A. africanus** (**A. umbellatus**). The most popular one is **A. 'Headbourne Hybrid'** — height 2½ ft (75 cm), spread 2 ft (60 cm) and flowers from July to September. For white flowers choose **A. 'Bressingham White'** or **A. campanulatus 'Albidus'**. **A. 'Lilliput'** is a 1½ ft (45 cm) dwarf and **A. 'Tinkerbell'** has silver-striped leaves.

SITE & SOIL: A well-drained, moisture-retentive soil in full sun is necessary.

PROPAGATION: Divide clumps in spring.

A. 'Headbourne Hybrid'

Agapanthus africanus

The traditional hanging basket contains a mixture of upright and pendent bedding plants in a wide assortment of leaf shapes, flower sizes and colours. But this is not the only way of using a hanging basket — in many situations a solid mass of a single colour can be more dramatic, as these yellow pansies show.

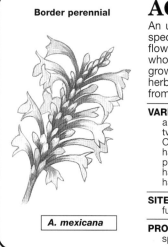

Border perennial

A. mexicana

AGASTACHE Giant Hyssop

An uncommon perennial — you will have to go to a specialist nursery or sow seeds for this one. The flowering spikes above the mint-like leaves bear whorls of small hooded blooms. It is an easy plant to grow and is useful for providing late colour in the herbaceous border — the flowering period extends from August to October.

VARIETIES: **A. foeniculum** is listed in many catalogues — a 3 ft (90 cm) high plant with violet-blue flowers. There are two white-flowered varieties — **'Alabaster'** and **'Alba'**. Other colours are available — **A. 'Firebird'** (2 ft/60 cm) has coppery flowers and the blooms on **A. cana** are pale pink. **A. mexicana** (height 2 ft/60 cm, spread 1 ft/30 cm) has pink flowers and is not fully hardy — grow it as a half-hardy annual in cold districts.

SITE & SOIL: Any well-drained soil will do — thrives best in full sun.

PROPAGATION: Sow seeds under glass or divide clumps in spring.

Agastache 'Firebird'

Bedding plant: half-hardy annual

A. houstonianum 'Blue Mink'

AGERATUM Floss Flower

The small powderpuff flower heads of Ageratum are a familiar sight in bedding schemes. There are several colours available but blue and mauve remain the favourite ones. White varieties turn brown with age and pink has never caught the public fancy.

VARIETIES: **A. houstonianum** has given rise to many varieties and hybrids. The old variety **'Blue Mink'** (9 in./22.5 cm, mid blue) remains popular, but there are many newer blues ranging from the pale blue **'Ocean'** to the deep blue **'Blue Cap'**. Both **'Blue Danube'** and **'Blue Blazer'** are excellent blue-mauves and the best pink is **'Pink Powderpuffs'**. For cutting choose one of the tall 1½-2½ ft (45-75 cm) varieties such as **'Blue Horizon'** or **'Tall Blue'**.

SITE & SOIL: Any reasonable soil in sun or light shade.

PROPAGATION: Sow seeds in February-March in gentle heat. Plant out in late May.

Ageratum houstonianum 'Blue Blazer'

Hardy annual

A. githago

A. githago 'Milas'

AGROSTEMMA Corn Cockle

Corn Cockle is not a popular garden plant but it is an excellent cottage garden annual, growing about 2½ ft (75 cm) high and bearing large flowers in June-August on top of slender stems. These stems withstand both wind and rain and Corn Cockle is recommended as a cut flower. It dislikes root disturbance — sow the seeds where they are to flower.

VARIETIES: The weed **A. githago** bears narrow hairy leaves and bright magenta blooms which close at night. The variety most usually grown as a garden plant is **'Milas'** — the 2 in. (5 cm) wide flowers are pale pink fading to white at the centre. Corn Cockle flowers attract bees and the seeds are a popular ingredient in wild flower mixtures.

SITE & SOIL: Any well-drained garden soil will do — low fertility is preferred. Thrives best in full sun.

PROPAGATION: Sow seeds in autumn or early spring in the garden. Do not transplant.

Agrostemma githago 'Milas'

AJUGA **Bugle**

Border perennial

A. reptans
'Multicolor'

In late spring or early summer small flowers on short stalks appear above the leaves of this easy-to-grow ground cover. Blue is the usual flower colour but there are also white and pink varieties. In some cases it is the floral display which is the main reason for growing this soil-hugging evergreen, but with most varieties it is the decorative foliage which is the main attraction.

VARIETIES: The Bugles available at the garden centre are varieties of **A. reptans** — height 4-6 in. (10-15 cm), flowering period April-June. Types grown for their floral display include **'Alba'** (white) and **'Pink Elf'** (pink). The coloured-leaf varieties are more widely available — look for **'Burgundy Glow'** (cream-edged red), **'Braunherz'** (purple), **'Atropurpurea'** (purple) and **'Multicolor'** (green/red/bronze/cream).

SITE & SOIL: Any reasonable soil will do — thrives in sun or partial shade.

PROPAGATION: Divide clumps in autumn or spring.

Ajuga reptans
'Burgundy Glow'

ALCAEA **Hollyhock**

Border perennial
•
**Bedding plant:
hardy annual or
hardy biennial**

A. rosea
'Powder Puffs'

Alcaea or Althaea — you will find both Latin names for hollyhocks in catalogues and textbooks. The tall spires of funnel-shaped flowers are a familiar sight in herbaceous borders, but after a couple of years rust disease weakens the plant. It is better to grow it as a biennial or annual bedding plant.

VARIETIES: **A. rosea** is the Common Hollyhock — height 5-9 ft (1.5-2.7 m), flowering period July-September. Single-flowered seed mixtures are available but double varieties are much more popular. Nearly all colours apart from blue are available and **'Chater's Double'** is the most popular. **'Powder Puffs'** is a ruffled 4 ft (1.2 m) variety. A number of dwarf annual varieties are offered as seeds — look for **'Carnival'** or **'Majorette'**.

SITE & SOIL: Any reasonable soil will do — thrives best in full sun. Stake if necessary.

PROPAGATION: Take cuttings in autumn. Sow biennials in May — plant out in September. With annuals sow in February in gentle heat. Plant out in May.

Alcaea rosea
'Chater's Double'

ALCHEMILLA **Lady's Mantle**

Border perennial
•
Rockery perennial

A. mollis

Alchemilla grows as a flat-topped clump of foliage, each lobed leaf bearing fine hairs which hold and turn raindrops into glistening orbs. It is a useful ground-cover plant with fluffy branching sprays of tiny greenish-yellow flowers in summer. Both leaves and floral sprays are widely used in flower arrangements. Cut the plants down to just above ground level when flowering has finished.

VARIETIES: **A. mollis** is the species grown in the herbaceous border — height 1½ ft (45 cm), flowering period June-July. Its pale green leaves are saw-edged and its flowers are about ⅛ in. (0.25 cm) across — self-sown seedlings can be a nuisance. There are several 6-8 in. (15-20 cm) dwarfs for the rockery — the best-known ones are **A. alpina**, **A. conjuncta** and **A. erythropoda**.

SITE & SOIL: Any well-drained soil will do — thrives in sun or light shade.

PROPAGATION: Divide clumps in spring.

Alchemilla mollis

ALLIUM Flowering Onion

There are dwarf Alliums for the rockery and tall ones for the back of the border. The flower heads last for about a month and most are easy to grow, but they have never become popular. Maybe the idea of having a strong onion odour in the bed or border is a deterrent, but there is no problem — the leaves only smell when crushed and some species have fragrant flowers. There is no standard shape — the leaves may be wide or narrow and the flowers may be wide- or narrow-petalled. There are two basic types of flower head. Some are spheres made up of many tightly-packed blooms — these are the *Ball-headed Alliums*. The rest bear loose clusters of upright or drooping blooms — these are the *Tufted Alliums*. Alliums are sold as dormant bulbs or growing plants.

Allium giganteum

VARIETIES: The giant among the Ball-headed Alliums is **A. giganteum** — 4 ft (1.2 m) high with 4 in. (10 cm) wide mauve heads in June. For the largest heads grow **A. albopilosum** — 2 ft (60 cm) high with 8 in. (20 cm) wide silver-lilac heads in June. Other examples include **A. hollandicum** (2 ft/60 cm, pale purple, May), **A. sphaerocephalon** (2 ft/60 cm, red, July) and **A. karataviense** (9 in./22.5 cm, pale purple, May). The Tufted Alliums are usually grown in the rockery or at the front of the border. The 9 in. (22.5 cm) **A. moly** is a popular choice, producing masses of loose yellow flowers in June. **A. cyaneum** bears small heads of blue flowers and **A. ostrowskianum** carries its pink starry flowers in wide clusters. For late summer blooms choose **A. amabile** (5 in./12.5 cm, reddish-purple). Some Tufted Alliums have drooping flowers — examples include **A. narcissiflorum** (pink), **A. triquetrum** (white) and **A. beesianum** (blue).

SITE & SOIL: Any well-drained soil will do — thrives best in full sun.

PROPAGATION: Divide overcrowded clumps every few years in autumn.

Bulb
•
Border perennial
•
Rockery perennial

Allium narcissiflorum

A. albopilosum

A. ostrowskianum

Allium moly

Bedding plant:
tender perennial

ALONSOA Mask Flower

This half-hardy shrubby perennial can be grown as a conservatory plant but it is more usual to treat it as a half-hardy annual and grow it outdoors. It is a rarity so you will have to search for a seed supplier — a plant for people who like the unusual. The branched stems bear racemes of 1 in. (2.5 cm) wide flat-faced flowers — these blooms appear all summer long.

VARIETIES: **A. warscewiczii** (height 2 ft/60 cm, spread 1 ft/30 cm) has serrated oval leaves and orange-red flowers — its variety **'Peachy-Keen'** has pale apricot blooms. Both flower profusely until autumn and so does **A. meridionalis** which has orange blooms. For other colours choose one of the varieties — there are **'Pink Beauty'** and **'Red Beauty'**.

SITE & SOIL: Any well-drained soil will do. Choose a sunny spot.

PROPAGATION: Sow seeds in February-March in gentle heat. Plant out in late May.

A. warscewiczii

Alonsoa warscewiczii

Border perennial

A. aurea

ALSTROEMERIA Peruvian Lily

This plant is best known as a commercial cut flower, but you can grow it in the garden if the soil is right. The usual flowering season is June-August. Unfortunately few flowers are produced in the first year and a crown-covering mulch is necessary over winter. It is easier to start with container-grown plants rather than tubers and faded blooms should be dead-headed.

VARIETIES: The 2 in. (5 cm) wide flowers are attractive with inner petals which are flecked with darker colours. They are borne in loose clusters and are long-lasting in water. For tall (3 ft/90 cm) plants grow **A. aurea** (**A. aurantiaca**) — named varieties include **'Orange King'**. **A. 'Ligtu Hybrids'** are shorter with a wider range of colours. There are many 'Royal Family' hybrids — **A. 'Princess Sarah'**, **'Princess Alice'** etc.

SITE & SOIL: Well-drained light soil rich in humus and in full sun is necessary.

PROPAGATION: Divide overcrowded clumps in early spring.

Alstroemeria 'Princess Alice'

ALYSSUM Alyssum

There are two distinct groups of plants labelled Alyssum at the garden centre. The *Bedding Alyssums* are hardy annuals which have long been the favourite partners for Lobelias to provide a floral edging around flower beds. White is the traditional colour but nowadays you can buy varieties with pink, purple or red flowers. The dwarf cushions are covered by the tiny honey-scented blooms and are widely used in window boxes, cracks between paving stones and for gaps in the rockery as well as in the flower bed. Trim off dead blooms and water copiously in dry weather. *Rockery Alyssums* are quite different — the flowers are usually yellow, the plants are perennial and the usual partner is Aubretia.

Alyssum saxatile

VARIETIES: When picking a Bedding Alyssum a white variety of **A. maritimum** (now renamed **Lobularia maritima**) is the usual choice — height 3-6 in. (7.5-15 cm), flowering period June-September. The low carpeting ones are **'Carpet of Snow'**, **'Snow Drift'** and **'Minimum'** — **'Snow Crystals'** is a Fleuroselect winner and **'Little Dorrit'** is more upright than the others. For a change of colour there are the purple Alyssums **'Royal Carpet'** and **'Oriental Night'**, the pink-flowered **'Rosie O'Day'** and the rich red **'Wonderland'**. For a mixture of colours sow **'Morning Mist'** or **'Easter Bonnet'**. By far the most popular Rockery Alyssum is **A. saxatile** (now renamed **Aurinia saxatilis**) — height 6 in.-1 ft (15-30 cm), spread 1½ ft (45 cm), flowering period April-June. The large heads of tiny yellow flowers may cover the grey foliage which persists all year. It is a rampant grower, so plant well away from delicate alpines. Varieties include **'Citrinum'** (pale yellow), **'Dudley Nevill'** (buff) and **'Compactum'** (dwarf). The best miniature for the rockery is **A. montanum** (6 in./15 cm, deep yellow).

SITE & SOIL: Any well-drained soil will do — thrives best in full sun.

PROPAGATION: Bedding Alyssum: Sow seeds in February under glass. Plant out in May. Rockery Alyssum: Plant cuttings in a cold frame in early summer.

Bedding plant: hardy annual
•
Rockery perennial

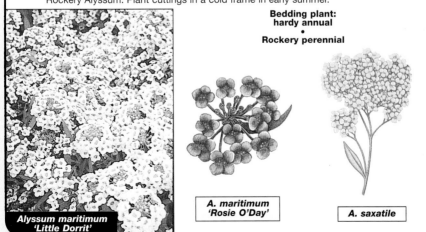

Alyssum maritimum 'Little Dorrit'

A. maritimum 'Rosie O'Day'

A. saxatile

Alyssum montanum

AMARANTHUS Love-lies-bleeding

Bedding plant: half-hardy annual

A showy plant for the centre of a formal bedding scheme or on its own in a large container. Between July and September 1½ ft (45 cm) long tassels of tiny blooms are a spectacular feature — use them fresh or dried for flower arranging. Keep the plants watered during dry spells to prolong flower life and to ensure an attractive foliage display. Support the stems if the site is exposed.

VARIETIES: **A. caudatus** is the popular species — height 2-3 ft (60-90 cm), spread 2 ft (60 cm). The large leaves are pale green and the tassels are crimson — for something different try the deep red variety **'Atropurpurea'** or the bright green **'Viridis'**. For a change of shape there are the 1-1½ ft (30-45 cm) dwarfs with erect flower heads — **'Pygmy Torch'** (red) and **'Green Thumb'** (green).

SITE & SOIL: Any well-drained, non-acid soil will do — thrives best in full sun.

PROPAGATION: Sow seeds in March in gentle heat. Plant out in late May.

A. caudatus

Amaranthus caudatus

AMARYLLIS Belladonna Lily

Bulb

Do not confuse this plant with the large 'Amaryllis' bulbs sold for growing indoors. These are varieties of Hippeastrum and have a different growth habit. Amaryllis can be grown outdoors in a sunny sheltered spot and unlike Hippeastrum the flower stalks topped by a cluster of blooms appear a month or two after the strap-like leaves have died down.

VARIETIES: The only species grown is **A. belladonna** — height 2 ft (60 cm), spread 1 ft (30 cm), flowering period September-October. The 3 in. (7.5 cm) wide flowers are fragrant and funnel shaped. Pink, salmon and white varieties are available and all require staking to prevent damage by strong winds. Cut down stalks when flowering is over and cover crowns with peat over winter.

SITE & SOIL: Well-drained, humus-rich soil is necessary — full sun is essential.

PROPAGATION: Plant shop-bought bulbs in August with tips level with the soil surface.

A. belladonna

Amaryllis belladonna

AMMOBIUM Winged Everlasting

Bedding plant: half-hardy annual

Ammobium is an easy plant to recognise. The upright stems have distinct wings and each button-like bloom has an outer ring of petal-like bracts — at the centre there is a prominent boss of tiny yellow true flowers. These 'everlasting' blooms appear from mid June to late September and are excellent for cutting and drying like Helichrysum for indoor decoration.

VARIETIES: The only species is **A. alatum** — height 2 ft (60 cm), spread 8 in. (20 cm). The blooms measure about 1 in. (2.5 cm) across — for larger blooms grow the variety **'Grandiflora'**. The problem with Ammobium is that it is a useful plant for the flower arranger but can look gaunt in the garden. The answer is to grow the compact 1¼ ft (37.5 cm) variety **'Bikini'**.

SITE & SOIL: Any well-drained garden soil will do — thrives best in full sun.

PROPAGATION: Sow seeds in April in gentle heat. Plant out in late May.

A. alatum

Ammobium alatum 'Grandiflora'

Border perennial

AMSONIA Blue Star

This is not a garden centre plant — you will have to order it from a comprehensive nursery catalogue. Obviously a good choice if you like rarities, but this hardy perennial is a useful addition and not just a novelty if you have a moist and shady spot to fill and have a particular liking for blue flowers. The star-faced funnel-shaped blooms appear in early summer on top of the upright stems.

VARIETIES: The Blue Star you are most likely to find is **A. tabernaemontana** — height 3 ft (90 cm), spread 1½ ft (45 cm). Arching stems bear willow-like leaves and small clusters of sky-blue flowers. These blooms are ¾ in. (1.5 cm) across — for darker but smaller flowers choose the species **A. orientalis**. Both these types of Blue Star form slow-growing leafy clumps.

SITE & SOIL: Any well-drained, moisture-retentive soil will do — thrives best in light shade.

PROPAGATION: Divide clumps in spring.

A. tabernaemontana

Amsonia tabernaemontana

Rockery perennial

ANACYCLUS Mt. Atlas Daisy

When seen in full flower it may seem surprising that this alpine is not more popular. The rosette of prostrate stems bears grey-green ferny foliage and the rich red buds open into large white daisies. It is hardy, but the problem is that it cannot stand waterlogging and so it will not survive the winter if the soil is heavy and the drainage is poor.

VARIETIES: The only one you will find at the garden centre is **A. depressus**, sometimes listed as **A. pyrethrum depressus**. The basic details are height 2 in. (5 cm), spread 1 ft (30 cm), flowers 1-2 in. (2.5-5 cm) across, flowering period May-August. If possible dead-head after flowering and protect from winter wet if soil is not free-draining. There is a yellow variety (**'Golden Gnome'**) but it is hard to find.

SITE & SOIL: Requires well-drained light soil — full sun is necessary.

PROPAGATION: Plant cuttings in a cold frame in spring.

A. depressus

Anacyclus depressus

Border perennial

ANAPHALIS Pearl Everlasting

Pearl Everlasting is grown as much for its appeal to flower arrangers as it is for its display in the border. It is a useful ground cover, the clumps of grey or silvery leaves spreading quite rapidly in nearly all situations. From July to September large clusters of small starry flowers appear. These white flower heads can be cut for indoor use — when dried both colour and texture are retained.

VARIETIES: **A. triplinervis** is the most important species — height 1½ ft (45 cm), spread 2 ft (60 cm) or more. For a more compact and neater growth habit choose the variety **'Summer Snow'**. For silvery rather than grey leaves grow **A. margaritacea** and for the largest plants with the largest flower heads look for **A. yedoensis**. All are easy to grow, but thorough watering is necessary when the weather is dry.

SITE & SOIL: Any well-drained soil will do — thrives in sun or light shade.

A. triplinervis

PROPAGATION: Divide clumps in autumn or spring.

Anaphalis yedoensis

ANCHUSA Anchusa

Few flowers can surpass the vivid blue of some Anchusas, so it is a must for bed or border for lovers of this colour. The Perennial Anchusa (Alkanet) is not an attractive plant. The straggly branching stems require support with canes or twigs and the large coarse leaves give rise to one of the common names — Ox Tongue. In addition the plants are short-lived, but these minor drawbacks are more than compensated for by the colour of the clusters of small-petalled flowers. Plant in the spring and mulch around the stems of established plants in May. Dead-head faded blooms and cut the stems down to ground level at the end of the flowering season. The Annual Anchusa (Summer Forget-me-not) is a bushy dwarf with branching stems and starry flowers. Keep well watered in dry weather.

VARIETIES: **A. azurea** (**A. italica**) is the only Perennial Anchusa species you are likely to find and **'Loddon Royalist'** is the most popular variety — height 3 ft (90 cm), spread 1½ ft (45 cm), flowering period June-August. **'Royal Blue'** grows to about the same height but you can have taller or smaller ones. **'Opal'** (pale blue) grows to about 4 ft (1.2 m) and both **'Morning Glory'** (white-eyed dark blue) and **'Dropmore'** (dark blue) can reach 5 ft (1.5 m). For smaller plants there are **'Feltham Pride'** (mid blue, 2½ ft / 75 cm) and **'Little John'** (dark blue, 1½ ft /45 cm). **A. capensis** is the Annual Anchusa — height 9 in. (22.5 cm) or 1½ ft (45 cm), spread 9 in. (22.5 cm), flowering period June-September. The leaves are narrow and hairy, and the white spots of mildew can be a problem. The short varieties include the popular **'Blue Angel'** (dark blue) and **'Dawn'** (white, pink, blue and mauve mixture). Taller ones include **'Blue Bird'** (indigo blue).

SITE & SOIL: Any well-drained soil will do — thrives best in a sunny open situation.

PROPAGATION: Perennials: Divide clumps in spring. Annuals: Sow seeds in March in gentle heat. Plant out in May.

Anchusa azurea 'Loddon Royalist'

Border perennial
•
Bedding plant:
hardy annual

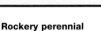

Anchusa azurea 'Royal Blue'

A. azurea 'Loddon Royalist'

A. capensis

Anchusa capensis 'Dawn'

ANDROSACE Rock Jasmine

Rockery perennial

You may be tempted to buy this alpine if you see it at the garden centre with its foliage covered by masses of tiny, primrose-like flowers. In the specialist catalogues you will find scores of species and varieties from which to make your choice. But take care — only a handful can be regarded as suitable for growing outdoors and even these types can be a challenge. They need moist soil but free drainage is essential, and protection against winter rain may be necessary.

VARIETIES: **A. carnea 'Rosea'** is the easiest — height 3 in. (7.5 cm), spread 8 in. (20 cm), pink flowers in late spring. **A. sarmentosa** is the most popular one — the leafy rosettes bear pink flowers. For late summer flowers choose the trailer **A. lanuginosa**.

SITE & SOIL: A well-drained gritty soil is essential. Thrives in sun or light shade.

PROPAGATION: Use rosettes or basal shoots as cuttings — plant in a cold frame in early summer.

A. sarmentosa

Androsace carnea 'Rosea'

ANEMONE Anemone

There is an Anemone for most situations from the wide range of types available. They can produce large drifts of blue daisies naturalised in country estates or small clumps of bright saucer-shaped blooms in tiny front gardens. There are Anemones for the middle or back of the herbaceous border and quite different ones for the rockery or woodland. There is no such thing as a 'typical' Anemone — the blooms may be starry or bowl-shaped, the leaves may be ferny or simply divided, the flowering season may be in spring, summer or autumn and below ground there may be tubers, rhizomes or fibrous roots. Despite this wide range of growth types the numerous species and varieties can be divided into three groups. The *Daisy-flowered Anemones* have many narrow petals surrounding a golden disc, the 1½ in. (3.5 cm) blooms appearing in spring. Plant the rhizomes or tubers about 2 in. (5 cm) deep in September — space them 4 in. (10 cm) apart. More popular but less permanent are the *Poppy-flowered Anemones*. The 2 in. (5 cm) bowl-shaped flowers are brightly coloured — white, pink, red, lavender or blue and they are favourite subjects for flower arranging. Soak the tubers overnight before planting — set them claws upwards 2 in. (5 cm) deep and 4 in. (10 cm) apart. Plant in September for March-April flowers or in March-April for June-September flowers. The final group are the *Japanese Anemones* — 2-5 ft (60 cm-1.5 m) high border perennials with 2 in. (5 cm) saucer-shaped blooms between August and October.

VARIETIES: The first of the Daisy-flowered Anemones to bloom is **A. blanda** (February-April). This is a plant for a dry and sunny site — for a moist and semi-shady spot **A. apennina** (March-April) is a better choice. Both these plants grow about 6 in. (15 cm) high and their usual colour is blue, although white and pink varieties are available. The Wood Anemone (**A. nemorosa**) belongs here, although the blooms are starry rather than daisy-like.

The Poppy-flowered Anemones are varieties of **A. coronaria** — height 6 in.-1 ft (15-30 cm), spread 6 in. (15 cm), all thrive in sun or light shade. The **de Caen** strain produces single flowers. It is usual to choose a multi-coloured mixture of this strain, but single-coloured varieties are available, such as **'The Bride'** (white), **'Mister Fokker'** (blue), **'Hollandia'** (red) and **'His Excellency'** (red). For semi-double or double flowers choose the **St. Brigid** strain — examples include **'The Admiral'** (mauve) and **'Lord Lieutenant'** (blue).

The Anemones described above are grown from rhizomes or tubers and very few grow more than 1 ft (30 cm) high. For late-flowering perennials which are suitable for the middle or back of the border you will have to grow one of the Japanese Anemones. There are two species from which to make your choice. The usual one is **A. japonica** (**A. hybrida**) — white or pink-petalled flowers on 3-5 ft (90 cm-1.5 m) high stems. **'Queen Charlotte'** (semi-double, pink) is a popular choice and so is **'Honorine Jobert'** (single, white). Others include **'Whirlwind'** (semi-double, white) and **'Richard Ahrens'** (semi-double, pink). For smaller plants grow a variety of the other Japanese Anemone species **A. hupehensis** (2-3 ft/ 60-90 cm). Examples are **'Hadspen Abundance'** (single, pink), **'September Charm'** (single, pink), **'Bressingham Glow'** (semi-double, rose-red) or **'Prince Henry'** (semi-double, rose-red).

SITE & SOIL: Any well-drained soil will do — for other requirements see above.

PROPAGATION: Daisy- and Poppy-flowered Anemones: Divide mature clumps in late summer. Japanese Anemones: Do not lift the plant. Cut away a rooted section from the side of the clump and plant in spring.

Bulb
•
Border perennial

A. coronaria
de Caen strain

A. coronaria
St. Brigid strain

A. nemorosa

A. japonica
'Queen Charlotte'

Anemone blanda

Anemone coronaria de Caen strain

Rockery perennial

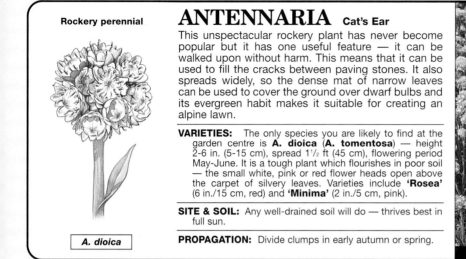

A. dioica

ANTENNARIA Cat's Ear

This unspectacular rockery plant has never become popular but it has one useful feature — it can be walked upon without harm. This means that it can be used to fill the cracks between paving stones. It also spreads widely, so the dense mat of narrow leaves can be used to cover the ground over dwarf bulbs and its evergreen habit makes it suitable for creating an alpine lawn.

VARIETIES: The only species you are likely to find at the garden centre is **A. dioica (A. tomentosa)** — height 2-6 in. (5-15 cm), spread 1½ ft (45 cm), flowering period May-June. It is a tough plant which flourishes in poor soil — the small white, pink or red flower heads open above the carpet of silvery leaves. Varieties include **'Rosea'** (6 in./15 cm, red) and **'Minima'** (2 in./5 cm, pink).

SITE & SOIL: Any well-drained soil will do — thrives best in full sun.

PROPAGATION: Divide clumps in early autumn or spring.

Antennaria dioica 'Rosea'

Border perennial
•
Rockery perennial

A. tinctoria 'Grallach Gold'

ANTHEMIS Chamomile

A bright hardy plant for the front or middle of the border — it flowers intermittently from early June until September. The foliage is finely divided and the daisy-like flowers are borne in large numbers. Each bloom has a central golden boss and the 'petals' are white, pale yellow or yellow depending on the variety. Support may be necessary — cut down the stems after flowering.

VARIETIES: **A. tinctoria** is the Golden Marguerite or Ox-eye Chamomile — height 2 ft (60 cm), flowers all-yellow, 2-3 in. (5-7.5 cm) wide. Varieties include **'E.C. Buxton'** (pale yellow) and **'Grallach Gold'** (golden-yellow). For the front of the border or large rockery choose **A. punctata 'Cupaniana'** — height 1 ft (30 cm), spread 1½ ft (45 cm). The flowers have white 'petals' and the foliage is grey.

SITE & SOIL: Any well-drained soil will do — thrives best in full sun.

PROPAGATION: Divide clumps in autumn or spring.

Anthemis tinctoria 'E.C. Buxton'

Bulb

A. liliago

ANTHERICUM St. Bernard's Lily

You will not find this summer-flowering bulb on prominent display at the garden centre, although it has been a garden plant for centuries. This lack of popularity is not due to any difficulty in cultivation — the problem is that it is a slow starter and so the heads of starry flowers do not appear until the second year after planting. A good subject for naturalising or open woodland.

VARIETIES: **A. liliago** is the species you are most likely to find — height 1½-2 ft (45-60 cm), flowering period May-July. The white starry blooms have prominent yellow anthers and give a cloud-like effect above the grassy leaves. The variety **'Major'** has the largest (1½ in./3.5 cm) flowers. **A. ramosum** has branching flower stems which reach 3 ft (90 cm). Both species can be cut for flower arranging.

SITE & SOIL: Well-drained, humus-rich soil is necessary — thrives in full sun or light shade.

PROPAGATION: Divide overcrowded clumps in spring.

Anthericum liliago

ANTIRRHINUM Snapdragon

The Snapdragon of the cottage garden is known to everyone — 1½ ft (45 cm) upright stems with spikes of lipped tubular flowers which open when squeezed. This garden favourite, however, has come a long way since Victorian times. Some newer varieties are open-faced — snapless flowers which may be single, semi-double or double. Pinch out the growing points when the plants are about 3 in. (7.5 cm) high, stake tall varieties and dead-head faded spikes. In the first edition of this book several 'rust resistant' varieties were recommended, but this tolerance has not persisted.

VARIETIES: Varieties of **A. majus** are available in all colours from white to near black and the flowering period extends from July to October. There are five groups. The Tall group (2-3 ft/60-90 cm) make a bold display — there are the trumpet-shaped **'Bright Butterflies'**, the ruffled **'Supreme Double'** and the open-faced **'Madame Butterfly'** with azalea-like flowers. The Intermediate group (1-2 ft/30-60 cm) is the most popular. The **'Coronette'** strain is renowned for its tolerance to poor weather conditions — **'Monarch'** is another reliable strain. Other mixtures include **'Vanity Fair'**, **'Bizarre'** and **'Cheerio'** — for single colours or bicolours look for **'Rembrandt'**, **'White Wonder'**, **'Purple King'**, **'Black Prince'** etc. For small beds look for the Short group (9 in.-1 ft/22.5-30 cm) — **'Tom Thumb'** and **'Floral Carpet'** are the basic ones and **'Peaches and Cream'** is an attractive bicolour. For open-faced flowers grow **'Pixie'** or **'Trumpet Serenade'**. The Dwarf group (4-9 in./10-22.5 cm) are compact bushes — examples include **'Magic Carpet'**, **'Bells'** and **'Little Gem'**. The latest introduction is the Trailing group — **'Chandelier'** and **'Candelabra'** are the names to look for.

SITE & SOIL: Any well-drained soil will do — thrives best in full sun.

PROPAGATION: Sow seeds in February-March in gentle heat. Plant out in late May.

Antirrhinum 'Madame Butterfly'

Bedding plant: half-hardy annual

A. 'Rembrandt'
Snap type

A. 'Trumpet Serenade'
Open-faced type

Antirrhinum 'Monarch'

Antirrhinum 'Magic Carpet'

The wisdom of underplanting rose beds is a matter of opinion. Some purists feel that roses should always be grown on their own, and others believe that only prostrate leafy ground cover should be used. The problem is that a bed of non-repeat flowering roses can look dull for most of the season and so many gardeners plant flowering ground cover round the shrubs to provide extended interest. The flowers should be neither bold nor bright — Alchemilla mollis has been used here.

AQUILEGIA Columbine

An old-fashioned plant which has produced many excellent varieties in recent years. The traditional Columbine of cottage gardens is a dainty perennial with grey-green ferny leaves and short-spurred flowers in blue or white on 2-3 ft (60-90 cm) stalks. These days there is a much wider choice. There are brightly-coloured long spurred species, fluffy double-flowered types and a range of Alpine Columbines which are suitable for a small rockery. Unfortunately Aquilegias are not long-lived, but they are easily raised by sowing seeds in the spring. May and June is the main flowering season, but some continue to flower in July. Dead-head faded blooms and water copiously in dry weather. Cut down the stems of border varieties once flowering is over.

VARIETIES: The old-fashioned Columbine described above is **A. vulgaris**, but the usual choice is a variety and not the species. There are the near-black and white **'Magpie'**, the all-white **'Nivea'** and the double-flowered **'Nora Barlow'**. In addition there are varieties such as the **'Vervaeneana'** group which have variegated leaves. These varieties of A. vulgaris have only short spurs or none at all and grow about 1½ ft (45 cm) high — for plants with long spurs choose **A. canadensis** (red/yellow flowers). The most popular of all the Aquilegias are the tall-growing **A. 'McKana Hybrids'**. Large flowers with long spurs are borne on 3 ft (90 cm) high stems — these blooms are a mixture of bright bicolours. Blue is the predominant colour of the rockery types. There are **A. bertolonii** (6 in./15 cm, blue), **A. flabellata pumila** (6 in./15 cm, violet/white) and the difficult **A. jonesii** (3 in./7.5 cm, blue). For a change in colour look for **A. canadensis 'Nana'** (8 in./20 cm, red/yellow).

SITE & SOIL: Any well-drained soil will do — thrives best in partial shade.

PROPAGATION: Sow seeds outdoors in April. Mature clumps can be divided but Aquilegias dislike transplanting.

Aquilegia 'McKana Hybrids'

Border perennial
•
Rockery perennial

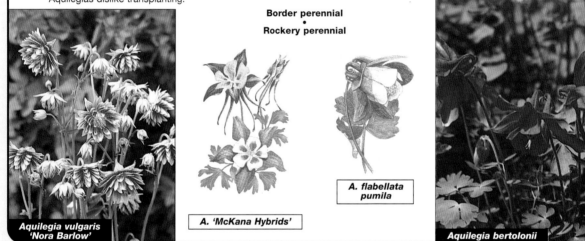

A. flabellata pumila

A. 'McKana Hybrids'

Aquilegia vulgaris 'Nora Barlow'

Aquilegia bertolonii

Rockery perennial

ARABIS Rock Cress

One of the three or four basic rockery plants — the grey-leaved carpets with white flowers in March and April are seen everywhere growing over rocks or tumbling over walls. The common types are invasive — cut back after flowering to keep them in check.

VARIETIES: The Common Rock Cress is **A. albida** (**A. caucasica**) — height 9 in. (22.5 cm), spread 2 ft (60 cm). The single flowers are white — for large double blooms choose the variety **'Flore Pleno'**. White is not the only colour — there are **'Pink Pearl'** (pink) and **'Coccinea'** (red). In addition there is **'Variegata'** with white-edged leaves. Not all species are as wide-spreading as A. albida — **A. blepharophylla 'Spring Charm'** is a crimson-flowered compact plant and **A. ferdinandi-coburgi 'Variegata'** has neat rosettes of brightly variegated leaves all year round.

SITE & SOIL: Any well-drained soil will do — thrives in sun or light shade.

PROPAGATION: Divide clumps in autumn or plant cuttings in a cold frame in summer.

A. albida

Arabis albida 'Flore Pleno'

ARCTOTIS African Daisy

You will find seeds of this showy plant in the comprehensive catalogues of large seed companies but you may not find them at the garden centre. The hybrids provide an eye-catching display of large daisy-like flowers in white, yellow, blue, orange, red and purple on long branching stems. The problem is that they close when the sun goes in and the stems require support.

VARIETIES: The only African Daisies you are likely to find are varieties of **A. hybrida** — height 1-1½ ft (30-45 cm), flowers 3 in. (7.5 cm) across, flowering period July-October. They are usually sold as **'Harlequin Mixed'** or **'Large-Flowered Hybrids'**. Pinch out growing tips when seedlings are 5 in. (12.5 cm) high. **A. venusta** is less easy to find — the 1 ft (30 cm) stems bear blue flowers.

SITE & SOIL: Well-drained light soil in full sun is necessary.

PROPAGATION: Sow seeds in March in gentle heat. Plant out in late May.

Bedding plant: half-hardy annual

A. hybrida

Arctotis hybrida 'Large-Flowered Hybrids'

ARENARIA Sandwort

Arenaria is a background plant in the rock garden rather than a focal point. The leafy prostrate stems form a mat over rocks or between paving stones and in late spring to early summer small white flowers appear on short stalks. There are two useful features. Some species will grow quite happily in shade and all are evergreen.

VARIETIES: The most popular species is **A. montana** — height 4 in. (10 cm), flowering period May-June. The leaves are grassy and the flowers are large for a Sandwort, but it does need a sunny situation. For covering rocks which receive little or no sun choose the mossy-leaved **A. balearica** — height 1 in. (2.5 cm), spread 1½ ft (45 cm), flowering period March-July. For pale purple instead of white flowers grow **A. purpurascens**.

SITE & SOIL: Well-drained moist soil is necessary — sun or shade requirement depends on the species.

PROPAGATION: Divide clumps in autumn or spring.

Rockery perennial

A. montana

Arenaria balearica

ARGYRANTHEMUM Marguerite

Marguerites were great favourites in Victorian times and are now coming back into favour as container plants. They are perennials, but are not hardy and so are grown from cuttings each year as bedding plants — the floral display lasts from late June to September. The daisy-like blooms are about 2 in. (5 cm) across and the foliage is feathery. Marguerites are often trained as standards.

VARIETIES: Marguerites with yellow discs and white 'petals' include **A. foeniculaceum**, **A. frutescens** and **A. 'Chelsea Girl'** — height 2-3 ft (60-90 cm), spread 3 ft (90 cm). Not all varieties bear single white flowers — **A. 'Jamaica Primrose'** has pale yellow blooms, **A. 'Powder Puff'** is pink and double, and **A. 'Vancouver'** is pink and anemone-centred. Argyranthemum may be labelled as **Chrysanthemum** or **Anthemis**.

SITE & SOIL: Any well-drained soil will do — thrives best in full sun.

PROPAGATION: Take cuttings in late summer and grow under glass. Plant out in late May.

Bedding plant: tender perennial

A. 'Jamaica Primrose'

Argyranthemum frutescens

Bulb

ARISAEMA Arisaema

This arum-like plant is not easy to find and is expensive to buy, but if you have an area of moist woodland in which you want to plant something unusual then Arisaema is worth the effort. The 'flowers' have a large tube (the spathe) which surrounds the pencil-like spadix. They appear in May-June — in late summer brightly-coloured berries appear on the spadix.

VARIETIES: **A. candidissimum** is the species which is usually offered — the 4 in. (10 cm) flower is on a 6 in. (15 cm) stalk. The broad shiny leaves appear after the pink- and white-striped flowers. Plant the tubers 6 in. (15 cm) deep in September. Other species include **A. ringens** with distinctly hooded flowers and the dramatic purple-netted **A. griffithii**.

SITE & SOIL: Well-drained, humus-rich soil in sun or partial shade is necessary.

PROPAGATION: Divide clumps or remove offset tubers and plant in autumn.

A. candidissimum

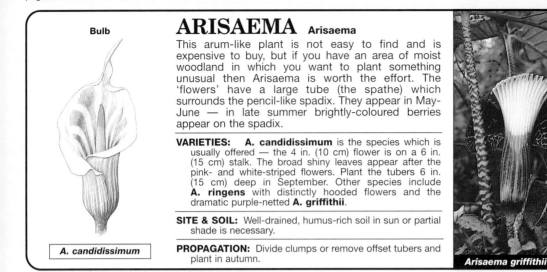

Arisaema griffithii

Bulb

ARISARUM Mouse Plant

Like Arisaema above this shade- and moisture-loving plant is a member of the arum family and is grown for its novelty value. Strange-looking flowers appear in March above the arrow-shaped leaves — it is these blooms which give the plant its common name. The long tail at the top and the colour of the spathe give the appearance of a mouse disappearing into a hole.

VARIETIES: The mouse-like Arisarum is **A. proboscideum**. As with all arums (see page 27) there are a spathe and a spadix. The spadix is insignificant and bears tiny flowers — surrounding it is the tubular spathe which is about 1 in. (2.5 cm) wide. The base is white, but the 'body' is purplish-brown and the 'tail' is a 6 in. (15 cm) long purple thread. **A. vulgare** is a tender green species.

SITE & SOIL: Well-drained, humus-rich soil in partial shade is necessary.

PROPAGATION: Divide clumps or remove offset tubers and plant in autumn.

A. proboscideum

Arisarum proboscideum

Rockery perennial
•
Border perennial

ARMERIA Thrift, Sea Pink

The grass-like leaves of Thrift, densely packed into hummocks, are a common sight in rock gardens and around the sea shore. It is also a good choice for the front of a dry and sunny border — in spring and summer the thin flower stalks appear, each one bearing a globular head of tiny papery blooms. These flower heads are long-lasting and may be numerous enough to cover the foliage.

VARIETIES: The native Thrift is **A. maritima** — height 8 in. (20 cm), spread 1 ft (30 cm), flowering period May-July. The pink flower heads are about 1 in. (2.5 cm) across — some varieties are pink (**'Laucheana'**, **'Vindictive'** etc) but there are other colours such as **'Bloodstone'** (red) and **'Alba'** (white). **A. juniperifolia** is a compact variety — height 3 in. (7.5 cm), pink flowers, flowering period April-May.

SITE & SOIL: Any well-drained soil will do — thrives best in full sun.

PROPAGATION: Divide clumps in spring or root cuttings under glass in summer.

A. maritima

Armeria maritima 'Vindictive'

Bulb

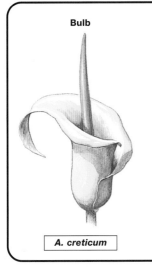

A. creticum

ARUM Cuckoo Pint

This curious flower has the standard pattern of all the Arum family — there are a spathe and a spadix. The Cuckoo Pint has a tube-like spathe and a pencil-like spadix, the flowers appearing above the arrow-shaped leaves between mid April and mid June. Open woodland is the usual site but Arum can be grown in the rockery or border — the flowers are usually eye-catching but both leaves and autumn berries may also be attractive features. Remember that the berries are poisonous.

VARIETIES: The most popular variety is **A. italicum 'Marmoratum'** — height 1¹/₂ ft (45 cm), spread 9 in. (22.5 cm). The wavy-edged leaves are veined and marbled with silver — this foliage is present during the winter months and the spring flowers are greenish-white. For floral display the brightest choice is the yellow-spathed **A. creticum**.

SITE & SOIL: Well-drained, humus-rich soil in sun or light shade.

PROPAGATION: Divide clumps or remove offset tubers and plant in autumn.

Arum italicum 'Marmoratum'

Border perennial

A. dioicus

ARUNCUS Goat's Beard

The large Aruncus by the pool looks like a giant Astilbe — feathery plumes of tiny creamy-white flowers tower above the sprays of pale green leaves. It is certainly not a plant for everyone — it needs moist soil with plenty of humus, plenty of space, plenty of water in dry weather and some shade. Cut down the stems in late autumn. Where space is limited choose a more compact type.

VARIETIES: A. dioicus (**A. sylvestris**) is the most impressive Aruncus — height 6 ft (1.8 m), flowering period June-July. It is a plant for the back of a large border or as a specimen plant on its own as well as for the edge of the pond. It is too large for most gardens and a better choice for the average plot is the variety **'Glasnevin'** (4 ft/1.2 m) or **'Kneiffii'** (3 ft/90 cm). The dwarf one is **A. aethusifolius** (1 ft/30 cm).

SITE & SOIL: Any water-holding soil will do — partial shade is necessary.

PROPAGATION: Divide clumps in autumn — mature plants are difficult to split.

Aruncus dioicus

Bedding plant: half-hardy annual

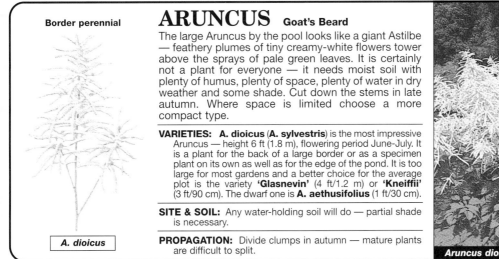

A. erubescens

ASARINA Asarina

This tender perennial of the conservatory is becoming increasingly popular as a half-hardy annual for bedding out into hanging baskets or in the garden against walls or fences. The stems bear large white, pink or lavender flowers from June to mid October. It is not a plant for all gardens — it needs a sunny and sheltered site.

VARIETIES: Nearly all types have twining but not self supporting stems with trumpet-shaped flowers. The shortest stems (length 4 ft/1.2 m, cream-throated pink flowers) are produced by **A. erubescens (Maurandya erubescens)** — the longest ones (10 ft/3 m) belong to **A. barclayana.** At the garden centre you will probably find packets of **A. scandens 'Mixed'** or **'Jewel Mixed'. A. antirrhiniflora** has snapdragon-like flowers.

SITE & SOIL: Any well-drained soil will do — a sheltered site in full sun is necessary.

PROPAGATION: Sow seeds in February-April in gentle heat. Plant out in late May.

Asarina scandens

Border perennial

A. incarnata

ASCLEPIAS Milkweed

This is definitely one to grow if you like unusual plants. There are tender Milkweeds but the two listed below are hardy. When not in flower they are nothing special — stout stems and plain lance-shaped leaves. The flowers and fruits, however, are eye-catching. Each 1 in. (2.5 cm) bloom in the cluster has a boss of upright 'horns' with reflexed petals below, and the fruits open to reveal silky hairs.

VARIETIES: **A. incarnata** (height 4 ft/1.2 m, spread 2 ft/ 60 cm, flowering period July-September) produces heads of pink flowers in the axils of the leaves. These flowers are followed by 3 in. (7.5 cm) erect fruits. **A. tuberosa** blooms at the same time, but it is smaller (3 ft/90 cm), less spreading (1 ft/30 cm) and with brighter flowers which may be yellow, orange or orange-red. Remember that the sap is irritating.

SITE & SOIL: Any well-drained, moisture-retentive soil will do — full sun is necessary.

PROPAGATION: Divide clumps in spring.

Asclepias tuberosa

Rockery perennial

A. lilaciflora

ASPERULA Woodruff

The Woodruffs are not popular alpines — they have none of the robustness of the old favourites although the smooth-leaved types described below are fairly easy to grow outdoors. The woolly-leaved ones such as A. suberosa cannot survive the cold and wet of winter and need the protection of an alpine house. The tubular flowers are usually pink but white and yellow varieties are available.

VARIETIES: **A. gussonii** (4 in./10 cm) is the easiest outdoor Asperula to find and the easiest to grow. The flesh pink flowers are borne above the leafy tufts in early summer. **A. lilaciflora** is a prostrate plant with 1 in. (2.5 cm) long lilac flowers above cushions of glossy green leaves. **A. odorata** (**Galium odoratum**) is quite different — starry white flowers above umbrella-like leaves.

SITE & SOIL: Well-drained gritty soil — full sun is necessary.

PROPAGATION: Divide clumps or take cuttings in spring.

Asperula gussonii

Bulb

A. lutea

ASPHODELUS Asphodel

The Asphodels bear tall spires of white or yellow starry flowers — showy, easy to grow but for most types you will have to order from a specialist bulb company. The tuber- or rhizome-like roots are despatched in spring or autumn and should be planted as soon as they are received. The usual flowering period is May and June after which the summer-long attractive seed heads appear.

VARIETIES: The only one you are likely to find at the garden centre is the Yellow Asphodel **A. lutea** (**Asphodeline lutea**). It grows 4 ft (1.2 m) high with dense spires of bright yellow flowers. For smaller plants and July flowers grow **A. liburnica**. The White Asphodel is **A. albus** — 3 ft (90 cm) high with 1½ in. (3.5 cm) wide flowers. **A. ramosus** is taller and blooms in midsummer.

SITE & SOIL: Any well-drained soil will do — thrives in full sun.

PROPAGATION: Divide overcrowded clumps in spring or autumn.

Asphodelus albus

ASTER Aster, Michaelmas Daisy

The *Michaelmas Daisy* group is by far the largest and most popular sector of this genus, but these plants are by no means the only group nor are they the easiest to grow. Michaelmas Daisies are particularly prone to powdery mildew which can cover the whole plant with pale grey mould if the summer is hot and dry. In addition it is necessary to lift the plants every other year and replant pieces taken from the outer healthy section of the clumps. If mildew has been a problem in the past or if regular lifting does not appeal to you then choose one of the more trouble-free types described below. Next in popularity is the *New England Aster* group — very similar to Michaelmas Daisies at first glance but the stems are stiff and hairy and the flower heads are wide-spreading. The most important difference is their mildew resistance, a feature shared with the *Italian Starwort* group. Another sector worth considering is the *Heath Aster* group — masses of small flowers on stiff wide-spreading stems which have good drought tolerance and some resistance to mildew. The remaining border perennials are collected together as the *Miscellaneous Aster* group. Here you will find some trouble-free types plus the earliest- and latest-flowering ones. The final sector is the *Mountain Aster* group for the rockery — spreading plants with greyish leaves and large, colourful flowers in late spring or summer. General care rules for all Asters include mulching in May, watering in dry weather and staking when necessary.

VARIETIES: The Michaelmas Daisy group are varieties of **A. novi-belgii** — height 1-4 ft (30 cm-1.2 m), flowering period September-October. The popular ones grow about 2-3 ft (60-90 cm) high and have 1½ in. (3.5 cm) wide flowers — examples include **'Winston S. Churchill'** (rich ruby), **'Crimson Brocade'** (double, red), **'Marie Ballard'** (double, blue) and **'Ada Ballard'** (lavender-blue). There are also 1 ft (30 cm) dwarfs for the front of the border — look for **'Snowsprite'** (white), **'Jenny'** (purplish-red) and **'Audrey'** (mauve). The New England Aster group (**A. novae-angliae** varieties) also has many varieties — height 3-5 ft (90 cm-1.5 m), flowering period August-October. **'Harrington's Pink'** (pale pink) is the favourite one — other widely available varieties include **'September Ruby'** (dark pink), **'Autumn Snow'** (white) and **'Andenken an Alma Potschke'** (salmon-pink).

The Italian Starwort group (varieties of **A. amellus**) are shorter, growing about 2 ft (60 cm) high with large flowers from late August to late October. **'King George'** (violet-blue) is the one you are most likely to find — other good ones are **'Violet Queen'** (violet-purple), **'Lady Hindlip'** (pink) and **'Brilliant'** (pink). Two species make up the Heath Aster group — there are **A. ericoides** (the 4 ft/1.2 m variety **'Pink Cloud'** is widely available) and **A. lateriflorus** ('Horizontalis' — height 2 ft/60 cm, pale pink is a popular variety).

There are some excellent varieties in the Miscellaneous Aster group. There is the mildew-resistant **A. frikartii** which blooms in July — look for the varieties **'Monch'** and **'Wonder of Stafa'**. **A. thomsonii 'Nanus'** is another mildew-free Aster which blooms in July — for November flowers there is **A. pringlei 'Monte Cassino'**. You will find just one species of Mountain Aster at the garden centre — **A. alpinus** (height 6 in./15 cm, pale purple flowers, flowering period May-July). Varieties include **'Albus'** (white) and **'Happy End'** (pink).

SITE & SOIL: Any well-drained soil will do — thrives best in full sun.

PROPAGATION: Divide clumps in autumn or spring.

Border perennial
•
Rockery perennial

A. novi-belgii **'Crimson Brocade'**

A. novae-angliae **'Harrington's Pink'**

A. amellus **'Lady Hindlip'**

A. frikartii **'Wonder of Stafa'**

A. thomsonii **'Nanus'**

Aster novi-belgii 'Winston S. Churchill'

Aster alpinus

ASTILBE Astilbe

Pass this one by if your soil is sandy and you live in a dry part of the country. Astilbe will only thrive if the ground is rich in humus so that it can hold the moisture that this plant requires at all times. It is a popular bog plant for the poolside, and is also suitable for peaty borders and open woodland. The foliage is deeply cut and often coppery in spring. The flowers are tiny, but what they lack in size is made up for in quantity. From June to August there are large feathery plumes in white, mauve, pink or red — these plumes can be left to provide autumn decoration. You will find many types to choose from in the catalogues or at large garden centres. Nearly all are middle-of-the-border perennials in height, but there are some dwarfs.

Astilbe chinensis 'Pumila'

VARIETIES: **A. chinensis** has produced two interesting species which can withstand dry conditions better than other Astilbes. There are **'Pumila'** (height 1 ft/30 cm, spread 1½ ft/45 cm, pink) and **'Superba'** (height 3 ft/90 cm, spread 2 ft/60 cm, mauve). Nearly all named Astilbes are hybrids and not varieties of a single species — important parents include **A. arendsii**, **A. japonica**, **A. chinensis** and **A. simplicifolia**. For a tall 3 ft (90 cm) hybrid look for **A. 'Bressingham Beauty'** (pink), **A. 'Fire'** (red), **A. 'Snowdrift'** (white), **A. 'Weisse Gloria'** (white), **A. 'Hyacinth'** (lilac-pink) and **A. 'Amethyst'** (lilac-pink). The most popular Astilbe in the medium 2 ft (60 cm) hybrid group is **A. 'Fanal'** (deep red) — others include **A. 'Deutschland'** (white), **A. 'Irrlicht'** (white) and **A. 'Federsee'** (rose-pink). Not all plumes are erect — **A. 'Ostrich Plume'** (3 ft/90 cm, pink) has arching flower heads. The dwarf hybrids are 1 ft (30 cm) or less — examples include **A. 'Sprite'** (pink), **A. 'Willie Buchanan'** (creamy-white), **A. 'Bronze Elegance'** (rose-pink) and **A. 'Perkeo'** (dark pink).

SITE & SOIL: Moist and humus-rich soil is required — thrives best in light shade.

PROPAGATION: Divide clumps every few years in autumn or spring.

Border perennial
•
Rockery perennial

Astilbe 'Deutschland'

A. 'Bressingham Beauty'

Astilbe 'Ostrich Plume'

ASTRANTIA Masterwort

Border perennial

Use this cottage garden plant in the border to provide a patch of pastel shades between the brightly-coloured blooms of modern hybrids. Each flower head is about 1 in. (2.5 cm) wide with a frill of papery bracts at the base and a cluster of tiny flowers above. The stems are wiry and the leaves deeply divided. Stake in exposed situations, keep watch for slugs and water freely in dry weather. The flowers are excellent for cutting.

VARIETIES: The most popular species is **A. major** — height 2 ft (60 cm), spread 1½ ft (45 cm), flowering period June-July. The flower heads are pinkish-green and not at all attractive — choose instead one of the brighter varieties such as **'Rubra'** (purplish-pink flowers) or **'Sunningdale Variegated'** (cream-splashed green leaves). **A. maxima** (2 ft/60 cm) has pink flowers.

SITE & SOIL: Any moisture-retentive soil will do — thrives best in partial shade.

PROPAGATION: Sow seeds in gentle heat in spring or divide clumps in autumn or spring.

A. major

Astrantia maxima

Rockery perennial

A. deltoidea

AUBRIETA   Aubretia, Rock Cress

Aubrieta in full flower cascading over a wall or growing over stones in a rockery is one of the heralds of spring. The grey-green evergreen leaves are downy and between late March and early June they are covered with masses of ³/₄ in. (1.5 cm) blooms. An easy and tolerant plant but it can be invasive — cut back hard after flowering.

VARIETIES: The basic species is **A. deltoidea** (height 3-5 in./ 7.5-12.5 cm, spread 2 ft/60 cm) but this form is not grown. The many garden varieties are hybrids of this and other species — pale purple and pink are the usual colours but both red and blue are available. Popular ones include **'Aureovariegata'** (gold-edged leaves, lavender flowers), **'Alix Brett'** (double crimson), **'Astolat'** (variegated leaves, purple), **'Bressingham Pink'** (double pink), **'Doctor Mules'** (purple) and **'Red Carpet'** (red).

SITE & SOIL: Any well-drained, non-acid soil — thrives best in full sun.

PROPAGATION: Divide clumps in autumn or take cuttings in summer and grow under glass.

Aubrieta deltoidea 'Doctor Mules'

Bedding plant: tender perennial

B. 'Snowflake'

BACOPA   Bacopa

One of the new generation of bedding plants — you will not find it in every garden centre and it is in very few textbooks. It is worth looking for if you are keen on hanging baskets — it is a semi-trailer with a wide spread and pendent stems which bear tiny flowers all summer long. It is used as an attractive foil to separate larger and brighter flowering types such as Petunia and Impatiens.

VARIETIES: Bacopa is available from the garden centre as rooted cuttings in the spring and not as packets of seeds. Until recently the only variety on offer was **B. 'Snowflake'** — length 1 ft (30 cm), spread 1¹/₂ ft (45 cm), flowering period late June-mid October. The starry white blooms appear in large numbers — lift and move indoors before the frosts arrive. A second variety (**B. 'Pink Domino'**) is now available.

SITE & SOIL: Any well-drained soil will do — thrives in sun or partial shade.

PROPAGATION: Take cuttings in spring and grow under glass. Plant out in late May.

Bacopa 'Snowflake'

Border perennial

B. australis

BAPTISIA   Baptisia

It is strange that lupins are seen in every herbaceous border and yet this tall and attractive cousin from the U.S is a rarity. It is a plant for the back of the border. The foliage is attractive, the long spikes bear eye-catching pea-like flowers in midsummer and the stems with black seed pods are useful flower arranging material. Staking will be necessary on exposed sites.

VARIETIES: The only one you are likely to find at the garden centre is **B. australis** — height 4 ft (1.2 m), spread 2 ft (60 cm), indigo blue flowers, flowering period June-August. The 3 in. (7.5 cm) leaves are made up of three leaflets and the 1 in. (2.5 cm) long flowers have orange stamens. **B. lactea** has purple-flecked white flowers. The one to grow in the wild flower garden is the yellow **B. tinctoria**.

SITE & SOIL: Any well-drained soil will do — thrives best in full sun.

PROPAGATION: Buy a new plant — Baptisia resents being lifted and divided.

Baptisia australis

BEGONIA Begonia

The Begonia genus is extensive and complex, but the garden ones fall neatly into two basic groups — the Fibrous-rooted Begonias and the Tuberous ones. They share a number of physical and cultural features — the leaves are fleshy or waxy, the soil should be enriched with humus before planting, you should wait until early June before planting out, some shade during the day is beneficial, and thorough watering is required when the soil is dry. Despite these similarities there are clear-cut differences. The leaves of the *Fibrous-rooted Begonias* are rounded and the main use of these plants is to provide a sheet of summer-long floral colour in bed, border or container. Their popularity has increased greatly in recent years as new free-flowering F$_1$ hybrids have appeared and gardeners have realised that only this plant can rival Impatiens as a source of colour in shady conditions. It is an easy plant to grow, but start with seedlings or plugs as seed propagation is difficult. *Tuberous Begonias* can also be bought as plugs or pot plants for bedding out in early summer, but many gardeners prefer to start with dormant tubers. These are pressed hollow side upwards into boxes of damp peat in March and kept at 60°-70°F (15°-21°C) — they are then transplanted into pots when the leafy shoots appear. The leaves are angular and serrated, and the use of these Begonias depends on which varieties are chosen. Lift tubers in late October — store in dry peat in a frost-free place.

VARIETIES: Fibrous-rooted Begonias (Bedding or Wax Begonias) are varieties of **B. semperflorens**. The usual height is 6-8 in. (15-20 cm) and compared to the tuberous types the colour range is limited — there are red, pink and white flowers plus one or two newer varieties which are salmon. **B. semperflorens 'Mixed'** will provide a selection of the standard colours at an economical price, but it is better to buy one of the F$_1$ hybrids — they are freer flowering and the growth habit is more even. Bed out in early June when the plants are in flower — blooms should continue to appear until mid October. There are 4-6 in. (10-15 cm) dwarfs such as **'Rusher Red'** and the **'Coco'** series — for 1 ft (30 cm) high plants choose **'Party Fun'**. In the 6-8 in. (15-20 cm) range you will find the **'Devil'**, **'Excel'** and **'Olympia'** series. For something different there are **'Frilly Pink'** and **'Frilly Red'** (ruffled flowers on tall stems), **'Olympia Salmon Orange'** (a novel Begonia colour) and **'Pink Avalanche'** (pink flowers on pendent stems for hanging baskets). Most people prefer the green-leaved types but there are other colours, ranging from pale green (**'Thousand Wonders'**, 8 in./20 cm) to chocolate brown (**'Cocktail'**, 6 in./15 cm). **'Devon Gems'** bears pink, red and white flowers above dark bronze foliage. The best-known Tuberous Begonia is the large-flowered **B. tuberhybrida** with 2-6 in. (5-15 cm) wide rose-like blooms in a wide array of shapes and colours from late June to late September. Named varieties include **'Diana Wynyard'** (white), **'Fairy Light'** (red-edged white), **'Sugar Candy'** (pink), **'Double Picotee'** (red-edged white) and **'Guardsman'** (red). These B. tuberhybrida varieties grow 9 in.-1¹/₂ ft (22.5-45 cm) high and should be spaced about 1 ft (30 cm) apart in beds or borders. Remember to pinch out the small female flowers under each showy male one. **B. multiflora** is smaller and bears masses of double flowers until the frosts arrive — **'Non Stop'** and **'Pin-up'** are popular types. For hanging baskets choose **B. pendula** — length 1-2 ft (30-60 cm), flowers 1-2 in. (2.5-5 cm) across. Varieties include **'Chanson'** (semi-double) and **'Picotee Cascade'** (double).

Bedding plant:
half-hardy annual
•
Bulb

B. 'Thousand Wonders'

B. 'Cocktail'

B. semperflorens

B. tuberhybrida

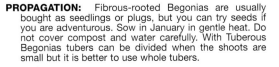

B. multiflora

B. pendula

SITE & SOIL: Any non-chalky, humus-rich soil will do — thrives best in light shade.

PROPAGATION: Fibrous-rooted Begonias are usually bought as seedlings or plugs, but you can try seeds if you are adventurous. Sow in January in gentle heat. Do not cover compost and water carefully. With Tuberous Begonias tubers can be divided when the shoots are small but it is better to use whole tubers.

BEGONIA continued

Begonia 'Devil Mixed'

Begonia 'Frilly Red'

Begonia 'Olympia Starlet'

Begonia 'Sugar Candy'

Begonia 'Guardsman'

Begonia 'Fairy Light'

Begonia 'Non Stop Yellow'

Begonia 'Pin-up'

Begonia 'Picotee Cascade'

Bulb

B. chinensis

BELAMCANDA Leopard Lily

You will have to order this one from the catalogue of a specialist bulb nursery. It is not a garden centre plant, probably because of its reputation for tenderness. Do not let this put you off — it will grow quite happily in the garden as a perennial if the crown is covered with a thick mulch in winter. The flowers are spotted (hence the common name) and in autumn the pods split open to reveal clusters of shiny black seeds.

VARIETIES: The only species you are likely to find is **B. chinensis** — height 2¹/₂ ft (75 cm), flowering period mid June-mid August. The leaves are grouped in a fan like an Iris, but the flowers are quite different. The flat-faced 2 in. (5 cm) wide blooms are borne on branched stalks — the yellow or orange petals are spotted or streaked with red. Each flower only lasts for a day, but new ones continue to appear.

SITE & SOIL: Well-drained, humus-rich soil in sun or light shade is necessary.

PROPAGATION: Divide overcrowded clumps in spring.

Belamcanda chinensis

Bedding plant: hardy biennial

B. perennis
Single variety

B. perennis
Double variety

BELLIS Daisy

The familiar daisy on the lawn has given rise to a large number of garden varieties. Nearly all are doubles in which the central yellow disc has been obliterated and the flower colours range from white to red. All are perennials but are generally grown as biennials — use Bellis for ground cover, edging, containers or to fill gaps in the rockery.

VARIETIES: The basic species is **B. perennis** (height 3-8 in./ 7.5-20 cm, spacing 6 in./15 cm, flowering period April-July). For large 2 in. (5 cm) blooms choose **'Monstrosa'**, **'Radar Red'** or **'Goliath'** — for masses of small blooms look for **'The Pearl'** or the **'Carpet'** series. Grow **'Spring Star'** or **'Pomponette'** for pompon-like blooms or for quilled red-tipped petals you can sow the tall-growing **'Habanera Blush'**.

SITE & SOIL: Any reasonable soil will do — thrives best in sun or partial shade.

PROPAGATION: Sow seeds in May-June — plant out in autumn.

*Bellis perennis
'Habanera Blush'*

Border perennial

B. cordifolia

BERGENIA Elephant's Ear

Bergenia is a splendid ground cover for a herbaceous or mixed border. It thrives under shrubs and trees, spreads rapidly, effectively keeps down weeds and provides colour all year round. Most green-leaved varieties turn red in autumn and above the foliage hyacinth-like flower heads in red, pink, purple or white appear in spring.

VARIETIES: The one you usually see in the garden is **B. cordifolia** — height 1¹/₂ ft (45 cm), flowering period March-April. Deep pink flowers are borne in drooping sprays — the variety **'Purpurea'** has pale purple flowers. One of the named hybrids is a better choice — good ones include **B. 'Sunningdale'** (rose-pink, red stems), **B. 'Baby Doll'** (pink, small leaves), **B. 'Evening Glow'** (crimson) and **B. 'Silberlicht'** (white).

SITE & SOIL: Any soil which does not waterlog will do — thrives in sun or partial shade.

PROPAGATION: Divide large and overcrowded clumps in autumn.

Bergenia 'Silberlicht'

**Bedding plant:
half-hardy annual**

**B. ferulifolia
'Golden Goddess'**

BIDENS Bidens

Not all the bedding plants introduced in the 1990s have proved to be successful, but Bidens has lived up to its promise. In both good and bad summers it has produced ferny-leaved stems studded with large starry flowers from the end of June until mid October. Growth is vigorous, so it is suitable for ground cover as well as for tubs and hanging baskets.

VARIETIES: The first variety to be offered for sale was **B. ferulifolia 'Golden Goddess'** — stem length 1½-2 ft (45-60 cm), bright yellow flowers. The 1½-2 in. (3.5-5 cm) wide blooms appear throughout the summer and autumn on the weak spreading stems. **B. aurea 'Sunshine'** has similar flowers and foliage but the growth habit is pendent rather than spreading and it is therefore a better choice for hanging baskets.

SITE & SOIL: Any well-drained soil will do — thrives in sun or light shade.

PROPAGATION: Sow seeds in February-March in gentle heat. Plant out in late May.

**Bidens ferulifolia
'Golden Goddess'**

Bulb

B. striata

BLETILLA Chinese Ground Orchid

Orchids are not plants for the open garden in this country, but there is one which can be grown if you are able to satisfy its three basic requirements. The soil must be free-draining, the site must be in a mild part of the country and the crowns must be covered with a thick mulch of pine needles or leaf mould over winter. For most areas it is better to grow Bletilla as a pot plant for summer display in the garden.

VARIETIES: The one to order is **B. striata (B. hyacinthina)** — height 1 ft (30 cm), flowers pink or mauve, flowering period mid June-mid July. Plant in spring as soon as the pseudobulbs (tuber-like stems) arrive — set them 6 in. (15 cm) apart and cover with a 1 in. (2.5 cm) layer of soil. Varieties are hard to find, but **'Albostriata'** (pink-striped white) and **'Alba'** (pink-flushed white) appear in some catalogues.

SITE & SOIL: Well-drained, humus-rich soil in full sun is necessary.

PROPAGATION: Divide clumps every other year in early spring.

Bletilla striata

Border perennial

B. asteroides

BOLTONIA False Chamomile

There are many narrow-petalled daisies for the herbaceous border — some are seen everywhere like Michaelmas Daisies and others are rarely seen like Boltonia. It is fully hardy and easy to grow, but its lack of popularity is no surprise. Boltonia is a giant, reaching 6 ft (1.8 m) or more with branching stems which require staking against the wind and spraying against mildew.

VARIETIES: **B. asteroides** is the only species — height 6 ft (1.8 m), spread 3 ft (90 cm), white or mauve 1 in. (2.5 cm) flowers, flowering period August-September. The variety **'Latisquama'** has lilac flowers and both plants bear their blooms in large clusters. Boltonia is a back-of-the-border plant, but perhaps it is better suited to the wild garden. Where space is a problem look for the dwarf variety **'Nana'** (3 ft/90 cm).

SITE & SOIL: Any well-drained soil will do — thrives in sun or partial shade.

PROPAGATION: Divide clumps in early spring.

Boltonia asteroides

**Bedding plant:
half-hardy annual**

B. iberidifolia

BRACHYCOME Swan River Daisy

Bright fragrant daisies on top of branching stems are the main feature of this Australasian plant. The feathery foliage gives it a delicate appearance but it is hardier than it looks with good drought tolerance. It is still not an easy plant, needing good soil and protection from strong winds. You will find several varieties listed in the catalogues and there will be seed packets in the stores, but it is not often seen among the bedding plant seedlings at the garden centre in spring.

VARIETIES: **B. iberidifolia** is generally sold as a mixture — height 1-2 ft (30-60 cm), spread 1½ ft (45 cm), white, pink, lilac and blue 1½ in. (3.5 cm) flowers, flowering period mid June-late September. The central disc may be black or yellow. Named varieties available as seeds include **'Blue Star'**, **'Purple Splendour'** and **'White Splendour'**.

SITE & SOIL: Rich, free-draining soil is necessary — thrives best in full sun.

PROPAGATION: Sow seeds in March in gentle heat. Plant out in May.

*Brachycome iberidifolia
'Purple Splendour'*

Bulb

B. amethystina

BRIMEURA Spanish Hyacinth

Unlike the ever-popular Dutch Hyacinth you will have to search for a supplier of the Spanish one. It looks more like a bluebell than a hyacinth and the search is only worth while if you like to collect unusual plants. The upright stalk with 10-15 delicate bells appears above the long and narrow leaves at the base. It will grow quite happily in a shady spot in the rockery.

VARIETIES: **B. amethystina** is the only species you are likely to find — height 6-8 in. (15-20 cm), pale blue ½ in. (1 cm) long tubular blooms in May-June. Plant 4 in. (10 cm) deep in early autumn — spacing 4 in. (10 cm). A dark blue form is available and there is also a white variety — **'Alba'**. This white Spanish Hyacinth is showy and more vigorous than the blue ones.

SITE & SOIL: Any well-drained soil will do — thrives in sun or partial shade.

PROPAGATION: Divide overcrowded clumps in autumn.

Brimeura amethystina

Bulb

B. laxa

BRODIAEA Brodiaea

A most confusing genus — one species may look quite different from another one and a single species may be given three different genus names! The slender flower stalk bears a cluster of starry or tubular blooms at the top — the leaves are narrow and strap-like. An excellent plant for cutting, but it requires light soil and you will need to protect it from strong winds.

VARIETIES: The species of Brodiaea may be listed under **Triteleia** or **Dichelostemma**. All are uncommon but you will find **B. laxa** in a number of catalogues — height 2 ft (60 cm), flowering period mid May-late July. The tubular blooms are white, blue or lilac. **B. coronaria** has blooms which are star-faced and the pendent flowers of **B. ida-maia** are bright red and green.

SITE & SOIL: Well-drained soil, a sheltered site and full sun are necessary.

PROPAGATION: Dislikes disturbance — buy new corms.

*Brodiaea laxa
'Queen Fabiola'*

Bedding plant: half-hardy annual

B. speciosa

BROWALLIA Bush Violet

Browallia has been sold for many years as a house plant. It is bought in flower and then placed in good light indoors to provide a floral display for many weeks. This bushy weak-stemmed plant has now moved out into the garden as a result of the boom in container growing. It is an attractive choice for hanging baskets or the edge of tubs and troughs in sheltered sites.

VARIETIES: **B. speciosa** is the usual species — height 8 in.-2 ft (20-60 cm), white-throated violet 2 in. (5 cm) wide flowers, flowering period mid June-late September. Popular varieties include **'Blue Troll'** (blue) and **'White Troll'** (all-white) — both are low-growing. For 2 ft (60 cm) plants grow **'Jingle Bells'** — a mixture of white, blue and lavender blooms.

SITE & SOIL: Any reasonable soil will do — choose a sunny, sheltered spot.

PROPAGATION: Sow seeds in February-March in gentle heat. Plant out in late May.

Browallia speciosa 'White Troll'

Border perennial

B. macrophylla

BRUNNERA Perennial Forget-me-not

An easy plant for difficult situations — it will grow as ground cover in the shade under leafy trees or provide an early floral display at the front of the border when little else is in flower. The large branching sprays of small starry flowers give the impression of a giant Forget-me-not, but the large heart-shaped leaves show that it is not related. Water thoroughly during dry spells.

VARIETIES: **B. macrophylla** is the only species — height 1½ ft (45 cm), spread 2 ft (60 cm), pale blue flowers, flowering period April-early June with a second flush in autumn. There are several popular varieties — look for **'Variegata'** or **'Dawson's White'** (white-edged leaves), **'Hadspen Cream'** (cream-edged leaves) and **'Aluminium Spot'** (silver-spotted leaves). Cut off stems after flowering.

SITE & SOIL: Any well-drained soil will do — thrives best in shade.

PROPAGATION: Divide clumps in autumn or spring.

Brunnera macrophylla 'Variegata'

Bulb

B. vernum

BULBOCODIUM Spring Saffron

At first glance the young goblet-shaped flower of this plant looks like a Crocus, but on closer inspection differences can be seen. Leaves are absent or are small when the bloom appears and the strap-like petals open wide as they mature. The 6 in. (15 cm) long narrow leaves die down in early summer. Lift and divide the clumps in early autumn every three years.

VARIETIES: **B. vernum** is the only species offered for sale — height 3 in. (7.5 cm), spacing 4 in. (10 cm), flowers lavender-pink with a white base, flowering period February-March. Up to three flowers push through the soil on short stalks. Bulbocodium is a member of the Colchicum and not the Iris family like Crocus — the petals open to produce a star-shaped flower. Plant the corms 3 in. (7.5 cm) deep in September or October.

SITE & SOIL: Any well-drained soil will do — thrives best in full sun.

PROPAGATION: Remove cormlets at lifting time and replant.

Bulbocodium vernum

Border perennial
•
Rockery perennial

C. nepetoides

CALAMINTHA Calamint

This member of the mint family is neither brightly coloured nor showy, but it is a useful addition to the herbaceous border where a foil between large flowers in primary colours is required. It is also recommended for growing around roses, in cottage gardens and anywhere you may wish to attract butterflies and bees. The small tubular flowers are arranged in whorls on upright spikes.

VARIETIES: **C. grandiflora** is the tallest species — height $1^{1}/_{2}$ ft (45 cm), spread $1^{1}/_{2}$ ft (45 cm), pink flowers, flowering period June-August. Grow **'Variegata'** for green-splashed cream leaves. **C. nepetoides** is smaller (1 ft x 1 ft/30 cm x 30 cm) and blooms later (August-October). The leaves are highly aromatic and the flowers are lilac. **C. cretica** forms a 9 in. (22.5 cm) white-flowered dome for the rockery.

SITE & SOIL: Any well-drained soil will do — thrives in sun or light shade.

PROPAGATION: Divide clumps in spring

Calamintha grandiflora

Bedding plant: half-hardy annual

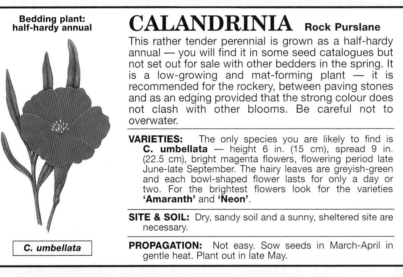

C. umbellata

CALANDRINIA Rock Purslane

This rather tender perennial is grown as a half-hardy annual — you will find it in some seed catalogues but not set out for sale with other bedders in the spring. It is a low-growing and mat-forming plant — it is recommended for the rockery, between paving stones and as an edging provided that the strong colour does not clash with other blooms. Be careful not to overwater.

VARIETIES: The only species you are likely to find is **C. umbellata** — height 6 in. (15 cm), spread 9 in. (22.5 cm), bright magenta flowers, flowering period late June-late September. The hairy leaves are greyish-green and each bowl-shaped flower lasts for only a day or two. For the brightest flowers look for the varieties **'Amaranth'** and **'Neon'**.

SITE & SOIL: Dry, sandy soil and a sunny, sheltered site are necessary.

PROPAGATION: Not easy. Sow seeds in March-April in gentle heat. Plant out in late May.

Calandrinia umbellata 'Amaranth'

Bedding plant: half-hardy annual
•
Rockery perennial

C. rugosa

CALCEOLARIA Slipper Flower

The Slipper Flower was a favourite bedding plant in Victorian times but is no longer popular. The French Marigold has taken over the yellow spot and before the F_1 hybrids appeared it was notoriously difficult to raise from seeds. It is making something of a comeback — you will find several varieties offered as seeds and also as young plants for bedding out in spring.

VARIETIES: Bedding Calceolarias are varieties of **C. rugosa** — height 8-15 in. (20-37.5 cm), spread 9 in. (22.5 cm), yellow or red flowers, flowering period June-mid October. The masses of pouched flowers provide a colourful display in beds or containers. **'Sunshine'** (yellow) is the most popular variety — **'Sunset'** has red and yellow flowers. **C. tenella** is a mat-forming hardy perennial for the rockery.

SITE & SOIL: Any reasonable soil will do — thrives in sun or light shade.

PROPAGATION: Not easy. Sow seeds in January-March in gentle heat. Plant out in late May.

Calceolaria 'Sunshine'

**Bedding plant:
hardy annual**

*C. officinalis
'Orange King'*

CALENDULA   Pot Marigold

This old garden plant was once widely grown as a kitchen herb but is now used as a summer-flowering annual. It is a favourite starter plant for children — a pinch of seeds in spring and in about 10 weeks masses of flowers appear above the hairy, pungent leaves. Pinch out the growing tips of young stems to induce bushiness — dead-head to prolong the flowering season.

VARIETIES: There are now many varieties of the basic species **C. officinalis** — height 9 in.-2 ft (22.5-60 cm), spacing 9 in.-1 ft (22.5-30 cm), flowering period late May-mid September. Flower colours range from cream to mahogany. The favourite dwarf is **'Fiesta Gitana'**. Popular 1½ ft (45 cm) ones include **'Lemon Queen'**, **'Orange King'** and **'Radio'** — the usual tall variety is **'Art Shades'**.

SITE & SOIL: Any reasonable soil will do — thrives in sun or partial shade.

PROPAGATION: Sow seeds in January-March in gentle heat. Plant out in April or May.

*Calendula officinalis
'Fiesta Gitana'*

CALLISTEPHUS   China Aster, Annual Aster

China Asters provide summer and autumn colour in flower beds and long-lasting blooms for indoor decoration. The leaves are hairy and deeply lobed, and the flowers look like large daisies or small chrysanthemums. You will find a bewildering selection in the seed catalogues — dwarf and tall, single and double and colours ranging from white to near black. Callistephus is almost hardy — it is usually bedded out in May but in mild districts the seeds can be sown outdoors in spring. They are not trouble-free — aster wilt is a serious soil disease. Do not grow these plants in the same spot year after year — choose a semi-resistant variety such as 'Roundabout' or 'Ostrich Plume' if you have had a wilt problem. Dead-head regularly, mulch in spring and stake tall varieties.

VARIETIES: **C. chinensis** is the basic species — height 6 in.-3 ft (15-90 cm), flowering period August-late September. The Single group are not often grown these days, but here you will find tall ones such as **'Super Sinensis'**. The double varieties have a number of flower forms. The Chrysanthemum group ranges from the tall **'Duchess'** strain with 4-5 in. (10-12.5 cm) incurved blooms to the 1 ft (30 cm) high **'Milady'** and even smaller **'Pinocchio'**. The Ball group is a limited one — look for **'Miss Europe'** and **'Milady Rose'**. Long feathery petals are the feature of the Plume group — examples include the old favourite **'Ostrich Plume'** (1½ ft/45 cm) and the large-flowered **'Totem Pole'**. Finally there is the Pompon group with button-like flowers — included here are **'Lilliput'** (1 ft/30 cm) and **'Pompon Mixed'** (1½ ft/45 cm). This list illustrates the wide range available but is by no means complete. There are excellent extra-short ones like **'Roundabout'** and extra-tall ones like **'Matsumoto'**.

SITE & SOIL: Any well-drained, non-acid soil will do. Choose a sunny, sheltered spot.

PROPAGATION: Sow seeds in March in gentle heat. Plant out in May.

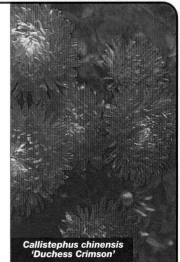

*Callistephus chinensis
'Duchess Crimson'*

**Bedding plant:
half-hardy annual**

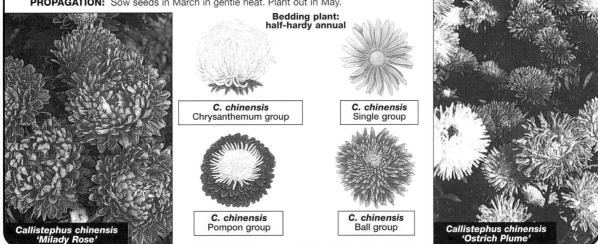

*Callistephus chinensis
'Milady Rose'*

C. chinensis
Chrysanthemum group

C. chinensis
Single group

C. chinensis
Pompon group

C. chinensis
Ball group

*Callistephus chinensis
'Ostrich Plume'*

CALTHA Kingcup, Marsh Marigold

Border perennial

Caltha is only suitable for boggy ground. It will grow in a damp border but it feels more at home in the marshy land around a pond. The dark green heart-shaped leaves have serrated edges and in spring the buttercup-like flowers appear on branching stems above the leaves. If grown in the border you must ensure that the ground is kept moist in dry weather.

VARIETIES: The basic species is **C. palustris** — height 1 ft (30 cm), spacing 1¹/₂ ft (45 cm), yellow flowers, flowering period April-June. The 1-2 in. (2.5-5 cm) wide single flowers are attractive, but there are variations. **'Plena'** and **'Flore Pleno'** have double flowers and **'Alba'** bears white single blooms. For a bold yellow-flowered Kingcup which will reach 2 ft (60 cm) or more choose **C. laeta.**

SITE & SOIL: An organic-rich moist or wet soil is essential — thrives in sun or partial shade.

PROPAGATION: Divide clumps in June.

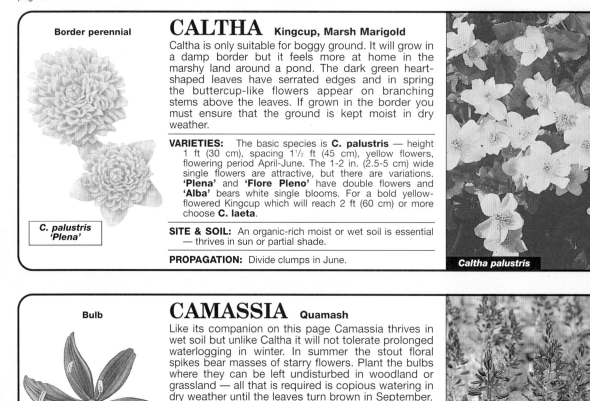

C. palustris 'Plena'

Caltha palustris

CAMASSIA Quamash

Bulb

Like its companion on this page Camassia thrives in wet soil but unlike Caltha it will not tolerate prolonged waterlogging in winter. In summer the stout floral spikes bear masses of starry flowers. Plant the bulbs where they can be left undisturbed in woodland or grassland — all that is required is copious watering in dry weather until the leaves turn brown in September.

VARIETIES: **C. leichtlinii** is the most widely available species — height 3 ft (90 cm), blue flowers, flowering period late May-June. Plant the bulbs 4 in. (10 cm) deep in October. The flowers are about 1¹/₂ in. (3.5 cm) wide — grow **'Electra'** for the largest flowers or **'Alba'** if you want white blooms. **C. quamash** (2 ft/60 cm) has white, blue or purple flowers — **C. cusickii** has up to 100 blue blooms on each spike.

SITE & SOIL: Any moisture-retentive soil will do — thrives in sun or partial shade.

PROPAGATION: Lift and divide overcrowded clumps in autumn.

C. cusickii

Camassia leichtlinii

The herbaceous border is one of Britain's major contributions to the world of gardening and it has few rivals as an impressive display in high summer. The problem is that it provides neither colour nor interest for several months of the year, and so its popularity has declined as the mixed border has steadily taken over. Here bulbs, evergreens, shrubs etc together with border perennials ensure that the border is never bare nor devoid of flowers and/or leaf colour.

CAMPANULA Bellflower

There are Campanulas for setting out in autumn as bedding plants, for growing in the border as hardy perennials and for filling in bare patches in the rockery. Most are easy to grow although some of the rarer rockery ones need winter protection — the major problem with Campanulas is slug damage and many popular ones are susceptible to the rust fungus. The bell-shaped or starry blooms are nearly always blue, white, lavender or purple and heights range from less than 6 in. (15 cm) to more than 6 ft (1.8 m). Staking is necessary for tall-growing varieties and dead-heading will prolong the floral display. The *Bedding Campanulas* are usually grown as biennials — here you will find the Canterbury Bell with its wavy-edged, hairy leaves and numerous spikes of bell-shaped flowers. The largest group are the *Border Campanulas* with varieties for the front, middle or back of the border. Flowering occurs some time between July and September and the arrangement of the flowers on the stem gives a clue to the species. Nearly all Border Campanulas are excellent for cutting. The final group are the *Rockery Campanulas* — easy and reliable but they do need a non-acid soil which is free draining. June and July are the peak flowering months and they have a well-earned reputation for producing masses of blooms.

VARIETIES: The most popular Bedding Campanula is the Canterbury Bell **C. medium** — flowers may be single, semi-double or double and there are rose-coloured varieties alongside the usual whites, blues and purples. The semi-double **'Calycanthema'** is the old favourite Cup and Saucer — height 2¹/₂ ft (75 cm), flowering period May-July. For single bell-shaped flowers on 1¹/₂ ft (45 cm) dome-shaped plants choose **'Bells of Holland'** — for double flowers grow **'Flore Pleno'** (3 ft/90 cm). The giant of the group is the Chimney Bellflower (**C. pyramidalis**) reaching 6 ft (1.8 m) or more. At the other end of the scale are the dainty half-hardy annual trailers such as **C. isophylla** bought in pots for the edges of containers. **C. persicifolia** was for many years the most widely-grown Border Campanula — the cup-shaped flowers are borne along the 2-3 ft (60-90 cm) high wiry stems. **'Telham Beauty'** (pale blue) is the usual choice but there are also double whites such as **'Boule de Neige'** and Cup and Saucer types. **C. latifolia** (4-5 ft/1.2-1.5 m) is a taller species and the blooms are shaped like long bells, but the best choice among taller Campanulas is **C. lactiflora** (3-5 ft/90 cm-1.5 m) with open-bell flowers in branched heads. The varieties have a long flowering period throughout the summer — look for **'Prichard's Variety'** (lavender), **'Loddon Anna'** (pink) and the 1 ft (30 cm) dwarf **'Pouffe'** (pale blue). The final Border Campanula species is **C. glomerata** — 2 ft (60 cm) high with small bells borne in round clusters. You will find a number of Rockery Campanulas at a large garden centre. **C. carpatica** will be one. Height 9 in. (22.5 cm), cup-shaped white or blue bells — the **'Clips'** series form free-flowering 6 in. (15 cm) mounds. **C. cochleariifolia** also bears open white or blue bells but it grows as a 3 in. (7.5 cm) high mat. **C. portenschlagiana** is a purple-flowered trailer which will grow in shade. For starry-flowered rockery plants look for **C. poscharskyana** or **C. garganica**.

SITE & SOIL: Any well-drained soil will do — thrives in sun or light shade.

PROPAGATION: Bedding Campanulas: Sow seeds in May-June — plant out in autumn. Alternatively sow in February in gentle heat and plant out in April. Border and Rockery Campanulas: Divide clumps in spring.

Bedding plant:
hardy annual
or hardy biennial
•
Border perennial
•
Rockery perennial

BEDDING CAMPANULAS

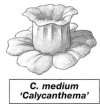

*C. medium
'Calycanthema'*

BORDER CAMPANULAS

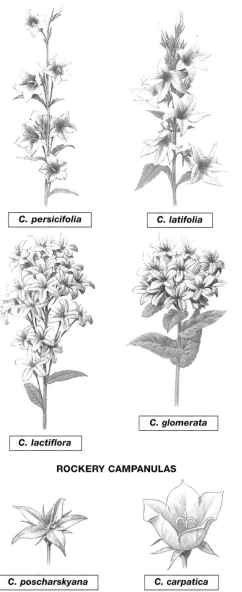

C. persicifolia

C. latifolia

C. lactiflora

C. glomerata

ROCKERY CAMPANULAS

C. poscharskyana

C. carpatica

CAMPANULA continued

Campanula medium 'Calycanthema'

Campanula pyramidalis

Campanula isophylla

Campanula latifolia 'Alba'

Campanula lactiflora 'Loddon Anna'

Campanula glomerata 'Superba'

Campanula carpatica

Campanula cochleariifolia

Campanula poscharskyana

Bulb

C. generalis

CANNA Canna Lily

There is hardly any other bedding plant which can rival Canna as an eye-catching focal point. The paddle-shaped leaves are 1 ft (30 cm) or more in length and are often coloured — the brightly-coloured blooms are up to 5 in. (12.5 cm) across and the display lasts from July until the first frosts. But it is not for everyone — it needs a sheltered spot in full sun.

VARIETIES: There are many named varieties of **C. generalis**. Coloured-leaved Cannas include **'Assault'** (4 ft/1.2 m, red flowers, purple foliage), **'Dazzler'** (4 ft/1.2 m, red flowers, bronze foliage) and **'Verdi'** (3 ft/90 cm, orange-splashed yellow and purple flowers, purple foliage). Green-leaved Cannas include **'Lucifer'** (2 ft/60 cm, yellow-edged red flowers) and **'President'** (3 ft/90 cm, red flowers). Start rhizomes in peat in March — plant out in early June and lift and store in autumn.

SITE & SOIL: Humus-rich soil and full sun are essential.

PROPAGATION: Cut up rhizomes once they have started into growth.

Canna generalis 'Lucifer'

Border perennial

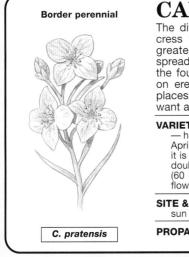

C. pratensis

CARDAMINE Bittercress

The difference between this modest member of the cress family and the plant above could hardly be greater. Cardamine is hardy, low-growing and spreading. The leaves have little decorative value and the four-petalled flowers are borne in large numbers on erect wiry stems. It is a plant for moist or wet places such as the pond edge or woodland where you want a wild flower look.

VARIETIES: **C. pratensis** (Lady's Smock) is a native plant — height 1½ ft (45 cm), pale lilac flowers, flowering period April-May. The variety **'Flore Pleno'** is a better choice — it is shorter, less invasive and the pink or lilac flowers are double. For a taller plant choose **C. latifolia** — height 2 ft (60 cm), white, lilac or violet ½ in. (1 cm) wide flowers, flowering period May-June.

SITE & SOIL: Any moisture-retentive soil will do — thrives in sun or partial shade.

PROPAGATION: Divide clumps in late autumn.

Cardamine pratensis 'Flore Pleno'

Bulb

C. giganteum

CARDIOCRINUM Giant Himalayan Lily

If you have the space and like to grow unusual things then the Giant Himalayan Lily is worth looking for in the catalogues. Plant the large bulbs 6 in. (15 cm) deep in October — space them 3 ft (90 cm) apart. In summer the stout stems will be above your head and lily-like trumpets about 6 in. (15 cm) long are borne in terminal clusters. After flowering the main bulb dies but offsets are produced.

VARIETIES: **C. giganteum** (**Lilium giganteum**) grows up to 9 ft (2.7 m) tall. The white flowers which appear in July and August have reddish markings on the inside and are strongly fragrant. The crown of about 20 large bells above the shiny leaves spiralling around the towering stem is an impressive sight. You will need patience — it may take a couple of years before the tall flowering stems are produced.

SITE & SOIL: Well-drained, moisture-retentive soil and light shade are essential.

PROPAGATION: Buy new bulbs. Offsets can be planted but will take several years to flower.

Cardiocrinum giganteum

Border perennial

CATANANCHE Cupid's Dart

Silvery buds on wiry stems open to produce 1½ in. (3.5 cm) wide daisy-like flowers with papery petals. The ends of these petals are blunt and serrated — a useful key to recognition. It has several virtues as a border plant — it will thrive in dry soil, the flowering season is a long one and the flowers can be cut and dried for use indoors. The problem is that it looks rather sparse and the stems need twigs for support — it is seen at its best in the cottage garden. Cut back the stems once flowering is over.

VARIETIES: **C. caerulea** is the basic species — height 2 ft (60 cm), spacing 1 ft (30 cm), blue cornflower-like flowers, flowering period June-September. The variety **'Major'** has the largest flowers — **'Alba'** is white and the blooms of **'Bicolor'** are blue with white edges.

SITE & SOIL: Any well-drained soil will do — thrives in sandy soil. A sunny spot is essential.

PROPAGATION: Divide clumps in spring or sow seeds in March in gentle heat — plant out in May.

| C. caerulea |

Catananche caerulea 'Major'

Bedding plant: half-hardy annual

CELOSIA Prince of Wales Feathers

The pots of Celosia on display at the garden centre have two distinct types of flower head. They will be mostly of the plumed type and can be grown outdoors if the site is sheltered and warm — this is not a plant for the cooler parts of the country. Their feathery flower spikes are quite different from the velvety cockscombs of the crested ones which are suitable only for the living room or conservatory.

VARIETIES: The Plumed Celosias are varieties of **C. plumosa** — height 9 in.-3 ft (22.5-90 cm), white, yellow, orange, red or purple flowers, flowering period July-September. Choose a tall one for the centre of a bed — look for **'Century'** (2 ft/60 cm), or **'Flamingo Feather'** (3 ft/90 cm). At the other end of the scale are the 9 in.-1 ft (22.5-30 cm) dwarfs — **'Rondo'**, **'Kimono'**, **'Olympia'** and **'Dwarf Geisha'**.

SITE & SOIL: The soil must not be heavy and the site must be warm and sunny.

PROPAGATION: Sow seeds in February-March in gentle heat. Plant out in early June.

| C. plumosa |

Celosia 'Dwarf Geisha'

The single herbaceous border (see page 40) in summer is an eye-catching feature in many gardens, and the double border as illustrated here is an even more spectacular sight. One of the basic rules, however, appears to have been overlooked here — the path should be wide enough and clear enough to allow easy walking and easy mowing. The spread of some of the plants on to the turf makes cutting difficult as does the ornament in the centre of the path.

CENTAUREA Cornflower, Knapweed

Blue annuals in the cottage garden and pink perennials in the border — Centaurea has long been a familiar sight in our gardens. The thistle-like flower heads are attractive to bees and butterflies — dead-head spent blooms and stake tall varieties. The blue of the native farm weed remains the most popular colour of Annual Cornflowers but shades from white to maroon are available. They are easy plants to grow and are often sown where they are to flower. The Perennial Cornflowers produce their main flush of blooms in midsummer with a second flush in autumn. They tend to spread rapidly and should be lifted and divided every three years. Cut the stems down to ground level in autumn.

Centaurea cyanus 'Blue Diadem'

VARIETIES: Annual Cornflowers are usually varieties of **C. cyanus** — height 1-3 ft (30-90 cm), 1-2 in. (2.5-5 cm) wide flowers, flowering period June-September. **'Blue Diadem'** (2-3 ft/60-90 cm) with deep blue extra-large flowers has long been the favourite tall variety and in more recent years the **'Florence'** series in a wide range of colours has dominated the 1½ ft (45 cm) range. The dwarfs grow about 1 ft (30 cm) high — choose from **'Polka Dot'** (mixed colours) or **'Jubilee Gem'** (blue). If you want something different there are the tall **'Frosty'** with white-edged petals and **C. moschata** (Sweet Sultan) with powderpuff flowers. Several species make up the Perennial Cornflowers or Knapweeds. **C. dealbata** has the fine variety **'Steenbergii'** (2 ft/60 cm, white-centred reddish-pink flowers) and **C. hypoleuca 'John Coutts'** has yellow-centred pink flowers. For yellow flowers on 3 ft (90 cm) stems choose **C. macrocephala** — for late spring flowers on sprawling stems pick **C. montana**.

SITE & SOIL: Any well-drained soil will do — thrives in sun or light shade.

PROPAGATION: Annual Cornflowers: Sow seeds in March in gentle heat. Plant out in May. Perennial Cornflowers: Divide clumps in autumn or spring.

Centaurea cyanus 'Polka Dot'

Bedding plant: hardy annual
•
Border perennial

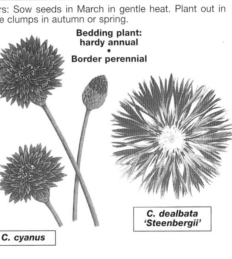
C. cyanus

C. dealbata 'Steenbergii'

Centaurea montana

CENTRANTHUS Red Valerian

Border perennial

C. ruber 'Coccineus'

Centranthus is part of the countryside — you will find it growing on old walls and in gravelly chalky ground. Obviously it is an undemanding plant and has just two basic needs — the soil must not waterlog in winter and the site should be a sunny one. The flowering season lasts from early summer to late autumn. The plants are short-lived but nearby self-sown seedlings are generally abundant.

VARIETIES: The basic species is **C. ruber** — height 1½ ft (45 cm), pink flowers. These small blooms are borne in large clusters above the shiny, lance-shaped leaves. Cut the stems down to ground level in autumn. The varieties are taller and generally more satisfactory — look for **'Albus'** (2 ft/60 cm, white flowers) and **'Coccineus'** (bright crimson flowers).

SITE & SOIL: Any well-drained soil will do — thrives best in full sun.

PROPAGATION: Sow seeds in gentle heat or plant cuttings in a cold frame in spring.

Centranthus ruber 'Albus'

Rockery perennial

CERASTIUM Snow-in-summer

So many plants in this book deserve to be more widely grown, but this one should be much more restricted. You will see the silvery-leaved sheets in rockeries everywhere, and when left unchecked it spreads like a weed and chokes out other plants. So it has earned a bad reputation and is offered by only a few alpine nurseries, but that does not mean it hasn't a job to do in the garden. There is little to beat it for covering a large dry bank.

VARIETIES: The ordinary Snow-in-summer is **C. tomentosum** — height 4 in. (10 cm), spread 2 ft (60 cm) or more, white ¹/₂-1 in. (1-2.5 cm) wide flowers, flowering period May-July. The flowers have notched petals and are borne in loose clusters above the oblong leaves. The dwarf variety **'Columnae'** is equally rampant — **C. alpinum** is more restrained but less free-flowering.

SITE & SOIL: Any well-drained soil will do — thrives best in full sun.

PROPAGATION: Sow seeds or divide clumps in spring.

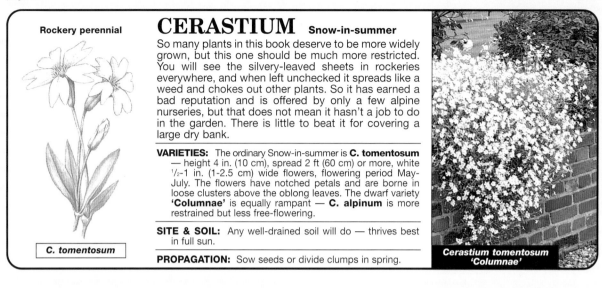

C. tomentosum

Cerastium tomentosum 'Columnae'

CHEIRANTHUS Wallflower

Wallflowers together with bulbs and primroses are the heralds of spring in countless gardens throughout the country. Millions are planted every year during October and the four-petalled flowers on erect spikes open in March or April (Common Wallflower) or May (Siberian Wallflower). Yellow and red are the favourite colours but the range extends from creamy-white to near-black, and there are varieties as small as 8 in. (20 cm) and as tall as 2 ft (60 cm). All branch freely and the flowers of many varieties are fragrant. It is an easy plant to grow — work peat into the soil in the nursery bed and sow seeds in early summer. Do not let the ground dry out and pinch out the tips of the seedlings before moving them to their final quarters in autumn. Plant firmly, and in early spring remove any broken side shoots.

VARIETIES: The Common Wallflower is **C. cheiri** — height 8 in.-2 ft (20-60 cm), spacing 9 in.-1 ft (22.5-30 cm), flowering period March-mid May. For small beds, edging or window boxes choose a dwarf variety — **'Tom Thumb Mixed'** was once the popular choice but the **'Prince'** series (8 in./20 cm) has taken over. The most popular Wallflowers in the 1 ft (30 cm) range are the **'Bedder'** series in yellow, orange and red, and in the 1¹/₂ ft (45 cm) range you will find many old favourites such as **'Cloth of Gold'** (golden yellow), **'Blood Red'** and **'Vulcan'** (deep red) and **'Fire King'** (vermilion). There are many others, such as **'Ivory White'** (creamy-white), **'Purple Queen'** (dark purple) and **'Fair Lady'** (pastel shades). The 2 ft (60 cm) Wallflower is **'Double-flowered Branching Mixture'**. For orange blooms in May to June choose the Siberian Wallflower (**C. allionii**) — **'Orange Queen'** (1 ft/30 cm) is the most popular variety.

SITE & SOIL: Any well-drained soil with adequate lime will do. Choose a sunny spot.

PROPAGATION: Sow seeds outdoors in May-June and plant out seedlings in October where they are to flower.

Cheiranthus cheiri 'Tom Thumb Mixed'

Bedding plant: hardy biennial

C. cheiri 'Vulcan'

C. allionii 'Orange Queen'

Cheiranthus cheiri 'Cloth of Gold'

Cheiranthus allionii

Border perennial

C. obliqua

CHELONE Turtlehead

An unusual plant for the border which you should be able to find at a large garden centre and in many nursery catalogues. It gets its common name from the shape of the 1 in. (2.5 cm) flower heads — snapdragon-like, although its close relative is Penstemon and not Antirrhinum. The blooms are borne on stiff and upright stems — support may be needed on an exposed site.

VARIETIES: **C. obliqua** is the most frequently seen species — height 2 ft (60 cm), spread 2 ft (60 cm), yellow-bearded pink flowers, flowering period August-October. It is not a grow-anywhere plant — it needs acid, humus-rich soil. Mulch in spring and do not remove dead stems until winter is over. Not all Chelones are deep pink — for white-bearded white flowers grow **C. glabra**.

SITE & SOIL: Well-drained, water-retentive soil is necessary — thrives in sun or partial shade.

PROPAGATION: Divide clumps in autumn or spring.

Chelone obliqua

Rockery perennial

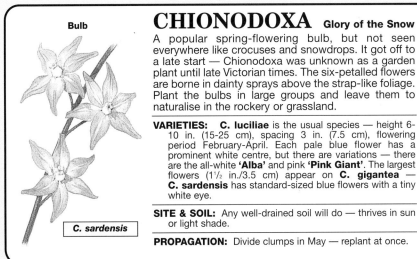

C. oppositifolium

CHIASTOPHYLLUM Lamb's Tail

You will have no difficulty in recognising this interesting alpine if you find one in full flower — the difficulty is in finding one. Despite its attractive growth habit and reliability it is still a plant for specialist collections rather than ordinary rock gardens. Unlike most rockery perennials it will happily grow in partial shade and its only hate is soggy soil.

VARIETIES: **C. oppositifolium** is the only species — height 6 in. (15 cm), spread 1½ ft (45 cm), yellow flowers, flowering period May-June. The tiny flowers are borne in arching sprays ('lamb's tails') well above the rosettes of serrated fleshy leaves. You may find this species labelled as **Cotyledon simplicifolia** — the variety **'Jim's Pride'** has cream-variegated foliage and bright yellow flowers.

SITE & SOIL: Any well-drained soil will do — thrives in sun or partial shade.

PROPAGATION: Divide overcrowded clumps after flowering.

Chiastophyllum oppositifolium 'Jim's Pride'

Bulb

C. sardensis

CHIONODOXA Glory of the Snow

A popular spring-flowering bulb, but not seen everywhere like crocuses and snowdrops. It got off to a late start — Chionodoxa was unknown as a garden plant until late Victorian times. The six-petalled flowers are borne in dainty sprays above the strap-like foliage. Plant the bulbs in large groups and leave them to naturalise in the rockery or grassland.

VARIETIES: **C. luciliae** is the usual species — height 6-10 in. (15-25 cm), spacing 3 in. (7.5 cm), flowering period February-April. Each pale blue flower has a prominent white centre, but there are variations — there are the all-white **'Alba'** and pink **'Pink Giant'**. The largest flowers (1½ in./3.5 cm) appear on **C. gigantea** — **C. sardensis** has standard-sized blue flowers with a tiny white eye.

SITE & SOIL: Any well-drained soil will do — thrives in sun or light shade.

PROPAGATION: Divide clumps in May — replant at once.

Chionodoxa luciliae

CHRYSANTHEMUM Annual Chrysanthemum

Until quite recently the genus Chrysanthemum contained a vast range of species and varieties ranging from bright annuals, pot plants and border perennials to the mop-headed giants of the show bench. A massive renaming operation has taken place, however, and only a trio of annual species now remain under the Latin name 'Chrysanthemum'. The remainder have been placed in other genera — the Florist Chrysanthemums are now listed under Dendranthema, Shasta Daisy is a species of Leucanthemum and so on. The picture is confused because some catalogues and garden centres have remained with all the old names while some textbooks and catalogues have changed over completely. The worst of all worlds is to use some new names and not others, and so the new naming system has been adopted in full in this book.

Chrysanthemum carinatum 'Court Jesters'

VARIETIES: The true Chrysanthemums are a small group of annuals which bloom in June-July. All are easily-grown hardy plants which are usually sown in spring where they are to flower. **C. carinatum** (**C. tricolor**) is the colourful Painted Daisy. The flowers on 2 ft (60 cm) stems are often boldly zoned around a central disc — **'Court Jesters'** is a popular variety. The Crown Daisy (**C. coronarium**) has yellow or mixed white and yellow flowers — the height ranges from 1 ft (30 cm) if you grow **'Golden Gem'** to 3 ft (90 cm) reached by **'Flore Plenum'**. **C. segetum** is the wild flower Corn Marigold — height 1½ ft (45 cm), 2 in. (5 cm) wide yellow flowers. It has given rise to a number of varieties, such as **'Prado'**, **'Eastern Star'** and **'Morning Star'**. No others remain in this genus — for plants listed under Chrysanthemum in earlier editions look under Argyranthemum, Dendranthema, Coleostephus, Tanacetum and Leucanthemum.

SITE & SOIL: Thrives best in non-acid light soil. Choose a sunny spot.

PROPAGATION: Sow seeds in March-April where they are to flower. Thin to required spacing.

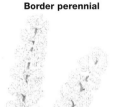

Chrysanthemum coronarium

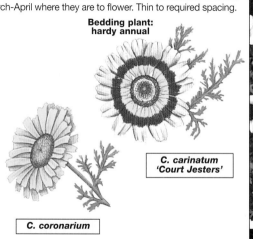

Bedding plant: hardy annual

C. carinatum 'Court Jesters'

C. coronarium

Chrysanthemum segetum 'Eastern Star'

Border perennial

CIMICIFUGA Bugbane

This unusual perennial is one for the middle or back of the border — plume-like flowering spikes appear in late summer or autumn above clumps of deeply-divided leaves. It has a number of specific needs — a humus-rich soil is necessary and so is some shade to protect the leaves from the midday sun. Mulch around the stems in May and provide support if necessary. Cut down to ground level in November.

VARIETIES: **C. simplex** is a middle-border plant — height 3-4 ft (90 cm-1.2 m), fluffy white flowers, flowering period September-October. **'White Pearl'** with arching stems is a well-known variety but it is hard to find a supplier of the bronze-leaved **'Brunette'**. **C. racemosa** is a taller plant producing slender flowering stems in July and August — **'Purpurea'** is the popular variety.

SITE & SOIL: Requires moisture-retentive soil — thrives best in light shade.

PROPAGATION: Divide clumps in autumn or spring.

C. simplex 'White Pearl'

Cimicifuga racemosa

Border perennial

C. japonicum

CIRSIUM Thistle

The increased interest in wild flower gardening has led to the appearance in some catalogues of one or two of our native thistles and some cultivated varieties. Nearly all types of Cirsium are too aggressive and too unattractive for the border, and species such as the Meadow Thistle (C. dissectum) and the Melancholy Thistle (C. heterophyllum) belong only in the wild garden. There are, however, two Cirsium species which do deserve a place in the border.

VARIETIES: **C. rivulare 'Atropurpureum'** has dark crimson flower heads — height 4 ft (1.2 m), 1 in. (2.5 cm) wide thistle-type flower heads, flowering period July-August. You will find this one offered as cuttings — if you wish to raise plants from seeds look for **C. japonicum** (height 5 ft/1.5 m, 2 in./5 cm wide white or pink flowers).

SITE & SOIL: Any well-drained, moisture-retentive soil will do — thrives in sun or light shade.

PROPAGATION: Divide clumps in autumn or spring, or sow seeds in gentle heat in spring.

Cirsium rivulare 'Atropurpureum'

Bedding plant: hardy annual

C. elegans

CLARKIA Clarkia

This popular annual may seem as if it has been around from early times but it was not discovered in the U.S until the last century. The flowers look like tiny hollyhocks and are borne on upright spikes. An easy plant but it does not like transplanting — where possible sow where it is to grow. Clarkias look best when they are set in bold groups — support the stems if necessary.

VARIETIES: The usual species is **C. elegans** (**C. unguiculata**) — height 1¹/₂-2¹/₂ ft (45-75 cm), 1¹/₂ in. (3.5 cm) red, pink, purple and white flowers in the axils of the leaves, flowering period July-September. Single-colour varieties are available but mixtures are much more usual — **'Rhapsody Mixed'**, **'Double Mixed'** etc. **C. pulchella** (1 ft/30 cm) is a semi-double daintier plant — look for **'Filigree'** and **'Lace Mixed'**.

SITE & SOIL: The soil should be neither heavy nor chalky. Thrives best in full sun.

PROPAGATION: Sow seeds in March in gentle heat. Prick out into individual pots and plant out in May.

Clarkia pulchella 'Filigree'

Border perennial

C. heracleifolia

CLEMATIS Clematis

All the popular Clematis varieties are climbers but there are a few hard-to-find ones which are suitable for the border where the weak stems can be left to scramble over low-growing shrubs. Alternatively you can support the stems with twigs — in summer there is a display of white or blue flowers and in autumn there are the silky seed heads. In November cut the stems down to near ground level.

VARIETIES: **C. heracleifolia** is the species you are most likely to find — height 3 ft (90 cm), 1 in. (2.5 cm) pale blue flowers, flowering period August-September. The fragrant blooms have curled-back petals — quite different from the large clusters of white starry flowers borne by **C. recta** in midsummer. **C. integrifolia** has blue bell-shaped blooms on top of 1¹/₂ ft (45 cm) stems in June-August.

SITE & SOIL: Any well-drained, non-acid soil will do — thrives in sun or light shade.

PROPAGATION: Take cuttings in April and grow under glass or divide clumps in autumn or spring.

Clematis integrifolia

CLEOME Spider Flower

Cleome can be planted as an unusual and exotic focal point at the centre of a flower bed. The bushy plant with seven lobed leaves can also be used to serve as a temporary hedge, but its appeal is with its floral display and not its foliage. The scented flowers are 3 in. (7.5 cm) in length and the long stamens give it a spidery appearance.

VARIETIES: **C. spinosa** is the only species — height 3-4 ft (90 cm-1.2 m), spread 2 ft (60 cm), white, pink, red or mauve flowers, flowering period July-October. The usual choice is the **'Colour Fountain'** mixture but you can get single-colour varieties from specialist seed suppliers. **'Helen Campbell'** is white, but the usual colour is rose or mauve. The name usually indicates the colour — **'Rose Queen'**, **'Violet Queen'** etc.

SITE & SOIL: Any well-drained soil will do — full sun is necessary.

PROPAGATION: Sow seeds in February-March in gentle heat. Plant out in late May.

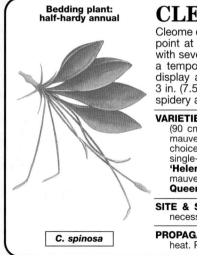

C. spinosa

Cleome spinosa

COBAEA Cup & Saucer Plant

Cobaea is an outstanding example of the small group of plants which can be used to provide a quick-growing but temporary screen. This climber may survive the winter in a mild district but the usual practice is to discard the plants in late autumn. The stems attach themselves to the supports by means of tendrils which arise from the leaf stalks.

VARIETIES: **C. scandens** is the only species — height 10 ft (3 m), spacing 2 ft (60 cm), 3 in. (7.5 cm) long violet flowers with prominent curved stamens, flowering period July-October. The display of bell-like flowers is sometimes disappointing — causes include poor drainage, underwatering and failure to harden off properly before planting out. **'Alba'** is a yellowish-green variety — not white as the name suggests.

SITE & SOIL: A well-drained soil is essential — thrives best in full sun.

PROPAGATION: Sow seeds in individual pots in February in gentle heat. Plant out in early June.

C. scandens

Cobaea scandens 'Alba'

CODONOPSIS Bonnet Bellflower

It is worth searching the catalogues for this one if you like flowers with unusual features. At first glance the 1-2 in. (2.5-5 cm) long greenish or pale blue bells may not seem special, but look inside. With the species described below you will find intricate markings in orange, violet, blue etc. Most are twining climbers which are grown against other shrubs — there are also upright dwarfs for the rockery.

VARIETIES: **C. clematidea** is the most popular one — height 6 ft (1.8 m), pale blue pendent flowers, flowering period July-September. **C. convolvulacea** is similar — the twining stems have lance-shaped leaves and the pale violet or off-white blooms are lined and ringed on the inside with orange, black, blue etc. The 1 ft (30 cm) dwarfs (**C. ovata** and **C. meleagris**) have flower bells which are chequered within.

SITE & SOIL: Any well-drained, humus-rich soil will do — thrives best in light shade.

PROPAGATION: Divide clumps in autumn.

C. clematidea

Codonopsis clematidea

Bulb

C. autumnale

COLCHICUM Autumn Crocus

Despite its common name and the shape of its flowers, Colchicum is not related to the true crocus. In autumn the wineglass-shaped blooms appear, the long tubes at the base of the petals extending down into the earth. The 2-8 in. (5-20 cm) wide blooms are gone before the onset of winter and in spring the large untidy leaves appear. All Colchicums are poisonous.

VARIETIES: **C. autumnale** is a popular small-flowered species — height 6 in. (15 cm), 2 in. (5 cm) wide lilac flowers, flowering period September-November. Varieties include **'Album'** (white) and **'Roseum Plenum'** (double, pink). **C. speciosum** (9 in./22.5 cm) is a stronger plant with 6-8 in. (15-20 cm) wide blooms. Well-known hybrids include **'Waterlily'** (double, pink), **'The Giant'** (violet) and **'Lilac Wonder'** (lilac).

SITE & SOIL: Well-drained, humus-rich soil is necessary — thrives in sun or light shade.

PROPAGATION: Divide clumps in midsummer — replant at once.

Colchicum 'Waterlily'

Bedding plant: half-hardy annual

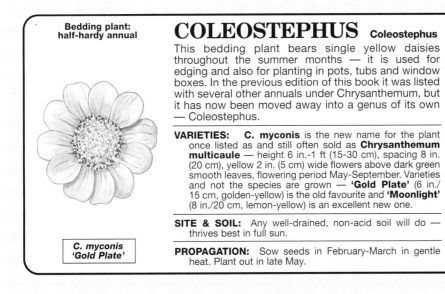

C. myconis 'Gold Plate'

COLEOSTEPHUS Coleostephus

This bedding plant bears single yellow daisies throughout the summer months — it is used for edging and also for planting in pots, tubs and window boxes. In the previous edition of this book it was listed with several other annuals under Chrysanthemum, but it has now been moved away into a genus of its own — Coleostephus.

VARIETIES: **C. myconis** is the new name for the plant once listed as and still often sold as **Chrysanthemum multicaule** — height 6 in.-1 ft (15-30 cm), spacing 8 in. (20 cm), yellow 2 in. (5 cm) wide flowers above dark green smooth leaves, flowering period May-September. Varieties and not the species are grown — **'Gold Plate'** (6 in./15 cm, golden-yellow) is the old favourite and **'Moonlight'** (8 in./20 cm, lemon-yellow) is an excellent new one.

SITE & SOIL: Any well-drained, non-acid soil will do — thrives best in full sun.

PROPAGATION: Sow seeds in February-March in gentle heat. Plant out in late May.

Coleostephus myconis 'Moonlight'

Bedding plant: hardy annual

C. 'Giant Imperial'

CONSOLIDA Larkspur

Larkspur is a close relative of the tall and stately Delphiniums of the herbaceous border. There are varieties which are suitable for the back or front of the annual border — choose a sheltered site if you can and stake tall varieties. The upright spikes bear densely-packed blooms in white, pink, red or blue.

VARIETIES: **C. ajacis** (**Delphinium consolida**) is the main parent of the many hybrids available — height 1-4 ft (30 cm-1.2 m), flowering period June-late August. The old favourite is **'Giant Imperial'** (3-4 ft/90 cm-1.2 m), but it is more usual these days to buy one of the **'Hyacinth-Flowered'** mixtures — dwarfs and giants are available. The **'Dwarf Rocket'** series grow 1-2 ft (30-60 cm) high.

SITE & SOIL: Any well-drained garden soil will do — thrives in sun or light shade.

PROPAGATION: If possible sow in spring where it is to flower. For bedding sow seeds in March under glass and prick out into individual pots. Plant out in May.

Consolida 'Dwarf Hyacinth-Flowered'

CONVALLARIA — Lily of the Valley

Bulb

Convallaria is an excellent choice for spring-flowering ground cover under trees or other shady sites. The small pendent bells on arching stems appear at the same time as the large lance-shaped leaves. The plant spreads by means of underground rhizomes which produce small shoots ('pips') which are used for propagation — plant in October-March.

VARIETIES: There is just one species — **C. majalis** (height 8 in.-1 ft/20-30 cm, spacing 4 in./10 cm, ¼ in./0.5 cm white fragrant flowers, flowering period April-May). There are a number of interesting varieties — **'Rosea'** has pink flowers, **'Fontin's Giant'** has unusually large blooms and **'Prolificans'** has double ones. For leaf colour try **'Albostriata'** (white-striped green) or **'Variegata'** (gold-striped green).

SITE & SOIL: Moisture-retentive soil is necessary — thrives best in partial shade.

PROPAGATION: Divide overcrowded clumps in October — replant at once.

C. majalis

Convallaria majalis 'Variegata'

CONVOLVULUS — Convolvulus

Bedding plant: hardy annual

The species used for bedding are compact or sprawling plants. There are two forms with different growth habits. C. tricolor (Dwarf Morning Glory) is a bushy plant which produces colourful flowers all summer long — wide-mouthed, yellow-hearted trumpets which last for only one day. C. sabatius is a more recent introduction with trailing stems.

VARIETIES: Several varieties of **C. tricolor** (**C. minor**) are available. **'Royal Ensign'** is the most popular one — height 1 ft (30 cm), 2 in. (5 cm) dark blue flowers, flowering period July-September. Others include **'Red Ensign'**, **'Blue Flash'** etc but most suppliers prefer to offer a mixture. The pendent stems of **C. sabatius** (**C. mauritanicus**) reach 1-1½ ft (30-45 cm) and bear masses of 1 in. (2.5 cm) wide lavender flowers.

SITE & SOIL: Any well-drained soil will do — it should not be too fertile. Thrives best in full sun.

PROPAGATION: Sow seeds of C. tricolor in individual pots in March in gentle heat. Plant out in late May.

C. tricolor
'Royal Ensign'

Convolvulus sabatius

COREOPSIS — Tickweed

Bedding plant: hardy annual
•
Border perennial

A free-flowering plant bearing large marigold-like flowers on wiry stems. In spring at the garden centre you will find seeds and later seedlings of several varieties which are used as bedding plants and you will also find containers of perennial types for planting in the border. Tall (2-3 ft/60-90 cm) varieties are available but most popular ones grow no higher than 1-1½ ft (30-45 cm).

VARIETIES: **C. tinctoria** is a typical annual species — height 1-3 ft (30-90 cm), 2 in. (5 cm) wide flowers, flowering period July-September. Dwarf varieties include **'Dwarf Dazzler'** and **'Mahogany Midget'**. Other popular annuals are **C. grandiflora 'Early Sunrise'**, **C. lanceolata 'Goldfink'** and **C. auriculata 'Cutting Gold'**. The best perennial is **C. verticillata** and the best tall variety **'Grandiflora'**.

SITE & SOIL: Any well-drained soil will do — thrives best in full sun.

PROPAGATION: Sow seeds in March in gentle heat — plant out in May. Divide perennial clumps in autumn or spring.

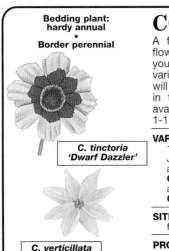

C. tinctoria
'Dwarf Dazzler'

C. verticillata

Coreopsis lanceolata 'Goldfink'

Border perennial

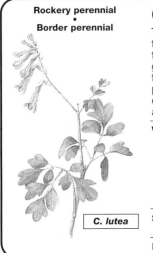

C. selloana

CORTADERIA   Pampas Grass

Wispy flower heads enhance the decorative effect of some garden grasses but only Cortaderia has the floral display as its main show feature. The silvery silky plumes are about 1½ ft (45 cm) long and their tips are up to 10 ft (3 m) above the ground. Female plants produce the best plumes and the display is always at its best after a hot and sunny season. Plant in April as a single specimen in the lawn or against a background of dark green evergreen foliage.

VARIETIES: C. selloana (C. argentea) is the species grown in the garden — narrow arching 6 ft (1.8 m) long leaves and showy plumes on stiff stalks about 7 ft (2.1 m) high. **'Sunningdale Silver'** has the largest plumes and **'Pumila'** is a 4 ft (1.2 m) dwarf. **'Gold Band'** has yellow-striped green leaves. Remove flowering stems in late autumn.

SITE & SOIL: Any well-drained soil will do — thrives in sun or light shade.

PROPAGATION: Divide clumps in April but it is better to buy new plants.

Cortaderia selloana 'Sunningdale Silver'

Rockery perennial
•
Border perennial

C. lutea

CORYDALIS   Corydalis

The foliage of Corydalis is ferny and delicate and each tubular bloom is spurred at the rear and lipped at the front. There the generalisations must end — below ground there may be fibrous roots or tubers and the flower colour may be blue, yellow, white, pink or purple. In addition some are very difficult to grow outdoors whereas the yellow C. lutea will self-seed and spread everywhere.

VARIETIES: C. flexuosa is widely available and a good one to choose — height 1 ft (30 cm), 1 in. (2.5 cm) long bright blue flowers, flowering period May-June. **C. cashmeriana** is another bright blue Corydalis — it is smaller and much more difficult to grow. **C. lutea** is the easiest — the yellow blooms appear from March to October. Others include **C. cheilanthifolia** (yellow) and **C. solida** (rose, purple or white).

SITE & SOIL: Requires well-drained soil — thrives in sun or partial shade.

PROPAGATION: Divide clumps in late spring.

Corydalis flexuosa

As shown in the photograph a rock garden should look like a natural outcrop of stone on a sloping site — a mound of earth in which a number of erect gravestone-like rocks are inserted is usually an eyesore and certainly not an ideal home for alpines. If your site is flat and you are keen on rockery plants then consider an alternative home such as a scree (page 71) or a raised bed (page 78).

COSMOS   Cosmea

Cosmea is a popular annual which is easily recognised by its slender shape, delicate ferny foliage and large flowers which look like single dahlias. Traditional types have white or pink flowers on 3 ft (90 cm) stalks, but there are several interesting variations these days. All thrive in poor, light soil — stake tall varieties and remove dead blooms to prolong the flowering season.

VARIETIES: Most garden cosmeas are varieties of **C. bipinnatus** and the **'Sensation'** series has been the popular choice — height 3 ft (90 cm), white, pink or red flowers, flowering period July-October. Other tall ones are **'Purity'** (white) and **'Candy Stripe'** (red-blotched). The popularity crown has now passed to the 1½ ft (45 cm) **'Sonata'** series. **C. 'Ladybird'** is yellow and **C. 'Hot Chocolate'** is chocolate-coloured with a chocolate odour.

SITE & SOIL: Any well-drained, non-heavy soil — choose a sunny spot.

PROPAGATION: Sow seeds in March-April in gentle heat. Plant out in late May.

C. bipinnatus 'Sensation'

Cosmos bipinnatus 'Sonata'

CRAMBE   Giant Seakale

Border perennial

Crambe can be grown at the back of a large border but it is perhaps seen at its best as a focal point against a dark background. The cloud effect of its mass of tiny white flowers is quite dramatic. Slugs and caterpillars can be a problem — keep watch and treat if necessary. The rough heart-shaped leaves at the base of the stalks are about 2 ft x 2 ft (60 cm x 60 cm) — cut down to ground level in autumn.

VARIETIES: **C. cordifolia** is widely available — height 6-8 ft (1.8-2.4 m), spread 6-8 ft (1.8-2.4 m), small white flowers borne on a tangled mass of stems, flowering period June-July. Make sure you give the plant enough space and mulch around the base in late spring. Where there is no room for Giant Seakale you can plant ordinary Seakale (**C. maritima**) — 3 ft x 2 ft (90 cm x 60 cm).

SITE & SOIL: Well-drained, fertile soil is necessary — thrives best in full sun.

PROPAGATION: Divide clumps in early spring.

C. cordifolia

Crambe cordifolia

CREPIS   Hawksbeard

Rockery perennial
•
Bedding plant:
hardy annual

Hawksbeard appears in nobody's list of favourite flowers — it isn't bold enough to attract that sort of attention. The blooms are dandelion-like and are borne on upright stalks above rosettes of lance-shaped leaves. There is a perennial one for the rockery and an annual for the front of the bed — both are easy to grow and are good for cutting.

VARIETIES: **C. rubra** is raised each year from seeds — height 1½ ft (45 cm), spread 1 ft (30 cm), 1 in. (2.5 cm) wide pink flowers, flowering period June-October. **'Alba'** is a white-flowered variety. The blooms on C. rubra are borne singly or in pairs — for clusters of flowers on shorter stems grow the rockery perennial **C. incana** — height 8 in. (20 cm), spread 8 in. (20 cm), 1½ in. (3.5 cm) wide pink flowers, flowering period July-October.

SITE & SOIL: Any well-drained soil will do — thrives best in full sun.

PROPAGATION: Sow seeds in March-April in open ground or under glass — thin out or plant in May.

C. incana

Crepis rubra

Bulb

*C. powellii
'Album'*

CRINUM Swamp Lily

It is a pity that Crinum does not have a hardier constitution as it is one of the showiest of the late summer bulbs. Everything about it is large, from the 6 in. (15 cm) bulbs to the 6 in. (15 cm) wide lily-like flowers. It needs the protection of a sheltered site during the growing season and a mulch over the crown in winter. Perhaps the best plan is to grow it in a container which is moved into the greenhouse in winter.

VARIETIES: **C. powellii** is the species to grow — height 3 ft (90 cm), 4 in. (10 cm) long fragrant pink flowers, flowering period August-September. The leaves are long and strap-like, and the stout flower stem bears a terminal cluster of flowers which open in succession. A white variety (**'Album'**) is available. Plant the bulbs about 8 in. (20 cm) deep, give them plenty of room and water copiously in dry weather.

SITE & SOIL: Well-drained, moisture-retentive soil and a south-facing position are essential.

PROPAGATION: Buy new bulbs — Crinum hates root disturbance.

Crinum powellii

**Border perennial
•
Bulb**

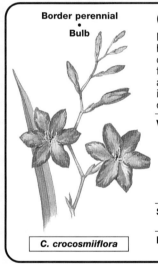

C. crocosmiiflora

CROCOSMIA Montbretia

Montbretia is highly decorative in the border and also highly regarded as a cut flower. It forms a spreading clump of sword-like leaves and in summer the arching flower stalks with their tubular or starry blooms appear. Unfortunately not all varieties are fully hardy so it is a good idea to leave the dead foliage on the plant over winter and to cover the crowns with a mulch.

VARIETIES: **C. crocosmiiflora** is the most popular species — height 2-3 ft (60-90 cm), trumpet-shaped 1½ in. (3.5 cm) flowers borne in zig-zag fashion on flower stalks, flowering period July-August. Many colours are available — look for **'Lucifer'** (red, hardy), **'Jenny Bloom'** (yellow, hardy), **'Emberglow'** (orange-red, hardy) and **'Solfaterre'** (yellow, semi-tender). Container-grown plants are usually used but corms can be planted in April.

SITE & SOIL: Well-drained, humus-rich soil in a sheltered sunny spot is necessary.

PROPAGATION: Divide clumps after flowering every three years.

Crocosmia 'Solfaterre'

A small clump of daffodils made up of a few bulbs can look attractive, especially if they are grown on their own in a container or if they are a dwarf variety grown in the rockery. In the open garden, however, they are seen at their best when planted as a drift of naturalised bulbs, which means growing them in a way and in a situation which make them look like wild flowers. In the photograph a large drift in grassland is illustrated, but informal planting under a single deciduous tree can create a wholly natural look.

CROCUS Crocus

Bulb

The crocuses most people buy are blue and yellow large-flowered Dutch Hybrids which bloom after the snowdrops and before the tulips. The range, however, is much wider — there are ones which flower in January and others which are in bloom in October. All are goblet-shaped with six petals. The flower becomes starry or cup-shaped when fully open and the narrow leaves continue to grow after the flowers have faded. Plant the corms in September-November, or July for the autumn-flowering ones. There are four basic groups, with a height range of 3-5 in. (7.5-12.5 cm). The showiest are the *Dutch* or *Large-flowered Hybrids* which bloom in March-April. They are generally blue, purple or white but yellows do occur. The *Chrysanthus Hybrids* flower earlier (February-March) and are medium-sized and fragrant. Most are yellow, but bicolours and blends with white, blue and mauve do occur. The *Spring-flowering Species* are also quite small and depending on the one you pick will bloom as early as January or as late as April. Finally there are the small *Autumn-flowering Species* which bloom in September-December.

DUTCH HYBRIDS

C. 'Pickwick'

CHRYSANTHUS HYBRIDS

C. 'Cream Beauty'

VARIETIES: All the Dutch Hybrids have been bred from **C. vernus** and a number of favourites belong here. Examples include **'Pickwick'** (purple-striped white), **'Joan of Arc'** (white), **'Mammoth Yellow'** (large yellow) and **'Remembrance'** (purple). The Chrysanthus Hybrids are generally smaller and earlier — look for **'E.A. Bowles'** (yellow), **'Snow Bunting'** (white with yellow base), **'Cream Beauty'** (pale yellow with orange stigmas), **'Blue Pearl'** (blue with gold base), **'Princess Beatrix'** (blue with yellow base) and **'Ladykiller'** (purple-backed white). The Spring-flowering Species are generally very early — the January-February bloomers include **C. ancyrensis** (gold), **C. angustifolius** (brown-backed gold) and **C. tommasinianus** (open blooms, various colours). Other Spring-flowering Species include **C. sieberi** (gold-throated lilac) and **C. imperati** (purple-striped white). Choose a sunny spot for the Autumn-flowering Species. **C. speciosus** (dark-veined white, blue or violet) is the earliest — **C. sativus** is the Saffron Crocus and for other colours look for **C. ochroleucus** (cream) and **C. nudiflorus** (purple).

SITE & SOIL: Any well-drained soil will do — thrives in sun or light shade.

PROPAGATION: Divide overcrowded clumps in autumn.

SPRING-FLOWERING SPECIES

C. tommasinianus

AUTUMN-FLOWERING SPECIES

C. speciosus

Crocus 'Mammoth Yellow'

Crocus sieberi 'Tricolor'

Crocus ochroleucus

**Bedding plant:
half-hardy annual**
•
**Bedding plant:
tender perennial**

C. miniata

CUPHEA Cuphea

Cuphea is more at home in the conservatory than in the outdoor garden but in recent years a few species have become available as bedding plants for sheltered situations. They are available as either seedlings or rooted cuttings in spring and the plants can be saved by lifting and taking indoors before the frosts arrive. Use cuphea in a window box, hanging basket, rockery or small raised bed.

VARIETIES: The brightest Cuphea is **C. miniata** — height 1½ ft (45 cm), 1½ in. (3.5 cm) long open-faced tubular red flowers, flowering period July-September. **C. ignea** (Mexican Cigar Plant) is better known as a house plant than a garden one and is rather more tender than C. miniata. It has small red cigar-shaped flowers tipped with red and white 'ash'. For blue or mauve blooms grow **C. hyssopifolia**.

SITE & SOIL: Any well-drained, non-acid soil will do — thrives best in full sun.

PROPAGATION: Take cuttings in early spring. Alternatively sow seeds in March-April in a propagator — plant out in late May.

Cuphea hyssopifolia

Rockery perennial

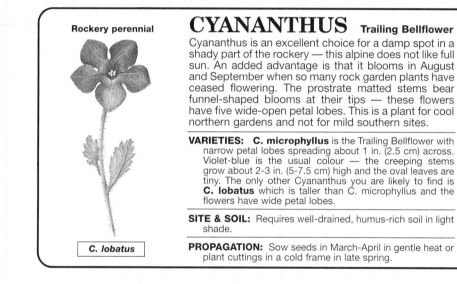

C. lobatus

CYANANTHUS Trailing Bellflower

Cyananthus is an excellent choice for a damp spot in a shady part of the rockery — this alpine does not like full sun. An added advantage is that it blooms in August and September when so many rock garden plants have ceased flowering. The prostrate matted stems bear funnel-shaped blooms at their tips — these flowers have five wide-open petal lobes. This is a plant for cool northern gardens and not for mild southern sites.

VARIETIES: **C. microphyllus** is the Trailing Bellflower with narrow petal lobes spreading about 1 in. (2.5 cm) across. Violet-blue is the usual colour — the creeping stems grow about 2-3 in. (5-7.5 cm) high and the oval leaves are tiny. The only other Cyananthus you are likely to find is **C. lobatus** which is taller than C. microphyllus and the flowers have wide petal lobes.

SITE & SOIL: Requires well-drained, humus-rich soil in light shade.

PROPAGATION: Sow seeds in March-April in gentle heat or plant cuttings in a cold frame in late spring.

Cyananthus microphyllus

Border perennial

C. scolymus

CYANARA Cyanara

Both species of Cyanara are perennial vegetables grown for their edible flower bases, but they are more often seen in the border than in the vegetable bed. As bold flowering plants they make eye-catching displays — the deeply-divided leaves are up to 3 ft (90 cm) long and in summer the thistle heads surrounded by spiny bracts appear. Use them as cut flowers for drying or eating.

VARIETIES: **C. cardunculus** (Cardoon) is the one to grow — height 6 ft (1.8 m), white, blue or lavender flowers, flowering period July-September. The spiny leaves are downy beneath. The other Cyanara is **C. scolymus** (Globe Artichoke) — more popular as a vegetable but with less decorative leaves and smaller stems (5 ft/1.5 m). Cover the crowns of both types with straw or peat in winter.

SITE & SOIL: Any well-drained soil will do — thrives best in full sun.

PROPAGATION: Sow seeds in April in gentle heat — plant out in May. Alternatively divide clumps in spring.

Cyanara cardunculus

Rockery perennial
•
Border perennial

C. hederifolium

CYCLAMEN   Cyclamen

For most of us cyclamen is a pot plant — large, long-stemmed flowers with swept-back petals rising above heart-shaped silver-patterned leaves. If this flower form appeals to you there are small hardy versions with 1 in. (2.5 cm) flowers to grow outdoors in the shady rock garden or for carpeting under trees. You can choose your own flowering time — there are spring, summer, autumn and winter varieties.

VARIETIES: **C. hederifolium** (**C. neapolitanum**) is the easiest to grow — the ivy-shaped marbled leaves appear after the first flowers. The flowering period is September-November — for January-March flowers grow **C. coum** (round leaves, white, pink or red flowers). **C. repandum** (purple twisted petals) blooms in April-May and **C. purpurascens** provides July-September blooms.

SITE & SOIL: Well-drained, humus-rich soil in partial shade is required.

PROPAGATION: Sow seeds under glass in late spring — plant out in early autumn.

Cyclamen coum

Border perennial
•
**Bedding plant:
hardy annual**

C. amabile

CYNOGLOSSUM   Cynoglossum

There are perennial and annual forms to grow. The border perennial is a clump-forming plant which looks like a giant forget-me-not — the leaves and stems are bristly and the flowers have the same attractive blue colour. The annual has grey-green leaves and is rather smaller — the flowers are usually blue but there are white and pink varieties.

VARIETIES: **C. nervosum** (Hound's Tongue) is a hardy perennial for the border or cottage garden — height 2 ft (60 cm), $\frac{1}{2}$ in. (1 cm) wide blue flowers, flowering period June-July. Cut back after flowering. **C. amabile** (Chinese Forget-me-not) is a biennial which is usually grown as an annual — height 1$\frac{1}{2}$ ft (45 cm), flowering period July-September.

SITE & SOIL: Any well-drained soil will do — thrives in sun or light shade.

PROPAGATION: C. nervosum: Divide clumps in spring. C. amabile: Sow seeds in March-April in gentle heat. Plant out in May.

Cynoglossum nervosum

Border perennial

D. elata

DACTYLORHIZA   Marsh Orchid

This plant is included because it is the easiest orchid to grow outdoors. In June upright spikes densely crowded with $\frac{3}{4}$ in. (1.5 cm) hooded flowers appear. Buy Dactylorhiza as growing plants or as tubers which should be set 3 in. (7.5 cm) deep. A water-retentive loamy soil with some shade during the day is ideal. Protect the young shoots from slugs, snails and rabbits.

VARIETIES: The most popular and probably the most reliable species is **D. foliosa** (Madeira Orchid) — height 2 ft (60 cm), pink or pale purple flowers, flowering period June-July. **D. elata** is taller (2$\frac{1}{2}$ ft/75 cm) and the flowers are darker (maroon-purple). **D. fuchsii** (Common Spotted Orchid) bears white, pink or lilac flowers in May and **D. incarnata** is the dwarf species, growing only 1 ft (30 cm) high.

SITE & SOIL: Humus-rich soil in a sheltered site and light shade are necessary.

PROPAGATION: Divide and replant tubers in autumn.

Dactylorhiza foliosa

DAHLIA Dahlia

From the end of July to the first frosts Dahlias provide large splashes of colour when so many flowers are past their best. The giant Border varieties with blooms which may be 10 in. (25 cm) across are the stars of the show, but you can also buy Bedding and Lilliput Dahlias with small flowers and a compact growth habit. The favourite types of Border Dahlia are the Decorative, Semi-Cactus and Cactus groups, and their usual home is the herbaceous border or in a bed of their own. The Bedding and Lilliput varieties are grown in rockeries, containers and bedded-out areas.

It is an accommodating plant. Dahlias relish good loam but will grow almost anywhere. They like sunshine, but can still do well in partial shade. There are various starting points. You can begin with tubers, rooted cuttings or seeds. Rooted cuttings and sprouted tubers are planted out in late May or early June, but it is more usual to plant dormant tubers and set them out about a month earlier — the crown of the tuber should be 3 in. (7.5 cm) below the surface for Border varieties and 2 in. (5 cm) below for Bedding and Lilliput types. Spacing should be 1-3 ft (30-90 cm) depending on the expected height of the variety you have chosen. Border Dahlias will require staking — insert a stout cane or stake to a depth of 1 ft (30 cm) before planting. You can increase bushiness by pinching out the tips of the main stems about three weeks after planting. Water thoroughly during dry spells — once the buds have appeared it will be necessary to water every few days if rain does not fall. Do not hoe — keep weeds down by applying a 2 in. (5 cm) mulch of peat or compost around the stems. For larger (but fewer) flowers it is necessary to remove the side buds in the cluster, leaving just the terminal flower bud. When the first frosts have blackened the foliage cut off the stems about 6 in. (15 cm) above the ground. Gently fork out the tubers and discard surplus soil and broken roots. Stand the tubers upside down for a week to drain off excess moisture and then place them on a bed of peat in a box and cover the roots but not the crowns with more peat. Store in a cool but frost-free place until planting time arrives.

Annual Dahlias share many cultural requirements with their taller and showier relatives. Organic matter should be dug into the soil before planting out and slug pellets should be put down to protect young shoots if these pests are a problem in your garden. All Dahlias are thirsty and hungry plants — water in dry weather and occasionally feed with a liquid fertilizer.

VARIETIES: The wide range of Border and Bedding Dahlias is illustrated on pages 60 and 61 — all colours but true blue are available. Choose a flower shape, colour and size which appeal to you but do check the expected final height. For the range of plant heights see page 60 — remember that the actual height achieved by a plant will depend upon location, weather and cultural conditions. Examples of the height range include Tall: **'Alva's Supreme'**, **'Daleko Jupiter'**. Medium: **'Athalie'**, **'Bishop of Llandaff'**. Small: **'Border Princess'**, **'Jescot Julie'**. Bedding: **'Yellow Hammer'**, **'Preston Park'**. In the seed catalogues you will find numerous varieties of Annual Dahlias for use as bedding plants. Once the single varieties dominated the scene, but these days you are more likely to find one of the dwarf semi-double or double types. Apart from these 1-2 ft (30-60 cm) Annual Dahlias for bedding there are several 3-5 ft (90 cm-1.5 m) Border Dahlias you can grow from seed and which will bloom in the first year.

Tender perennial
•
Bedding plant: half-hardy annual

BORDER DAHLIAS

BEDDING DAHLIAS

D. 'Yellow Hammer'

LILLIPUT DAHLIAS

D. 'Athalie'

D. 'Little John'

ANNUAL DAHLIAS

D. 'Dandy'

SITE & SOIL: Any well-drained soil will do — choose a spot which receives at least a few hours direct sunshine on a bright day.

PROPAGATION: Divide tubers every two years — make sure each division has a piece of stem with swollen tubers attached. With Annual Dahlias sow seeds in March in gentle heat — prick out into individual pots. Plant out in late May.

DAHLIA continued

PLANT HEIGHT	BORDER & BEDDING DAHLIAS		FLOWER SIZE

PLANT HEIGHT

Some catalogues use words to describe the average height of a variety grown under good conditions.

Tall Border variety
  More than 4 ft (1.2 m)

Medium Border variety
  3-4 ft (90 cm-1.2 m)

Small Border variety
  2-3 ft (60-90 cm)

Bedding variety
  1-2 ft (30-60 cm)

BORDER & BEDDING DAHLIAS

SINGLE-FLOWERED
One ring of ray florets. Central group of disc florets. Height 1½-2 ft (45-60 cm). Blooms up to 4 in. (10 cm). Examples: **'Yellow Hammer'** (Small yellow), **'Preston Park'** (Small red), **'Murillo'** (Small red)

ANEMONE-FLOWERED
One or more rings of ray florets. Central group of tubular florets. Height 2-3 ft (60-90 cm). Blooms up to 4 in. (10 cm). Examples: **'Comet'** (Small red), **'Lemon Puff'** (Small white and yellow), **'Vera Higgins'** (Small bronze)

FLOWER SIZE

Some catalogues use words to describe the bloom diameters of well-grown Decorative and Cactus varieties.

Giant   More than 10 in. (25 cm)

Large   8-10 in. (20-25 cm)

Medium   6-8 in. (15-20 cm)

Small   4-6 in. (10-15 cm)

Miniature Less than 4 in. (10 cm)

COLLERETTE
One outer ring of flat ray florets plus an inner ring of collar florets and a central group of disc florets. Height 2½-4 ft (75 cm-1.2 m). Blooms up to 4 in. (10 cm). Examples: **'Chimborazo'** (Small maroon and yellow), **'Claire de Lune'** (Small yellow), **'La Cierva'** (Small purple and white)

WATER-LILY
Fully double, flattened shape. Ray florets are flat or with slightly curved margins. Height up to 4 ft (1.2 m). Blooms up to 6 in. (15 cm). Examples: **'Abridge Natalie'** (Small pink), **'Christopher Taylor'** (Small red and silver), **'Gerrie Hoek'** (Small pink)

DECORATIVE
Fully double. Flat ray florets are broad and blunt-ended. Height up to 5 ft (1.5 m). Blooms up to 10 in. (25 cm) or more. Examples: **'Alva's Supreme'** (Giant yellow), **'David Howard'** (Miniature orange-yellow), **'House of Orange'** (Medium orange)

BALL
Fully double, ball-shaped — often flattened. Involute ray florets are blunt- or round-ended. Height up to 4 ft (1.2 m). Blooms up to 6 in. (15 cm). Examples: **'Alltami Cherry'** (Small red), **'Candy Cupid'** (Miniature lavender-pink), **'Wootton Cupid'** (Miniature pink)

POMPON
Fully double, globe-shaped. Involute ray florets are blunt- or round-ended. Height 2½-4 ft (75 cm-1.2 m). Blooms less than 2 in. (5 cm). Examples: **'Moor Place'** (Miniature purple), **'Small World'** (Miniature white), **'Willo's Surprise'** (Miniature red), **'Wendy's Place'** (Miniature pale purple)

CACTUS
Fully double. Revolute ray florets are narrow and pointed. Height up to 5 ft (1.5 m). Blooms up to 10 in. (25 cm) or more. Examples: **'Athalie'** (Small pink), **'Border Princess'** (Small gold), **'Doris Day'** (Small red)

SEMI-CACTUS
Fully double. Pointed ray florets are revolute for half their length or less. Height up to 5 ft (1.5 m). Blooms up to 10 in. (25 cm) or more. Examples: **'Alltami Apollo'** (Giant white), **'Daleko Jupiter'** (Giant red and yellow), **'Show and Tell'** (Medium red)

MISCELLANEOUS
Flower form not belonging to any of the other nine groups. Examples: **'Bishop of Llandaff'** (Small red), **'Jescot Julie'** (Small orange), **D. merckii** (Small lilac)

DAHLIA continued

LILLIPUT DAHLIAS	ANNUAL DAHLIAS

LILLIPUT DAHLIAS

Single — one ring of ray florets. Central group of ray florets. Height less than 1 ft (30 cm). Blooms up to 1¹/₂ in. (3.5 cm).
Examples: **'Little John'** (Miniature yellow), **'Omo'** (Miniature white), **'Harvest Inflammation'** (Miniature orange)

ANNUAL DAHLIAS

Several flower types — single, semi-double, double, collerette, quill-petalled etc. Height 1-2 ft (30-60 cm). Blooms up to 4 in. (10 cm).
Examples: Varieties with single flowers include the old favourite **'Coltness Mixture'** (height 1¹/₂ ft/45 cm), **'Sunburst'** (height 2 ft/60 cm, 4 in./10 cm wide blooms) and **'Piccolo'** (height 1 ft/30 cm, 2 in./5 cm wide blooms). For semi-double or double flowers grow **'Rigoletto'** (height 1¹/₂ ft/45 cm), **'Figaro'** (height 1 ft/30 cm) or the bronze-leaved **'Redskin'** (height 1¹/₂ ft/45 cm). For something different try the quill-petalled **'Disco'** or the collerette-flowered **'Dandy'**.

Dahlia 'Comet'

Dahlia 'Gerrie Hoek'

Dahlia 'House of Orange'

Dahlia 'Doris Day'

Dahlia 'Bishop of Llandaff'

Dahlia 'Rigoletto'

DELPHINIUM Delphinium

Border perennial

For most people the delphinium is the stately queen of the herbaceous border. When grown by an experienced gardener the spikes of large flowers in white, blue, pink or purple on top of leafy stems tower above the surrounding plants — a fine sight in midsummer in the border or cottage garden. Unfortunately it is not an easy plant to grow really well. You will have to ensure that the soil is fertile and well-drained, and you should plant good-quality stock in April. You will have to take measures to control slugs and to keep powdery mildew in check. You must not neglect watering in dry weather and staking with strong canes is needed with tall varieties. Pinching out the tips when the stems are 1-2 ft (30-60 cm) high results in bushier and shorter plants. When the main flowering season is over in July cut back the spikes to induce another flush of flowers in autumn. The plants will deteriorate with age — the answer is to lift the clumps in spring every few years and divide them, replanting the most vigorous sections.

VARIETIES: The most popular varieties belong to the Elatum group which have **D. elatum** (4-5 ft/1.2-1.5 m) as the parent species. These plants have the classical delphinium shape and flower form with upright spikes bearing large flat flowers which may be semi-double or double. The tall ones (height 5-6 ft/1.5-1.8 m) include **'Gordon Forsyth'** (blue), **'Bruce'** (purple), **'Fanfare'** (mauve), **'Faust'** (blue), **'Michael Ayres'** (purple) and **'Nimrod'** (purple). The medium varieties are numerous — look for **'Blue Nile'** (blue), **'Royal Flush'** (pink), **'Sungleam'** (pale yellow), **'Min'** (pale purple), **'Spindrift'** (blue/lilac) and **'Turkish Delight'** (pink/mauve). The dwarfs grow 3-4 ft (90 cm-1.2 m) high — examples are **'Lord Butler'** (blue), **'Tiddles'** (mauve) and **'Mighty Atom'** (blue). The second major section is the Belladonna group — height 3-4 ft (90 cm-1.2 m), slender stems, branching flower heads, cupped (not flat) blooms which are small and wide spreading. Popular varieties include **'Pink Sensation'**, **'Casa Blanca'** and **'Blue Bees'**. The third section is the Pacific group — tall, large-flowered plants which are grown from seeds as annuals or biennials. Look for **'Galahad'** (white), **'King Arthur'** (purple) and **'Guinevere'** (pale purple).

SITE & SOIL: Well-drained fertile soil is necessary — thrives best in a sunny and sheltered site.

PROPAGATION: Divide clumps in spring. With Pacific Delphiniums sow seeds in March in gentle heat — plant out in May.

D. elatum
Elatum group

D. elatum
Pacific group

D. elatum
Belladonna group

Delphinium 'Lord Butler'

Delphinium 'Pink Sensation'

Delphinium 'King Arthur'

DENDRANTHEMA Chrysanthemum

Tender perennial
•
Border perennial

If you look at Chrysanthemum in this A-Z chapter you will find just a few annual species — all the others which were found under this heading in the previous edition have now been put into different genera. Nearly all of the 'Chrysanthemum' varieties of old are now listed under Dendranthema. The main block of these varieties are the *Florist Chrysanthemums*. In this group you will find the showiest types — plants usually grown for the beauty of the blooms rather than the beauty of the plant. This is the chrysanthemum of the exhibitor, cut flower enthusiast and lover of large blooms in the garden. The two types of Florist Chrysanthemum are the early-flowering outdoor varieties and the late-flowering indoor varieties. The latter group are grown under glass for October-December blooms and so are not dealt with in this book on garden flowers. The other group of Florist Chrysanthemums do concern us as they are garden plants flowering outdoors in September and October. When choosing one of these varieties the basic alternative is between a Small-flowered type for general garden display or a Decorative type for cutting, showing or for just admiring the large blooms.

A stout bamboo cane is inserted to a depth of 1 ft (30 cm) before planting — the stem is attached fairly loosely to the stake. The plant will also require stopping (the removal of the growing tip) — the growing point is pinched out when the plant is 8 in. (20 cm) tall. This stimulates the early growth of flower-bearing side shoots (breaks). When growing for exhibition these breaks are reduced to three. Disbudding is another technique used by the exhibitor — every small shoot and flower bud clustered under the central main bud is removed to allow the chosen bud to develop to its full potential. For ordinary garden display a Spray variety is the usual choice, with many small flowers on each branched stem. Your choice, then, is to grow a Florist Chrysanthemum for top-quality single blooms or for a mass of smaller flowers, but in both cases there is a problem. These plants are not hardy and this means that the rootstocks (stools) have to be stored over winter.

To avoid this need to store stools over winter you can grow a variety of *Garden Chrysanthemum*. These plants are hardy, but in winter you should cut the stems down to about 4 in. (10 cm) and cover with a mulch. There are three groups from which to make your choice. Korean Chrysanthemums grow 2-3 ft (60-90 cm) high and bloom from October until the first frosts. There are single, semi-double and double varieties in a range of colours. A similar range of choices is offered by the second group — the Rubellum Hybrids. These are bushy, profusely-branched plants growing about 3 ft (90 cm) high. The third group of hardy Garden Chrysanthemums are the Garden (Cushion) Mums which have become popular in recent years. The leafy mounds are about 1¹/₂ ft (45 cm) high and the multibranched stems are covered with flowers from August to the first frosts. With all chrysanthemums plant out rooted cuttings in late May — do not plant too deeply. Water thoroughly during dry spells — feed until the buds begin to swell.

VARIETIES: Some examples of the varieties in each of the flower forms of Florist Chrysanthemums are given on page 64, but a general book of this size cannot do justice to the enormous range available — consult a specialist catalogue. Among the Garden Chrysanthemums the choice is much smaller. Examples of Korean Chrysanthemums are **'Raquel'** (Single pink), **'Ruby Mound'** (Double red) and **'Starlet'** (Double bronze). The Rubellum Hybrids include **'Nancy Perry'** (Semi-double pink), **'Emperor of China'** (Double pink) and **'Mary Stoker'** (Single cream). Finally there are the Garden Mums with **'Debonair'** (Intermediate pale purple), **'Holly'** (Pompon yellow) and **'Nicole'** (Incurved white) as examples.

SITE & SOIL: Any well-drained reasonable soil will do — pick a spot which receives at least a few hours sunshine on a bright day.

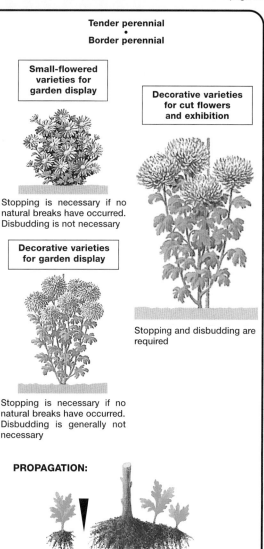

Small-flowered varieties for garden display

Stopping is necessary if no natural breaks have occurred. Disbudding is not necessary

Decorative varieties for cut flowers and exhibition

Stopping and disbudding are required

Decorative varieties for garden display

Stopping is necessary if no natural breaks have occurred. Disbudding is generally not necessary

PROPAGATION:

Root division
This method is used to propagate Korean and Rubellum Hybrids. In spring last year's stools can be lifted and the outer portions detached. Each piece should bear new shoots and roots.

Rooted cuttings
This method is used to propagate Florist Chrysanthemums. Last season's stools are kept in a greenhouse. Cuttings 2-3 in. (5-7.5 cm) long are taken in February-April from the shoots at the base (not the side) of the stems. These are rooted at 50°-60° F (10°-15° C) and then transferred to 3 in. (7.5 cm) pots.

DENDRANTHEMA continued

GARDEN CHRYSANTHEMUMS

Dendranthema 'Ruby Mound'

Dendranthema 'Emperor of China'

Dendranthema 'Holly'

FLORIST CHRYSANTHEMUMS

INCURVED
Florets are turned towards the centre. Blooms form a tight ball.
Examples: **'Alison Kirk'** (white), **'Martin Riley'** (yellow)

INTERMEDIATE
Florets are loosely and irregularly incurved or partly reflexed.
Examples: **'Cricket'** (white), **'White Allouise'** (white)

REFLEXED
Florets are turned outwards and downwards from the centre.
Examples: **'Regalia'** (rosy-purple), **'Dorridge Beauty'** (red)

SINGLE
Not more than five rings of ray florets.
Examples: **'Enbee Wedding'** (pink), **'Pennine Jade'** (bronze)

ANEMONE-CENTRED
Not more than five rings of ray florets. Central cushion of tubular florets.
Examples: **'Pennine Oriel'** (cream), **'Yellow Pennine Oriel'** (yellow)

POMPON
Florets are tightly packed (not curled) forming a small globular bloom.
Examples: **'Denise'** (yellow), **'Bronze Elegance'** (bronze)

MISCELLANEOUS
Florets are spidery, quilled or spooned as illustrated.
Examples: **'Pennine Ace'** (pink, spooned), **'Yellow Rayonnante'** (yellow, spider form), **'Pennine Flute'** (pink, quilled)

spider form

quilled

spooned

DENDRANTHEMA continued

FLORIST CHRYSANTHEMUMS

Dendranthema 'Martin Riley'

Dendranthema 'White Allouise'

Dendranthema 'Regalia'

Dendranthema 'Enbee Wedding'

Dendranthema 'Yellow Pennine Oriel'

Dendranthema 'Denise'

Dendranthema 'Yellow Rayonnante'

Dendranthema 'Pennine Flute'

Dendranthema 'Pennine Ace'

DIANTHUS Carnation, Pink

The Ancient Greeks loved them and the Elizabethans grew a wide variety of 'gillyflowers'. Carnations and pinks may have lost some of their popularity over the years but they remain important plants for beds, borders, containers, rockeries and cottage gardens. Dianthus leaves are grass-like and often tinged with blue or grey. The flowers are borne on upright stems and many have a distinctive perfume. All will flourish in chalky soil but an alkaline site is not essential. Pinks have more delicate stems, narrower leaves, smaller flowers and a more dainty appearance than carnations, and a typical carnation is quite different from a typical pink, but the dividing line is not clear cut.

There are thousands of varieties of Dianthus — to make things a little easier they are divided into several groups. The showiest ones are the *Florist Carnations* — the Perpetual flowering types with their double flowers and serrated petals, together with the strongly fragrant Malmaison varieties. These plants are tender and are grown in the greenhouse and so do not concern us — the hardy garden ones with stout stems and large flowers are the *Border Carnations* and the smaller hardy ones are the pinks. The *Old-fashioned Pinks* are slow-growing and have a single flush of flowers but the *Modern Pinks* have largely taken over because they grow more quickly and they have a 'perpetual-flowering' habit with early summer and autumn flushes. The *Rockery Pinks* are smaller than ordinary pinks — neat cushions or spreading carpets of leaves studded in early summer with sweet-smelling flowers.

Finally we have the annuals and biennials which are grown from seeds. There are three distinct groups — the *Sweet Williams* with densely-packed, flattened heads of flowers, the *Indian Pinks* with bright single blooms and the *Annual Carnations* with double flowers.

VARIETIES: The basic details of the Border Carnation are height 2-3 ft (60-90 cm), spacing 1¹/₂ ft (45 cm), flowering period July-August. These hybrids of **D. caryophyllus** have flowers with petals which are smooth-edged, unlike the serrated petals of the Florist Carnation, and there are selfs (single colour), fancies (two or more colours) and picotees (pale colour with a darker edging). Examples include **'Hannah Louise'** (yellow/red), **'Bookham Fancy'** (yellow/purple), **'Catherine Glover'** (yellow/red) and **'Lavender Clove'** (lavender-pink). Old-fashioned Pinks have **D. plumarius** as a parent — height 1 ft (30 cm), flowering period June. **'Mrs. Sinkins'** (white) is the old favourite, but you can also find many others such as **'Sam Barlow'** (white/purple), **'Inchmery'** (pink) and **'Dad's Favourite'** (white/red/purple). The Modern Pinks are hybrids of **D. allwoodii** — height 9 in.-1¹/₂ ft (22.5-45 cm), flowering period June-September. Choose your pinks from this group — there are **'Doris'** (salmon-pink), **'Devon Glow'** (red), **'Laced Monarch'** (red) and many others. Among the Rockery Pinks choose **D. alpinus** if you want large 1 in. (2.5 cm) flowers on neat cushions of green foliage — height 4 in. (10 cm), flowering period May-August. **D. deltoides** is an old favourite — height 8 in. (20 cm), flowering period June-September. Other Rockery Pinks include **D. caesius, D. erinaceus** and **D. pavonius** — in addition to these species there are miniature hybrids such as **'La Bourboule'** (pink) and **'Little Jock'** (pink). You will find numerous annuals and biennials in the catalogues. Sweet William (**D. barbatus**) is the biennial — height 1-2 ft (30-60 cm), flowering period June-July. Varieties include **'Auricula-eyed'** and **'Monarch'** — to grow it as an annual choose **'Roundabout'**. **D. chinensis** is the Indian Pink — height 6 in.-1¹/₂ ft (15-45 cm), 1¹/₂ in. (3.5 cm) wide flowers, flowering period July-October. There are all sorts of colour combinations — look for **'Baby Doll'** (mixed), **'Strawberry Parfait'** (pink/red), **'Snowflake'** (white) and the bushy **'Telstar'** (mixed). The Annual Carnations are hybrids of **D. caryophyllus** — height 1 ft (30 cm), 2 in. (5 cm) wide double flowers, flowering period July-October. Reliable strains include **'Chabaud'**, **'Knight'** and **'Raoul Martin'**.

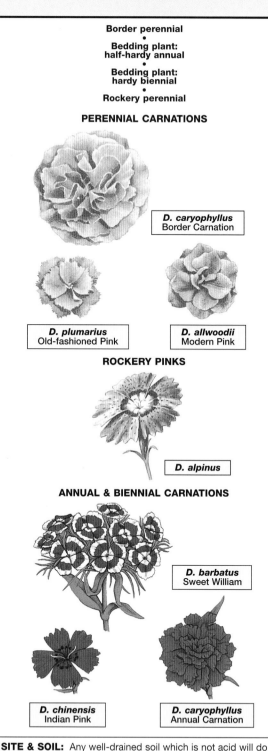

- Border perennial
- Bedding plant: half-hardy annual
- Bedding plant: hardy biennial
- Rockery perennial

PERENNIAL CARNATIONS

D. caryophyllus
Border Carnation

D. plumarius
Old-fashioned Pink

D. allwoodii
Modern Pink

ROCKERY PINKS

D. alpinus

ANNUAL & BIENNIAL CARNATIONS

D. barbatus
Sweet William

D. chinensis
Indian Pink

D. caryophyllus
Annual Carnation

SITE & SOIL: Any well-drained soil which is not acid will do — choose a sunny spot.

PROPAGATION: Border Carnations and perennial pinks: Take cuttings in July and grow in a cold frame or layer side shoots in August. Annual Carnations: Sow seeds in February-March in gentle heat — plant out in late May. Sweet William: Sow seeds outdoors in May-June — plant out in autumn.

DIANTHUS continued

Dianthus 'Hannah Louise'

Dianthus 'Mrs. Sinkins'

Dianthus allwoodii 'Doris'

Dianthus deltoides 'Flashing Light'

Dianthus caesius

Dianthus 'Little Jock'

Dianthus barbatus

Dianthus chinensis 'Baby Doll'

Dianthus caryophyllus 'Chabaud'

DIASCIA Diascia

Bedding plant: half-hardy annual
• Border perennial •
Rockery perennial

D. 'Pink Queen'

Once a rarity and now seen in garden centres everywhere — the reason is the boom in container growing in the 1990s. Above a sprawling mat of leaves the lax stems appear with slender spikes of open-faced flowers. The flowering period lasts from early July to the first frosts, but it is necessary to cut back the stems between flushes. It is usually grown as an annual, but it can be used as a perennial in mild regions.

VARIETIES: Several species are available for the front of the border — look for **D. integerrima** (1½ ft/45 cm, rose-pink), **D. cordata** (1 ft/30 cm, pink) and **D. fetcaniensis** (1 ft/30 cm, pink). For hanging baskets named hybrids are the usual choice — look for **D. 'Pink Queen'**, **D. 'Ruby Field'**, **D. 'Lilac Belle'** and **D. 'Joyce's Choice'**.

SITE & SOIL: Any well-drained soil will do — thrives best in full sun.

PROPAGATION: Sow seeds in March in gentle heat — plant out in late May. Alternatively plant cuttings in a cold frame in spring.

Diascia 'Ruby Field'

DICENTRA Bleeding Heart

Border perennial

D. spectabilis

A useful plant for growing under trees — the leaves are ferny and the arching stems bear pendent locket-like flowers. Choose a sheltered spot as the early leaves and flowers can be damaged by cold spring winds. Do not hoe close to the stems as the roots grow near to the surface — apply a mulch in May.

VARIETIES: **D. spectabilis** is the most popular and also the tallest Dicentra — height 2 ft (60 cm), rosy-red flowers, flowering period May-June. It may not be the best choice as it dies down in summer — named varieties of **D. formosa** and **D. eximia** are shorter (1 ft/30 cm) and may flower until autumn. Examples are **'Bountiful'** (pink), **'Adrian Bloom'** (red), **'Pearl Drops'** (pink-tinged white) and **'Bacchanal'** (red).

SITE & SOIL: Any well-drained soil will do — thrives best in light shade.

PROPAGATION: Divide clumps in autumn or spring — be careful not to break the brittle roots.

Dicentra 'Adrian Bloom'

DICTAMNUS Burning Bush

Border perennial

D. albus 'Purpureus'

On a warm still day you can discover how this plant got its common name — strike a match close to one of the flower heads and the volatile oils will ignite. A blue flame will surround the upper part of the bush but it will not be damaged. Unfortunately these oils can cause a rash so wear gloves when handling this plant. It will take a couple of years to become established but after that it is a reliable and attractive perennial.

VARIETIES: **D. albus** is the only species sold for the garden — height 2 ft (60 cm), 1½ in. (3.5 cm) wide white or pale purple flowers, flowering period June-August. The starry flowers have long stamens and are borne on tall spikes. The flowers of the variety **'Purpureus'** are more colourful — pink petals streaked with purple.

SITE & SOIL: Any well-drained, non-acid soil will do — thrives in sun or light shade.

PROPAGATION: Do not divide the clumps. Buy a container-grown plant or sow seeds in spring under glass if you are willing to wait three years for flowers.

Dictamnus albus

Bulb

DIERAMA Wand Flower

An eye-catching plant in the right place, but not often seen. It needs space — the most popular one (D. pulcherrimum) grows 4-5 ft (1.2-1.5 m) high. It can be raised by planting corms in late autumn or spring, but it is more usual to buy a pot-grown specimen. The long grassy leaves are semi-evergreen and in late summer tubular or bell-shaped flowers appear on wiry arching stems.

VARIETIES: **D. pulcherrimum** bears deep pink or purplish-red blooms — the stems are bowed down by the weight of the 2 in. (5 cm) long flowers. For other colours look for the varieties **'Album'** (white) and **'Blackbird'** (violet). **D. pendulum** is a tall-growing species with open bell-like flowers — the one to grow where space is limited is **D. dracomontanum** (height 2 ft/60 cm, spread 1 ft/30 cm).

SITE & SOIL: Well-drained soil and full sun are necessary.

PROPAGATION: Divide and replant corms in spring.

D. pulcherrimum

Dierama pulcherrimum

DIGITALIS Foxglove

For most gardeners foxgloves are biennials for planting out in the autumn for flowers in the following summer. It is a plant for shady borders, cottage gardens and woodland areas — there are not many annuals and biennials which can be used to add height and colour to a damp and shady bed. Seeds of *Biennial Foxgloves* are readily available from any garden centre — the wild species D. purpurea and its varieties are sometimes grown but it is more usual to choose a showy hybrid. Tall spikes bearing bell-like flowers appear above the basal rosette of large downy leaves. These biennials are not the only foxgloves — there are *Perennial Foxgloves* which will come up year after year.

VARIETIES: By far the most popular choice among the Biennial Foxgloves are the **D. 'Excelsior'** hybrids — height 5 ft (1.5 m), spacing 2 ft (60 cm), flowering period June-August. The blooms are borne almost horizontally all round the spike so that you can clearly see the maroon mottling inside each bell. Flower colours are white, yellow, pink, red and purple. If you like a single colour try the apricot-pink **D. 'Sutton's Apricot'** (5 ft/1.5 m). **D. 'Foxy'** grows about 3 ft (90 cm) high and can be grown as an annual. In general the Perennial Foxgloves are shorter than the biennial ones — the most popular perennial is **D. grandiflora** — it grows about 2 ft (60 cm) high with spikes of 2 in. (5 cm) long pale yellow flowers in early summer. **D. mertonensis** grows to about the same height — this hybrid of D. grandiflora and D. purpurea has spotted dark pink flowers. For other colours look for **D. viridiflora** (2 ft/60 cm, greenish-yellow), **D. parviflora** (2 ft/60 cm, reddish-brown) and **D. lanata** (2½ ft/75 cm, buff).

SITE & SOIL: Humus-rich soil is required — thrives best in partial shade.

PROPAGATION: Biennials: Sow seeds in April-June — plant out in autumn. Perennials: Divide clumps every few years or sow seeds in a cold frame in late spring.

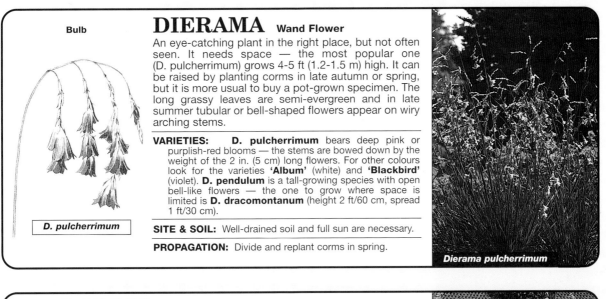

Digitalis 'Excelsior'

Bedding plant:
hardy biennial
•
Border perennial

Digitalis 'Foxy'

D. 'Foxy'

D. grandiflora

Digitalis mertonensis

Bedding plant: hardy annual

D. 'Goliath'

DIMORPHOTHECA Star of the Veldt

In the right situation this South African daisy is an excellent choice — few plants can provide such a sheet of colour to cover the ground. The right situation is well-drained, light soil in full sun — put it in a shady spot and the flowers will refuse to open. It will grow under drier conditions than almost any other bedding plant — dead-head occasionally to prolong the floral display.

VARIETIES: The garden varieties are hybrids of **D. aurantiaca** — height 1 ft (30 cm), 2 in. (5 cm) wide scented flowers, flowering period June-September. Around the dark disc the petals may be white, yellow, orange or pink. In most cases a multicoloured mixture such as **'Aurantiaca Hybrids'** is chosen. White varieties include **'Glistening White'** and **'Tetra Polestar'** — **'Goliath'** and **'Dwarf Salmon'** are orange.

SITE & SOIL: Well-drained sandy soil is necessary — a sunny location is essential.

PROPAGATION: Sow seeds in April where they are to flower or sow under glass in March and plant out in late May.

Dimorphotheca 'Glistening White'

Rockery perennial

D. pulchellum 'Red Wings'

DODECATHEON Shooting Star

The Shooting Star gets its name from the shape of its showy flowers. The petals are swept backwards to reveal the golden anthers — these blooms are borne in a cluster on top of an upright stalk. It is an easy plant to grow if the site is damp and shady. Eye-catching in early summer when the flowers are present but in winter the leaves die down and there is nothing to be seen.

VARIETIES: The most popular species is **D. meadia** — height 1½ ft (45 cm), rose-purple flowers, flowering period May-June. A white variety (**'Album'**) is available. **D. pulchellum** is a better choice than D. meadia — the foliage is neater, the flower stems are shorter and the crimson variety (**'Red Wings'**) grows only 8 in. (20 cm) high. The stamens at the centre of the flower are purple.

SITE & SOIL: A moist but well-drained soil is necessary — thrives best in light shade.

PROPAGATION: Sow seeds under glass or divide clumps in spring.

Dodecatheon meadia

Border perennial
•
Rockery perennial

D. excelsum 'Harpur Crewe'

DORONICUM Leopard's Bane

There are many yellow daisy-like flowers suitable for the border but this is the one to pick if you want flowers in spring rather than summer. In many borders this plant provides the first splash of colour. There are few problems — keep watch for slug damage and remove the spent blooms to obtain a second flush of flowers in autumn.

VARIETIES: **D. excelsum 'Harpur Crewe'** is a tall variety — height 3 ft (90 cm), 3 in. (7.5 cm) wide flowers, flowering period April-June. For a more compact plant with 2 in. (5 cm) blooms you can grow **D. 'Miss Mason'** (2 ft/60 cm) or **D. orientale** (1 ft/30 cm). There is a fully double-flowered variety (**D. 'Spring Beauty'**) and also dwarfs (6-9 in./15-22.5 cm) for the rockery. These rock garden ones such as **D. columnae** which start to flower in March are hard to find.

SITE & SOIL: Any reasonable soil will do — thrives in sun or partial shade.

PROPAGATION: Divide clumps in autumn or spring.

Doronicum 'Spring Beauty'

Rockery perennial

| D. aizoides |

DRABA   Whitlow Grass

Some alpines are too large or too invasive to be suitable for growing in a trough garden or small rockery, but Draba is perfectly at home in these surroundings. Its small cushions of foliage would be overlooked in a large rock garden — grow it in the crevices between rocks or in a small scree. In spring clusters of white or yellow flowers appear. Take care when buying — some species are not suitable for outdoors.

VARIETIES: The easiest one to grow is also the largest and most popular — **D. aizoides**. Basic details are height 3-4 in. (7.5-10 cm), spread 6 in. (15 cm), yellow flowers, flowering period April. The leaves are borne in tight rosettes and the 1/4 in. (0.5 cm) flowers are carried on wiry stems. **D. bryoides 'Imbricata'** is a smaller yellow-flowered species with a height and spread of only 2 in. (5 cm).

SITE & SOIL: Any well-drained soil will do — thrives best in full sun.

PROPAGATION: Sow seeds in spring in gentle heat or plant rosettes as cuttings in summer in a cold frame.

Draba aizoides

Border perennial
•
Bulb

| D. vulgaris |

DRACUNCULUS   Dragon Arum

This is an easy plant to grow and it is eye-catching, but you will almost certainly never have seen one. It is curious rather than beautiful — the large leaves spread out like a fan and the large flowers have the spathe and spadix arrangement of the arum family (page 27). The odour is attractive to moths but not to people. It is not completely hardy, so cover the crown with a mulch over winter.

VARIETIES: **D. vulgaris (Arum dracunculus)** appears in the catalogues of numerous suppliers of unusual plants. The leaves are about 8 in. (20 cm) long and are divided into finger-like sections with a snakeskin appearance. The early summer flowers have a 1 1/2 ft (45 cm) spathe which is pale green on the outside and maroon-purple within. The spadix is dark purple.

SITE & SOIL: Any well-drained soil will do — thrives best in full sun.

PROPAGATION: Remove offsets from the base and plant in autumn or spring.

Dracunculus vulgaris

A scree in nature is an area of loose rock at the bottom of a gully or cliff. In the garden it is a gravel-covered area in which alpines can flourish. The area chosen must be weed-free, shade-free and well-drained — fill the dug-out area with a mixture of 1 part topsoil, 1 part leaf-mould or peat and 3 parts grit. Shake off much of the compost from the roots before planting — surround plants with a 1 in. (2.5 cm) layer of gravel when planting is finished. A few small rocks may improve the appearance.

D. octopetala

DRYAS   Mountain Avens

An attractive creeping plant for clothing rocks in the alpine garden and for covering bare ground in the border. The woody stems bear leathery evergreen leaves which are shiny above and silvery below. Above these oak-like leaves the flowers appear in late spring on short stalks — the blooms are followed by silky seed heads in summer. A good choice for a sunny and starved site.

VARIETIES: The popular species is **D. octopetala** — height 4 in. (10 cm), spread 2 ft (60 cm), 1½ in. (3.5 cm) wide golden-centred white flowers, flowering period May-June. **D. drummondii** has pendent bell-shaped flowers which are all-yellow and there is a hybrid of the two species (**D. suendermannii**) with cup-shaped cream-coloured flowers. All are fully hardy and easy to grow.

SITE & SOIL: Any well-drained, non-acid soil will do — full sun is necessary.

PROPAGATION: Plant cuttings in summer in a cold frame.

Dryas octopetala

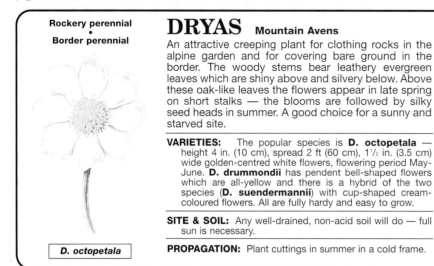

E. scaber

ECCREMOCARPUS

Chilean Glory Flower

This self-clinging climber grows quickly to cover walls or trelliswork, and during the summer months clusters of small tubular flowers in yellow, pink or red appear. Unfortunately the stems are killed by frost and so it is generally grown as a half-hardy annual. This means beginning again each year, although the plants can be brought into the greenhouse over winter.

VARIETIES: You will find Chilean Glory Flower listed in many seed catalogues these days. The basic species is **E. scaber** — height 10 ft (3 m), spread 3 ft (90 cm), 1 in. (2.5 cm) long flowers, flowering period July-October. **E. 'Tresco Hybrids'** and **E. 'Anglian Hybrids'** are sometimes offered instead of the species.

SITE & SOIL: Rather fussy — needs well-drained light and fertile soil. Full sun is necessary.

PROPAGATION: Sow seeds in February in gentle heat. Plant out in May.

Eccremocarpus scaber

E. purpurea
'The King'

ECHINACEA   Coneflower

This late-flowering border perennial is closely related to Rudbeckia. Both have a prominent cone-like disc at the centre of each large daisy-like flower, but the petals of Rudbeckia are yellow or orange and those of Echinacea are purple, pink or white. It is an easy plant to grow but it does need compost in the soil before planting and then feeding in summer.

VARIETIES: **E. purpurea** is the popular species — height 3-5 ft (90 cm-1.5 m), brown-centred purple flowers, flowering period July-October. The toothed leaves are rough and the flowers are excellent for cutting. The varieties offer different colours — **'Magnus'** is purple with an orange cone, **'The King'** has pink petals with a brown cone and there are two white-petalled varieties with yellow cones — **'White Swan'** and **'White Lustre'**.

SITE & SOIL: Any well-drained soil will do — thrives best in full sun.

PROPAGATION: Divide clumps in spring.

Echinacea purpurea

Border perennial

E. ritro

ECHINOPS Globe Thistle

A good back-of-the-border plant, described in the catalogues as stately, architectural or statuesque. The stout stems bear grey-green deeply lobed leaves with globular flower heads in summer. It is an undemanding plant, thriving in dry as well as chalky soil, but it does not do well in shade or shallow soil. Wear gloves when handling the stems and leaves.

VARIETIES: The one to choose for the back of the border is **E. bannaticus 'Taplow Blue'** — height 5 ft (1.5 m), spread 2 ft (60 cm), 2-3 in. (5-7.5 cm) wide pale blue flower heads, flowering period July-September. For dark blue flowers look for **E. ritro** — the varieties **'Veitch's Blue'** and **'Ruthenicus'** grow about 3 ft (90 cm) high. **E. 'Nivalis'** bears pale grey flower heads on grey stems. All Echinops blooms can be cut for drying just before they are fully open.

SITE & SOIL: Any well-drained soil will do — thrives best in full sun.

PROPAGATION: Divide clumps in autumn or spring.

*Echinops ritro
'Veitch's Blue'*

Hardy annual

E. plantagineum
'Dwarf Hybrids'

ECHIUM Annual Borage

If your flower bed is in an open sunny situation and the soil drains freely then this plant is worth considering. It makes a welcome change from the popular range of low-growing annuals, and the flowers which look like upturned bells are fragrant and attractive to bees. The freely-branching stems bear narrow leaves and throughout the summer the long-lasting blooms appear in large numbers. Staking is not necessary.

VARIETIES: **E. plantagineum** is the basic species — height 1 ft (30 cm), spacing 9 in. (22.5 cm), flowering period June-October. The garden varieties have been improved in recent years and are no longer restricted to blue — white, rose, red, mauve and purple are available. **'Blue Bedder'** provides blue flowers — for a mixture of white, pink and blue look for **'Dwarf Hybrids'**.

SITE & SOIL: Any well-drained soil will do, but light or medium land is preferred. Choose a sunny spot.

PROPAGATION: Sow seeds in April where they are to flower. Thin to the required spacing.

*Echium plantagineum
'Blue Bedder'*

Rockery perennial

E. pumilio

EDRAIANTHUS Edraianthus

This attractive alpine is not difficult to grow but it is difficult to find in the catalogues. It produces tight clumps of tufted leaves from which trailing stems arise. The flowers are open bells of blue, white or occasionally purple — they appear on short stalks in midsummer. Its deep-rooting habit makes it a good choice for dry situations but it is unfortunately sometimes short-lived.

VARIETIES: **E. pumilio** is the one to choose — height 3 in. (7.5 cm), spread 6 in. (15 cm), 1 in. (2.5 cm) wide violet-blue flowers, flowering period June-July. Where the conditions are right the almost stemless blooms cover much of the silvery-grey foliage. **E. serpyllifolius** is larger — height 6 in. (15 cm), spread 1 ft (30 cm), 2 in. (5 cm) wide violet flowers. **E. graminifolius** has grassy leaves and almost stemless blue-purple flowers.

SITE & SOIL: Requires well-drained gritty soil — thrives in full sun.

PROPAGATION: Sow seeds or plant cuttings in a cold frame in summer.

Edraianthus serpyllifolius

Border perennial
•
Rockery perennial

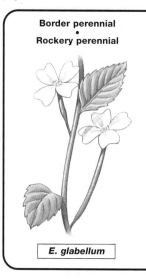

| E. glabellum |

EPILOBIUM Willow

The garden Epilobiums are relatives of the common weed Rosebay Willow Herb. Choose with care as the types on offer differ quite widely. Heights range from 1 ft (30 cm) to 5 ft (1.5 m), flowers are borne singly or grouped in racemes and some but not all are invasive. The four-petalled flowers are followed by long seed pods which open to reveal masses of woolly seeds.

VARIETIES: The most popular variety is **E. angustifolium 'Album'** — height 5 ft (1.5 m), ½ in. (1 cm) wide white flowers, flowering period July-September. It spreads by means of rhizomes but it is not as invasive as the pink-flowered species. There is a 1 ft (30 cm) high species for the front of the border — the rose-red **E. fleischeri**. For the middle there is the rose-purple **E. dodonaei** (2½ ft /75 cm) and its white variety **'Album'**. For the rockery choose **E. glabellum** (8 in./20 cm, white).

SITE & SOIL: Any well-drained soil will do — thrives best in full sun.

PROPAGATION: Divide clumps in autumn or spring.

Epilobium angustifolium 'Album'

Border perennial

| E. grandiflorum |

EPIMEDIUM Bishop's Hat

This ground cover perennial which flourishes in the light shade under shrubs and trees only just qualifies for a place in a book on flowers. It is grown primarily for its foliage — leathery heart- or arrow-shaped leaves which change colour as the season progresses. The flowers appear before the new leaves — pink, red, yellow, purple or white on long stalks.

VARIETIES: Some but not all are evergreens. **E. perralchicum 'Frohnleiten'** is a typical evergreen — height 1½ ft (45 cm), yellow flowers, flowering period April-May. Other yellows include **E. pinnatum colchicum** and **E. perralderianum** — for mauve flowers grow **E. acuminatum**. In the deciduous group there are the large-flowered **E. grandiflorum**, the rose-coloured **E. youngianum 'Roseum'** (8 in./20 cm) and the red/yellow **E. rubrum**.

SITE & SOIL: Any reasonable garden soil will do — thrives best in partial shade.

PROPAGATION: Divide clumps in autumn or spring.

Epimedium perralchicum 'Frohnleiten'

Bulb

| E. hyemalis |

ERANTHIS Winter Aconite

Plant a group of tubers under shrubs or deciduous trees in September — in February or even earlier you will be rewarded with a glossy yellow carpet of flowers. These blooms are borne on 3 in. (7.5 cm) stems and bear a frilly green collar of bracts — the true leaves appear later. The recommended planting depth is 2 in. (5 cm) and spacing 4 in. (10 cm). Eranthis is often planted with snowdrops.

VARIETIES: **E. hyemalis** is the most popular species — the 1 in. (2.5 cm) wide flowers are lemon-yellow. This is the one to choose for early flowers but it can become a nuisance as it produces an abundance of self-sown plants. The hybrid **E. tubergenii** is less invasive, more robust and the flowers are larger. **E. cilicica** is another large-flowered one — the leaves have a bronzy tinge.

SITE & SOIL: Any well-drained soil will do — thrives in sun or partial shade.

PROPAGATION: Lift and divide clumps in early summer every few years — replant immediately.

Eranthis cilicica

Border perennial

EREMURUS Foxtail Lily

The Foxtail Lily rivals the Delphinium in stateliness — bold upright spikes rising above head-height. Their make-up, however, is quite unlike the Delphinium — Eremurus heads are made up of countless starry flowers. It is not an adaptable plant and you will have to choose the site carefully. It needs good drainage, sun, shelter and copious watering in dry weather. Mulch the crowns in autumn.

VARIETIES: The giant Eremurus is **E. robustus** — height 8 ft (2.4 m), spacing 3 ft (90 cm), pale peach flowers, flowering period May-June. **E. bungei** (**E. stenophyllus**) is a more popular species — 3 ft (90 cm) high with yellow flowers. The easiest ones to grow are the **'Shelford'** and **'Ruiter'** hybrids — another easy one is **E. himalaicus** (4 ft/1.2 m). All the Foxtail Lilies die down after flowering.

SITE & SOIL: Well-drained soil with full sun in the afternoon and evening is necessary.

PROPAGATION: Divide clumps in autumn or early spring.

E. bungei

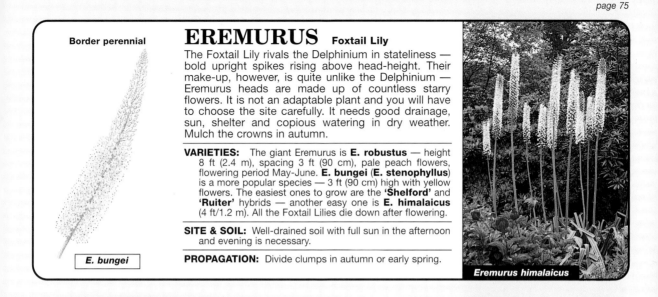
Eremurus himalaicus

ERIGERON Fleabane

Fleabanes have been popular cottage garden plants for hundreds of years and are easy to grow. At first glance they look like miniature Michaelmas Daisies but the petals are more numerous and they bloom earlier in the season. The flowers are single or semi-double and the central disc is always yellow. The most widely-grown Erigerons are the hardy perennials which are used at the front of the border — the stems will need some form of support and the blooms can be cut for indoor decoration. There are some smaller hardy perennials which are suitable for the rockery — they are usually short-lived and one or two are very invasive. Finally there is the annual variety which is easily raised from seed.

VARIETIES: The old-fashioned fleabane was the purple **E. speciosus** but nowadays its hybrids are preferred. The flowers are larger, brighter and do not droop — height 1-2 ft (30-60 cm), spacing 1 ft (30 cm), 2-3 in. (5-7.5 cm) wide flowers, flowering period June-August. Popular varieties include **'Foerster's Liebling'** (pink), **'Darkest of All'** (violet), **'Dignity'** (lilac), **'Prosperity'** (light blue) and **'Rosa Juwel'** (lilac). Cut the stems down to ground level in autumn. The most popular rockery species is **E. karvinskianus** — height 6 in. (15 cm), spread 1½ ft (45 cm), flowering period June-October. Unfortunately it is the most invasive of the dwarfs — more restrained ones include the rather difficult **E. aureus** (height 4 in./10 cm, yellow flowers) and **E. aurantiacus** (height 1 ft/30 cm, orange flowers). The annual for bedding out is **E. 'Profusion'**. It grows about 1 ft (30 cm) high and from June to October the foliage is smothered by white flowers which turn pink and then purple as they age.

SITE & SOIL: Any well-drained soil will do — thrives best in full sun.

PROPAGATION: Perennials: Divide clumps in spring. Annuals: Sow seeds in March in gentle heat — plant out in May.

Erigeron 'Rosa Juwel'

Border perennial
•
Rockery perennial
•
Bedding plant: hardy annual

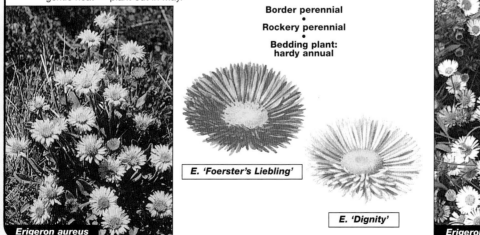
E. 'Foerster's Liebling'

E. 'Dignity'

Erigeron aureus

Erigeron 'Profusion'

Rockery perennial

E. alpinus

ERINUS Summer Starwort

This little alpine is for cracks and crannies in paving and walls and for planting in the rock garden. It is easy to grow but the plants are rather short-lived. This is not really a problem as self-sown seedlings take over, providing small mounds of tiny green leaves. In spring clusters of star-shaped flowers appear on short stalks and continue until midsummer or later.

VARIETIES: **E. alpinus** is the only species you are likely to find — height 3 in. (7.5 cm), spread 4 in. (10 cm), 1/2 in. (1 cm) wide flowers, flowering period April-August. The toothed leaves are dark green and the flower colour is pink. You can buy named varieties in different colours which come true from seed — look for **'Albus'** (white), **'Dr. Hahnle'** (crimson) and **'Mrs. Charles Boyle'** (pink).

SITE & SOIL: Requires well-drained infertile soil — thrives in sun or light shade.

PROPAGATION: Sow seeds in spring where the plants are to flower.

Erinus alpinus 'Albus'

Rockery perennial
Border perennial

E. corsicum

ERODIUM Stork's Bill

The common name of this hardy geranium-like plant refers to the long and beaked fruits. There are a few tall ones for the border but it is the dwarf rockery varieties which are more usually grown. Erodium is a long-lived plant with foliage which is generally attractive. The usual flower colour is white or pink with red veins, but there are exceptions.

VARIETIES: The most popular Erodium for the border is **E. manescaui** — height 1 1/2 ft (45 cm), magenta flowers, flowering period June-August. For the rockery look for a variety of **E. variabile** — height 8 in. (20 cm), 1/2 in. (1 cm) wide flowers, flowering period June-July. Popular ones are **'Album'** (white), **'Roseum'** (pale pink) and **'Bishop's Form'** (deep pink) — other rockery species include **E. corsicum** (pink) and **E. chrysanthum** (yellow).

SITE & SOIL: Any well-drained soil will do — thrives best in full sun.

PROPAGATION: Sow seeds or divide clumps in spring.

Erodium variabile 'Roseum'

Border perennial

E. oliverianum

ERYNGIUM Sea Holly

The Sea Holly in bloom is unmistakable. The rosette of thistle-like leaves and the branching stems usually have a bluish tinge, and each thimble-shaped flower head has an intricately-spined ruff. These plants stay in flower for about three months and the seed heads can be left over winter as a decorative feature.

VARIETIES: There are deciduous and evergreen varieties. **E. planum** is a middle-of-the-border evergreen — height 2 1/2 ft (75 cm), blue flowers, flowering period July-September. Others include the deciduous **E. oliverianum** and **E. tripartitum**. Low-growing ones (1 1/2-2 ft/45-60 cm) for the front of the border include **E. variifolium**, **E. alpinum** and **E. bourgatii**. For 4 ft (1.2 m) high ones look for **E. giganteum**, **E. paniculatum** and **E. agavifolium**.

SITE & SOIL: Any well-drained, non-acid soil will do — thrives best in full sun.

PROPAGATION: Clumps can be divided in spring, but Eryngium dislikes root disturbance.

Eryngium bourgatii

ERYSIMUM   Perennial Wallflower

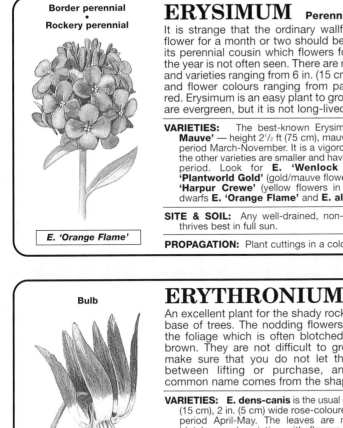

It is strange that the ordinary wallflower which is in flower for a month or two should be so popular while its perennial cousin which flowers for nine months of the year is not often seen. There are numerous species and varieties ranging from 6 in. (15 cm) to 2¹/₂ ft (75 cm) and flower colours ranging from pale yellow to dark red. Erysimum is an easy plant to grow and most types are evergreen, but it is not long-lived.

VARIETIES: The best-known Erysimum is **E. 'Bowles Mauve'** — height 2¹/₂ ft (75 cm), mauve flowers, flowering period March-November. It is a vigorous shrubby plant — the other varieties are smaller and have a shorter flowering period. Look for **E. 'Wenlock Beauty'** and **E. 'Plantworld Gold'** (gold/mauve flowers in April-June), **E. 'Harpur Crewe'** (yellow flowers in April-May) and the dwarfs **E. 'Orange Flame'** and **E. alpinum**.

SITE & SOIL: Any well-drained, non-acid soil will do — thrives best in full sun.

PROPAGATION: Plant cuttings in a cold frame in spring.

E. 'Orange Flame'

Erysimum 'Bowles Mauve'

ERYTHRONIUM   Dog's Tooth Violet

Bulb

An excellent plant for the shady rockery or around the base of trees. The nodding flowers are borne above the foliage which is often blotched or streaked with brown. They are not difficult to grow but you must make sure that you do not let the tubers dry out between lifting or purchase, and planting. The common name comes from the shape of the tubers.

VARIETIES: **E. dens-canis** is the usual choice — height 6 in. (15 cm), 2 in. (5 cm) wide rose-coloured flowers, flowering period April-May. The leaves are marked with brown blotches and varieties with flowers in white, pink and violet are available. For taller plants with yellow flowers grow **E. 'Pagoda'** — a smaller yellow is **E. americanum**. The showiest variety is **E. californicum 'White Beauty'** (1 ft/30 cm, red-eyed white flowers).

SITE & SOIL: Well-drained, humus-rich soil is required — thrives best in partial shade.

PROPAGATION: Resents root disturbance — divide overcrowded clumps in late summer.

E. dens-canis

Erythronium 'Pagoda'

ESCHSCHOLZIA   Californian Poppy

Hardy annual

It is easier to grow this annual than to spell it — a sprinkling of seed over bare ground in autumn or spring produces a drift of silky-petalled flowers from June to September. The much-branched stems bear blue-grey deeply-cut leaves and the flowers flutter in the breeze. Dead-head regularly to prolong the flowering season.

VARIETIES: The deep yellow flowers of **E. californica** cover large areas of the 'Golden West' (hence the name) of the U.S. There are now hybrids in many colours — for a mixture of shades look for **'Single Mixed'**, **'Monarch Art Shades'** (semi-double) and **'Prima Ballerina'** (double). All grow to 1 ft (30 cm) as do **'Alba'** (white), **'Dalli'** (red/yellow), **'Golden Values'** (orange/yellow), **'Mikado'** (red/orange) and **'Rose Chiffon'** (rose/cream). Dwarfs (6 in./15 cm) include the yellow varieties **'Moonlight'** and **'Sundew'**.

SITE & SOIL: A well-drained soil and full sun are necessary.

PROPAGATION: Dislikes root disturbance. Sow seeds in April or September where they are to flower.

E. californica

Eschscholzia californica

Bulb

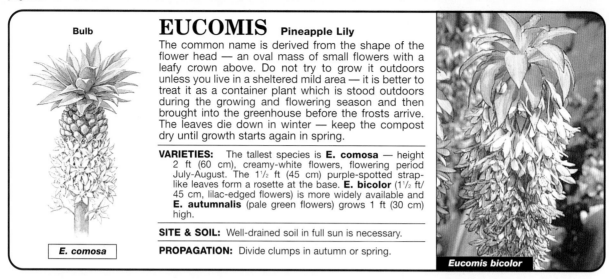

E. comosa

EUCOMIS   Pineapple Lily

The common name is derived from the shape of the flower head — an oval mass of small flowers with a leafy crown above. Do not try to grow it outdoors unless you live in a sheltered mild area — it is better to treat it as a container plant which is stood outdoors during the growing and flowering season and then brought into the greenhouse before the frosts arrive. The leaves die down in winter — keep the compost dry until growth starts again in spring.

VARIETIES: The tallest species is **E. comosa** — height 2 ft (60 cm), creamy-white flowers, flowering period July-August. The 1½ ft (45 cm) purple-spotted strap-like leaves form a rosette at the base. **E. bicolor** (1½ ft/ 45 cm, lilac-edged flowers) is more widely available and **E. autumnalis** (pale green flowers) grows 1 ft (30 cm) high.

SITE & SOIL: Well-drained soil in full sun is necessary.

PROPAGATION: Divide clumps in autumn or spring.

Eucomis bicolor

Border perennial

E. purpureum

EUPATORIUM   Eupatorium

The Eupatorium species and varieties are tall and erect plants which are easy to grow in moist soil. This is not a plant for a small and formal border — it belongs in a semi-wild area or bog garden. In late summer and autumn clusters of tiny fluffy flowers are borne in dense heads on top of leafy stems. Cut down to nearly ground level after flowering.

VARIETIES: **E. cannabinum** is our native Hemp Agrimony — height 6 ft (1.8 m), spread 3 ft (90 cm), reddish-purple flowers, flowering period August-September. The variety **'Flore Pleno'** has pink double flowers. **E. purpureum** (Joe Pye Weed) is a better choice — rose-purple flower heads up to 9 in. (22.5 cm) across are borne on top of 6 ft (1.8 m) purple stems — the variety **'Atropurpureum'** has purple leaves. **E. rugosum** is a 4 ft (1.2 m) high species with white flowers.

SITE & SOIL: Moist soil is essential — thrives in sun or light shade.

PROPAGATION: Divide clumps in autumn.

Eupatorium purpureum

Raised beds were once an unusual feature but are now becoming more popular as people realise the advantages they bring to the garden. Drainage is improved in heavy soil, the plants are brought closer to the eye which is important with small plants like alpines and closer to the hand which makes weeding, planting, dead-heading etc much easier. Finally, a third dimension is added to flat sites.

EUPHORBIA Spurge

The Euphorbias are a vast genus of plants with about 2000 varieties and a number of uses. Some of them such as the well-known Poinsettia and the Crown of Thorns are grown as house plants, but here we are concerned with the garden varieties. Almost all are hardy perennials for the border or in one or two cases for the rockery, and there is a species which is grown as a half-hardy annual. Euphorbias were once rather plain plants and were largely ignored when choosing subjects for the border, but things have changed. There are now varieties with colourful leaves, brightly coloured flower heads and excellent winter foliage displays. The true flowers are insignificant — the floral display comes from the petal-like bracts which surround each bloom. They should certainly be more widely grown, but there are one or two precautions to remember. Some varieties are extremely invasive, and all parts are poisonous. In addition the milky sap can cause severe skin irritation.

VARIETIES: **E. amygdaloides** is a typical evergreen Euphorbia — height 1½ ft (45 cm), flowering period April-May. The variety **'Robbiae'** is one of the best of all ground covers for growing under trees — tight-fitting rosettes of dark leaves spread quite rapidly. The purple-leaved **'Purpurea'** is another shade-lover. **E. myrsinites** is a semi-prostrate evergreen for the rockery or the front of the border and at the other end of the scale is **E. characias 'Wulfenii'** (5 ft/1.5 m) with blue-green foliage and 1 ft (30 cm) long flower heads. **E. martinii** has red-centred flowers and forms 2 ft x 2 ft (60 cm x 60 cm) domes — **E. nicaeensis** (2 ft/ 60 cm) has midsummer flowers. One of the most popular deciduous species is **E. polychroma** — height 1½ ft (45 cm), flowering period April-May. The flower heads are yellow — for orange or red clusters and bronzy young foliage grow **E. griffithii**. Other colourful deciduous ones include **E. cyparissias** and **E. dulcis 'Chameleon'**. **E. marginata** (Snow on the Mountain) is a half-hardy annual used for bedding — height 1½ ft (45 cm), white-edged foliage, green-striped white flower heads, flowering period September.

SITE & SOIL: Any well-drained soil will do — thrives in sun or partial shade.

PROPAGATION: Perennials: Plant cuttings in a cold frame in spring or divide clumps in autumn or spring. Annuals: Sow seeds in March in gentle heat. Plant out in late May.

Border perennial
•
Rockery perennial
•
Bedding plant:
half-hardy annual

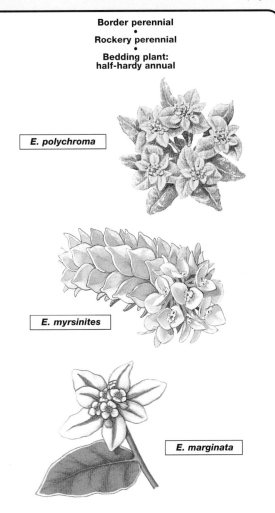

E. polychroma

E. myrsinites

E. marginata

Euphorbia amygdaloides 'Robbiae'

Euphorbia characias 'Wulfenii'

Euphorbia griffithii

Bedding plant: half-hardy annual

E. russellianum

EUSTOMA **Prairie Gentian**

Eustoma was introduced at the end of the 1980s, first as a house plant and then as a bedding plant. The single or double blooms are showy and have a long vase life when cut for flower arranging. If buying from a garden centre make sure the plants have been hardened off for outdoors and are not meant for indoor cultivation.

VARIETIES: **E. russellianum (E. grandiflorum)** is the basic species — 2-3 ft (60-90 cm) high, 2 in. (5 cm) wide blue or purple flowers, flowering period July-September. The species has been replaced by a number of hybrids — the **'Yodel'** series grow 1-2 ft (30-60 cm) high with white, pink and blue single flowers and the **'Echo'** series (2½ ft/ 75 cm) have velvety double flowers. **'Mermaid Blue'** is a 6 in. (15 cm) dwarf.

SITE & SOIL: Any well-drained soil will do — thrives best in full sun.

PROPAGATION: Sow in a propagator in February — plant out in late May.

Eustoma 'Mermaid Blue'

Bedding plant: half-hardy annual

F. bergeriana

FELICIA **Kingfisher Daisy**

These South African daisies do need full sun and good drainage but they are not difficult to grow. The dwarf F. bergeriana will succeed on windy and exposed sites, and when grown in light soil the blue flowers cover almost all the foliage when the sun is shining. Unfortunately the petals close up in dull weather as with other daisies from South Africa.

VARIETIES: The tall one is **F. amelloides** — height 1½ ft (45 cm), 1½ in. (3.5 cm) wide kingfisher blue flowers, flowering period July-October. Varieties include **'Santa Anita'** (large flowers) and **'Variegata'** (cream-edged leaves). This plant is more suited to the conservatory than the flower bed — the low-growing **F. bergeriana** (4 in./10 cm) with bright blue flowers and grey-green leaves is a better choice.

SITE & SOIL: A well-drained site in full sun is essential.

PROPAGATION: Sow seeds in March in gentle heat. Plant out in late May.

Felicia amelloides

Border perennial

F. hexapetala 'Plena'

FILIPENDULA **Meadowsweet**

The Meadowsweets are usually grown in boggy areas or damp woodland, but they can be grown in the border if the soil is enriched with humus and watered in dry weather. The leaves are often fern-like and the stems bear terminal clusters of small flowers. The blooms can be cut for indoor decoration.

VARIETIES: **F. hexapetala** (Dropwort) is grown for its heads of white or pink-tinged flowers and ferny foliage — height 2½ ft (75 cm), flowering period June-July. The double-flowered variety **'Plena'** is more eye-catching than the species. **F. purpurea** (4 ft/1.2 m) has large flat heads of rosy flowers and the giant **F. rubra 'Venusta'** (6 ft/1.8 m) has wide heads of feathery pink flowers. The most popular Meadowsweet (**F. ulmaria 'Aurea'**) is grown solely for its yellow leaves.

SITE & SOIL: Any well-drained soil will do — thrives best in light shade.

PROPAGATION: Divide clumps in autumn or spring.

Filipendula purpurea

Border perennial

F. chiloensis

FRAGARIA Ornamental Strawberry

The flowers are strawberry-like and so are the fruits, but these very hardy ground-cover plants are grown for display and not for their produce. The leaves are made up of three toothed leaflets and the flowers are about 1 in. (2.5 cm) across. They are shade-lovers, and in fertile soil can spread rapidly and become invasive.

VARIETIES: The species you are most likely to find is **F. indica** which may be listed as **Duchesnea indica** (Indian Strawberry) — height 4 in. (10 cm), yellow flowers, flowering period May-September. Popular varieties are **'Harlequin'** (speckled foliage) and **'Pink Panda'** (pink flowers). The small red fruits which follow the flowers are tasteless — for edible fruits there is **F. chiloensis** which is a taller but less invasive species and bears white flowers.

SITE & SOIL: Well-drained, humus-rich soil is necessary — thrives best in partial shade.

PROPAGATION: Remove and plant rooted plantlets in autumn.

Fragaria indica 'Pink Panda'

Rockery perennial

F. laevis

FRANKENIA Sea Heath

You will find this unusual rockery plant in some catalogues but not at the garden centre — a collector's item rather than a plant for the ordinary rock garden. It is at home at the seaside and has a heather-like appearance — hence the common name. Frankenia has wiry stems and a prostrate growth habit — the leaves are tiny and small pink flowers appear in summer above the foliage, each one bearing five petals around a yellow centre.

VARIETIES: Two species are available. **F. thymifolia** is the one you are more likely to find — height 3 in. (7.5 cm), pale pink flowers, flowering period July-August. **F. laevis** is smaller and more difficult to grow. The narrow leaves have inrolled edges and unlike the flower clusters of F. thymifolia there is just one ¼ in. (0.5 cm) wide flower per stem.

SITE & SOIL: Requires well-drained light soil in full sun.

PROPAGATION: Divide clumps in autumn.

Frankenia thymifolia

Bulb

F. hybrida

FREESIA Outdoor Freesia

The Florist Freesias are well-known as cut flowers for indoor decoration — less well-known are the Outdoor Freesias which can be grown in a sheltered sunny garden. These corms have been specially prepared to enable them to grow in our climate. They provide a bright display of fragrant blooms but unfortunately the corms have to be discarded once flowering has finished.

VARIETIES: Buy prepared corms of **F. hybrida** — height 1-1½ ft (30-45 cm), 2 in. (5 cm) long tubular flowers, flowering period August-October. The flowers are borne on one side of the wiry stems — the key to success is to provide a warm spot and to water regularly in dry weather. A mixture will provide white, yellow, orange, red, blue and lilac flowers. Plant the corms 2 in. (5 cm) deep in late April or May.

SITE & SOIL: Well-drained sandy soil in full sun is essential.

PROPAGATION: Not practical — buy new corms.

Freesia 'Everett'

FRITILLARIA Fritillary

The bell-like flowers of Fritillaria open in spring, hanging downwards from the top of upright stems which bear narrow leaves. There the family likeness ends as the species vary widely in shape, size and cultural needs. It is hard to believe that the stately Crown Imperial and the dainty Snake's Head Fritillary are so closely related. Both are easy to grow — all they need is a free-draining site and some sunshine on bright days, but at the other end of the scale F. grayana needs the shelter of an alpine house. Plant fritillaries in September-November — do not let the bulbs dry out and handle carefully. Put some coarse sand in the hole and place the bulbs sideways 5-8 in. (12.5-20 cm) deep. Cover with sand and replace the soil.

VARIETIES: **F. meleagris** (Snake's Head Fritillary) is a plant for the rockery or front of the border — height 1 ft (30 cm), 1½ in. (3.5 cm) pendent white or checkerboard flowers, flowering period April-May. **'Alba'** and **'Aphrodite'** are the all-white varieties. **F. imperialis** (Crown Imperial) is a much more imposing plant — height 2-3 ft (60-90 cm) with 2 in. (5 cm) cup-like blooms clustered at the top of each stout stem. Above the blooms is a crown of short green leaves — flower colours include yellow (**'Maxima Lutea'**), orange (**'Aurora'**) and red (**'Rubra'**). This is a plant for the border as is the equally imposing **F. persica** with tall green stems from which hang purple bell-like blooms. In contrast there is the 6 in. (15 cm) high **F. michailovskyi** which bears yellow-edged purple bells. Another colourful species is **F. acmopetala** — 1½ ft (45 cm) high with purple- and yellow-striped flowers.

SITE & SOIL: Any well-drained sunny soil will do.

PROPAGATION: Divide clumps every few years in summer.

Fritillaria meleagris 'Alba'

Bulb

Fritillaria persica

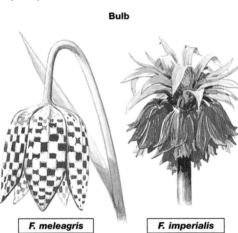

F. meleagris

F. imperialis

Fritillaria michailovskyi

The patio has become a basic feature of the garden in recent years — a hard-surfaced area close to or attached to the house to serve as an outside room in good weather. Many patios can be improved by introducing flowers to enliven the concrete, stone or brick surface — these can be in containers or in beds created by removing some of the paving material. These flowers are subject to close inspection, so dead-heading, pest control etc are essential.

FUCHSIA Fuchsia

For some people the fuchsia is the most beautiful flower in the garden. This may seem strange as the blooms are small compared with a rose or lily and the colour range is limited to white, pink, red, mauve and violet. Its charm lies in the general flower pattern of a skirt of four swept-back sepals with the petals and stamens hanging below to give a bell-like effect. Not all varieties have this shape — the clustered fuchsias have a long tubular calyx with the petals insignificant or absent.

There are many sorts of fuchsias, ranging from tall shrubby ones to delicate greenhouse types. There are a number of varieties and hybrids which can be relied upon to produce graceful arching branches and pendent flowers year after year in the border. In the mildest areas the woody stems are permanent and the plants can be regarded as flowering shrubs, but in nearly all areas the stems are cut down by frost and so are classed as border perennials. Some fuchsias are less hardy than these *Border Fuchsias* and the plants and not just the stems cannot survive the winter. These are the *Bedding Fuchsias* which are raised from cuttings or seeds for planting out when the frosts have passed. They grow about 1-2 ft (30-60 cm) high and like the hardy ones bloom from July to mid October. An important group of non-hardy varieties are the *Trailing Fuchsias* with weak stems for use in hanging baskets.

With all fuchsias organic matter should be added to the soil before planting — put in the hardy types with about 4 in. (10 cm) of stem below ground level. To induce bushiness, pinch out the tip after three sets of leaves have formed. When each side shoot has developed three sets of leaves pinch out the growing tips again. Support with twigs or stakes as necessary. Water thoroughly when the weather is dry and feed occasionally — with hardy varieties which have spent the winter outdoors, cut down the stems to 1 in. (2.5 cm) above ground level in March. The bedding varieties will need to be taken indoors during winter. In October lift the plants carefully and transfer them to pots. Store these pots in a greenhouse or well-lit shed for the winter. Keep cool, do not feed and water very sparingly until spring arrives.

Border perennial
•
Bedding plant:
tender perennial
•
Bedding plant:
half-hardy annual

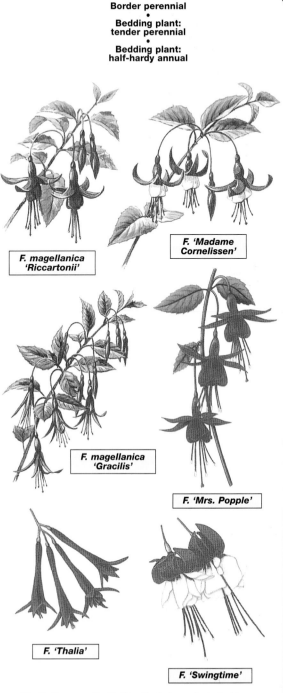

F. magellanica 'Riccartonii'

F. 'Madame Cornelissen'

F. magellanica 'Gracilis'

F. 'Mrs. Popple'

F. 'Thalia'

F. 'Swingtime'

VARIETIES: **F. magellanica** is the most popular species of Border Fuchsia — height 4 ft (1.2 m), 1½ in. (3.5 cm) long red-sepalled/purple-petalled flowers. It is usual to grow a variety rather than the species, and there are several from which to choose. **'Riccartonii'** is an old favourite with a good reputation for hardiness, **'Gracilis'** has small and narrow blooms and **'Alba'** has white/pale mauve flowers. **'Variegata'** has cream-edged leaves and **'Versicolor'** has red/violet flowers and cream-splashed grey-green leaves. Apart from the species and its varieties there is a host of hybrids — the list below is far from complete. **F. 'Alice Hoffman'** (scarlet sepals/white petals, compact), **F. 'Blue Gown'** (scarlet/purple, compact), **F. 'Chillerton Beauty'** (white/mauve), **F. 'Lady Thumb'** (pink/white, 1½ ft/45 cm dwarf), **F. 'Madame Cornelissen'** (red/white), **F. 'Margaret'** (crimson/purple), **F. 'Mrs. Popple'** (scarlet/violet) and **F. 'Tom Thumb'** (pale red/violet, dwarf).

The choice of Bedding Fuchsia is even wider — there are hundreds of **F. hybrida** varieties with large and colourful flowers. Bushy types with bell-like flowers include **F. 'Avocet'** (red sepals/white petals), **F. 'Bon Accorde'** (white/lilac), **F. 'Checkerboard'** (red/white), **F. 'Dancing Flame'** (orange/carmine), **F. 'Mission Bells'** (red/purple), **F. 'Rufus'** (red), **F. 'Winston Churchill'** (red/lavender) and **F. 'Royal Velvet'** (crimson/purple). A few have colourful foliage — look for **F. 'Golden Treasure'** (green and gold leaves) and **F. 'Sunray'** (yellow, pink and green leaves). If you want to raise fuchsias from seeds you will find one or two in the catalogues — there are **F. 'Florabelle'**, **F. 'Chimes'** and **F. 'Fuseedia Mixed'**. The usual choice for a cluster-flowered fuchsia is **F. triphylla** or one of its hybrids such as **F. 'Thalia'**, **F. 'Mary'** and **F. 'Trumpeter'**.

Finally there are the Trailing Fuchsias — included here are **F. 'Cascade'** (white sepals/red petals), **F. 'Marinka'** (red/purple), **F. 'Pink Galore'** (pink/pale pink), **F. 'Swingtime'** (red/white) and **F. 'Summer Snow'** (white). For variegated leaves grow **F. 'Tom West'**.

SITE & SOIL: Any well-drained soil in sun or light shade will do. Thrives best in soil which is rich in humus and well-fed.

PROPAGATION: Cuttings: Use 3 in. (7.5 cm) tips of non-flowering shoots — plant in a propagator in summer. Seeds: Sow in February-March — plant out in late May.

FUCHSIA continued

FLOWER FORMS

Fuchsia magellanica 'Alba'

Fuchsia 'Alice Hoffman'

SINGLE
F. 'Checkerboard'
F. 'Bon Accorde'
F. magellanica
F. 'Rufus'

SEMI-DOUBLE
F. 'Lady Thumb'
F. 'Snowcap'
F. 'Pink Flamingo'
F. 'Margaret'

DOUBLE
F. 'Alice Hoffman'
F. 'Blue Gown'
F. 'Swingtime'
F. 'Prosperity'

CLUSTERED
F. 'Thalia'
F. 'Mary'
F. 'Trumpeter'
F. 'Coralle'

Fuchsia 'Sunray'

Fuchsia 'Florabelle'

Fuchsia 'Thalia'

Fuchsia 'Pink Galore'

GAILLARDIA Blanket Flower

Most Gaillardias can be raised from seeds to flower in the first year — the perennial varieties are kept in the border to flower in subsequent years. The ones bought as annuals are raised for bedding out as a temporary summer display. The perennials are by far the more popular — the large 2-4 in. (5-10 cm) wide daisy-like flowers are a familiar sight in herbaceous borders everywhere. The blooms continue to appear from early summer until autumn but there is one major drawback. In badly-drained soil it will die in the first winter and even in ideal conditions the plants deteriorate, so divide the clumps every three years. The annuals have an even longer flowering period but are not popular as the growth habit is untidy.

VARIETIES: The popular perennial Gaillardias are varieties of the hybrid **G. grandiflora** — height 1-3 ft (30-90 cm), yellow-tipped orange or red flowers, flowering period June-September. The taller varieties need support and dead-heading is necessary to prolong the display. **'Dazzler'** (2-3 ft/60-90 cm) is a tall variety with red-centred golden flowers — **'Wirral Flame'** is similar in growth habit but the yellow of the petals is confined to the tips. Not all perennial Gaillardias are bicolours — **'Croftway Yellow'** is all-yellow and **'Burgunder'** is all-red. The tall **'Torchlight'** with very large yellow-edged red flowers and the dwarf **'Goblin'** (1 ft/30 cm) are often grown as annuals, but the true annuals are varieties of **G. pulchella** — height 1-1½ ft (30-45 cm), flowering period June-October. The usual choice is one of the double forms — the ball-like heads are extremely showy. Examples include **'Lollipops'**, **'Gaiety'** and the **'Plume'** series.

SITE & SOIL: Any well-drained soil will do — light land is preferred. Choose a sunny spot.

PROPAGATION: Perennials: Sow seeds or divide clumps in spring. Annuals: Sow seeds in March in gentle heat — plant out in late May.

Gaillardia 'Dazzler'

Border perennial
•
Bedding plant:
hardy annual or
half-hardy annual

Gaillardia 'Goblin'

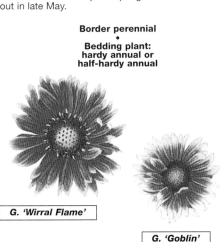

G. 'Wirral Flame'

G. 'Goblin'

Gaillardia pulchella 'Lollipops'

GALANTHUS Snowdrop

The snowdrop is the curtain-raiser for the gardening year — small white flowers hanging on 6 in. (15 cm) stems from January onwards. The date you will see the first blooms in your garden will depend on the variety, locality and the weather. The flower can be distinguished from the Snowflake (Leucojeum) by the three green-tipped petals and the three outer all-white ones. Plant the bulbs as soon as possible after purchase in September or October.

VARIETIES: The Common Snowdrop is **G. nivalis** — height 6 in. (15 cm), 1 in. (2.5 cm) long flowers, flowering period January-March. Varieties include the double-flowered **'Ophelia'**, **'Flore Pleno'** and **'Pusey Green Tip'** and the yellow-marked **'Lutescens'**. G. elwesii has 10 in. (25 cm) stems and the two choice hybrids are **G. 'Atkinsii'** (early, tall) and **G. 'S. Arnott'** (large-flowered, scented).

SITE & SOIL: Moist soil and light shade are required.

PROPAGATION: Divide mature clumps immediately after flowering and replant at once.

Bulb

G. nivalis

Galanthus 'Atkinsii'

Border perennial

G. 'His Majesty'

GALEGA Goat's Rue

Galega is an easy perennial which will grow in any reasonable soil in sun or shade. There is an abundance of flower heads bearing pea-like blooms throughout the summer, but it is an untidy sprawling plant which is more at home in the wild or cottage garden than the herbaceous border. In the mixed border it can be used for growing through tall shrubs.

VARIETIES: The species you are most likely to find is **G. officinalis** — height 3-5 ft (90 cm-1.5 m), mauve or purple flowers on branched spikes, flowering period June-September. The variety **'Alba'** has white flowers and there are a number of colourful hybrids including **'His Majesty'** (pink) and **'Lady Wilson'** (mauve/cream). **G. orientalis** is a shorter plant with violet-blue flowers.

SITE & SOIL: Any well-drained soil will do — thrives in sun or partial shade.

PROPAGATION: Divide clumps in autumn.

Galega officinalis

Bulb

G. candicans

GALTONIA Summer Hyacinth

Galtonia is an imposing plant for the herbaceous border or for growing between shrubs. In summer the tall flower stalk is clothed with 20 or more pendulous white bells. The leaves are long and strap-like — the effect is that of a giant and elongated hyacinth. Cut off the stalks once they have withered and cover the crown with a thick mulch to protect it from frost.

VARIETIES: The popular species is **G. candicans** — height 3 ft (90 cm), 1½ in. (3.5 cm) long white flowers, flowering period August-September. It is an easy plant to grow if you remember to plant the bulbs deeply enough (6-8 in./15-20 cm) in March-April and leave the clumps to grow undisturbed. **G. viridiflora** is an equally tall species but the leaves are wide and the flowers are pale green.

SITE & SOIL: Well-drained, humus-rich soil is required — thrives best in full sun.

PROPAGATION: Dislikes disturbance — buy new bulbs.

Galtonia candicans

Border perennial

G. lindheimeri

GAURA Gaura

This tall and bushy perennial is often described as 'graceful'. Slender spikes of pale-coloured flowers stand above the narrow leaves from midsummer to the first frosts. It is not an easy plant to place — you need a large patch in sandy soil to see it at its best. It will flower in the first year from spring-sown seeds — do not bother with Gaura if your soil is heavy.

VARIETIES: **G. lindheimeri** is the only species you will find — height 5 ft (1.5 m), 1½ in. (3.5 cm) wide flowers, flowering period July-October. The flowers are borne in loose panicles on branched stems — self-sown seedlings can make this plant invasive. Varieties include **'Corrie's Gold'** (gold-edged green leaves) and **'Whirling Butterflies'** (3 ft/90 cm, white/red flowers, grey-green leaves).

SITE & SOIL: Well-drained light soil is necessary — thrives best in full sun.

PROPAGATION: Sow seeds in spring or take cuttings in gentle heat in summer.

Gaura lindheimeri

**Bedding plant:
half-hardy annual**

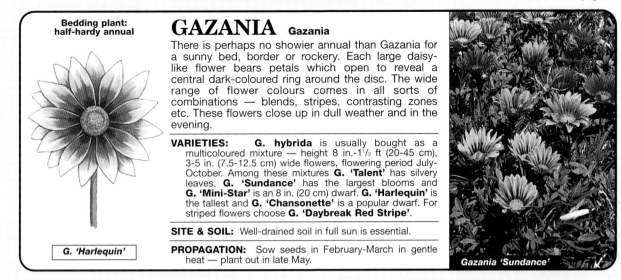

G. 'Harlequin'

GAZANIA Gazania

There is perhaps no showier annual than Gazania for a sunny bed, border or rockery. Each large daisy-like flower bears petals which open to reveal a central dark-coloured ring around the disc. The wide range of flower colours comes in all sorts of combinations — blends, stripes, contrasting zones etc. These flowers close up in dull weather and in the evening.

VARIETIES: **G. hybrida** is usually bought as a multicoloured mixture — height 8 in.-1½ ft (20-45 cm), 3-5 in. (7.5-12.5 cm) wide flowers, flowering period July-October. Among these mixtures **G. 'Talent'** has silvery leaves, **G. 'Sundance'** has the largest blooms and **G. 'Mini-Star'** is an 8 in. (20 cm) dwarf. **G. 'Harlequin'** is the tallest and **G. 'Chansonette'** is a popular dwarf. For striped flowers choose **G. 'Daybreak Red Stripe'**.

SITE & SOIL: Well-drained soil in full sun is essential.

PROPAGATION: Sow seeds in February-March in gentle heat — plant out in late May.

Gazania 'Sundance'

GENTIANA Gentian

A comprehensive rock garden must contain at least one species of gentian. The blue trumpets of this alpine can provide colour from May to October if you grow spring-, summer- and autumn-flowering types. Unfortunately most gentians are rather temperamental and cannot be regarded as 'grow-anywhere' plants. You should always check the likes and dislikes of a particular species before you buy it, and even then it can refuse to flower for no particular reason. Lime is often the problem — spring-flowering types may either tolerate it or require it, but autumn-flowering gentians hate it. All of them require free-draining but not impoverished soil.

VARIETIES: The easiest one to grow is **G. septemfida** — height 9 in. (22.5 cm), spread 1 ft (30 cm), 1-2 in. (2.5-5 cm) long blue-purple trumpets, flowering period July-August. **G. asclepiadea** is another July-August flowering gentian, but it is much taller and is a plant for the mixed border rather than the rockery — height 2½ ft (75 cm), 2 in. (5 cm) long blue trumpets. **G. lutea** is even taller — a 5 ft (1.5 m) plant with yellow flowers. The popular **G. acaulis** (Trumpet Gentian) is a much smaller plant (3 in./7.5 cm high) than the ones above and it blooms earlier (May-June), but its flowers are much more eye-catching — 3 in. (7.5 cm) long almost stemless trumpets standing upright above the glossy leaves. In some situations it may not bloom — if this happens move it to another spot in the autumn. **G. verna** is another spring-flowering species with bright blue starry blooms. The most popular autumn-flowering gentian is **G. sino-ornata** — height 6 in. (15 cm), green-striped blue trumpets, flowering period September-October. **G. farreri** is an attractive white-throated autumn-flowering species.

SITE & SOIL: Well-drained soil is essential — thrives in sun or light shade.

PROPAGATION: Summer- and autumn-flowering species: Divide clumps in spring. Spring-flowering species: Divide clumps in midsummer. Propagation from seeds is difficult.

Gentiana septemfida

**Rockery perennial
•
Border perennial**

G. verna

G. acaulis

Gentiana acaulis

Gentiana farreri

GERANIUM Crane's Bill

Border perennial
•
Rockery perennial

The Geranium or Crane's Bill should not be confused with the half-hardy Pelargonium which is popularly referred to as a 'geranium'. The plants described here are hardy perennials which are grown as ground cover in borders, cottage gardens, woodland gardens and rockeries. They are invaluable in many situations — there are varieties to provide both weed-suppressing mounds of leaves together with flowers in dense shade and there are many varieties to provide bright floral displays or colourful foliage displays in sunny situations. There are tall ones for the herbaceous border and dwarfs for the rockery — Geraniums have few rivals if you are looking for easy-to-grow and drought-tolerant ground cover. The leaves are deeply divided or lobed and the colour may be green, red, grey or bronze. The blooms are usually saucer-shaped and there are varieties in white, pink, blue, mauve and red with petals which may be prominently veined. Many types lose their leaves in winter but there are numerous varieties which cover the ground with foliage all year round.

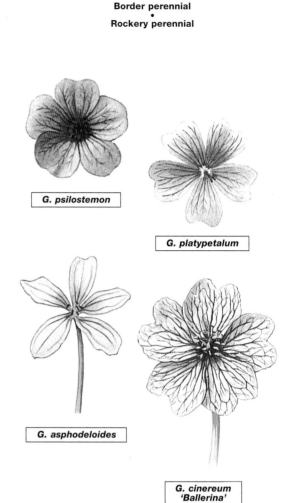

G. psilostemon

G. platypetalum

G. asphodeloides

G. cinereum 'Ballerina'

VARIETIES: Making a choice is not easy — you will find a number of different types at the garden centre and scores of varieties in the catalogues. Height is an important consideration and the range is the key feature of the selection below. The tall one for the border is **G. psilostemon** — height 3 ft (90 cm), magenta flowers, deciduous, flowering period June-August. There is a large number of varieties in the medium (1-2 ft/30-60 cm) range — included here are the excellent evergreens **G. endressii** and the varieties of **G. oxonianum** such as **'Wargrave Pink'** (salmon-pink), **'Winscombe'** (dark-veined pink) and **'A.T. Johnson'** (silvery-pink). These all flower from May to September and so does the magenta-flowered herbaceous variety **G. 'Ann Folkard'**. **G. platypetalum** bears violet-blue flowers in July and August. An important member of the low-growing (less than 1 ft/30 cm) group is the evergreen **G. macrorrhizum** which flourishes in dry shade — popular varieties include **'Variegatum'** (cream-splashed leaves, mauve flowers) and **'Ingwersen's Variety'** (pale green leaves, pink flowers). **G. wallichianum 'Buxton's Variety'** produces trailing stems — for mounds of foliage there are **G. asphodeloides**, **G. renardii** and **G. sanguineum**. Dwarfs which grow less than 6 in. (15 cm) high include the evergreens **G. dalmaticum** (pink), **G. cinereum 'Ballerina'** (dark-veined pink) and **G. cinereum 'Subcaulescens'** (magenta).

SITE & SOIL: Any well-drained soil will do — thrives in sun or shade, depending on the variety.

PROPAGATION: Divide clumps in autumn or spring.

Geranium oxonianum 'Wargrave Pink'

Geranium cinereum 'Subcaulescens'

Geranium sanguineum

GEUM Avens

The popular varieties of Geum form dense clumps at the front of the border and in early summer wiry stems appear which bear bright, bowl-shaped flowers. These blooms are about 1½ in. (3.5 cm) across — single, semi-double or double and in shades of yellow, orange or red. There is a long flowering season and it is an easy plant to grow, but it does benefit from organic matter being added to the soil before planting — the clumps should be divided every few years. In addition to these border types there are a few dwarfs for the rockery. These alpines have saucer-shaped blooms like the popular varieties, but G. rivale (Water Avens) is quite different — it is a moisture-loving plant with pendent flowers.

VARIETIES: The border species is **G. chiloense** — height 1-2 ft (30-60 cm), flowering period May-September. You will find a number of named hybrids in the catalogues and garden centres but two have remained the firm favourites for many years — **G. 'Mrs. J. Bradshaw'** (1½ ft/45 cm, semi-double, scarlet) and **G. 'Lady Stratheden'** (semi-double, yellow). If you want something a little less common there are **G. 'Fire Opal'** (semi-double, orange), **G. 'Princess Juliana'** (semi-double, red-flushed yellow) and **G. 'Georgenberg'** (single, pale orange). **G. 'Borisii'** is shorter than the G. chiloense hybrids described above — it has 1 ft (30 cm) high stems and masses of single bright orange flowers. The most popular rockery Geum is **G. montanum** (Alpine Avens) — height 6 in. (15 cm), yellow flowers, flowering period May-July. It is an easy plant to grow, but **G. reptans** (height 6 in./15 cm, yellow flowers) is not. **G. rivale** is a plant for the bog garden — height 1½ ft (45 cm), ½ in. (1 cm) wide dusky pink bell-like flowers, flowering period May-October.

SITE & SOIL: Any well-drained soil will do — thrives in sun or light shade.

PROPAGATION: Sow seeds under glass in spring or divide clumps in autumn or spring.

Geum 'Mrs. J. Bradshaw'

Border perennial
•
Rockery perennial

Geum 'Borisii'

G. 'Fire Opal'

G. 'Lady Stratheden'

G. montanum

Geum rivale

Hardy annual

GILIA Gilia

This easily grown annual has never become popular despite its attractive flowers and feathery foliage. It has a long flowering season and is not fussy about soil type, but you will find it in few textbooks and not many seed catalogues. The problem is that it needs to be sown where it is to flower and is not grown for sale in spring as a bedding plant. Well worth trying if you like plants which are unusual.

VARIETIES: There are two species with flowers which look nothing like each other. The larger flowers are borne by **G. tricolor** (Bird's Eyes) — height 1 ft (30 cm), pale lilac flowers with creamy-white centres and purple-spotted throats, flowering period June-September. **G. capitata** (Queen Anne's Thimbles) is larger — height 1½ ft (45 cm), 1 in. (2.5 cm) wide globular flower heads made up of tiny lavender flowers, flowering period June-September.

SITE & SOIL: Any well-drained soil in a sunny spot will do.

PROPAGATION: Sow seeds in March-May where they are to grow — thin out as necessary.

G. tricolor

Gilia capitata

GLADIOLUS Sword Lily

Gladiolus like the hyacinth and tulip is a bulbous plant which any gardener can recognise. Its sword-like leaves, upright stems and one-sided spikes of irregular-shaped open trumpets are a common sight in borders outside and vases inside the house during the summer months. All quite similar at first glance, perhaps, but the differences between the various types are surprisingly large. The height of the flower stalk which arises from the corm may reach little more than 1 ft (30 cm) or as much as 4 ft (1.2 m). Flowers range from the width of an egg cup to the size of a saucer and the colours span the rainbow. The petal edge is often plain, but it may be hooded, frilled or ruffled. There are one or two species which are hardy but the popular hybrids are half-hardy.

The hybrids are planted 4-5 in. (10-12.5 cm) deep between March and May for blooms in July-September. The corms are lifted in October — shake off the soil and dry for a few days in a warm room before storing in a cool but frost-free place until the spring. They are easy to grow in good soil and a sunny spot — water thoroughly during dry weather once the flower spikes have appeared. The Large-flowered Hybrids do have a few drawbacks as bedding plants — staking is usually necessary and the flowering period for an individual spike may be as little as two weeks. The trick is to plant at fortnightly intervals so that a succession of blooms is obtained. The routine for the hardy Species Gladioli is different — corms are planted in October and the flowering period is May-June.

VARIETIES: There are several ways of classifying Gladioli, depending on whether you are a botanist, exhibitor or a gardener. For the gardener the following division will help when looking around the garden centre or in the catalogues. There are five basic groups. The first and by far the most popular one consists of the *Large-flowered Hybrids*. Here are the large plants which grow 3-4 ft (90 cm-1.2 m) high with triangular flowers measuring 4-7 in. (10-17.5 cm) across. The flower spikes are about 1½ ft (45 cm) high. The range of varieties available is vast — a few popular ones are **G. 'White Friendship'** (Giant, white), **G. 'Peter Pears'** (Large, red-throated salmon), **G. 'Royal Dutch'** (Large, white-throated lavender), **G. 'Flower Song'** (Large, frilled yellow), **G. 'Spic and Span'** (Large, yellow-blotched pink) and **G. 'White Ice'** (Medium, white).

The *Primulinus Hybrids* grow 1½-3 ft (45-90 cm) high — the flowers are loosely arranged on the stem and the top petal is hooded (bent forward). The average bloom width is 3 in. (7.5 cm) and examples are **G. 'White City'** (white), **G. 'Robin'** (rose-purple), **G. 'Leonore'** (yellow), **G. 'Columbine'** (pink and white) and **G. 'Essex'** (red). Staking is not necessary and it is not often needed for the third group — the *Butterfly Hybrids*. These grow 2-4 ft (60 cm-1.2 m) high with 3-4 in. (7.5-10 cm) wide flowers. The two basic features of most of these hybrids are the close packing of the ruffled flowers on the stem and the striking colours of the throats. These features can be clearly seen in such varieties as **G. 'Tinkerbell'** (yellow-throated orange), **G. 'Melodie'** (red-throated pink), **G. 'Georgette'** (yellow-throated red) and **G. 'Seraphin'** (white-throated pink).

The *Miniature Hybrids* are like small Primulinus varieties — height 1½-2 ft (45-60 cm), flower size 2 in. (5 cm) across with petals which are frequently frilled or ruffled. Examples include **G. 'Bo Peep'** (apricot), **G. 'Robinetta'** (cream-blotched dark red) and **G. 'Greenbird'** (yellowish-green). The final group consists of the *Species Gladioli* which flower in spring and early summer. **G. colvillei 'The Bride'** (height 2 ft/60 cm, white flowers) is quite tender and needs a winter mulch to protect the crown — **G. papilio** (purple/yellow) is hardier but **G. byzantinus** (magenta) is the only popular one which can be relied upon to be fully hardy.

Bulb

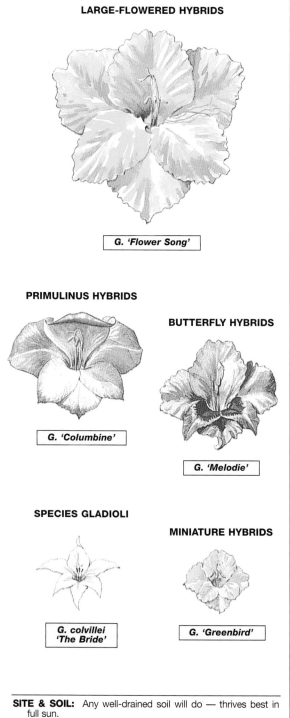

LARGE-FLOWERED HYBRIDS

G. 'Flower Song'

PRIMULINUS HYBRIDS

G. 'Columbine'

BUTTERFLY HYBRIDS

G. 'Melodie'

SPECIES GLADIOLI

G. colvillei 'The Bride'

MINIATURE HYBRIDS

G. 'Greenbird'

SITE & SOIL: Any well-drained soil will do — thrives best in full sun.

PROPAGATION: At lifting time remove the cormlets attached to the corms and store in a frost-free place. Plant in spring — these cormlets will take two to three years to flower.

GLADIOLUS continued

Gladiolus 'Peter Pears'

Gladiolus 'Columbine'

FLOWER SIZE
Catalogues sometimes express the size of Gladioli flowers in words rather than figures. These terms refer to the width of the bottom flower in the spike when it is fully open and when grown under good conditions.

GIANT
over 5½ in. (14 cm)

LARGE
4½-5½ in. (11-14 cm)

MEDIUM
3½-4½ in. (9-11 cm)

SMALL
2½-3½ in. (6-9 cm)

MINIATURE
less than 2½ in. (6 cm)

Gladiolus 'Flower Song'

Gladiolus 'Melodie'

Gladiolus 'Greenbird'

Gladiolus colvillei 'The Bride'

Gladiolus byzantinus

Hardy annual

GODETIA Godetia

Godetia was once a great favourite for the annual bed or border, but it has lost much of its popularity with the trend away from sowing seeds in the place where they are to grow and flower. It does not like transplanting, but the technique described below for raising bedding plants is quite successful. The large flowers have fluted papery petals and are borne on leafy spikes.

VARIETIES: The garden varieties are hybrids of **G. grandiflora** (**Clarkia grandiflora**) — height 8 in.-2 ft (20-60 cm), 2-4 in. (5-10 cm) wide flowers, flowering period July-September. Choose **'Tall Double Mixed'** or **'Grace Mixed'** (2 ft/ 60 cm) for the middle of the border — **'Sybil Sherwood'** is shorter and **'Azalea-flowered Mixed'** is the showiest variety. **'Salmon Princess'** and **'Dwarf Satin'** are 8 in. (20 cm) dwarfs.

SITE & SOIL: The soil should be neither heavy nor chalky. Thrives best in full sun.

PROPAGATION: For bedding sow seeds in March in gentle heat. Prick out into individual pots and plant out in May.

G. 'Sybil Sherwood'

Godetia 'Salmon Princess'

Bedding plant: half-hardy annual

GOMPHRENA Globe Amaranth

You will not find Gomphrena in the bedding plant section of your garden centre, but it is worth raising from seed if you like dried flowers — the preserved blooms are small colourful cones and not strawy daisies like many other 'everlasting' flowers. Apart from their use as dried material the flowers make an attractive feature in beds or containers. Feed occasionally during the flowering season.

VARIETIES: The basic species is **G. globosa** — height 1 ft (30 cm), ball-like flower heads, flowering period July-October. The pink, red or purple heads are borne on stiff stems. There is a dwarf variety **'Buddy'** which is about 6 in. (15 cm) high and also a showy 2 ft (60 cm) hybrid **G. 'Strawberry Fields'** with rich red 2 in. (5 cm) round flower heads. **G. 'Pink Pinheads'** has trailing stems and dark pink flowers.

SITE & SOIL: Any well-drained soil will do — thrives best in full sun.

PROPAGATION: Sow seeds in February in gentle heat. Plant out in late May.

G. 'Strawberry Fields'

Gomphrena globosa

Tubs and large pots are often used to house a single tree or specimen shrub, but with floral displays it is more usual to plant a mixture of different annuals and/or perennials in the container. The use of a single variety is, however, sometimes a better choice when you want the pot to serve as a focal point. In the illustration Lilium regale has been employed to good effect.

Bog plant

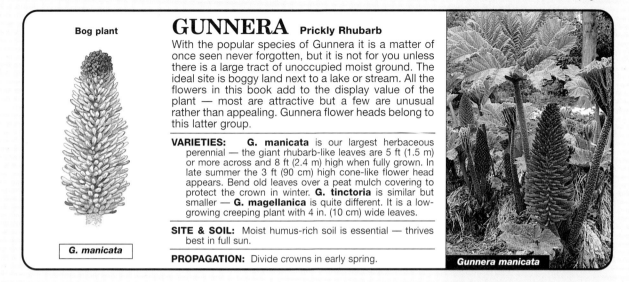

G. manicata

Gunnera manicata

GUNNERA Prickly Rhubarb

With the popular species of Gunnera it is a matter of once seen never forgotten, but it is not for you unless there is a large tract of unoccupied moist ground. The ideal site is boggy land next to a lake or stream. All the flowers in this book add to the display value of the plant — most are attractive but a few are unusual rather than appealing. Gunnera flower heads belong to this latter group.

VARIETIES: **G. manicata** is our largest herbaceous perennial — the giant rhubarb-like leaves are 5 ft (1.5 m) or more across and 8 ft (2.4 m) high when fully grown. In late summer the 3 ft (90 cm) high cone-like flower head appears. Bend old leaves over a peat mulch covering to protect the crown in winter. **G. tinctoria** is similar but smaller — **G. magellanica** is quite different. It is a low-growing creeping plant with 4 in. (10 cm) wide leaves.

SITE & SOIL: Moist humus-rich soil is essential — thrives best in full sun.

PROPAGATION: Divide crowns in early spring.

GYPSOPHILA Baby's Breath

Loose clusters of small flowers on thin stems form a billowy cloud above the grey-green leaves — hence the common name. Gypsophila is a great favourite with flower arrangers but it also has a useful job to do in the garden where it provides a welcome contrast to large and bright blooms. The lax stems should be supported with twigs. There are both perennial and annual varieties — all are quite easy to grow if your soil is neutral or alkaline. With perennials do not divide or transplant once established and cut the stems down to ground level in autumn. Gypsophila has its limitations. The flowering period is quite short — with annual varieties successional sowing is necessary.

VARIETIES: **G. paniculata** is the border species and the usual choice is **'Bristol Fairy'** — height 3 ft (90 cm), double white flowers, flowering period July-August. For similar-sized plants with double pink flowers grow **'Flamingo'**. There are a number of more compact varieties such as **'Compacta Plena'** (height 1½ ft/45 cm, double white) and **'Rosy Veil'** (height 1 ft/30 cm, double pink). For the rockery there are several dwarf varieties headed by **G. repens** — height 6 in. (15 cm), flowering period June-August. The stems and grey-tinged foliage soon carpet a large area — varieties include **'Dorothy Teacher'** (single pink), **'Fratensis'** (single pink), **'Rosea'** (double pink) and **'Dubia'** (single white). Other dwarfs include **G. cerastioides** and **G. aretioides**. The annual Gypsophilas are usually varieties of **G. elegans** — the usual height is 1½ ft (45 cm). Look for **'Covent Garden'** (white), **'Monarch'** (white) and **'Bright Rose'** (pink). There are also **G. muralis 'Garden Bride'** (single pink) and **'Gypsy'** (double pink).

SITE & SOIL: Any well-drained, non-acid soil will do — choose a sunny spot.

PROPAGATION: Perennials: Plant cuttings in a cold frame in summer. Annuals: Sow seeds in February-March — plant out in May.

Gypsophila paniculata 'Bristol Fairy'

Gypsophila repens 'Dorothy Teacher'

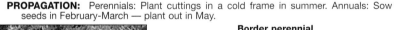

Border perennial
•
Rockery perennial
•
Hardy annual

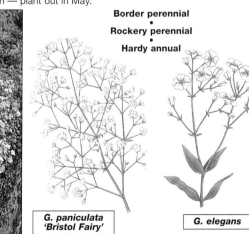

G. paniculata 'Bristol Fairy'

G. elegans

Gypsophila elegans 'Covent Garden'

Rockery perennial

H. rhodopensis

HABERLEA Haberlea

Haberlea is a pretty lilac alpine which offers a challenge. It is fussy about its environment and will not succeed unless given the right set of conditions. It needs acid soil in a shady spot, and water must not be left to stand in the heart of the leafy rosette in winter. The best plan is to plant it sideways in a crack between stones or bricks in a north-facing rockery or wall.

VARIETIES: The one you are most likely to find is **H. rhodopensis** — height 4 in. (10 cm), spread 8 in. (20 cm), flowering period May-June. The stalks bearing clusters of flowers arise from the centre of the rosette composed of dark green leaves. The 1 in. (2.5 cm) wide lilac blooms are tubular. A white variety (**'Virginalis'**) is available. **H. ferdinandi-coburgii** is larger and the lilac flowers are flecked with gold.

SITE & SOIL: Well-drained but damp soil with little or no direct sun is necessary.

PROPAGATION: Divide clumps in autumn or plant leaf cuttings in a cold frame in summer.

Haberlea rhodopensis

Bulb

H. robustus

HABRANTHUS Habranthus

This dainty bulb is related to Hippeastrum, but it has none of the grandeur of its showy cousin. Instead it looks like a crocus borne on top of an upright stalk — a characteristic feature is that the bloom is held at an angle. There are several species but most are tender — the two which can be grown outdoors are to be found in some specialist catalogues but not at the garden centre.

VARIETIES: **H. tubispathus** is the only species which is reliably hardy — height 1 ft (30 cm), 1 in. (2.5 cm) long trumpet-like flowers, flowering period June-July. The blooms are borne singly on top of each stalk — yellow inside and coppery-orange outside. Plant bulbs in October. **H. robustus** bears larger blooms between July and September, but it is not reliably hardy and needs a sunny and sheltered site.

SITE & SOIL: Well-drained, humus-rich soil is necessary — thrives best in full sun.

PROPAGATION: Divide clumps in autumn.

Habranthus tubispathus

Rockery perennial
•
Border perennial

H. epipactis

HACQUETIA Hacquetia

Buy this one if you have a moist and partially shady spot which needs to be clothed with a low-growing mound-forming plant — a woodland garden or a damp rockery is ideal. The flower is unusual — there is a central cluster of tiny yellow true flowers surrounded by leafy bracts which are yellow at first but become green as they age. Hacquetia is listed in many catalogues but it has never been popular and you will not find it at your garden centre.

VARIETIES: **H. epipactis** (**Dondia epipactis**) is the only species. In late winter or early spring the flowers appear, forming a 6 in.-1 ft (15-30 cm) wide clump which is about 2 in. (5 cm) high. These flowers are followed by the deeply-lobed 3 in. (7.5 cm) long leaves which are bright green and glossy. Hacquetia produces self-sown seedlings and so it can be invasive in a small rockery.

SITE & SOIL: Damp soil in partial shade is necessary.

PROPAGATION: Divide clumps after flowering.

Hacquetia epipactis

HEDYCHIUM Ginger Lily

Bulb

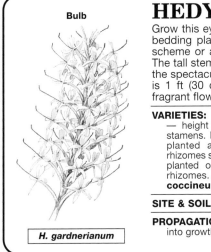

H. gardnerianum

Grow this eye-catching plant from India as a summer bedding plant — use it as a dot plant in a bedding scheme or as a specimen plant in a large container. The tall stem bears long leaves and at the top there is the spectacular flower head in July-September — this is 1 ft (30 cm) high with rows of 2 in. (5 cm) long fragrant flowers bearing prominent stamens.

VARIETIES: **H. gardnerianum** is the easiest one to grow — height 4 ft (1.2 m), yellow flowers with bright red stamens. In mild areas it can be grown as a perennial if planted against a south-facing wall. Elsewhere the rhizomes should be started each year in peat in March and planted out in June — in autumn lift and store the rhizomes. **H. coronarium** has white flowers — **H. coccineum** blooms are red, pink or orange.

SITE & SOIL: Humus-rich soil and full sun are essential.

PROPAGATION: Cut up rhizomes once they have started into growth.

Hedychium coronarium

HELENIUM Sneezewort

Border perennial

H. 'Butterpat'

H. 'Moerheim Beauty'

The late summer herbaceous border relies on Helenium as a basic source of reds and yellows. Each large daisy-like flower has a prominent central disc and is borne on an erect stem which is 2-5 ft (60 cm-1.5 m) high — the tall varieties will need support on exposed sites. Mulch around the stems in spring and water in dry weather — dead-head spent blooms and divide the clumps every few years.

VARIETIES: Almost all garden Heleniums are hybrids of **H. autumnale**. By far the most popular one is **'Moerheim Beauty'** — height 3 ft (90 cm), copper-red flowers, flowering period July-September. Others include **'Butterpat'** (gold), **'Coppelia'** (orange and red) and **'Waldtraut'** (orange-brown). Tall ones include **'Chipperfield Orange'** and there are dwarfs like **'Crimson Beauty'**. **H. hoopesii** (yellow) blooms in June.

SITE & SOIL: Any well-drained soil will do — thrives in sun or light shade.

PROPAGATION: Divide clumps in autumn or spring.

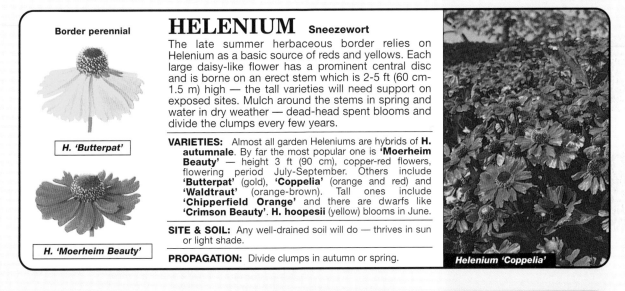

Helenium 'Coppelia'

HELIANTHEMUM Rock Rose

Rockery perennial

H. 'Ben Hope'

Few plants can match the Rock Rose in providing such a long-lasting sheet of white, yellow, pink, orange or red flowers during the summer months. Each flower lasts for only a day or two, but new ones are borne in profusion. It can be invasive — once the first flush of flowers has faded you must cut them back hard to induce another flush of flowers and to prolong the life of the plant.

VARIETIES: The named varieties at the garden centre are hybrids of **H. nummularium** and **H. apenninum**. There are a few 4 in. x 1 ft (10 cm x 30 cm) dwarfs such as **'Amy Baring'** but most grow to 8 in. (20 cm). The Wisley Series (**'Wisley White'**, **'Wisley Pink'** and **'Wisley Primrose'**) have grey leaves. **'Jubilee'** and **'Mrs. C.W. Earle'** have double flowers and the Ben Series (**'Ben Hope'** etc) are the hardiest.

SITE & SOIL: Well-drained light soil and full sun are necessary.

PROPAGATION: Plant cuttings in a cold frame in summer.

Helianthemum 'Wisley Pink'

HELIANTHUS   Sunflower

For garden display it is better to choose one of the more compact annuals than the familiar coarse-leaved giant. They are usually more colourful and have flowers at a level where they can be seen at close quarters. Seeds may be sown 1 in. (2.5 cm) deep in April where they are to flower, but for earlier blooms it is better to raise seedlings under glass for planting out in spring. Tall varieties will require staking and all Sunflowers respond to occasional feeding. The perennial varieties are less popular — they grow 4-6 ft (1.2-1.8 m) high with 2-3 in. (5-7.5 cm) wide flowers. They are plants for the back of the border with yellow blooms on strong stems in late summer and autumn.

VARIETIES: The Annual Sunflowers are varieties of **H. annuus** — height 1-10 ft (30 cm-3 m), flowering period July-October. Always check the height in the catalogues or on the label before you buy. The giants such as **'Russian Giant'**, **'Tall Single'** and **'Giant Yellow'** reach 6-10 ft (1.8-3 m) with flowers 1 ft (30 cm) across. In the medium-sized range (4-5 ft/1.2-1.5 m) there is **'Autumn Beauty'** in yellow, orange and red — for all-yellow blooms there are **'Sunburst'** and **'Full Sun'**. The dwarf varieties (1-2 ft/ 30-60 cm) have become increasingly popular for beds and containers — **'Teddy Bear'** has furry flowers, **'Pacino'** bears single golden flowers, **'Music Box'** is a mixture of cream, yellow and red blooms and **'Sunspot'** has 8 in. (20 cm) wide blooms. The most popular perennial variety is **H. 'Loddon Gold'** — height 5 ft (1.5 m), double golden flowers, flowering period July-September. **H. decapetalus 'Soleil d'Or'** has semi-double yellow blooms and **H. salicifolius** bears branched heads of yellow flowers.

Helianthus annuus
'Tall Single'

SITE & SOIL: Any well-drained soil will do — thrives best in full sun.

PROPAGATION: Sow seeds in March-April in gentle heat — plant out in May. Divide clumps of perennial varieties in autumn or spring.

Bedding plant:
hardy annual
●
Border perennial

Helianthus annuus
'Teddy Bear'

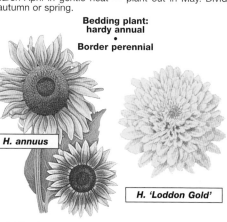

H. annuus

H. 'Loddon Gold'

H. annuus 'Autumn Beauty'

Helianthus decapetalus
'Soleil d'Or'

Bedding schemes have become more dramatic as the choice of plants at the garden centre has increased. Canna, Abutilon etc are readily available for sale in spring to give an exotic touch when used as dot plants in the scheme. You can go even further by creating a Mediterranean mixed border in a sunny and sheltered spot as illustrated here.

HELICHRYSUM   Helichrysum

There are annuals which produce 'everlasting' flowers and also dwarf perennials for the rockery. The annuals look like double daisies but there is an important difference. True flowers are found only at the centre of each bloom — the display comes from the surrounding petal-like strawy bracts. It is dried by cutting just before the flowers are fully open and the stems are hung upside down in a cool place. The perennials are dwarfs used for ground cover. They are usually grown for their silvery foliage but there are two species which have attractive flowers.

VARIETIES: The annual Helichrysum is **H. bracteatum** (Straw Flower) — height 1-3 ft (30-90 cm), 2-3 in. (5-7.5 cm) wide flowers, flowering period July-September. Each plant bears about 25 blooms and a wide range of heights and colours is available. Mixtures are available as **'Tall Mixed'**, **'Double Mixed'** etc or you can buy single colours such as **'Terracotta'**, **'White'** and **'Rose'**. Unfortunately these tall plants are gaunt and it has been the introduction of the 1 ft (30 cm) bushy dwarfs which has changed Helichrysum into an attractive bedding plant. There are **'Bright Bikini'** (mixed bright colours), **'Hot Bikini'** (scarlet/gold), **'Spangle Mixed'** (mixed bright colours) and **'Pastel Mixed'** (pink, yellow, salmon etc). **'Golden Baby'** bears heads of small yellow flowers. The rockery perennial you are most likely to find is **H. bellidioides** — height 3 in. (7.5 cm), white flowers on short stalks, flowering period June-August. The flowers appear above a mat of woolly grey leaves. **H. milfordiae** is more colourful — red buds which open into large white flowers.

SITE & SOIL: Any well-drained soil in a sunny spot will do.

PROPAGATION: Annuals: Sow seeds in March in gentle heat — plant out in May. Perennials: Divide clumps in summer.

Helichrysum bracteatum 'Tall Mixed'

Bedding plant:
hardy annual
•
Rockery perennial

Helichrysum bracteatum 'Hot Bikini'

H. bracteatum

H. milfordiae

Helichrysum bellidioides

Bedding plant:
hardy annual

HELIOPHILA   Heliophila

This uncommon bedding plant can be found in some but not all the seed catalogues. The best way to see Heliophila is as a wide area of massed plants — sow it outdoors in spring where it is to flower or raise seedlings under glass and bed out later. The flowers have the four-petal arrangement of the cress family and are borne in clusters on top of the stems in midsummer.

VARIETIES: The only garden annual is **H. longifolia** (**H. coronopifolia**) — height 1 ft (30 cm), ½ in. (1 cm) wide white- or yellow-eyed blue flowers, flowering period July-September. The papery-petalled flowers or the ornamental long green pods are useful for flower arranging — use them fresh or dry them for winter display. The usual variety is **'Blue Bird'** which has bright blue flowers.

SITE & SOIL: Any well-drained soil will do — thrives best in full sun.

PROPAGATION: Sow outdoors in April where they are to flower. Alternatively sow in March-April in gentle heat and plant out in May.

H. longifolia

Heliophila longifolia

Border perennial

HELIOPSIS Heliopsis

There are several summer-flowering yellow daisies for the herbaceous border and choice may be difficult, but heliopsis has three points in its favour. The bushy plants are compact, they do not have to be lifted and divided every few years, and the flowers are long-lasting. Single, semi-double and double varieties are available. At the end of the season cut the stems down to ground level.

VARIETIES: **H. scabra** is the basic species — height 3-4 ft (90 cm-1.2 m), 3 in. (7.5 cm) wide yellow or orange flowers, flowering period July-August. The most popular variety is **'Summer Sun'** — a 3 ft (90 cm) high plant with golden single flowers. The favourite double flower is **'Golden Plume'** (4 ft/1.2 m) and **'Goldgreenheart'** is a lime-centred novelty.

SITE & SOIL: Any reasonable soil will do — thrives best in full sun.

PROPAGATION: Divide clumps in autumn or spring.

H. scabra 'Golden Plume'

Heliopsis scabra

Bedding plant: half-hardy annual

HELIOTROPIUM Heliotrope

Once heliotrope was a popular summer-bedding plant but not any more. It is a shrubby tender perennial which is grown as a half-hardy annual and the range of varieties is strictly limited these days. Each individual flower is tiny, but they are massed in large heads. It is noted for its evening fragrance and is worth considering for hanging baskets, tubs etc.

VARIETIES: Several varieties of **H. peruvianum** (Cherry Pie) are available — height 1-1½ ft (30-45 cm), white, mauve, purple or blue flowers, flowering period June-September. The one you will find in the seed catalogues is **'Marine'** or **'Mini Marine'** (violet-purple flowers, dark green wrinkled foliage). Types grown from cuttings include **'White Lady'** (white) and **'Lord Roberts'** (dark blue).

SITE & SOIL: Any well-drained soil will do — thrives best in full sun.

PROPAGATION: Sow seeds in February-March in gentle heat. Plant out in early June.

H. peruvianum

Heliotropium peruvianum 'Marine'

Hardy annual

HELIPTERUM Everlasting Flower

This Australian flower is often called Acroclinum in seed catalogues, but its Latin name is Helipterum. The strawy-petalled daisy-like flowers are borne on slender stems and they belong to a group of 'everlasting' flowers which can be dried for winter decoration. The blooms may be single, semi-double or double. Cut stems for drying before the flowers are fully open.

VARIETIES: The usual species is **H. roseum** (Rhodanthe roseum) — height 1-1½ ft (30-45 cm), 2 in. (5 cm) wide white or pink flowers, flowering period July-September. It is usually sold as a mixture of white and pink semi-double and double varieties (**'Special Mixture'**, **'Large-Flowered Mixture'** etc). **'Goliath'** is a pink, dark-centred variety. For a change in colour there is the yellow-flowered **H. humboldtianum**.

SITE & SOIL: Any well-drained soil will do — thrives best in full sun.

PROPAGATION: Dislikes root disturbance. Sow seeds in April where they are to flower — thin to required spacing.

H. roseum

Helipterum roseum

HELLEBORUS   Hellebore

The ideal place for hellebores is in a mixed or shrub border. The large saucer-shaped blooms are usually white, green, pink or purple depending on the variety, and the time of flowering ranges from mid winter to late spring. The deeply-lobed leaves provide good ground cover and the flowers last well when cut for indoor decoration. Hellebores need very little attention — dig in compost, leaf mould or peat before planting, water in dry weather and watch for slugs in spring. Two words of warning — hellebores take a long time to recover if dug up and divided, and all parts are poisonous.

VARIETIES: The Christmas Rose is **H. niger** — height 1-1½ ft (30-45 cm), 2-3 in. (5-7.5 cm) wide white flowers with a central boss of golden stamens, flowering period January-March (despite the common name). For the largest flowers choose **'Potter's Wheel'**. The Lenten Rose (**H. orientalis**) is rather easier to grow and has varieties in a wide range of colours — the pendent blooms may be white, cream, yellow, green, pink, red, purple or black. These blooms appear in February-April and they are often marked or spotted with other colours. Both these species are evergreen or semi-evergreen — another evergreen is the Stinking Hellebore (**H. foetidus**). This is a 1½ ft (45 cm) shrubby plant which bears evil-smelling purple-rimmed yellow flowers from February to April. An improved form is sold as the **'Wester Flisk Group'** — look for their red-tinted leaves and stems. Deciduous hellebores include **H. sternii** and its variety **'Blackthorn'** which bear purple-stained green flowers, the green-flowering **H. viridis** and the rather tender **H. lividus** which produces its flowers in January.

SITE & SOIL: Well-drained, humus-rich soil is necessary — thrives best in partial shade.

PROPAGATION: Overcrowded clumps can be divided in spring, but it is better to buy young plants from your garden shop or nursery.

Border perennial

Helleborus niger

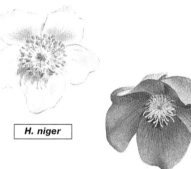

H. niger

H. orientalis

Helleborus orientalis

Helleborus lividus

The true cottage garden has two essential features. The plant arrangement is crowded, strictly informal and apparently chaotic — in addition there are herbs and vegetables as well as flowers. The flower species and varieties should be mainly or entirely old established ones rather than modern hybrids, although the old and new do sometimes blend quite well as in this cottage garden.

HEMEROCALLIS Day Lily

In recent years a vast array of hybrids have been developed. No longer are plain orange and yellow the only colours and no longer is the open-faced trumpet the only flower shape. There are now 1½ ft (45 cm) dwarfs and 4 ft (1.2 m) giants as well as the more traditional 2½-3 ft (75-90 cm) varieties. There has also been a wider appreciation of how easy they are to grow — all that is required is a moisture-retentive soil and they will grow almost anywhere. Above the strap-like leaves arise the branching flower stalks in summer. Each bloom usually lasts for a single day but new ones continue to open for many weeks.

VARIETIES: The flowers of Hemerocallis hybrids appear between June and August and are available in a range of shapes and opening times. The older types are usually lily-like or star-shaped while the modern ones tend to be fuller and ruffled with a more rounded look — double and spider-petalled varieties are also available. Most types have flowers which open in the morning but there are also nocturnal ones which open in late afternoon — obviously with Day Lilies you should read the label or catalogue description carefully to see what you are buying. Listed below are a number of varieties which are widely available, but you will find many more in the catalogues. **H. 'Black Magic'** (3 ft/90 cm, 3 in./7.5 cm dark red flowers), **H. 'Bonanza'** (3 ft/90 cm, 3 in./7.5 cm golden flowers), **H. 'Catherine Woodbery'** (2½ ft/75 cm, 5 in./12.5 cm lavender/green flowers), **H. 'Golden Chimes'** (2 ft/60 cm, 2 in./5 cm yellow flowers), **H. 'Little Wine Cup'** (1½ ft/45 cm, 2 in./5 cm wine-red/green flowers), **H. 'Pink Damask'** (3 ft/90 cm, 5 in./12.5 cm pink/yellow flowers) and **H. 'Stafford'** (2½ ft/75 cm, 4 in./10 cm red/yellow flowers).

SITE & SOIL: Any reasonable soil will do — thrives in sun or light shade.

PROPAGATION: Divide overcrowded clumps in autumn or spring.

Border perennial

Hemerocallis 'Bonanza'

Hemerocallis 'Golden Chimes'

H. 'Stafford'

Hemerocallis 'Pink Damask'

HEPATICA Hepatica

Rockery perennial

Hepatica sounds as if it would be a most welcome addition to the rockery — it comes into flower before Alyssum, Aubrieta and the usual spring flowers and it is quite happy in partial shade. Unfortunately it does have a special need — the soil must be kept moist at all times. Add peat or compost to the soil before planting.

VARIETIES: **H. nobilis** is the most popular species — height 3 in. (7.5 cm), spread 1 ft (30 cm), 1 in. (2.5 cm) wide mauve starry flowers, flowering period February-April. The blooms are borne on short stalks above the tri-lobed leaves. Single and double varieties are available in white (**'Alba'**), blue, pink and purple. **H. transsilvanica** is similar in appearance but it is larger and the leaves are rounded. Best of all is the hybrid **H. media 'Ballardii'** but it is hard to find.

SITE & SOIL: Well-drained but damp soil is necessary — thrives best in light shade.

PROPAGATION: Divide clumps in autumn.

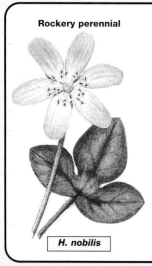

H. nobilis

Hepatica transsilvanica

HERMODACTYLUS Widow Iris

Bulb

H. tuberosus

Widow Iris is small and its blooms are not colourful but it has its uses. It will grow in chalky soil and its blooms which appear early in the year make an excellent addition to spring flower arrangements. It is regarded as being rather tender but it will grow quite happily in the rockery if provided with a mulch in winter. The foliage dies down in summer.

VARIETIES: **H. tuberosus** is the only species — height 1 ft (30 cm), 2 in. (5 cm) wide flowers, flowering period March-April. The blooms appear singly on the stalks — the upright inner petals are green and the outer ones are brown or purple. The grey-green leaves are long and narrow. Do not disturb the clumps unless it is really necessary — divide overcrowded ones in spring.

SITE & SOIL: Any well-drained, non-acid soil will do — full sun is essential.

PROPAGATION: Plant tubers 2 in. (5 cm) deep in October-November.

Hermodactylus tuberosus

HESPERIS Sweet Rocket

Border perennial
•
Hardy annual

H. matronalis
'Lilacina Flore Pleno'

This cottage garden plant makes a welcome contribution to the border, woodland garden or containers where fragrance is important — the perfume is strongest in the evening. Loose spikes of four-petalled flowers are borne on slender branching stems above the lance-shaped evergreen leaves. Grow it from seeds or cuttings as a short-lived perennial or as an annual.

VARIETIES: The only species available is **H. matronalis** — height 2 ft (60 cm), ³/₄ in. (1.5 cm) wide white, pink or mauve flowers, flowering period June-July. The flower heads which are about 1 ft (30 cm) tall are attractive to butterflies and the plant readily produces self-sown seedlings. Varieties include **'Albiflora'** (pure white) and **'Lilacina Flore Pleno'** (double lilac).

SITE & SOIL: Any well-drained soil will do — thrives best in light shade.

PROPAGATION: Sow species seeds outdoors in April-May where they are to grow — raise varieties from cuttings.

Hesperis matronalis

HEUCHERA Coral Flower

Border perennial

H. sanguinea

Heuchera, Tellima and Tiarella are a group of evergreen or semi-evergreen plants which are used as ground cover. They all have lobed, hairy and veined leaves with small flowers on upright stalks. You may confuse these plants at the all-leaf stage but not when in flower — Heuchera blooms are small bells borne in panicles.

VARIETIES: **H. sanguinea** is a typical Heuchera — height 2 ft (60 cm), ¹/₂ in. (1 cm) long pink flowers, silver-marbled green leaves, flowering period June-August. There are many other species, varieties and hybrids — look for **H. micrantha diversifolia 'Palace Purple'** (white flowers, purple leaves), **H. 'Red Spangles'** (crimson flowers), **H. 'Pewter Moon'** (pink flowers, grey-marbled leaves) and **H. 'Rachel'** (pink flowers).

SITE & SOIL: Any well-drained soil will do — thrives in sun or light shade.

PROPAGATION: Divide clumps in autumn or spring.

Heuchera 'Pewter Moon'

HIBISCUS Hibiscus

Bedding plant:
hardy annual
•
Bedding plant:
half-hardy annual

H. trionum

Unlike its perennial relatives the annual varieties of hibiscus are sadly neglected. The flowers have a brief life, a day at the most, but they appear freely and continually on the bushy plants for many weeks. The short-lived flowers are followed by attractive seed pods. Keep watch for greenfly — spray if necessary.

VARIETIES: The hardy annual variety of hibiscus is **H. trionum** (Flower of an Hour) — height 2 ft (60 cm), dark-centred white or cream flowers, flowering period June-September. Sow seeds in April where they are to flower. The most popular half-hardy variety is **H. 'Disco Belle'** — height 2 ft (60 cm), white, pink or red flowers, flowering period July-September. The blooms measure up to 7 in. (17.5 cm) across. Others to grow as half-hardy annuals are **H. manihot** and **H. 'Dixie Belle'**.

SITE & SOIL: A well-drained sheltered spot in full sun is necessary.

PROPAGATION: Sow seeds in February in gentle heat. Prick out into pots and plant out in June.

Hibiscus 'Disco Belle Mixed'

HIERACIUM Hawkweed

Border perennial
•
Rockery perennial

Hawkweed is included in this book as it is offered by numerous garden centres, but it is not a plant which can be generally recommended. It is excellent in a wild flower garden, but in the border or rockery the dandelion-like flowers give the plant a weedy look and the profusion of self-sown seedlings can pose a problem. Its main advantages are the silvery leaves of some species and its ability to grow in dry starved soil.

VARIETIES: **H. villosum** is the most popular species — height 1 ft (30 cm), 1½ in. (3.5 cm) wide yellow flowers, woolly grey leaves, flowering period June-August. **H. maculatum** has smaller flowers and purple-blotched leaves — it self-seeds very freely. **H. aurantiaca** has bright orange flowers.

SITE & SOIL: Any well-drained soil will do — thrives best in full sun.

PROPAGATION: Divide clumps in autumn or spring.

H. villosum

Hieracium aurantiaca

HOMERIA Homeria

Bulb

These spring- and summer-flowering plants are rarities — you will have to search through the catalogues to find a supplier. The leaves are long and narrow and the starry or cup-shaped blooms are borne on top of wiry stems. It is a tender plant which is usually grown indoors, but if you have a well-drained sunny site you can try it in the garden. Plant the corms 3 in. (7.5 cm) deep in January and lift again in October. Store in dry peat until replanting time.

VARIETIES: There are three species in the specialist catalogues. **H. collina** grows about 1 ft (30 cm) high and has 2-3 in. (5-7.5 cm) wide flowers in spring — these open-faced cups are orange with a yellow centre. The yellow-flowered **H. ochroleuca** grows taller and blooms later — **H. flaccida** has red and yellow flowers.

SITE & SOIL: Well-drained soil in a warm and sheltered site is necessary.

PROPAGATION: Remove and store cormlets at lifting time.

H. collina

Homeria ochroleuca

HOSTA Plantain Lily

Hosta is a dual-purpose plant — it is grown for its spikes of trumpet-shaped flowers and for its attractive leaves. The bell- or trumpet-shaped blooms measure 1-2½ in. (2.5-6 cm) long and are borne on one side of the flower stalk which is usually leafless. The usual flower colour is lilac, but there are white, violet and purple varieties. These blooms provide a colourful summer feature but Hostas are grown mainly for their leaves. These range from lance-shaped to almost round and there are colours from pure yellow to near blue. In addition there are all sorts of variegations. The place you are most likely to see them is under trees or shrubs in a mixed border where they provide effective ground cover in summer. They can be used elsewhere if the site is partially shady — they can be grown in boggy ground around the pond and small varieties give leaf colour to the rockery. In addition varieties with big and bold leaves can be grown as specimen plants in containers. Hostas have two drawbacks — they lose their leaves in winter so they are only part-year ground-covering plants, and the young foliage in spring can be badly damaged by slugs and strong winds.

VARIETIES: Catalogues and garden centres offer a large selection of Hostas — always read the label as the mature foliage may differ from the young leaves in the pot. Basic details are leaf mound height 6 in.-3 ft (15-90 cm), flowering period June-August. For deep shade choose an all-green variety such as **H. 'Royal Standard'** (heart-shaped leaves, white flowers), **H. ventricosa** (heart-shaped leaves, lilac flowers), **H. sieboldiana 'Elegans'** (heart-shaped leaves, white flowers) and **H. lancifolia** (lance-shaped leaves, purple flowers). Variegated and blue-leaved types flourish in partial shade — widely available ones include **H. fortunei 'Albopicta'** (green-edged cream leaves) and **'Aureomarginata'** (cream-edged green leaves), **H. 'Ground Master'** (white-edged green leaves), **H. 'Halcyon'** (blue leaves), **H. 'Blue Angel'** (blue leaves), **H. 'Francee'** (white-edged green leaves) and **H. 'Wide Brim'** (cream-edged green leaves). All-yellow varieties need a sunny spot with some shade at midday — look for **H. 'Golden Prayers'**, **H. 'Piedmont Gold'** and **H. 'Zounds'**. Dwarfs for the rockery include **H. 'Blue Moon'** (4 in./10 cm, blue leaves) and **H. 'Ginko Craig'** (9 in./22.5 cm, white-edged green leaves).

SITE & SOIL: Any reasonable soil will do — thrives best in partial shade.

PROPAGATION: Divide clumps in spring.

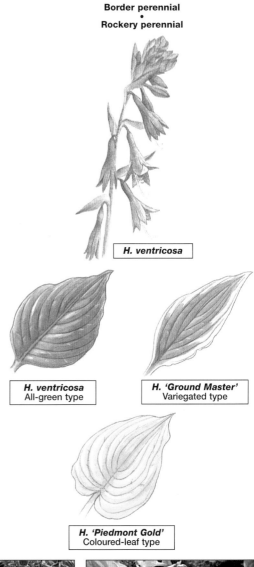

Border perennial
•
Rockery perennial

H. ventricosa

H. ventricosa
All-green type

H. 'Ground Master'
Variegated type

H. 'Piedmont Gold'
Coloured-leaf type

Hosta sieboldiana 'Elegans'

Hosta fortunei 'Aureomarginata'

Hosta 'Golden Prayers'

Rockery perennial

HOUSTONIA Bluets

It is worth sending away for this one if you want something out of the ordinary for the rock garden. Bluets forms a clump or mat of ½ in. (1 cm) long glossy leaves and from late spring to early autumn the four-petalled flowers appear on slender stalks above the foliage. Unlike most alpines it likes damp soil and some shade — a good subject for a woodland garden. It is fully hardy and the foliage is evergreen.

VARIETIES: There are two species and much confusion over names. **H. caerulea** is the taller one which grows in clumps — height 6 in. (15 cm), yellow-eyed blue flowers, flowering period May-September. The variety **'Alba'** has white flowers. Creeping Bluets (**H. michauxii**, **H. serpyllifolia** or **Hedyotis michauxii**) is mat-forming (3 in. x 1½ ft/7.5 cm x 45 cm) and has deeper blue flowers. Choose the variety **'Fred Mullard'**.

SITE & SOIL: Well-drained, humus-rich soil in partial shade is necessary.

PROPAGATION: Divide clumps or mats in autumn.

H. michauxii

Houstonia caerulea

Rockery perennial

HUTCHINSIA Chamois Cress

This alpine is related to Arabis and Iberis but its blooms are much smaller. Clusters of these white flowers cover the foliage in early summer and it readily self-seeds. This is an easy plant to grow but is a difficult one to find — you will have to look through the catalogues of nurseries which specialise in alpines. It will be lost if planted between large rocks — grow it in a raised bed or in crevices in an old wall.

VARIETIES: **H. alpina** (**Thlaspi alpinum**) is the only species — height 3 in. (7.5 cm), spread 9 in. (22.5 cm), flowering period May-July. The foliage is dark green, shiny and divided into small leaflets. The short flower stalks appear in profusion and at the top of each one is a crowded 1 in. (2.5 cm) cluster of small, white flowers. The variety **'Brevicaulis'** (1 in./2.5 cm) is even smaller.

SITE & SOIL: Requires well-drained gritty soil — thrives in sun or light shade.

PROPAGATION: Sow fresh seeds in summer in gentle heat.

H. alpina

Hutchinsia alpina

Bulb

HYACINTHELLA Hyacinthella

This is a page of rarities — Hyacinthella, like the plants above, will not be found in your local garden centre but is listed in a few specialist catalogues. It is a low-growing plant for the rockery — depending on the variety the short flower spikes carry a few or a mass of bell-shaped blooms. Each flower is somewhere between a Hyacinth and a Grape Hyacinth in shape.

VARIETIES: **H. acutiloba** is the species you are most likely to find — height 4 in. (10 cm), mid blue flowers, flowering period April-May. A couple of strap-like leaves occur at the base of the flower stalk. Plant the bulbs 2 in. (5 cm) deep in September-October. For a mass of small blue flowers look for **H. pallens** — in contrast **H. leucophaea** bears just a few white flowers on the top of each stalk.

SITE & SOIL: Well-drained light soil is essential — thrives best in full sun.

PROPAGATION: Divide clumps every few years in autumn.

H. pallens

Hyacinthella leucophaea

HYACINTHUS Hyacinth

Bulb

Hyacinths are plants with a lot of merit in the garden — neat growth, a long flowering period, a wide range of colours and a strong sweet fragrance. Despite these merits they have never been able to match tulips, daffodils and crocuses in popularity. The probable reasons are that they cost more than the other spring favourites and there is little variety apart from colour among the popular types. In most soils you can leave the bulbs of Dutch Hyacinths in the soil over winter, but the display in the second year will not be as good. It is generally better to let the foliage die down, lift the bulbs and then store them in dry peat until planting time comes round again. Plant the bulbs 6 in. (15 cm) deep in September-October. There are two points to remember at planting time. Don't choose the large bulbs which are for planting in bowls for indoor decoration — buy instead the medium-sized ones (Bedding Hyacinths) which produce flower stalks that are less susceptible to weather damage. Secondly, add peat or well-rotted compost to the soil before putting in the bulbs.

VARIETIES: By far the most popular hyacinths are the Dutch hybrids of **H. orientalis**. In April or early May the tightly-packed flower heads appear in colours ranging from white to dark purple. The stem is 10-12 in. (25-30 cm) high of which about half is clothed with 1 in. (2.5 cm) long waxy flowers. Varieties include **'Amethyst'** (early, lilac), **'Amsterdam'** (early, red), **'Anna Marie'** (early, lilac), **'Blue Magic'** (mid-season, purple-blue), **'Carnegie'** (late, white), **'City of Haarlem'** (late, yellow), **'Delft Blue'** (mid-season, pale blue), **'Jan Bos'** (early, red), **'Lady Derby'** (mid-season, pink), **'Lord Balfour'** (mid-season, wine red), **'L'Innocence'** (mid-season, white), **'Ostara'** (mid-season, dark blue), **'Pink Pearl'** (early, pink) and **'Violet Pearl'** (early, silver-edged rose-lilac). The flowers of Roman Hyacinths (**H. orientalis albulus** or **Bellevalia romana**) are less tightly packed on the stalks than the blooms of the Dutch ones. Colours are restricted to white, pink and blue — they are early flowering but are rather tender. A third group, the Multiflora Hyacinths, also have their flowers loosely arranged on the stems and each bulb produces several flower stalks. Both Roman and Multiflora Hyacinths are rarely grown these days.

SITE & SOIL: Any reasonable soil will do — thrives in sun or light shade.

PROPAGATION: Remove offsets at lifting time — plant in autumn.

DUTCH HYACINTHS

H. orientalis 'Pink Pearl'

MULTIFLORA HYACINTHS

H. orientalis 'Multiflora'

ROMAN HYACINTHS

H. orientalis albulus

Hyacinthus 'Anna Marie'

Hyacinthus 'Carnegie'

Hyacinthus orientalis albulus 'Pale Blue'

Border perennial
•
Rockery perennial

H. officinalis

HYSSOPUS   Hyssop

Hyssop is usually regarded as a subject for the herb garden, but its flowers are decorative enough for it to earn a place in the border, larger rock garden or container. The tubular blooms are borne in whorls at the top of the flower stalks — they are fragrant and are attractive to bees and butterflies. One of its advantages is the ability to flourish in dry and chalky soil.

VARIETIES: **H. officinalis** is a shrub-like plant with 1½ in. (3.5 cm) long lance-shaped leaves — height 1½ ft (45 cm), spread 2 ft (60 cm), ½ in. (1 cm) long blue flowers, flowering period June-September. The fragrant blooms are funnel-shaped and lipped. Hyssop is completely hardy and is a welcome addition in the cottage or wild garden. Varieties include **'Albus'** (white) and **'Roseus'** (pink).

SITE & SOIL: Any well-drained light soil will do — thrives best in full sun.

PROPAGATION: Plant cuttings in a cold frame in summer.

Hyssopus officinalis
'Roseus'

IBERIS   Candytuft

The clusters of candytuft flowers are often numerous enough to cover the foliage — each bloom has the four-petalled arrangement of the cabbage family, but there are two long petals and two short ones. Iberis does need room to spread — it is best grown where it can tumble over rocks, spread over paving or grow down a wall. Dead-head regularly to extend the flowering season. White is the only colour, but the Annual Candytuft is available in white, pink, red, purple and mauve. It is one of the most tolerant of all annuals and will grow quite happily in poor soil but it should be sown in autumn or spring where it is to flower and not transplanted at the seedling stage like a bedding plant.

VARIETIES: Perennial Candytuft is **I. sempervirens** — height 9 in. (22.5 cm), spread 2 ft (60 cm), 2 in. (5 cm) wide flower clusters, flowering period April-June. It is better to choose a variety rather than the species — **'Snowflake'** is the one which is usually recommended. Where space is a problem grow one of the dwarfs, such as **'Little Gem'** (4 in./10 cm) or **'Pygmaea'** (3 in./7.5 cm). Nearly all types of Annual Candytuft are varieties of **I. umbellata** — height 9 in. (22.5 cm), spread 9 in. (22.5 cm), flowering period June-September. The old favourite is **'Fairy Mixture'** which is a mixture of white, pink and red flowers. For a mixture of brighter blooms including purple and cream grow **'Flash Mixed'**. Single-colour varieties such as **'Pink Queen'** and **'Red Flash'** are listed in some catalogues. For something different grow the Hyacinth-flowered Candytuft which bears spikes of blooms on 1½ ft (45 cm) stems — look for the varieties **'Iceberg'**, **'White Empress'** and **'White Pinnacle'**.

SITE & SOIL: Any well-drained soil will do — thrives best in full sun.

PROPAGATION: Perennials: Plant cuttings in a cold frame in summer. Annuals: Sow seeds in September or April where they are to flower.

Iberis sempervirens
'Snowflake'

Rockery perennial
•
Hardy annual

Iberis umbellata
'Fairy Mixture'

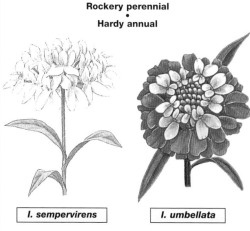

I. sempervirens   **I. umbellata**

Iberis umbellata
'White Pinnacle'

IMPATIENS Busy Lizzie, Balsam

Busy Lizzie is one of the top ten bedding plants in both Britain and the U.S. It is therefore surprising that it was not until the late 1970s when it began to appear in the garden and not just on the windowsill of the drawing room. This remarkable change was due to the work of the plant breeders who produced the compact and showy F_1 hybrids which are such a feature of present day bedding schemes. Only Begonia semperflorens can rival its ability to provide solid sheets of colour for months on end when planted under trees or in damp shady places. Shade isn't essential — Impatiens will stay in flower in a sunny situation and it comes into flower when the seedlings are only a few inches high. The drawbacks and difficulties are few — you will have to water the plants during dry spells and it is not easy to raise from seed. The main criticism levelled at Busy Lizzies is that there is not much variation between the types apart from colour. This was true at the start of the garden Impatiens boom but it no longer applies. Orange and lilac have joined the familiar white, pink and red flowers. There are now bicolours, double flowers and the bright-leaved New Guinea hybrids — enough variation for anyone.

Balsam (I. balsamina) is closely related to Busy Lizzie but there are some differences. It needs full sun in order to thrive, it does not do well in cool and wet summers, and the blooms are borne on the stems and are half-hidden by the leaves. The large blooms are azalea- or camellia-like and are available in a wide range of colours.

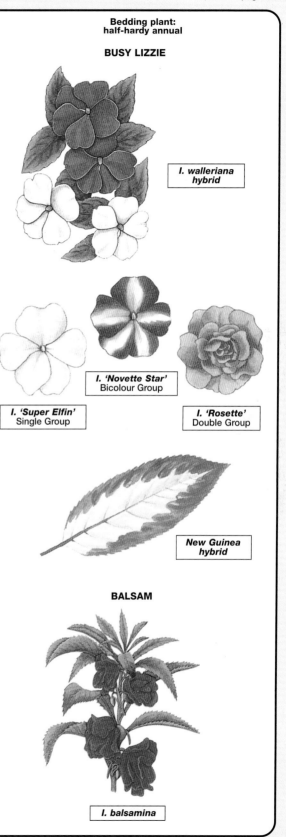

**Bedding plant:
half-hardy annual**

BUSY LIZZIE

I. walleriana hybrid

I. 'Super Elfin' Single Group

I. 'Novette Star' Bicolour Group

I. 'Rosette' Double Group

New Guinea hybrid

BALSAM

I. balsamina

VARIETIES: The Busy Lizzies you will see at the garden centre in spring are hybrids of **I. walleriana**. A wide range is available these days, but fortunately they fall into a few distinct groups. Firstly there are the green-leaved, single-flowered varieties which are generally self-coloured. These bushy plants grow 8-10 in. (20-25 cm) high and the group is dominated by the **'Accent'** and **'Super Elfin'** series. You can buy single-colour varieties in white, orange, pink, salmon, coral, red or violet, but many people prefer a multicoloured mixture for bedding, hanging baskets or tubs. The **'Imp'** strain is similar but the flowers are larger — for even larger flowers look for **'Blitz 2000'**, **'Bruno'** or the **'Expo'** strain. The next group contains the bicolours with flowers which have white stripes or centres. The blooms of **'Starbright'** and **'Novette Star'** have a large white star on the face of the bloom — the largest flowers in this white-star section are borne by **'Mega Orange Star'**. Other bicolours include the bronzy-leaved **'Deco'** strain, the red-eyed **'Pantomime'** and the picotee-edged **'Swirls'** and **'Chelsea Girl'**. The third group contains the double varieties, which you must expect to contain a few singles and semi-doubles. **'Rosette'** is the old-established one but it is claimed that **'Carousel'** and **'Confection'** are better — **'Double Duet'** is a bicoloured double. The final group consists of the New Guinea hybrids — these 1-1½ ft (30-45 cm) high plants are the showiest Busy Lizzies of all. The long leaves are green or an eye-catching mixture of green, yellow and red. In the seed catalogues you will find **'Tango'** (orange) and **'Spectra'** (mixed colours) — on the garden centre bench you will find other varieties such as **'Arabesque'** and **'Fanfare'**.

You will find **I. balsamina** (Balsam) seed packets at the garden centre and there may be seedlings for bedding out in spring, but this Impatiens is much less popular than Busy Lizzie. The **'Camellia Flowered'** strain is the usual type — height 1½ ft (45 cm), 3 in. (7.5 cm) wide double flowers, flowering period July-October. For smaller plants choose **'Tom Thumb'** (9 in./22.5 cm). Other balsams include **'Double Blackberry Ice'** (white-splashed purple flowers) and **'Topknot'** (flowers borne above the foliage).

SITE & SOIL: Any well-drained soil will do — thrives in sun or partial shade. Add organic material before planting.

PROPAGATION: Sow seeds in March under glass at 70°-75°F (21°-24°C). Seed propagation is not easy — it is better to buy seedlings for potting on. Plant out in late May.

IMPATIENS continued

Impatiens 'Accent Lilac'

Impatiens 'Blitz 2000'

Impatiens 'Mega Orange Star'

Impatiens 'Swirls'

Impatiens 'Rosette'

Impatiens 'Double Duet'

Impatiens 'Tango'

Impatiens 'Fanfare'

Impatiens balsamina 'Tom Thumb'

Border perennial

I. delavayi

INCARVILLEA Chinese Trumpet Flower

There is nothing difficult about Incarvillea despite its odd growth habit and its exotic appearance. In early May the flower stalks appear and in early summer the gloxinia-like blooms open. The plant's peculiar feature is the emergence of the leaves *after* the flowers. Mark the position with a stick in autumn — all growth disappears in winter. Add compost to the soil before planting.

VARIETIES: **I. delavayi** is a popular species — height 2 ft (60 cm), 3 in. (7.5 cm) wide trumpet-shaped deep pink flowers, flowering period May-June. The ferny leaves are dark green. A pale pink variety (**'Bees Pink'**) is available. **I. mairei** is a smaller plant (1-1½ ft/30-45 cm) with yellow-throated rose-red flowers and leaves which are not ferny. Popular varieties are **'Grandiflora'** and **'Frank Ludlow'**.

SITE & SOIL: Well-drained soil and full sun are essential.

PROPAGATION: Sow seeds outdoors in spring. Division of clumps in autumn is possible but difficult.

Incarvillea mairei

Border perennial

I. hookeri

INULA Inula

There are many yellow daisy-like perennials — some are seen in every herbaceous border and others are less usual like this one. Choose Inula if your soil is heavy, the site is shady and if you prefer finely-rayed blooms rather than the broad-petalled ones. It is long-lived and free-flowering — apply a mulch in spring and water during dry spells.

VARIETIES: There are several varieties in the catalogues but you may not find one at the garden centre. For the middle of the border there is **I. hookeri** — height 2 ft (60 cm), 3 in. (7.5 cm) wide flowers, flowering period July-August. The disc turns brown with age and the plant spreads rapidly — for more controlled growth choose **I. orientalis**. **I. ensifolia** is a late-flowering 1 ft (30 cm) dwarf — **I. magnifica** is a 6 ft (1.8 m) giant with August-September blooms.

SITE & SOIL: Any reasonable soil will do — thrives in sun or partial shade.

PROPAGATION: Divide clumps in autumn or spring.

Inula orientalis

Where a dense screen is required to cover an upright support or to hide an unsightly view the usual choice is a woody perennial climber. Annual and herbaceous perennial flowering climbers are generally used for their floral display and not for the sake of their leaf cover which might be quite sparse as with the Sweet Peas on the right.

Bulb

I. uniflorum

IPHEION   Spring Starflower

A bulb for a sunny rockery or the front of the border. It is an easy plant with 6 in. (15 cm) strap-like leaves with star-shaped blooms crowning each stalk in spring. These flowers have a pleasant smell, but the leaves emit a pungent garlic odour when crushed. It may be disappointing in the first year, but after a few years a large clump is formed which blooms profusely.

VARIETIES: The basic species is **I. uniflorum** — height 6 in. (15 cm), 1 in. (2.5 cm) wide pale blue flowers, flowering period April-May. Few plants have been given more alternative Latin names — **Brodiaea uniflora**, **Milla uniflora**, **Triteleia uniflora** and **Tristigma uniflorum**! Varieties include **'Album'** (white), **'Froyle Mill'** (violet) and **'Wisley Blue'** (blue-violet). Brightest of all is **I. 'Rolf Fiedler'**.

SITE & SOIL: Any well-drained soil will do — thrives in sun or light shade.

PROPAGATION: Lift and divide clumps in autumn every few years. Replant at once.

Ipheion 'Rolf Fiedler'

Bedding plant: half-hardy annual

I. tricolor **'Heavenly Blue'**

IPOMOEA   Morning Glory

Morning Glory is a beautiful climber — its wiry stems twine around upright supports and the large trumpet-like flowers appear throughout the summer months. One basic problem is that the leaves are not plentiful and so Morning Glory does not make an effective screen for hiding an unsightly view. The flowers last for only a day, but they are borne continually.

VARIETIES: **I. purpurea** (**Convolvulus major**) bears 3 in. (7.5 cm) wide purple trumpets in summer. The named types are varieties of the tender perennial **I. tricolor** which is treated as a half-hardy annual. **'Heavenly Blue'** has 3-5 in. (7.5-12.5 cm) wide blue trumpets — the hybrids **'Flying Saucers'** and **'Sapphire Cross'** have blue and white stripes. **'Cardinal'** is a red variety — all grow 8-10 ft (2.4-3 m) high.

SITE & SOIL: Any well-drained soil will do — sun and shelter are necessary.

PROPAGATION: Sow seeds in individual pots in March under glass — plant out in late May.

Ipomoea tricolor

Window boxes are widely used to add colour and interest to dull walls and windows, and the usual practice is to grow a mixture of multicoloured flowers and foliage plants. All too often the face of the window box is left bare — another drab feature alongside the adjacent wall and window. Avoid this problem by growing trailing plants at the front of the box to form a screen — Thunbergia and Hedera have been used in the example illustrated here.

IRIS Iris

Irises are a vast group of plants ranging from bold-flowering specimens with 4 ft (1.2 m) stems to tiny alpines peeping above the ground. Colours span the rainbow and the flowering season spans from November to July, depending on the variety. Classification is complex, but getting a working knowledge of the main types is not difficult. There are two basic groups — the Rhizome Group described below and the Bulb Group (see page 113).

RHIZOME GROUP

These irises spread by means of a thickened underground or partially underground stem which creeps along horizontally. The most popular varieties belong here and the *Bearded Irises* are the ones you are most likely to see. These are the irises you will find in every herbaceous border — the recognition feature is the presence of fleshy hairs on the falls. The thick rhizomes bear a fan of flat, broad leaves at the tips and should be planted soon after the flowers have faded, choosing a day when the soil is moist. Set the rhizomes about 1 ft (30 cm) apart, leaving the top half uncovered — trim the tops off the leaves. Most gardeners look no further than the Bearded Irises but there is a wide range of other varieties in the Rhizome Group. The *Beardless Irises* have falls which are smooth and rhizomes which are generally under the soil surface — plant 1-2 in. (2.5-5 cm) deep. Many varieties with a wide range of sizes, shapes and cultural needs are found here and some of the more important ones are described below. The third section of the Rhizome Group is the smallest as only a few species and varieties are available — these *Crested Irises* have a raised strip of tissue rather than hairs along the falls.

VARIETIES: The Bearded Irises have been given many names — Flag Iris, German Iris, June Iris etc. They are divided into four sections in the list below — this is a simplified version of the official classification which is somewhat complex. The Tall section (2½ ft/75 cm or over, June flowering) includes thousands of hybrids — some of the ones you are likely to find in the catalogues and the garden centre are **'Jane Phillips'** (pale blue), **'Frost and Flame'** (white, red beard), **'Top Flight'** (apricot), **'Staten Island'** (gold standards, red falls) and **'Black Swan'** (dark maroon standards, black falls). The Intermediate section (1½-2½ ft/45-75 cm, May flowering) also has many named hybrids such as **'Golden Fair'** (yellow), **'Arctic Fancy'** (violet and white) and **'Black Watch'** (deep purple). The Dwarf section (8 in.-1½ ft/20-45 cm, May flowering) contains Irises for the rockery or front of the border — examples include **'Blue Pools'** (white, pale blue beard), **'Pygmy Gold'** (yellow) and **'Gingerbread Man'** (brown, purple beard). Finally there is the Miniature section (up to 8 in./20 cm, April flowering) — look for **I. pumila** (4 in./10 cm).

The Beardless Irises are separated into various sections. The Pacific Coast Irises have attractively-veined petals and evergreen leaves — **I. innominata** and its hybrids are the only ones you are likely to find. The Siberian Irises are varieties and hybrids of **I. sanguinea** and **I. sibirica**, and many varieties are available — popular ones include **I. sibirica 'Perry's Blue'** (blue) and **'Butter and Sugar'** (white and yellow). The Winter Irises bloom during mild periods between November and March. The species to look for is **I. unguicularis** (**I. stylosa**) — 9 in. (22.5 cm), grassy leaves, violet flowers. The Water Irises need boggy ground — examples include **I. pseudacorus** (yellow), **I. kaempferi** (purple) and **I. laevigata** (blue-purple). Finally there is the Miscellaneous section of the Bearded Irises — the most popular one is **I. foetidissima** which is grown for its decorative orange seeds. The Bearded and Beardless Irises dominate the plant lists but there are also the Crested Irises represented by **I. cristata** (4 in./10 cm, lavender, orange crest) and **I. japonica 'Ledger's Variety'** (3 ft/90 cm, lavender, orange crest).

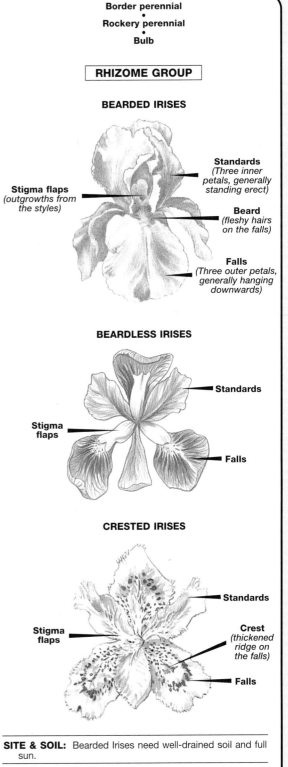

Border perennial
•
Rockery perennial
•
Bulb

RHIZOME GROUP

BEARDED IRISES

Standards
(Three inner petals, generally standing erect)

Stigma flaps
(outgrowths from the styles)

Beard
(fleshy hairs on the falls)

Falls
(Three outer petals, generally hanging downwards)

BEARDLESS IRISES

Standards

Stigma flaps

Falls

CRESTED IRISES

Standards

Crest
(thickened ridge on the falls)

Stigma flaps

Falls

SITE & SOIL: Bearded Irises need well-drained soil and full sun.

PROPAGATION: Divide rhizomes every few years — discard old and damaged portions.

IRIS continued

Iris 'Jane Phillips'

Iris 'Arctic Fancy'

Iris 'Gingerbread Man'

Iris innominata

Iris sibirica

Iris unguicularis

Iris laevigata 'Midnight'

Iris foetidissima

Iris japonica 'Ledger's Variety'

IRIS continued

BULB GROUP

The Bulb Group are smaller than most of the Rhizome ones and are grown in the rockery or the front of the border. Flowers appear in winter, spring or summer depending on the species grown. Survival over winter can be a problem — a few types are rather tender and nearly all require well-drained light soil. Do not disturb the clumps — lifting and dividing should not take place for at least four to five years after planting. The varieties and species in the Bulb Group are divided into three sections. The first one consists of the *Reticulata Irises* — the popular dwarfs which grow 3-6 in. (7.5-15 cm) high and bloom in February or March. The *Xiphium Irises* are quite different — they flower in June-July and the stems are 1½-2 ft (45-60 cm) tall. Finally there are the *Juno Irises* with 2-3 in. (5-7.5 cm) wide flowers in April-May — these irises are far less popular than the Reticulata and Xiphium ones.

VARIETIES: Reticulata Irises are a basic feature of the rock garden and there are two fragrant favourites. **I. danfordiae** has brown-spotted yellow flowers and the even more popular **I. reticulata** bears orange- or yellow-marked blue, mauve or purple flowers. There are several named varieties of I. reticulata including **'J.S. Dijt'** (orange-marked purple) and **'Cantab'** (orange-marked pale blue). The flowers of these species are about 3 in. (7.5 cm) across — for larger and earlier blooms grow **I. histrioides 'Major'** (white- and gold-marked blue). Plant Reticulata Irises 3 in. (7.5 cm) deep in September-October. The tall Xiphium Irises are border plants. The earliest ones to bloom are the June-flowering Dutch hybrids — popular varieties include **I. 'Lemon Queen'** (yellow) and **I. 'Wedgwood'** (blue). The English Iris (**I. latifolia**) bears 5 in. (12.5 cm) wide blooms and flowers a little later — the remaining Xiphium Iris is the Spanish Iris (**I. xiphium**) which produces blue-violet flowers in July. Plant these Xiphiums 4-6 in. (10-15 cm) deep in September-October. The Juno Irises are rather tender and need humus-rich soil and full sun. Examples include **I. bucharica** (1 ft/ 30 cm, ivory and yellow) and **I. magnifica** (2 ft/60 cm, lavender and white). Junos should be planted 2 in. (5 cm) deep in September.

SITE & SOIL: For most types well-drained sandy soil is necessary — thrives best in full sun.

PROPAGATION: Divide clumps when lifting is necessary.

BULB GROUP

RETICULATA IRISES
Leaves narrow, round, pointed

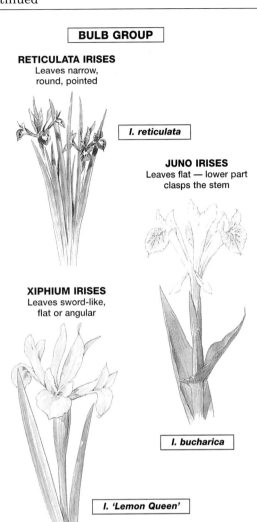

I. reticulata

JUNO IRISES
Leaves flat — lower part clasps the stem

XIPHIUM IRISES
Leaves sword-like, flat or angular

I. bucharica

I. 'Lemon Queen'

Iris danfordiae

Iris 'Wedgwood'

Iris magnifica

Bulb

I. viridiflora

IXIA Corn Lily

Ixia produces starry flowers on wiry stems in early summer. These blooms close when the sun goes in. In a mild region and sandy soil you can leave it in the garden over winter — in other areas you will have to plant the corms 3 in. (7.5 cm) deep in March and then lift when the foliage has died down. The corms are stored until planting time next year.

VARIETIES: The colours are usually bright — yellow, orange, pink or red and the centre is generally dark. Several species are listed in specialist catalogues, including **I. maculata** (yellow) and **I. viridiflora** (green). The hybrids are preferred as they are easier to grow — height 1-1½ ft (30-45 cm), 1-2 in. (2.5-5 cm) wide flowers, flowering period June-July. Examples include **I. 'Mabel'** (rose-red) and **'Hogarth'** (yellow).

SITE & SOIL: Well-drained light soil in a sheltered sunny spot.

PROPAGATION: Remove cormlets after lifting — store and then plant in spring.

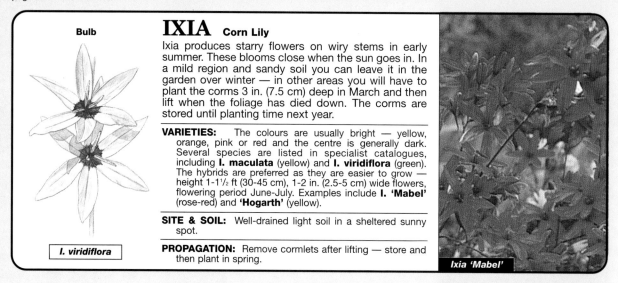

Ixia 'Mabel'

Bulb

I. pallasii

IXIOLIRION Ixia Lily

Despite the common name of this hard-to-find bulb and its similar cultural needs it is not related to Ixia. It can be grown outdoors in a warm and sunny spot but it is preferable to follow the Ixia procedure and plant in March for a floral display in early summer. Lift and store the bulbs in autumn until planting time next year.

VARIETIES: **I. pallasii** (**I. tataricum**) is the only species in the catalogues — height 1½ ft (45 cm), 2 in. (5 cm) wide funnel-shaped lavender or violet-blue flowers, flowering period June. The six petals have dark longitudinal stripes and are reflexed to produce an open-faced bloom which is sought after by flower arrangers. A cluster of these blooms is borne loosely on top of each thin stem.

SITE & SOIL: Well-drained light soil in a sheltered sunny spot.

PROPAGATION: Remove bulblets after lifting — store and then plant in spring.

Ixiolirion pallasii

**Bedding plant:
half-hardy annual**

K. blossfeldiana

KALANCHOE Flaming Katy

You will not find this one in the outdoor plant section of your garden centre — it is generally regarded as a house plant and so pots of Kalanchoe are sold in the indoor section. However, if you like the unusual in your window box, plant tub etc, then there is no reason why you should not bed out Flaming Katy in mid June to provide clusters of flowers for months.

VARIETIES: The basic species is **K. blossfeldiana** — height 1-1½ ft (30-45 cm), flower heads of 25-50 tiny blooms, flowering period June-September. The oval leaves are fleshy and hybrids in many flower colours are available. If space is limited dwarfs (6 in./15 cm) such as **K. 'Tom Thumb'** and **K. 'Tetra Vulcan'** are available. After flowering you can bring the plants indoors over winter.

SITE & SOIL: Any well-drained soil will do — choose a sheltered and sunny spot.

PROPAGATION: Buy plants from a garden centre.

Kalanchoe 'Tetra Vulcan'

Border perennial

KNAUTIA Knautia

This scabious-like plant is not often found in herbaceous borders although it is not difficult to grow and the more popular species has richly-coloured flowers. The leafy rosette at the base of each plant is evergreen and in summer the branched stalks bear 'pincushion' flower heads made up of masses of tiny flowers. The seed heads are useful for flower arranging.

VARIETIES: **K. macedonica** (**Scabiosa rumelica**) is the species you are more likely to find — height 2 ft (60 cm), 2 in. (5 cm) wide bright red flower heads, flowering period June-August. Plant it in a cottage garden or the middle of the border — the thin stalks will need support. **K. arvensis** (Field Scabious) is taller (5 ft/1.5 m) and the flower heads are lilac.

SITE & SOIL: Any well-drained soil will do — thrives best in full sun.

PROPAGATION: Take cuttings in spring and grow under glass.

K. macedonica

Knautia macedonica

Border perennial

KNIPHOFIA Red Hot Poker

Kniphofia is an old favourite in the herbaceous border and one which everyone can recognise — a clump of grass-like leaves and spikes of long tubular flowers. Some but not all have the traditional 'red-hot poker' appearance — a flower head which is red at the top and yellow at the base. Other colours include white, yellow, orange, red and even green. Cover the crowns with peat in winter.

VARIETIES: The popular choice is a variety or hybrid of **K. uvaria** — height 2½-5 ft (75 cm-1.5 m), flowering period July-September. For a true poker choose **K. 'Royal Standard'**, **'Samuel's Sensation'**, **'Springtime'** or **'Atlanta'**. For single colours pick **K. 'Alcazar'** (red), **'Bees' Sunset'** (orange) or **'Ice Queen'** (cream). Other species include **K. caulescens** (orange/yellow) and the orange dwarf **K. galpinii**.

SITE & SOIL: Any well-drained soil will do — thrives best in full sun.

PROPAGATION: Divide mature clumps in spring.

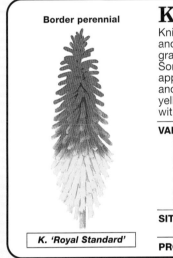

K. 'Royal Standard'

Kniphofia 'Springtime'

Border perennial
• Rockery perennial

LAMIUM Dead Nettle

This ground cover plant is grown mainly for its foliage, but in late spring or early summer there is a display of white, pink, mauve or yellow flowers. The nettle-like leaves are usually prominently striped or splashed with silver. Lamium is useful for covering the ground in partial or full shade — it is suitable for the rockery but it can be invasive. Cut back after flowering is over.

VARIETIES: **L. maculatum** is the most popular species — height 8 in.-1 ft (20-30 cm), spread up to 3 ft (90 cm), flowering period May-June. A variety rather than the species is usually chosen and the brightest carpeter is the pink-flowered **'Beacon Silver'**. Others include **'White Nancy'** and the pink-flowered, yellow-leaved **'Aureum'**. **'Elizabeth de Haas'** is a good mauve variety and **L. galeobdolon** has yellow flowers.

SITE & SOIL: Any well-drained soil will do — thrives best in partial shade.

PROPAGATION: Divide clumps in autumn or spring.

L. maculatum 'Beacon Silver'

Lamium maculatum

LATHYRUS **Sweet Pea, Everlasting Pea**

The original Sweet Pea was introduced from Sicily in 1699, but it was not until the Victorian era that the tall garden varieties in a multitude of colours appeared. The tall climbers remain the favourite group, but you can now buy knee-high ones and even dwarfs which do not require support. The colour range is vast, from white to near black with only the true yellows missing. Modern varieties generally have flowers which are larger than the old favourites, with petals which are frilly and with stripes, bicolours and blends as well as attractive single colours. Unfortunately some of the old-fashioned fragrance has been lost in the newer types, and so many gardeners prefer the dainty and older small-flowered varieties which are renowned for their scent. There are several books devoted entirely to Sweet Peas, but these are for exhibitors. For them thorough soil preparation is essential, sowing and planting are carefully timed, and protection against weather and pests is important. For the ordinary gardener who just wants a colourful screen, a covering for an arch, a way of bringing old trees to life or a source of cut flowers then the Sweet Pea is an easy plant to grow. Soak the seeds overnight and sow in pots or in the open ground where they are to flower. Pinch out the tips when the stems are about 4 in. (10 cm) high, provide support for the tendrils and water thoroughly in dry weather. Remove dead blooms regularly.

Sweet Peas are by far the most popular type of Lathyrus, but they are not the only ones. The perennial species are a group of bushes and climbers which are fully hardy and deserve to be more widely grown.

VARIETIES: Annual Sweet Peas are varieties of **L. odoratus** — height 6 in.-8 ft (15 cm-2.4 m), spacing 6 in.-1 ft (15-30 cm), 1-2 in. (2.5-5 cm) wide flowers borne singly or in small clusters, flowering period June-September. Most of the varieties offered for sale belong to the Tall Group (5-8 ft/1.5-2.4 m) and the Spencer varieties dominate the catalogues and our gardens. Large flowers, frilly petals, clusters containing four or five blooms and attractive colours are features of the Spencers — examples are **'Beaujolais'** (maroon), **'Winston Churchill'** (crimson), **'Swan Lake'** (white), **'Leamington'** (mauve), **'Southbourne'** (pink), **'Royal Wedding'** (white) and **'Noel Sutton'** (blue). For maximum fragrance move away from the Spencers and buy an **'Old-Fashioned Mixture'** or the oldest named variety of all — **'Painted Lady'** (red and white). Alternatively you can grow one of the highly scented Grandifloras such as **'Flora Norton'** (blue) or **'King Edward VII'** (red). For more flowers per stem than you will find on a Spencer there are the **'Galaxy'** strain and the **'Royal'** varieties — the **'Bouquet'** series is claimed to be the best of the non-Spencers. The Intermediate Group are much more compact, growing 2-3 ft (60-90 cm) high and needing little support. Here you will find **'Knee-hi'**, **'Jet Set'**, **'Snoopea'**, **'Continental'** and **'Explorer'** — these are sold as mixtures rather than single colours. Smallest of all is the Dwarf Group growing only 6 in.-1¹/₂ ft (15-45 cm) high. They are not climbers — **'Bijou'** reaches about 1¹/₂ ft (45 cm) and the strongly-scented **'Patio'** is a 1 ft (30 cm) upright plant. Smallest of all is the carpeting variety **'Cupid'** which grows just 6 in. (15 cm) high.

There are several perennial species. **L. grandiflorus** (Everlasting Pea) is a spreading climber with 1 in. (2.5 cm) wide pink-purple flowers in July-September. **L. latifolius** (Perennial Pea) bears smaller flowers in larger clusters — varieties include **'White Pearl'** and **'Pink Pearl'**. For a bushy non-climbing plant choose **L. vernus** (Spring Vetch) — height 1¹/₂ ft (45 cm), purple flowers, flowering period April-May.

SITE & SOIL: Any well-drained soil will do — choose a sunny situation.

PROPAGATION: Sow seeds in pots in October and overwinter in a cold frame — plant out in March or April. Alternatively sow seeds outdoors in March or April.

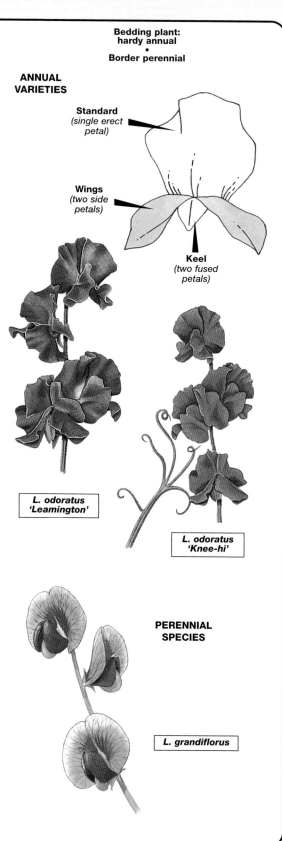

Bedding plant: hardy annual
•
Border perennial

ANNUAL VARIETIES

Standard
(single erect petal)

Wings
(two side petals)

Keel
(two fused petals)

L. odoratus 'Leamington'

L. odoratus 'Knee-hi'

PERENNIAL SPECIES

L. grandiflorus

LATHYRUS continued

Lathyrus odoratus 'Winston Churchill'

Lathyrus odoratus 'Southbourne'

Lathyrus odoratus 'Painted Lady'

Lathyrus odoratus 'Jet Set'

Lathyrus odoratus 'Bijou'

Lathyrus odoratus 'Cupid'

Lathyrus grandiflorus

Lathyrus latifolius 'White Pearl'

Lathyrus vernus

LAURENTIA Laurentia

Bedding plant: half-hardy annual

A bedding plant which came to the fore in the late 1990s — you will now find seeds listed in the popular catalogues and young plants at the garden centre for bedding out. Each fine-leaved dome bears masses of narrow-petalled starry flowers throughout the summer months — a good choice for both bedding and planting in containers. Wear gloves when handling — the leaves can irritate sensitive skin.

VARIETIES: There is only one species offered for sale — it is usually listed as **L. axillaris** but in the textbooks it may be called **Solenopsis axillaris** or **Isotoma axillaris**. Details are height 9 in.-1 ft (22.5-30 cm), 1 in. (2.5 cm) wide flowers, flowering period June-October. The varieties include **'Fantasy Blue'** (blue), **'Blue Star'** (blue), **'Mill Toy'** (mauve) and **'Pink Charm'** (pink).

SITE & SOIL: Any well-drained soil will do — thrives best in full sun.

PROPAGATION: Sow seeds in March-April in gentle heat. Plant out in late May.

L. axillaris 'Pink Charm'

Laurentia axillaris 'Fantasy Blue'

LAVATERA Annual Mallow

Hardy annual

If you are looking for a bushy plant to provide a temporary hedge or a back-of-the-border specimen covered in bloom during summer then Annual Mallow is a suitable choice. For these jobs you will need one of the older tall varieties — these days it is the compact 2 ft (60 cm) ones which dominate the catalogues.

VARIETIES: **L. trimestris** has produced numerous garden varieties — height 2-4 ft (60 cm-1.2 m), 3-4 in. (7.5-10 cm) wide trumpet-shaped flowers, flowering period July-September. **'Tanagra'** and **'Loveliness'** are the popular tall pink ones — **'Silver Cup'** (pink) is generally regarded as the best of the compact ones. Other 2 ft (60 cm) varieties include **'Mont Blanc'** (white), **'Ruby Regis'** (rose-red) and **'Pink Beauty'** (dark-veined pink).

SITE & SOIL: Any reasonable soil will do — thrives in sun or light shade.

PROPAGATION: Where possible, sow seeds in autumn or spring where they are to flower. Alternatively sow in March and bed out in May.

L. trimestris 'Silver Cup'

Lavatera trimestris 'Loveliness'

LEONTOPODIUM Edelweiss

Rockery perennial

Edelweiss is the symbol of the Alps and their flowers. It grows high on the slopes but it will flourish in your lowland garden if the site is sunny and the drainage is good. There are many alpines which are more difficult to grow, but there are also many which are more attractive. Edelweiss is interesting rather than beautiful — the flower heads are borne on short stalks above the grey-green leaves.

VARIETIES: **L. alpinum** is the popular species — height 6 in. (15 cm), spread 9 in. (22.5 cm), 2 in. (5 cm) wide flower heads, flowering period June-July. The leaves are hoary on top and densely woolly below — they form rosettes from which the flower stems arise. Each flower head has a central group of small rayless daisies surrounded by flannel-like bracts. **'Mignon'** is the variety to buy.

SITE & SOIL: Any well-drained soil in full sun will do.

PROPAGATION: Sow seeds under glass in early spring.

L. alpinum

Leontopodium alpinum

Border perennial

LEUCANTHEMUM Shasta Daisy

This popular herbaceous border plant used to be listed under Chrysanthemum but not any more. Now listed as Leucanthemum, the Shasta Daisy bears large flowers which may be single, semi-double or double — the petals are white and at the centre of each single flower is a prominent yellow eye. Divide the plants every two or three years and mulch in May. Cut the stems down to ground level in autumn.

VARIETIES: There are many varieties of **L. superbum** — height 6 in.-3 ft (15-90 cm), 2-4 in. (5-10 cm) wide flowers, flowering period June-August. The two varieties you are most likely to find are the 3 ft (90 cm) semi-double **'Wirral Supreme'** which needs staking and the 2 ft (60 cm) double **'Esther Read'**. If you want something different there are the 6 in. (15 cm) dwarf **'Snowcap'** and the attractive single **'Alaska'**.

SITE & SOIL: Any well-drained, non-acid soil will do — thrives best in full sun.

PROPAGATION: Divide clumps in spring.

L. superbum 'Wirral Supreme'

Leucanthemum superbum 'Esther Read'

Bulb

LEUCOJUM Snowflake

It is easy to mistake the Spring Snowflake for a tall-growing snowdrop. Both appear in early spring and both bear nodding flowers made up of six white petals. You will know it is Leucojum if all the petals are the same size and all have a green or yellow spot at the tip. There are spring-, summer- and autumn-flowering varieties.

VARIETIES: The Spring Snowflake is **L. vernum** — height 8 in. (20 cm), ³/₄ in. (1.5 cm) wide flowers, flowering period February-March. It is a tolerant plant which thrives in both shade and moist soil — the variety **'Carpathicum'** has yellow- rather than green-spotted petals. The Summer Snowflake (**L. aestivum**) has 2 ft (60 cm) flower stalks in April-May. The Autumn Snowflake (**L. autumnale**) grows only 5 in. (12.5 cm) high and unlike the others requires full sun and sandy soil — it blooms in September.

SITE & SOIL: Moisture-retentive soil in sun or partial shade is required.

PROPAGATION: Divide mature clumps when foliage has died down — replant at once.

L. vernum

Leucojum aestivum

Rockery perennial

LEWISIA Lewisia

Lewisia is one of the most colourful of rockery plants — flowers in pink, peach, orange or white with petals which are often striped. Unfortunately this American plant is not easy to keep alive in the rockery as water in the heart of the plant causes it to rot in winter. The answer is to plant it sideways in a crevice between rocks or in a crack between bricks.

VARIETIES: The varieties you will find at the garden centre are hybrids of **L. cotyledon** — height 8 in.-1 ft (20-30 cm), 1¹/₂ in. (3.5 cm) wide flowers, flowering period May-June. Choose one of the showy types, such as **'Sunset'**, **'George Henley'** or **'Ashwood Ruby'**. **L. tweedyi** has larger white or pale pink flowers but it is more difficult to overwinter, and so is **L. rediviva**. These Lewisias are evergreens — deciduous species include the white-flowered **L. brachycalyx** and the dwarf (3 in./7.5 cm) **L. pygmaea**.

SITE & SOIL: Well-drained gritty soil in full sun is necessary.

PROPAGATION: Sow seeds under glass in early spring.

L. cotyledon

Lewisia cotyledon

Border perennial

LIATRIS Gayfeather

In late summer and early autumn the erect spikes appear, densely clothed with small fluffy flowers in white, pink or pale purple. An unusual feature is that the blooms open from the top downwards. Add peat or compost before planting and mulch in spring. Water in dry weather and remove the spikes when the flowers have faded. Mark the position with a stick in autumn as all traces disappear in winter.

VARIETIES: **L. spicata** is the species at the garden centre — height 2½-3 ft (75-90 cm), flowering period July-September. The ½ in. (1 cm) wide pink or pale purple flowers are borne on 1½ ft (45 cm) spikes. Varieties include **'Floristan Weiss'** (white) and **'Floristan Violett'** (purple) which grow about 3 ft (90 cm) high — for a shorter plant choose **'Kobold'** (2 ft/60 cm, mauve).

SITE & SOIL: Any well-drained, humus-rich soil will do — thrives in sun or light shade.

PROPAGATION: Divide clumps in autumn or spring.

L. spicata

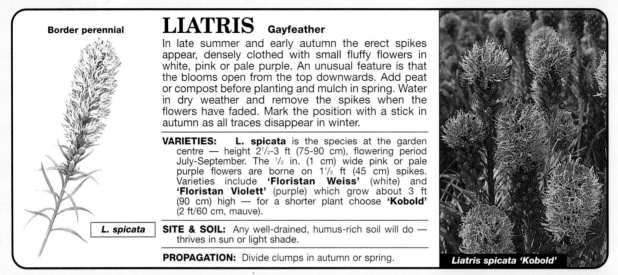
Liatris spicata 'Kobold'

Border perennial

LIBERTIA Libertia

Most plants in the herbaceous border are absent or brown and lifeless during the winter months — the claim to fame for this perennial is that its sword-like leaves are evergreen. In late spring the 2½ ft (75 cm) flower stalks appear above the clumps of foliage and from early to midsummer these stalks bear sprays of flowers — each bloom has three large inner petals and three smaller outer ones.

VARIETIES: The most popular species is **L. formosa** — the leathery leaves are about 1 ft (30 cm) long and the saucer-shaped white flowers are 1½ in. (3.5 cm) wide. In autumn showy brown seed heads appear. **L. grandiflora** is very similar, but the leaves are longer and they turn an attractive brown colour in winter. For pale blue flowers on 2 ft (60 cm) stalks look for **L. caerulescens** in the catalogues.

SITE & SOIL: Well-drained, humus-rich soil in full sun is necessary.

PROPAGATION: Divide clumps in spring.

L. grandiflora

Libertia formosa

Border perennial

LIGULARIA Golden Rays

Ligularia needs space, moisture-retentive soil and some shade. The large, deeply-cut leaves cover the ground and smother weeds, and in summer the yellow or orange daisy-like flowers appear. The size and arrangement of each bloom on the stem depend on the species. Mulch in May and water copiously in dry weather. Lift and divide the clumps every three years.

VARIETIES: **L. dentata** is the species with large rounded leaves — height 3 ft (90 cm), 3-4 in. (7.5-10 cm) wide golden-yellow flowers, flowering period July-September. **'Desdemona'** (brownish-green leaves) is a popular variety. **L. 'The Rocket'** has masses of small yellow flowers on erect black-stalked spikes. It grows 5 ft (1.5 m) high — for a 6 ft (1.8 m) plant with orange flowers grow **L. 'Gregynog Gold'**.

SITE & SOIL: Moist soil and a partially shaded site are essential.

PROPAGATION: Divide clumps in autumn or spring.

L. dentata

Ligularia 'The Rocket'

LILIUM Lily

The majority of ordinary gardeners regard the lily as a difficult plant and leave it at that. It cannot be expected to produce abundant blooms in the first year and it will quickly rot if the soil is not free-draining. The fleshy bulbs must be planted as soon as they arrive, so the average gardener prefers to turn to tulips, iris and gladioli. These days, however, the 'hard-to-grow' reputation for all lilies is quite unfounded. During this century a number of trouble-free species have been discovered and the Hybrid Lilies introduced during the past 50 years have set new standards in size, vigour and disease resistance. There is now a lily for every garden.

It is impossible to generalise about a group of plants as large and diverse as the lily genus. Flowers range from 1 in. (2.5 cm) to 1 ft (30 cm) in diameter and have a scent which extends from delightful to disagreeable. The colour range spans the whole floral spectrum with the exception of blue. There are dwarfs such as the 1 ft (30 cm) L. pumilum for the container or rock garden and the 8 ft (2.4 m) giants such as L. henryi which are suitable for the back of the border. Most are 3-5 ft (90 cm-1.5 m) high and are at home in the herbaceous and mixed border or in a bed on their own. By selecting the right varieties there are flowers to be seen and admired from June to October.

The basic requirement is for free-draining soil — waterlogging in winter will quickly lead to rot. Another essential is to make sure the bulbs are not allowed to dry out before planting. Depth of planting depends on the rooting habit of the variety. Stem-rooting Lilies produce roots just above the bulb as well as at the base, and so need to be planted deeply at 6-8 in. (15-20 cm). A few species are Basal-rooting Lilies and so need shallow planting in autumn at 2 in. (5 cm). Sprinkle coarse sand in the bottom of the hole before planting. Spread out the roots and sprinkle sand between them. Once the plants are actively growing they must not be allowed to dry out at the roots — water thoroughly and regularly during dry weather and feed occasionally with a liquid fertilizer. Do not hoe — place a peat or compost mulch around the stems instead. Not all lilies require staking, but it is advisable for any variety likely to grow over 3 ft (90 cm) high. Dead-head faded blooms and cut off the stems at ground level when they have died down at the end of the season. Apply a fresh mulch of peat or leafmould for the winter. Many species and hybrids can be grown in containers outdoors — use a large pot or tub and plant three or four bulbs. Remember that Stem-rooting Lilies require deep planting. Dwarf varieties such as 'Golden Pixie' in bud or flower have become a common sight at the garden centre in June — bed them out or plant in a container.

SITE & SOIL: A well-drained site is essential — enrich the soil with well-rotted organic matter. A few lilies such as L. auratum require lime but most species will not thrive if chalk is present — the modern hybrids are not bothered either way. Choose a sunny spot but a little shade during the day will not be a problem. Shade the lower part of the plant if possible by growing short plants around the base.

PROPAGATION: The easiest method is to divide the mature clumps in autumn and replant immediately. Another method is scaling — pull off plump scales from a bulb and place them in a sealed bag of moist peat until rooted. Plant in compost-filled pots.

Bulb

TURK'S-CAP SHAPED LILIES
The petals are rolled and swept back. The flowers are usually small.

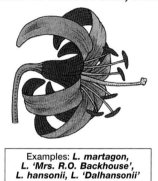

Examples: **L. martagon,
L. 'Mrs. R.O. Backhouse',
L. hansonii, L. 'Dalhansonii'**

TRUMPET SHAPED LILIES
The petals are grouped together for part of the length of the flower to produce a basal tube.

Examples: **L. regale,
L. 'Limelight',
L. candidum, L. longiflorum**

BOWL SHAPED LILIES
The petals flare open to produce a wide bowl. The flowers are usually large.

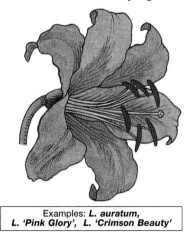

Examples: **L. auratum,
L. 'Pink Glory', L. 'Crimson Beauty'**

LILIUM continued

ASIATIC HYBRIDS

Height 2-5 ft (60 cm-1.5 m). Spacing 1¹/₂ ft (45 cm). Flowers 4-5 in. (10-12.5 cm) across — Turk's-cap, Trumpet or Bowl shaped. Flowering period June-July.

By far the most numerous group. Many have upright or outward-facing blooms — examples are **'Sterling Star'** (white), **'Orange Pixie'** (golden-yellow), **'Corsage'** (ivory-shaded pink), **'Orange Triumph'** (violet-spotted gold) and the Mid-Century Hybrids such as **'Enchantment'** (red), **'Harmony'** (orange-yellow), **'Red Lion'** (red), **'Destiny'** (yellow), **'Brandywine'** (orange), **'Cinnabar'** (maroon) and **'Paprika'** (deep red). The Turk's-cap Asiatic Hybrids have pendent flowers — examples include **'Citronella'** (yellow) and **'Connecticut Yankee'** (orange-red).

MARTAGON HYBRIDS

Height 4-6 ft (1.2-1.8 m). Spacing 1 ft (30 cm). Flowers 2-3 in. (5-7.5 cm) across — Turk's-cap shaped. Flowering period June-July.

About 25 pendent blooms are borne at the top of the flower stalk — the petals are usually spotted and varieties are available in a wide range of colours. These hybrids thrive best in partial shade and can tolerate alkaline soil. The usual parents are L. martagon and L. hansonii. Not many types are available — look for **L. 'Dalhansonii'** (orange-spotted maroon, unpleasant smell), the Backhouse Hybrids such as **'Mrs. R.O. Backhouse'** (purple-spotted gold), **'Marhan'** (brown-spotted orange) and **'Jacques S. Dijt'** (purple-spotted ivory). The Paisley Hybrids (red-spotted white, yellow, orange etc) also belong here.

CANDIDUM HYBRIDS

Height 4-6 ft (1.2-1.8 m). Spacing 1 ft (30 cm). Flowers 4-5 in. (10-12.5 cm) across — Trumpet shaped with strongly reflexed petals. Flowering period June-July.

The oldest known lily hybrid belongs here — **L. testaceum** or Nankeen Lily. The fragrant flowers have a Turk's-cap appearance — about ten are borne at the top of the flower stalk. These pendulous blooms have bright red anthers and the waxy petals are in various shades of yellow ranging from cream to deep apricot. This lily is basal-rooting so shallow planting in autumn is necessary — it is lime tolerant. Other Candidum Hybrids include **'Apollo'** (white), **'Artemis'** (apricot), **'Prelude'** (vermilion) and **'Ares'** (orange).

AMERICAN HYBRIDS

Height 4-7 ft (1.2-2.1 m). Spacing 1¹/₂ ft (45 cm). Flowers 4-5 in. (10-12.5 cm) across — most are Turk's-cap shaped. Flowering period July.

These hybrids have been bred from American species such as L. pardalinum. The nodding blooms are borne in a pyramid-shaped head. The best-known varieties are the Bellingham Hybrids which flourish in lime-free soil and light shade — yellow, orange or red bicolours with prominent dark red or black spots. **'Shuksan'** is the favourite choice — the golden petals are spotted with brown and may be tipped with pink. Another group are the Bullwood Hybrids such as the red **'Cherrywood'**. The American Hybrids produce rhizomes.

TRUMPET HYBRIDS

Height 4-6 ft (1.2-1.8 m). Spacing 1¹/₂ ft (45 cm). Flowers up to 8 in. (20 cm) long — Trumpet or Bowl shaped. Flowering period July-August.

The Trumpet group includes the Aurelian and Olympic Hybrids. Typical examples are **'African Queen'** (orange), **'Pink Perfection'** (pink), **'Black Dragon'** (white inside, purple-brown outside), **'Golden Splendour'** (golden-yellow), **'Green Dragon'** (white inside, green outside) and **'Limelight'** (lime-yellow). For Bowl-shaped blooms there are **'Heart's Desire'** (orange-throated ivory) and **'Thunderbolt'** (orange). For nodding Bowl-shaped flowers grow **'Golden Showers'** — for starry Bowl-shaped flowers with flat-faced blooms choose one of the **'Sunburst'** varieties.

ORIENTAL HYBRIDS

Height 2-8 ft (60 cm-2.4 m). Spacing 1-1¹/₂ ft (30-45 cm). Flowers up to 1 ft (30 cm) across — Bowl shaped. Flowering period August-September.

Here you will find the largest flowers, but they are harder to grow than many others. The Orientals need well-drained, acid and rich soil in a sunny sheltered position. Bowl-shaped varieties include **'Crimson Beauty'** (red-striped white), **'Empress of China'** (red-spotted white), **'Pink Glory'** (white-edged pink) and **'Bonfire'** (red and white). For starry Bowl-shaped flowers grow one of the Imperial varieties such as **'Imperial Silver'** (red-spotted white) or the popular **'Stargazer'** (white-edged pink). **'Journey's End'** has white-edged recurved pink petals.

SPECIES

L. amabile Height 4 ft (1.2 m). Spacing 1¹/₂ ft (45 cm). Stem-rooting. 3 in. (7.5 cm) Turk's-cap flowers — red with black spots. Disagreeable odour. June-July.

L. auratum (Golden-rayed Lily) Height 5-8 ft (1.5-2.4 m). Spacing 1 ft (30 cm). Stem-rooting. 8-10 in. (20-25 cm) Bowl-shaped flowers — white with yellow stripes, brown spots. August-September.

L. bulbiferum (Orange Lily) Height 2-4 ft (60 cm-1.2 m). Spacing 9 in. (22.5 cm). Stem-rooting. 3 in. (7.5 cm) Trumpet-shaped flowers — orange with purple spots. June-July.

L. canadense (Canada Lily) Height 4-6 ft (1.2-1.8 m). Spacing 1 ft (30 cm). Basal-rooting. 2 in. (5 cm) Trumpet-shaped flowers — yellow with brown spots. September.

L. candidum (Madonna Lily) Height 4-5 ft (1.2-1.5 m). Spacing 9 in. (22.5 cm). Basal-rooting. 3 in. (7.5 cm) Trumpet-shaped flowers — pure white. June-July.

L. henryi (Henry's Lily) Height 6-8 ft (1.8-2.4 m). Spacing 1¹/₂ ft (45 cm). Stem-rooting. 3 in. (7.5 cm) Turk's-cap flowers — yellow with dark red spots. August-September.

L. longiflorum (Easter Lily) Height 2¹/₂-3 ft (75-90 cm). Spacing 9 in. (22.5 cm). Stem-rooting. 5-6 in. (12.5-15 cm) Trumpet-shaped flowers — white. July-August. Half hardy.

L. martagon (Turk's-cap Lily) Height 3-5 ft (90 cm-1.5 m). Spacing 1 ft (30 cm). Basal-rooting. 1¹/₂ in. (3.5 cm) Turk's-cap flowers — purplish-brown with dark spots. Disagreeable odour. June-July.

L. pardalinum (Leopard Lily) Height 3-6 ft (90 cm-1.8 m). Spacing 1 ft (30 cm). Basal-rooting. 2¹/₂ in. (6 cm) Turk's-cap flowers — dark orange with purple spots. July.

L. pumilum (Coral Lily) Height 1-1¹/₂ ft (30-45 cm). Spacing 6 in. (15 cm). Stem-rooting. 1¹/₂ in. (3.5 cm) Turk's-cap flowers — scarlet. June.

L. regale (Regal Lily) Height 3-6 ft (90 cm-1.8 m). Spacing 1¹/₂ ft (45 cm). Stem-rooting. 5 in. (12.5 cm) Trumpet-shaped flowers — white with yellow throat. July-August.

L. tigrinum (Tiger Lily) Height 4 ft (1.2 m). Spacing 1¹/₂ ft (45 cm). Stem-rooting. 3 in. (7.5 cm) Turk's-cap flowers — orange with purple spots. July-September.

LILIUM continued

Lilium 'Cinnabar'

Lilium 'Mrs. R.O. Backhouse'

Lilium testaceum

Lilium 'Shuksan'

Lilium 'Thunderbolt'

Lilium 'Stargazer'

Lilium auratum

Lilium regale

Lilium tigrinum

Hardy annual

LIMNANTHES Poached Egg Flower

There are several reasons for choosing Limnanthes as an edging plant for the front of the border. It makes a welcome change from Aubrieta and Lobelia which are seen everywhere, and the two-toned flowers are both abundant and colourful. In addition the blooms are highly attractive to bees. The ferny foliage is pale green and the low-growing spreading habit makes it suitable for the rockery.

VARIETIES: **L. douglasii** is the only species you will find in the catalogues — height 6 in. (15 cm), 1 in. (2.5 cm) wide flowers, flowering period June-October. The yellow petals of each bloom have a distinct white edge — hence the common name. It is an easy plant to grow and the flowers cover almost all the foliage when grown in full sun. The fragrance is sweet but not strong.

SITE & SOIL: Any reasonable soil will do — thrives best in a sunny spot.

PROPAGATION: Sow seeds in March where they are to flower.

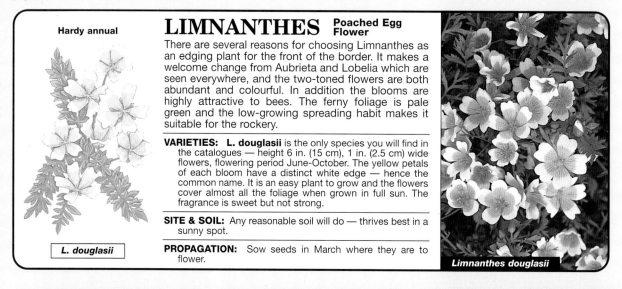

L. douglasii

Limnanthes douglasii

LIMONIUM Statice, Sea Lavender

Limonium is grown as either an annual or perennial in the garden. Nearly all of the annual varieties are 'everlasting' flowers which retain their colour after drying. For this reason these plants are a great favourite with flower arrangers, but the modern varieties are showy enough to be used in bedding schemes for their fresh floral display. The perennial Limonium is a double-purpose plant — it is grown for its summer-long show of frothy clouds of tiny blooms in beds and borders, and it is also cut to provide a supply of dried flowers for indoor decoration. Do not propagate by dividing established clumps.

VARIETIES: **L. sinuatum** (Statice) is the basic annual species with 'everlasting' flowers — height 1-2 ft (30-60 cm), 4 in. (10 cm) wide clusters of tiny papery-petalled flowers, flowering period July-September. The usual practice is to buy a mixture such as **'Sunset Shades'** or **'Fortress Mixed'** — dwarf (1 ft/30 cm) mixtures include **'Biedermeier Mixed'** and **'Petite Bouquet'**. Single colours are available — examples are **'Forever Gold'** (yellow), **'Gold Coast'** (yellow), **'American Beauty'** (pink) and **'Blue Peter'** (blue). **L. suworowii** is quite different — flowering stems are tall spikes densely covered with tiny flowers. It is good for flower arranging but not for drying. **L. latifolium** (Sea Lavender) is the basic perennial species — height 2½ ft (75 cm), flowering period July-September. The spreading flower panicles appear above the rosettes of oval leaves — varieties include **'Violetta'** (violet-blue) and **'Blue Cloud'** (lavender). To dry both annual and perennial varieties cut just before the flowers fully open and tie the stems in bunches. Hang upside down in a cool place away from direct sunlight.

SITE & SOIL: Any well-drained soil will do — thrives best in full sun.

PROPAGATION: Annuals: Sow seeds in February-March in gentle heat — plant out in late May. Perennials: Sow seeds under glass in spring.

Limonium sinuatum

Bedding plant: half-hardy annual
•
Border perennial

L. sinuatum

L. latifolium

Limonium suworowii

Limonium latifolium

Border perennial · Rockery perennial · Hardy annual

L. alpina

LINARIA   Toadflax

Toadflax is not one of the run-of-the-mill hardy perennials you can find at every garden centre. There are basically two types — the tall ones with long racemes of snapdragon-like flowers for the herbaceous border and low-growing trailing types for the rockery. The perennials tend to be short-lived — as an alternative you can grow one of the annual varieties from seed.

VARIETIES: The most popular perennial species is **L. purpurea** — height 1½-2½ ft (45-75 cm), ½ in. (1 cm) long spurred flowers, flowering period May-September. Varieties include **'Springside White'** (white) and **'Canon Went'** (pink and orange). **L. alpina** is quite different but has the same long flowering season — the violet and orange flowers are borne in clusters on 6 in. (15 cm) plants. The usual annual is **L. 'Fairy Bouquet'** (9 in./22.5 cm).

SITE & SOIL: Any well-drained soil will do — thrives in full sun.

PROPAGATION: Perennials: Divide clumps in spring. Annuals: Sow seeds in March-May where they are to flower.

Linaria 'Fairy Bouquet'

Rockery perennial

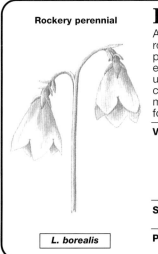

L. borealis

LINNAEA   Twin Flower

An uncommon plant for woodland, a moist and shady rockery or for growing under shrubs and trees. It produces a tangled mat of slender stems and rounded evergreen leaves. It spreads quickly and so can be used for ground cover, but it can be readily kept in check where space is limited. During the summer months dainty bell-like flowers appear above the foliage.

VARIETIES: There is just one species — **L. borealis**. Basic details are height 2 in. (5 cm), spread 2 ft (60 cm), flowering period May-July. Each flower stalk is topped by a pair of pale pink blooms — hence the common name. An easy plant, but a disappointment in sandy soil or a sunny site. The variety **'Americana'** is larger and the flowers are deeper pink.

SITE & SOIL: Requires moist humus-rich soil in partial shade.

PROPAGATION: Sow seeds or plant cuttings in a cold frame in spring.

Linnaea borealis

Most herbaceous borders are multicoloured features with flowers ranging from white to deep red. The monochrome border is seen much less often, although examples can be found at numerous famous gardens such as Wisley and Sissinghurst. The white and the blue border are the two most popular types — the white one illustrated here is either colourless or stylish depending on your personal taste.

LINUM Flax

Nearly all of the species and varieties of flax have the same general form — wiry stems bearing five-petalled flat or bowl-shaped flowers. Each bloom is short-lived, but there are always more buds to open. The annual types look gaunt and spindly as single plants — grow them in a large group for an impressive display of large flowers in summer. The perennials bear their blue or yellow flowers on 6 in.-2 ft (15-60 cm) stems — the floral display is seen at its best in sandy soil and hot weather. Mulch in spring and water during dry spells in summer, but no matter how careful you are the plants will be short-lived.

Linum grandiflorum 'Rubrum'

VARIETIES: **L. grandiflorum** is the parent of the annual varieties — height 9 in.-1½ ft (22.5-45 cm), 2 in. (5 cm) wide flowers, flowering period June-August. **'Rubrum'** (Scarlet Flax) is the brightest variety — the vivid red petals have a satin-like sheen. Other single-coloured ones include **'Album'** (white), **'Roseum'** (pink) and **'Blue Flax'** (blue). For red-centred white flowers buy **'Bright Eyes'**. **L. perenne** is the most popular perennial — height 1 ft (30 cm), 1 in. (2.5 cm) wide flowers, flowering period June-August. Blue, white, pink and red varieties are available. **'Blue Sapphire'** has deep blue flowers — **'Alpinum'** is a 6 in. (15 cm) sky blue dwarf for the rockery. **L. 'Gemmell's Hybrid'** is another dwarf for the rockery, trough garden or raised bed — the large yellow flowers are borne on mounds of grey-green leaves. Another yellow-flowered dwarf is **L. flavum 'Compactum'**. **L. narbonense** produces 1 in. (2.5 cm) white-centred rich blue flowers — **'Heavenly Blue'** is the recommended variety. Choose with care when buying a perennial flax — some species such as **L. arboreum** are not fully hardy.

SITE & SOIL: Any well-drained soil will do — thrives best in full sun.

PROPAGATION: Annuals: Sow seeds in March-April where they are to flower. Perennials: Sow seeds under glass in spring or plant cuttings in a cold frame in May.

Hardy annual
•
Border perennial
•
Rockery perennial

Linum arboreum

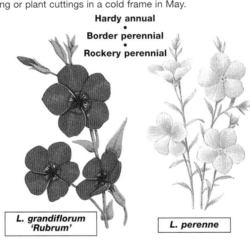

L. grandiflorum 'Rubrum'

L. perenne

Linum narbonense

Border perennial

Liriope muscari

LIRIOPE Lily Turf

This ground-cover plant looks like an oversized Grape Hyacinth when in flower. The arching grassy leaves grow in clumps or mats and in late summer or autumn the upright stems bear spikes of tiny bell-shaped flowers. It can be used for edging in the herbaceous border but it is invasive and requires lifting and dividing every few years to limit the spread. Dead-head when flowers fade.

VARIETIES: **L. muscari** is the basic species — height 1-1½ ft (30-45 cm), flowering period August-November. The leaves are dark green and the usual flower colour is mauve, lavender or violet. There are varieties in other colours, such as **'Monroe White'** (white), **'Royal Purple'** (purple) and **'Variegata'** (gold-striped leaves). **L. spicata** is a mat-forming narrower-leaved species.

SITE & SOIL: Any lime-free soil will do — thrives in sun or partial shade.

PROPAGATION: Divide clumps in spring.

L. muscari

Rockery perennial

L. oleifolium

LITHOSPERMUM Gromwell

Lithospermum (Lithodora) is a ground-cover plant with creeping stems which are clothed with narrow leaves. The blue, funnel-shaped flowers of the most popular gromwell are as bright as anything you will find in the summer rock garden. It requires a sunny spot and humus-rich soil — add peat or compost at planting time. Do not grow L. diffusum if your soil is chalky — choose instead the lime-tolerant L. oleifolium.

VARIETIES: The best-known species is **L. diffusum** — height 6 in. (15 cm), spread 2 ft (60 cm), ½ in. (1 cm) wide pure blue flowers, flowering period June-September. The species is rarely grown — the choice is between the varieties **'Heavenly Blue'** and **'Grace Ward'**. **L. oleifolium** is quite different — the leaves are silvery-grey and the flowers change from pink when in bud to pale blue when fully open.

SITE & SOIL: Well-drained, moisture-retentive soil is necessary — thrives best in full sun.

PROPAGATION: Plant cuttings in a cold frame in midsummer.

Lithospermum diffusum 'Heavenly Blue'

LOBELIA Lobelia

The annual varieties are to be seen everywhere in summer — but it is a more demanding plant than many less popular annuals. The soil needs to be enriched with humus, the tips must be pinched out to induce bushiness and a thorough soaking is essential when the soil is dry. The popular perennial lobelias are quite different — they are upright plants growing 2-5 ft (60 cm-1.5 m) high with showy spikes of pink, red or purple flowers. Damp soil is essential and so is a thick mulch to cover the crown in winter.

VARIETIES: Blue remains the favourite colour for the Edging Lobelia **L. erinus** — height 4-6 in. (10-15 cm), ¼ in. (0.5 cm) wide flowers, flowering period June-September. Popular varieties include **'Mrs. Clibran Improved'** (white-eyed deep blue), **'Crystal Palace'** (all-blue, bronzy leaves) and **'Cambridge Blue'** (pale blue) — the earliest one is **'Blue Pearl'**. For other colours choose **'White Lady'** (white) or **'Rosamund'** (red) — for a mixture of colours sow **'String of Pearls'** or **'Riviera Mixture'**. Grow the Trailing Lobelia **L. erinus pendula** in hanging baskets — varieties include **'Sapphire'** (white-eyed violet), **'Fountain Mixed'** and **'Cascade Mixed'**. The most popular perennial is **L. 'Queen Victoria'** — height 3 ft (90 cm), 1 in. (2.5 cm) wide flowers, dark red leaves, flowering period July-August. **L. cardinalis** is similar but the flowers are larger and the leaves are green. **L. siphilitica** is a shade-loving leafy plant with blue flowers. A few perennials make excellent bedding plants when grown as half-hardy annuals — examples include **L. 'Compliment Scarlet'** and **L. 'Fan Scarlet'**.

SITE & SOIL: Any reasonable humus-rich soil will do — perennials require constantly moist soil. Thrives in sun or light shade.

PROPAGATION: Annuals: Sow seeds in January-March in gentle heat — plant out in late May. Perennials: Divide clumps in spring or take cuttings in summer.

Lobelia erinus 'Cambridge Blue'

Bedding plant: half-hardy annual
•
Border perennial

Lobelia erinus pendula 'Sapphire'

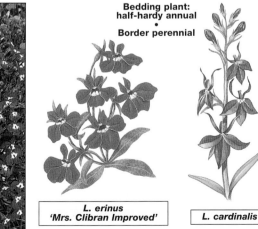

L. erinus 'Mrs. Clibran Improved'

L. cardinalis

Lobelia siphilitica

Bedding plant: hardy biennial

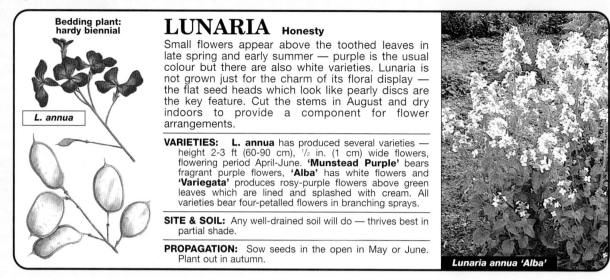

L. annua

LUNARIA Honesty

Small flowers appear above the toothed leaves in late spring and early summer — purple is the usual colour but there are also white varieties. Lunaria is not grown just for the charm of its floral display — the flat seed heads which look like pearly discs are the key feature. Cut the stems in August and dry indoors to provide a component for flower arrangements.

VARIETIES: **L. annua** has produced several varieties — height 2-3 ft (60-90 cm), ½ in. (1 cm) wide flowers, flowering period April-June. **'Munstead Purple'** bears fragrant purple flowers, **'Alba'** has white flowers and **'Variegata'** produces rosy-purple flowers above green leaves which are lined and splashed with cream. All varieties bear four-petalled flowers in branching sprays.

SITE & SOIL: Any well-drained soil will do — thrives best in partial shade.

PROPAGATION: Sow seeds in the open in May or June. Plant out in autumn.

Lunaria annua 'Alba'

LUPINUS Lupin

Before the 1930s lupins were nothing special, but the introduction of the Russell Hybrids changed all that. Their large spires of pea-like flowers provide bright splashes of colour in early summer. They are accommodating plants — quick-growing, tolerant of light shade and town conditions but they are short-lived and need replacing every few years. Add peat before planting and cover the crowns in winter if you live in a frost pocket. Enemies include virus, slugs and mildew. These perennials are not the only lupins — there are annuals to grow from seed. You will not get the height, bloom size or bright colours of the Russell Lupins but their daintiness can be an advantage in a small plot.

VARIETIES: **L. polyphyllus** has produced a wide range of hybrids. The **'Russell Hybrids'** are the most popular — height 3-4 ft (90 cm-1.2 m), flowering period June-July. Remove the first flush when the flowers have faded for a second flush later in the summer. Named ones in a wide range of shades are available. Some are single-coloured, such as **'Lady Fayre'** (pink), **'Noble Maiden'** (creamy-white), **'My Castle'** (red), **'The Page'** (red) and **'Chandelier'** (yellow). Others are bicoloured — examples are **'Blue Jacket'** (blue/white), **'The Governor'** (blue/white), **'The Chatelaine'** (pink/white) and **'Monarch'** (purple/yellow). The popular annuals are hybrids of a number of species, including **L. hartwegii**, **L. luteus** and **L. pubescens** — height 1-2 ft (30-60 cm), flowering period June-September. The best known varieties belong to the **L. 'Pixie'** strain. Some perennials such as **L. 'Lulu'** and **L. 'Gallery'** can be grown as annuals. **L. subcarnosus** (Texas Bluebonnet) bears blue flowers.

SITE & SOIL: Any well-drained, non-acid soil will do. Thrives in sun or light shade.

PROPAGATION: Perennials: Sow seeds under glass in spring or plant cuttings in March. Annuals: Sow seeds in February-March in gentle heat — plant out in May.

Lupinus 'Monarch'

Border perennial
•
Bedding plant: hardy annual

Lupinus 'Gallery Yellow'

L. 'Russell Hybrid'

L. 'Pixie Delight'

Lupinus 'Lulu'

LYCHNIS Campion

The campions are sun-lovers bearing flowers which are generally red or pink. The petals may be hardly notched or deeply incised, the flowers may be borne singly, in small clusters or in tight heads, and heights range from 4 in. (10 cm) to 3 ft (90 cm). Most campions belong in the border, but the Alpine Campion is small enough to be grown in the cracks between paving stones. Both the border and rockery varieties need well-drained soil but there is one for the bog garden — Ragged Robin grows wild in wet areas and it is useful for the land around a pond. Although differing so markedly the various campions have a few cultural features in common — all need copious watering in dry weather and dead-heading prolongs the floral display.

VARIETIES: The best border campion to grow is **L. chalcedonica** (Jerusalem Cross) — height 3 ft (90 cm), flowering period June-August. Large heads of bright red flowers are borne on long leaf stalks — varieties in other colours include **'Rosea'** (pink) and **'Albiflora'** (white). The flowers of **L. coronaria** (Rose Campion) are borne in loose sprays above the grey foliage — it grows about 1½ ft (45 cm) high and both red and white varieties are available as well as the more usual pink. **L. flos-jovis** (Flower of Jove) is a mat-forming perennial which bears pink flowers above the silvery leaves and **L. viscaria 'Splendens Plena'** (1½ ft/45 cm) has clusters of double pink flowers in early summer. The Alpine Campion **L. alpina** is easily raised from seed for the rockery — height 4 in. (10 cm), spread 4 in. (10 cm), flowering period May-July. **L. flos-cuculi** (Ragged Robin) is a plant for wet land — it grows about 2 ft (60 cm) high and in summer the stalks are topped with numerous pink flowers.

SITE & SOIL: Border and rockery varieties require well-drained soil in a sunny spot.

PROPAGATION: Sow seeds under glass in spring or divide clumps in autumn.

Lychnis chalcedonica

Border perennial
•
Rockery perennial
•
Bog plant

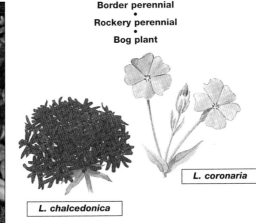

L. coronaria

L. chalcedonica

Lychnis viscaria 'Splendens Plena'

Lychnis flos-cuculi

LYSICHITON Skunk Cabbage

Lysichiton is not difficult to grow in either a bog garden or when covered with water on the marginal shelf of a pond. It is a bold and eye-catching plant, and so it is surprising that it is hard to find. This lack of popularity may be due to its size or its unpleasant smell — hence the common name. The seeds germinate readily so self-sown seedlings can be a problem.

VARIETIES: **L. americanus** (Yellow Skunk Cabbage) is the one you are more likely to find. In April the dramatic arum-like flowers appear — each one with a 1 ft (30 cm) yellow spathe on top of a stout 1½ ft (45 cm) stalk. The blooms are followed by 3 ft (90 cm) long leaves — where space is limited it is better to grow the White Skunk Cabbage **L. camtschatcensis** which has 2 ft (60 cm) leaves.

SITE & SOIL: Moist or wet soil is essential — thrives in sun or partial shade.

PROPAGATION: Remove and plant offsets in spring.

Bog plant

L. americanus

Lysichiton americanus

LYSIMACHIA   Lysimachia

Lysimachias are useful plants for damp sites. The border species have erect stems and white or yellow flowers — the arrangement of these flowers on the stem differs from one type to the other. Dig in plenty of compost or well-rotted manure and remember that some lysimachias can be invasive — dig up the clumps, divide and replant every three years to prevent them crowding out more delicate plants. The most popular rockery species is Creeping Jenny — its vigorous trailing stems will soon spread everywhere if not cut back after flowering. However, it is a good choice if you want to cover a large area of bare soil, especially at the edge of a pond. The yellow flowers are bowl-shaped.

Lysimachia ciliata

VARIETIES: **L. punctata** (Yellow Loosestrife) is an old favourite — height 2½ ft (75 cm), 1 in. (2.5 cm) wide yellow cup-shaped flowers, flowering period June-August. The blooms are borne in whorls around the stalks — it is an invasive plant which is more suited to the cottage or wild garden rather than the herbaceous border. A better choice for the border is **L. ciliata** with yellow blooms borne singly on the 3 ft (90 cm) high flower stalks. For white flowers there are two choices. **L. ephemerum** bears purple-eyed starry white flowers on upright narrow racemes — **L. clethroides** (Chinese Loosestrife).grows to the same height (3 ft/90 cm) but the 5 in. (12.5 cm) long flower spikes are curved. The flowering period is July-September. Creeping Jenny is **L. nummularia** — height 2 in. (5 cm), ½ in. (1 cm) wide yellow flowers, flowering period May-August. It is far too invasive for a small rockery — choose instead the less invasive, yellow-leaved variety **'Aurea'**. For a ground-hugging shade-lover look for **L. japonica 'Minutissima'**.

SITE & SOIL: Any moisture-retentive soil will do — thrives in sun or partial shade.

PROPAGATION: Divide clumps in autumn or spring.

Border perennial
•
Rockery perennial

Lysimachia clethroides

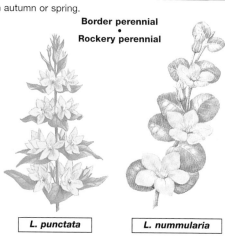

| L. punctata | L. nummularia |

Lysimachia nummularia

Border perennial
•
Bog plant

LYTHRUM   Purple Loosestrife

This water-loving plant is at its best in boggy ground, but it will grow quite happily in humus-rich soil in the herbaceous border. The leaves are dark green and elongated — above them rise the narrow flower spikes, densely packed with pink or red starry blooms. Mulch in spring, water copiously in dry weather and cut the stems down to ground level in autumn. Young growth is prone to slug damage.

VARIETIES: The basic species is **L. salicaria**. It can reach 6 ft (1.8 m) but the named varieties are shorter and generally more attractive — flowering period June-September. Popular ones include **'The Beacon'** (3 ft/ 90 cm, crimson), **'Lady Sackville'** (4 ft/1.2 m, rose-red) and **'Firecandle'** (3 ft/90 cm, rose-red). **L. virgatum** grows 1½-2 ft (45-60 cm) high.

SITE & SOIL: Any moisture-retentive soil will do — thrives in sun or partial shade.

PROPAGATION: Divide clumps in autumn or spring.

| L. salicaria |

Lythrum salicaria 'Firecandle'

Border perennial

| M. cordata |

MACLEAYA Plume Poppy

This plant needs space — not only does it grow more than head-high but its underground suckers are invasive. Not for a small garden, but a good choice for the back of an extensive herbaceous border or as a specimen plant in a large lawn. The deeply-cut leaves are grey-brown above and hoary white below, and in summer large plume-like panicles of tiny flowers appear.

VARIETIES: **M. cordata** is the main species — height 6-8 ft (1.8-2.4 m), flowering period July-August. The 3 ft (90 cm) plumes bear pearly white flowers which provide a greyish haze above the foliage. Cut down the stems in autumn. Plants which produce buff-coloured flowers with a pink tinge are often sold as M. cordata but are really **M. microcarpa 'Kelway's Coral Plume'**.

SITE & SOIL: Any reasonable soil will do — thrives in sun or partial shade.

PROPAGATION: Remove and plant rooted suckers in spring.

Macleaya cordata

Hardy annual

| M. maritima |

MALCOLMIA Virginia Stock

Many of today's gardeners began with a packet of Virginia Stock, but many gardening text books don't even bother to mention it. The reason is the ease with which it can be grown. A thin scattering anywhere — infertile soil, semi-shady bed, cracks between paving stones and so on, and in a month or two the plants are in flower and remain in bloom for several weeks.

VARIETIES: The usual practice is to buy a packet of mixed seed of **M. maritima** — height 8 in. (20 cm), $^1/_2$ in. (1 cm) wide four-petalled flowers. The slender stems bear 2 in. (5 cm) long grey-green leaves and the sweet-smelling flowers are white, pink, red, mauve and occasionally yellow. Single-coloured varieties such as **'Crimson King'** are available in some catalogues. Malcolmia may disappoint in a warm rainy summer.

SITE & SOIL: Any well-drained soil will do — thrives in sun or partial shade.

PROPAGATION: Sow seeds in spring for summer flowers — repeat every month for a succession of blooms.

Malcolmia maritima

Some bedding plants and border perennials are particularly sought after by butterflies which are attracted by the nectar of the flowers. In the photograph small Tortoiseshells flutter over the blooms of Sedum spectabile — other 'butterfly flowers' include Alyssum saxatile, Aubrieta, Aster, Calendula, Centranthus, Dianthus barbatus, Heliotrope, Iberis, Lunaria, Myosotis, Muscari and Scabious.

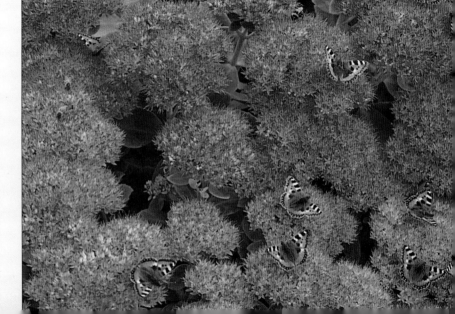

MALOPE Malope

Hardy annual

M. trifida
'Grandiflora'

Malope can be confused with Annual Mallow (Lavatera trimestris). Both have a bushy growth habit and bear 3-4 in. (7.5-10 cm) wide trumpet-shaped flowers during the summer months. The major differences are that Malope has a wider range of colours and it is a more reliable plant. It can be used to fill a large area in an annual bed or mixed border.

VARIETIES: Malope is listed on the seed package as either **M. trifida** or the large-flowered strain **M. trifida 'Grandiflora'** — height 3 ft (90 cm), spacing 1½ ft (45 cm), flowering period July-October. A good mixture such as **'Excelsior Mixed'** will produce plants bearing white, pink and crimson flowers — some of these flowers will be prominently veined. Blooms are borne abundantly and little staking is required.

SITE & SOIL: Any well-drained soil will do — choose a sunny spot.

PROPAGATION: Sow seeds in March-May where they are to flower — thin to the required spacing.

Malope trifida

MALVA Mallow

Border perennial

M. sylvestris
'Primley Blue'

The flowers of Malva can be mistaken for Lavatera — both are large and usually bowl-shaped. This border perennial is much less popular than the shrubby Lavatera we see everywhere these days, although it is easy to grow and the flowers are long-lasting. The taller varieties may need staking and self-sown seedlings can be a nuisance.

VARIETIES: The species you are most likely to find is **M. moschata** (Musk Mallow) — height 2 ft (60 cm), 2 in. (5 cm) wide pink or lavender flowers, flowering period June-September. The white variety **'Alba'** is popular. **M. sylvestris** has several interesting varieties. **'Mauritanica'** (5 ft/1.5 m) has large, ruffled magenta flowers and the 8 in. (20 cm) **'Primley Blue'** bears sky blue flowers. **'Zebrina'** has dark-centred lilac blooms.

SITE & SOIL: Any well-drained soil will do — thrives best in full sun.

PROPAGATION: Sow seeds or plant cuttings in a cold frame in spring.

Malva moschata 'Alba'

Blanket bedding involves the use of a single variety to fill a bed or border — a bright cultivar of Pelargonium, Begonia semperflorens or Impatiens is the favourite subject. This scheme is sometimes regarded as too uninteresting for general use. This may be true for a small front garden, but it can look most impressive over a large area as in this formal arrangement. It need not be formal — bedded-out 'meadows' are popular in Scandinavia and some other European countries.

MATTHIOLA Stock

In former times stocks were one of the mainstays in the flower bed and cottage garden, but these days they are more often bought as cut flowers for indoor arrangements rather than as seeds for raising bedding plants. This is unfortunate as their charm as a garden flower remains — soft grey-green foliage, densely-clustered flower spikes and an outstanding fragrance which fills the air. The decline in popularity is due to several inherent problems. The annual types tend to have a relatively short flowering period and the biennials may need some winter protection in the colder parts of the country. Raising all-double plants from seed calls for a fair degree of skill with selectable seed (see 'Propagation' below), and the classification of stocks often leads to confusion. Despite these difficulties you should certainly grow them if fragrance in the garden is important to you.

VARIETIES: There are four basic groups. The first one is the *Ten Week Stock* group with **M. incana** as a parent. These plants are grown as half-hardy annuals, sown in February or March in gentle heat and then planted out in late May for a June-August display. **'Dwarf Ten Week Mixed'** (1 ft/30 cm) will produce a high proportion of doubles. For longer flowering and more compact plants pick **'Cinderella'** — for taller (1½-2 ft/45-60 cm) but later-flowering plants choose **'Beauty of Nice'**. The most imposing types are the Column Stocks which grow 2-3 ft (60-90 cm) high — look for **'Giant Imperial'** or the selectable **'Giant Excelsior'** and **'Record'** strains. The second group is another important one — the *Brompton Stocks* bought as **'Brompton Mixed'**. These are biennials, sown outdoors in May-July and then pricked out into small pots before overwintering in a cold frame. Plant out in February-March for an April-May display. The usual height of the bushy, branching plants is 1½ ft (45 cm) — selectable strains are available. The third group is only a small one. It contains the *East Lothian Stock* — dwarf (1 ft/ 30 cm) plants which look like small Brompton Stocks and can be grown as either half-hardy annuals or biennials. Selectable strains are not available, but most plants are double. The fourth group is quite different from the others. This is the *Night-scented Stock* (**M. bicornis**) — a hardy annual which is sown in spring where it is to flower. The 1 ft (30 cm) plants bear insignificant blooms which close during the day, but at night the fragrance is outstanding.

SITE & SOIL: Any well-drained, non-acid soil will do — thrives in sun or light shade.

PROPAGATION: Follow the hardy annual, half-hardy annual or hardy biennial technique depending on the variety chosen — see above. Some double varieties are offered as selectable seed. With these it is necessary to keep them at 45°-50°F (7°-10°C) after germination. Dark-leaved seedlings will produce only single plants — prick out only the yellowish-green ones which will grow into double-flowered plants.

Bedding plant:
hardy annual
•
Bedding plant:
half-hardy annual
•
Bedding plant:
hardy biennial

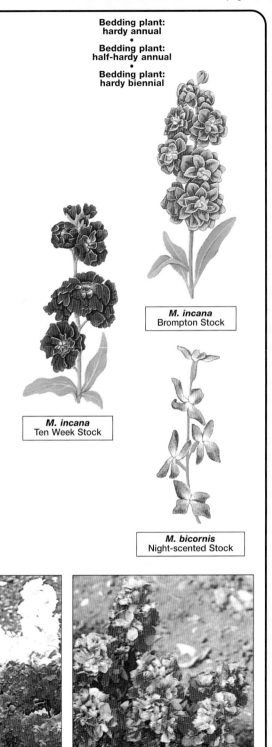

M. incana
Brompton Stock

M. incana
Ten Week Stock

M. bicornis
Night-scented Stock

Matthiola incana 'Ten Week Stock'

Matthiola incana 'Brompton Stock'

Matthiola incana 'East Lothian Stock'

MAZUS   Mazus

Rockery perennial

Mazus is a ground-cover plant which does not appear in many gardening books, but it is available at large garden centres. The creeping stems spread rapidly and it is an easy plant to grow if the soil is reasonably fertile and is not allowed to dry out in periods of drought. The flowers are two-lipped with the bottom petal spotted with white and gold. Slugs and snails can be a problem in spring.

VARIETIES: The only one you are likely to find is **M. reptans** — height 2 in. (5 cm), spread 1¹/₂ ft (45 cm), ³/₄ in. (1.5 cm) long lilac flowers, flowering period June-August. There is a white-flowered variety **'Albus'** — like the species it is a lime-hater. **M. radicans** has bronzy-green foliage and purple-centred white flowers in June-July. For yellow-centred white flowers in August grow **M. pumilio**.

SITE & SOIL: Requires well-drained soil — thrives in sun or light shade.

PROPAGATION: Sow seeds or divide clumps in spring.

M. reptans

Mazus reptans

MECONOPSIS   Meconopsis

Border perennial

There are numerous species of this poppy for the collector of unusual plants, but for the ordinary gardener there are just two — the Himalayan Blue Poppy and the Welsh Poppy. Both need humus-rich soil which must be kept moist in summer. Provide some support for taller types. The blooms are short-lived and unfortunately so are the plants. Replenish your stock regularly from seed.

VARIETIES: The Himalayan Poppy, once called **M. baileyi** but now referred to as **M. betonicifolia**, has been much admired since its introduction in the 1930s — height 3 ft (90 cm), 3 in. (7.5 cm) wide sky blue flowers, flowering period June-July. The Welsh Poppy **M. cambrica** is smaller and easier to grow — height 1 ft (30 cm), 2 in. (5 cm) wide yellow or orange flowers, flowering period June-September.

SITE & SOIL: Requires well-drained, lime-free soil in light shade.

PROPAGATION: Sow seeds under glass in spring.

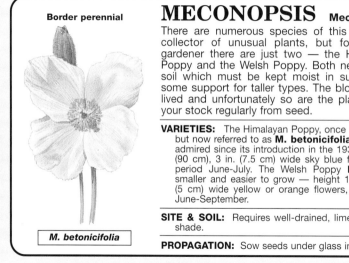

M. betonicifolia

Meconopsis cambrica

MERTENSIA   Mertensia

Border perennial

The two species you are most likely to find are hardy perennials for the border. Clusters of blue tubular flowers are borne above the blue-green foliage — a good choice if you like blue flowers and there is dappled shade and water-retentive soil at the planting site. The problem is that you will have to look through the catalogues — don't expect to find Mertensia at your local garden centre.

VARIETIES: **M. pulmonarioides** (Virginia Cowslip) is listed in numerous catalogues — height 1¹/₂ ft (45 cm), spread 1 ft (30 cm), 1 in. (2.5 cm) long blue flowers, flowering period April-May. The flowers are borne in drooping clusters and the stems die down in summer. **M. simplicissima** has smaller flowers on taller stems which appear later in the season between June and September. Do not let the plants dry out.

SITE & SOIL: Any well-drained, humus-rich soil will do — thrives in light shade.

PROPAGATION: Divide clumps in autumn or spring.

M. pulmonarioides

Mertensia pulmonarioides

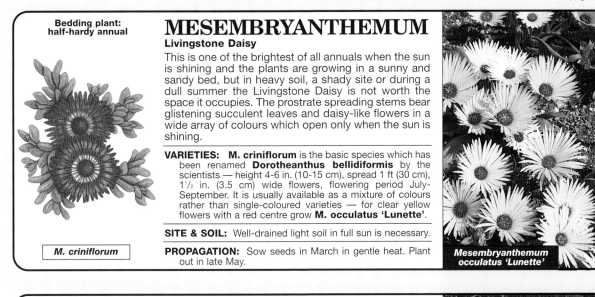

**Bedding plant:
half-hardy annual**

MESEMBRYANTHEMUM
Livingstone Daisy

This is one of the brightest of all annuals when the sun is shining and the plants are growing in a sunny and sandy bed, but in heavy soil, a shady site or during a dull summer the Livingstone Daisy is not worth the space it occupies. The prostrate spreading stems bear glistening succulent leaves and daisy-like flowers in a wide array of colours which open only when the sun is shining.

VARIETIES: **M. criniflorum** is the basic species which has been renamed **Dorotheanthus bellidiformis** by the scientists — height 4-6 in. (10-15 cm), spread 1 ft (30 cm), 1½ in. (3.5 cm) wide flowers, flowering period July-September. It is usually available as a mixture of colours rather than single-coloured varieties — for clear yellow flowers with a red centre grow **M. occulatus 'Lunette'**.

SITE & SOIL: Well-drained light soil in full sun is necessary.

PROPAGATION: Sow seeds in March in gentle heat. Plant out in late May.

M. criniflorum

Mesembryanthemum occulatus 'Lunette'

MIMULUS Monkey Flower

Mimulus can be found in several parts of the garden — in the annual bed, herbaceous border, rockery, boggy ground around the pond and even in the water in the pond. They all have a general liking for moist and shady conditions, but not all the perennials are hardy so pick with care. The annuals are the most popular type and will thrive in the shade of a north-facing wall. Impatiens and Bedding Begonias remain the popular bedding plants for such shady spots, despite the bright colours of the Mimulus F_1 hybrids.

VARIETIES: There are numerous varieties of **M. hybridus** which are grown as half-hardy annuals, and the modern ones are a great advance on the older types. **'Malibu'** is a compact dwarf (6 in./15 cm) with small flowers — **'Magic'** is another dwarf available in various colours. **'Calypso'** (9 in./22.5 cm) has the widest range of colours and **'Viva'** (1 ft/30 cm) is the largest and showiest of the F_1 hybrids. These annuals have 1-2 in. (2.5-5 cm) wide flowers and a flowering period from June to September. One of the best hardy perennials for the border is **M. cardinalis** — height 3 ft (90 cm), 2 in. (5 cm) long tubular red flowers, flowering period June-September. **M. lewisii** (2 ft/60 cm) has white-throated pink or magenta flowers. For the rockery there are a number of perennial hybrids such as **M. 'Whitecroft Scarlet'**, **M. 'Red Emperor'**, **M. 'Highland Red'** etc — height 9 in. (22.5 cm), flowering period June-September. The cream and pink **M. 'Andean Nymph'** is not reliably hardy and **M. burnetii** is a rockery species with copper-spotted yellow blooms. Species for wet ground around the pond include **M. bartonianus** (rose-red), **M. ringens** (lavender), **M. guttatus** (yellow) and **M. luteus** (yellow).

SITE & SOIL: Moisture-retentive soil is essential — some shade is desirable.

PROPAGATION: Annuals: Sow seeds in March in gentle heat — plant out in late May. Perennials: Sow seeds under glass or divide clumps in spring.

Mimulus cardinalis

**Bedding plant:
half-hardy annual**
•
Border perennial
•
Rockery perennial
•
Bog plant

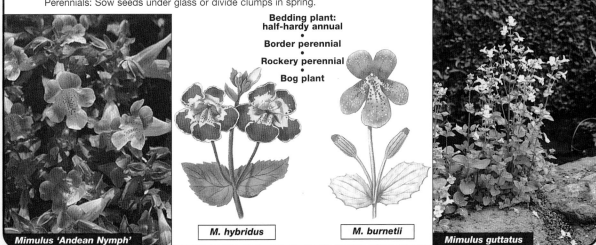

Mimulus 'Andean Nymph'

M. hybridus

M. burnetii

Mimulus guttatus

Bedding plant: half-hardy annual

MINA Spanish Flag

An annual climber to provide a change from the usual Climbing Nasturtium, Morning Glory etc. The twining stems will clothe a trellis or fence and throughout the summer sprays of banana-shaped blooms are produced. The flowers of the popular species change colour as they age so that a well-grown plant is covered with blooms in every shade from pure white to deep red.

VARIETIES: **M. lobata (Ipomoea lobata)** is the species in the seed catalogues — pot-grown specimens are available at some garden centres in spring. Basic details are height 4-6 ft (1.2-1.8 m), spacing 2 ft (60 cm), 1 in. (2.5 cm) long flowers, flowering period July-October. At first flowers are red, changing to orange and yellow and finally white. **M. pennata** has red starry flowers.

SITE & SOIL: Any well-drained soil will do — thrives best in full sun.

PROPAGATION: Sow seeds in February in gentle heat. Plant out in late May.

M. lobata

Mina lobata

Bedding plant: half-hardy annual

MIRABILIS Marvel of Peru

A bright out-of-the-ordinary shrubby plant for the annual bed or border. Trumpet-shaped flowers are borne above the oval leaves all summer long and these are followed by small green fruits containing large black seeds. A notable feature is that the blooms do not open until mid-afternoon, hence the alternative common name 'Four O'clock Plant'.

VARIETIES: You will find **M. jalapa** in some but not all catalogues — height 2-3 ft (60-90 cm), 2 in. (5 cm) long flared tubular flowers, flowering period July-October. It is usually grown as a mixture to provide white, yellow, orange, pink and purple flowers which may be plain or striped. The evening fragrance is strong — a feature shared with the magenta-flowered **M. viscosa**.

SITE & SOIL: Any well-drained soil will do — thrives in sun or light shade.

PROPAGATION: Sow seeds in February-April in gentle heat. Plant out in late May.

M. jalapa

Mirabilis jalapa

Bedding plant: half-hardy annual

MOLUCELLA Bells of Ireland

A plant which is interesting rather than beautiful — it came to us from Syria and not Ireland despite its common name. The petals are white and insignificant but are surrounded by a large, green and bell-like calyx. These floral bells are borne on graceful stems — somewhat colourless in the garden but a joy for the flower arranger.

VARIETIES: There is a single species (**M. laevis**) which is sometimes listed as the Shell Flower — height 2 ft (60 cm), spacing 1½ ft (45 cm), 2 in. (5 cm) wide flowers, flowering period August-September. If you want to use it for indoor decoration, cut the stems when the bells are fully open and dry them in a cool and airy place away from direct sunlight. These dried flowers are useful for winter decorations.

SITE & SOIL: Any well-drained soil will do — thrives in sun or light shade.

PROPAGATION: Sow seeds in February-April in gentle heat. Plant out in late May. Alternatively in mild areas sow seeds outdoors in April.

M. laevis

Molucella laevis

MONARDA Bergamot

Bergamot hybrids are at home in the herbaceous border where they need moist soil and some shade from the midday sun in order to flourish. Add compost or well-rotted manure at planting time, avoid a full-sun site, mulch in spring and water copiously in dry weather. The flower heads on top of the upright stems are made up of whorls of tubular flowers. Cut down to ground level in autumn.

VARIETIES: The hybrids have been derived from **M. didyma** — height 2-3 ft (60-90 cm), spacing 2 ft (60 cm), 1½ in. (3.5 cm) wide clusters of hooded flowers, flowering period June-September. Numerous named types are available. **M. 'Cambridge Scarlet'** (red), **'Prairie Night'** (lilac) and **'Croftway Pink'** (pale pink) are popular — others include **'Aquarius'** (mauve), **'Beauty of Cobham'** (pink), **'Fishes'** (pink) and **'Snow White'** (white).

SITE & SOIL: Any humus-rich soil will do — thrives best in light shade.

PROPAGATION: Divide clumps in autumn or spring.

M. 'Croftway Pink'

Monarda 'Cambridge Scarlet'

MORINA Morina

An unusual evergreen member of the scabious family with flowers which are quite unmistakable. The stems are about 3 ft (90 cm) tall and in midsummer each one bears a spike of showy flowers. The waxy blooms are borne in whorls with a collar of spiny green bracts below — these whorls of flowers are borne in tiers. Worth looking for, but only if you can provide cover against rain for the crown in winter.

VARIETIES: **M. longifolia** produces a basal rosette of 1 ft (30 cm) long thistle-like leaves — the leaves on the stems are smaller. The blooms are white when they open — waxy tubes with a five-lobed mouth. As they mature the colour changes to pink and finally to crimson. This species (common name Whorlflower) is widely available but **M. persica** is a rarity. The leaves are lobed, it grows about 4 ft (1.2 m) high and the final flower colour is pink and not red.

SITE & SOIL: Any well-drained, humus-rich soil will do — thrives in sun or light shade.

PROPAGATION: Sow seeds in a cold frame in spring.

M. longifolia

Morina longifolia

MORISIA Morisia

This low-growing rockery plant is a native of the Mediterranean coast and not a true alpine. It requires sandy soil and an absence of shade as you would expect from its natural habitat. Where conditions are right it forms a neat and compact cushion with numerous flowers on short stalks arising among the foliage — these leaves are made up of tiny leaflets. Do not feed Morisia — it does best in infertile soil.

VARIETIES: There is a single species **M. monanthos** which is sometimes listed as **M. hypogaea** — height 1 in. (2.5 cm), spread 6 in. (15 cm), ½ in. (1 cm) wide bright yellow flowers, flowering period March-May. The early-flowering habit is welcome but it is a small plant which can be lost in a large rockery. The variety **'Fred Hemingway'** has larger flowers (¾ in./1.5 cm) which are darker yellow — it is more popular than the species.

SITE & SOIL: Requires well-drained light soil in full sun.

PROPAGATION: Sow seeds in a cold frame in spring.

M. monanthos

Morisia monanthos

MUSCARI Grape Hyacinth

Muscari is a useful and popular clump-forming plant, producing splashes of colour in the rockery or at the edges of beds and borders. The flower colour is usually but not always blue, and they are frequently planted between taller bulbs such as tulips and daffodils. In addition they can be used for naturalising in woodland and grassy areas, and they are a good subject for small containers to provide a spring display. Nobody sings the praises of this old favourite because it has none of the glamour of the showier bulbs — the tiny bell- or flask-shaped flowers are clustered on top of a leafless and fleshy stem. The strap-like leaves appear before the flowers and the blooms can be cut for small-scale flower arrangements.

Muscari armeniacum 'Blue Spike'

VARIETIES: The usual choice is **M. armeniacum** — height 6-9 in. (15-22.5 cm), ¹/₄ in. (0.5 cm) long white-rimmed blue flowers, flowering period April-May. Plant the bulbs 3 in. (7.5 cm) deep in September-October — the usual spacing is 4 in. (10 cm). The foliage season is quite long, starting in autumn and lasting until after the blooms have withered. The varieties offer alternatives to the size and colour of the species — **'Blue Spike'** is shorter with double flowers and **'Fantasy Creation'** has double greeny-blue flowers. **M. azureum** bears dark-striped blue flowers in March — **'Album'** is a white-flowered dwarf variety. **M. botryoides 'Album'** is another white grape hyacinth. There are several species which differ from the standard pattern. **M. comosum 'Plumosum'** (1 ft/ 30 cm) has feathery violet blooms, **M. macrocarpum** bears brown-rimmed yellow flowers and **M. ambrosiacum** has purple blooms which fade to pale green and then cream with age — all these novelties bloom in May. The Oxford & Cambridge Muscari (**M. tubergenianum**) has pale blue flowers above dark blue ones on the stalk.

SITE & SOIL: Any well-drained soil will do — thrives best in full sun.

PROPAGATION: Divide clumps every three years in autumn — replant at once.

Muscari comosum 'Plumosum'

Bulb

M. armeniacum

M. botryoides 'Album'

Muscari macrocarpum

Bedding plant: hardy biennial
•
Border perennial
•
Rockery perennial

M. sylvatica 'Ultramarine'

MYOSOTIS Forget-me-not

One of the traditional plants used for carpeting the ground between tulips and wallflowers is the dwarf biennial forget-me-not — clusters of blue flowers appear above the grey-green downy leaves in spring. Other types are available — taller ones for the border, short-lived perennials for the rockery and flowers in white and pink as a change from blue.

VARIETIES: The popular forget-me-nots are varieties of **M. sylvatica** — 6 in.-1 ft (15-30 cm), ¹/₄ in. (0.5 cm) wide yellow-eyed flowers, flowering period April-May. Compact (6 in./15 cm) ones include **'Blue Ball'** (indigo), **'Ultramarine'** (rich blue) and **'White Ball'** (white) — pink dwarfs include **'Carmine King'** and **'Victoria Rose'**. Taller (1 ft/30 cm) varieties include **'Blue Basket'** and **'Royal Blue'** — **M. alpestris** is a short-lived perennial alpine.

SITE & SOIL: Any reasonable soil will do — thrives best in light shade.

PROPAGATION: Sow seeds in the open in May or June. Plant out in autumn.

Myosotis sylvatica 'Royal Blue'

NARCISSUS Narcissus, Daffodil

Narcissi are seen everywhere in spring — in window boxes, along the roadside, in tiny gardens and grand estates, and naturalised in grassland and wooded areas. It is no surprise that it is our favourite spring flower, but it is perhaps surprising that there are more Narcissi growing in the average garden than any other plant. Before dealing with this universally-loved genus in detail it might be useful to clear up any confusion over their common names. Narcissus is the Latin name of the genus, irrespective of the shape or size of the trumpet. As noted on page 140 the common name 'daffodil' is restricted to those varieties with a trumpet which is as long or longer than the petals — all varieties with shorter trumpets or cups have the common name 'narcissus'.

Everyone can recognise a daffodil or narcissus, of course, but the flower parts have special names (see the illustration on the right). Not everyone realises the range of shapes, sizes and colours among the many hundreds of varieties which are commercially available. The heights vary from 3 in. (7.5 cm) to 2 ft (60 cm) and the colours include oranges, pinks, apricots and reds as well as the familiar white and yellows. You can also find split corona and double varieties as well as the simple perianth/corona arrangement illustrated on the right. With all varieties the leafless flower stalk arises among the strap-like leaves. The flowers range from 1-3 in. (2.5-7.5 cm) across and are generally but not always borne singly on the top of the stalk. The flowering period is mid February-mid March — flowers are early, mid-season or late, depending on the variety.

They are easy to grow, which is one of the reasons for their great popularity. They will succeed in any reasonable soil, although they prefer fertile moist soil, and apart from the Tazetta varieties are fully hardy. This means that Narcissi can be left in the ground over winter and will spread into large clumps in a few years. They have all sorts of uses in the garden — the dwarfs are excellent in rockeries, pots, bed and border edges etc and the taller ones can be used in beds, borders, under trees, in grassland and so on. As a general rule Narcissi are better grown in informal groups than in regular-spaced neat rows, but it is a matter of personal taste. Dwarf varieties are popular as container plants — N. bulbocodium and N. 'Minnow' are typical examples. To make a start in the garden, look through the bulb catalogues or the wide selection at your garden centre in early autumn. To make your choice easier this genus has been split into 12 groups, and the Division numbers appear in the rest of this section and in many catalogues.

Choose your bulbs carefully — look for a firm basal plate, a firm neck and a covering of scale leaves which is not torn away nor mouldy. Plant them as soon as possible after buying — the recommended planting period is from August to October and the bulbs should be covered with soil to twice the height of the bulb. Set the bulbs 4-8 in. (10-20 cm) apart, depending on the expected height of the flower. Do not use offsets or multiple offsets if you want blooms next spring. If your soil is heavy sprinkle some coarse sand in the hole before planting. The time to feed the soil is before planting or in February — there is little point in feeding at or after flowering. Remove dead flower heads if practical and let the foliage die down naturally. Don't tie it into a knot and do not cut the grass above the bulbs for at least a month after the flowers have faded. The clumps should not be disturbed unless it is necessary — they can be lifted every four or five years in July or August for division and then replanted immediately.

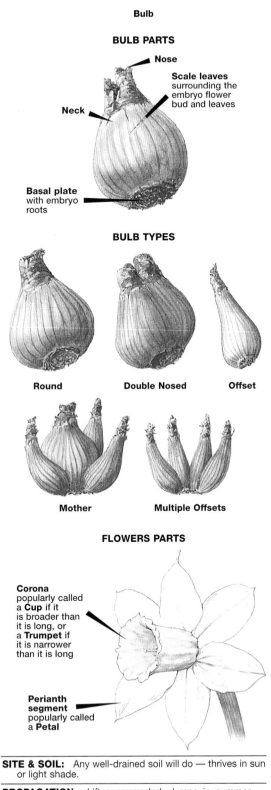

Bulb

BULB PARTS

Nose

Scale leaves surrounding the embryo flower bud and leaves

Neck

Basal plate with embryo roots

BULB TYPES

Round

Double Nosed

Offset

Mother

Multiple Offsets

FLOWERS PARTS

Corona popularly called a **Cup** if it is broader than it is long, or a **Trumpet** if it is narrower than it is long

Perianth segment popularly called a **Petal**

SITE & SOIL: Any well-drained soil will do — thrives in sun or light shade.

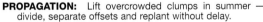

PROPAGATION: Lift overcrowded clumps in summer — divide, separate offsets and replant without delay.

NARCISSUS continued

Division 1:
TRUMPET DAFFODILS

One flower per stem — trumpet at least as long as the petals. Height 6 in.-1½ ft (15-45 cm).

The word 'daffodil' is the common name for all the varieties in this Division. **'King Alfred'** (golden-yellow, early) once dominated this group, but it has died out although the name is used by some suppliers for other all-yellow varieties. Its place has been taken by **'Golden Harvest'** (golden-yellow, very early), **'Dutch Master'** (golden-yellow, early), **'Rembrandt'** (yellow, early) and **'Unsurpassable'** (yellow, mid-season). The best-known all-white is **'Mount Hood'** (mid-season) — others include **'Empress of Ireland'** (large, early), **'April Love'** (large, early) and **'Beersheba'** (early). There are numerous bicolours — examples are **'Magnet'** (white with yellow trumpet, early) and **'Spellbinder'** (yellow, trumpet fading to white, early). There are some 6 in. (15 cm) dwarfs such as **'Topolino'** (white with yellow trumpet, early).

Division 2:
LARGE-CUPPED NARCISSI

One flower per stem — cup more than ⅓ the length of the petals. Height 1-2 ft (30-60 cm).

There are some fine yellows, including **'Carlton'** (early), **'Yellow Sun'** (very early), the narrow-cupped **'St. Keverne'** (early) and **'Gigantic Star'** (early). All-whites are less common, but you should be able to find **'Easter Moon'** (mid-season) and **'Desdemona'** (mid-season). For something different look for the all-white **'Sea Urchin'** (late) with its deeply serrated cup. This group has many splendid bicolours — examples include **'Carbineer'** (yellow with orange-red cup, late), **'Professor Einstein'** (white with orange cup, very early), **'Sempre Avanti'** (cream with orange cup, early) and **'Flower Record'** (white with orange-rimmed yellow cup, early). The first white variety with a pink cup was **'Mrs. R.O. Backhouse'** — modern ones include **'Salome'**, **'Rosy Sunrise'** and **'Salmon Trout'**.

Narcissus 'Golden Harvest'

Narcissus 'Professor Einstein'

Narcissus 'Texas'

Division 3:
SMALL-CUPPED NARCISSI

One flower per stem — cup less than ⅓ the length of the petals. Height 1-1½ ft (30-45 cm).

There are a number of all-white varieties such as **'Angel'** (very late) and **'Frigid'** (late) but most types are bicolours. The petals may be yellow, as with **'Birma'** (mid-season) and **'Edward Buxton'** (early), or white like **'Barrett Browning'** (early) and **'Aflame'** (early).

Division 4:
DOUBLE NARCISSI

One or more flowers per stem — more than one ring of petals. Height 6 in.-1½ ft (15-45 cm).

The old **'Telamonius Plenus'** (all-yellow, early) continues to be one of the most reliable. The more popular yellow these days is **'Golden Ducat'** (mid-season). There are several all-whites with one flower on each stem, including **'Ice King'** (mid-season). Most people pick a bicolour — look for **'Irene Copeland'** (white and apricot, mid-season) and **'Texas'** (yellow and orange, early). Some have several blooms on each stem — popular ones include **'Cheerfulness'** (pale cream, mid-season), **'White Marvel'** (white, late) and **'Sir Winston Churchill'** (white and orange-red, mid-season). There are several 6 in. (15 cm) dwarfs such as **'Rip Van Winkle'** (yellow, mid-season).

Division 5:
TRIANDRUS NARCISSI

Usually several flowers per stem — drooping flowers and slightly reflexed petals. Height 6 in.-1½ ft (15-45 cm).

'Thalia' is the popular one, but there are others. **'Angel's Tears'** (mid-season) is creamy-white, **'Ice Wings'** (mid-season) is pure white and **'Liberty Bells'** (late) is yellow.

NARCISSUS continued

Division 6:
CYCLAMINEUS NARCISSI

Nearly always one flower per stem — drooping flowers with long trumpets and strongly reflexed petals. Height 6 in.-1 ft (15-30 cm).

The frilly trumpets and swept-back petals of **'February Gold'** (all-yellow) and **'Peeping Tom'** (all-yellow) appear in late February. Shortly afterwards the March ones appear — **'Jack Snipe'** and **'February Silver'** with their white petals and yellow trumpets, and the all-yellow **'Tete-a-Tete'** with several flowers on each stem. **'Jenny'** is white and cream — **'Garden Princess'** is all-yellow. The first pink and white one was **'Foundling'** and more recent ones include **'Lilac Charm'** and **'Lavender Lace'**.

Division 7:
JONQUILLA NARCISSI

Usually more than one flower per stem — cup shorter than the petals. Height 6 in.-1 ft (15-30 cm).

The fragrant flowers have broad petals. All-yellows include **'Sun Disc'** (late) and **'Trevithian'** (mid-season). Other Jonquils include **'Suzy'** (yellow and orange, mid-season) and **'Waterperry'** (white and pink, mid-season).

Division 8:
TAZETTA NARCISSI

Several flowers per stem — small flowers with short cups and rounded petals. Height 6 in.-1½ ft (15-45 cm).

These varieties are only suitable outdoors in mild areas. The flowers are fragrant. **'Paper White'** (white, very early) and **'Grand Soleil d'Or'** (yellow and orange, early) are popular early varieties. New ones include **'Chinese Sacred Lily'** (white and gold) and **'Matador'** (yellow and orange, early). Included in this Division are the Poetaz Narcissi which are much hardier and can be grown outdoors. Look for **'Cragford'** (white and orange, early), **'Silver Chimes'** (white and pale yellow, mid-season) and the dwarf **'Minnow'** (cream and yellow, mid-season).

Narcissus 'Actaea'

Narcissus bulbocodium

Narcissus 'Orangery'

Division 9:
POETICUS NARCISSI

Usually one flower per stem — white petals with a frilled red-edged cup. Height 1-1½ ft (30-45 cm).

Popular varieties include **'Actaea'** (yellow cup, mid-season) and **'Pheasant's Eye'** (orange cup, late). Others include **'Cantabile'** (green cup, late) and **'Double White Poeticus'** (white cup, late). All are sweetly scented.

Division 10:
WILD NARCISSI

All species, varieties and natural hybrids found in the wild. Height less than 1 ft (30 cm).

Examples are **N. asturiensis** with its tiny yellow trumpets, **N. canaliculatus** (white and yellow) which is a tiny Tazetta Narcissus, **N. cyclamineus** with swept-back petals and the Hoop Petticoat (**N. bulbocodium**) with its wide trumpet and narrow petals. **N. pseudonarcissus** is the Wild Daffodil which grows 6-9 in. (15-22.5 cm) high. The Tenby Daffodil **N. obvallaris** is a small golden Trumpet Daffodil. Most are very early.

Division 11:
SPLIT-CORONA NARCISSI

One flower per stem — corona split for at least ⅓ of its length. Height 1-1½ ft (30-45 cm).

The split sections of the corona usually spread outwards. Examples include **'Chanterelle'** (white petals and yellow corona), **'Orangery'** (white and orange), **'Papillon Blanc'** (all-white) and **'Lemon Beauty'** (yellow and orange).

Division 12:
MISCELLANEOUS NARCISSI

Types which belong nowhere else.

Very uncommon. Specialist catalogues list some **N. bulbocodium** hybrids such as **'Kenellis'** and **'Taffeta'**.

Bulb

N. siculum

NECTAROSCORDUM
Nectaroscordum

A stately plant for the wild garden or herbaceous border which is closely related to Allium. The leaves have a distinct keel along their length, and in late spring the tall and leafless stems appear. From the top of these stems the flowers hang down on thin stalks. As the seed pods form the stalks stiffen and turn upwards, so that the seed head has a shuttlecock-like appearance.

VARIETIES: **N. siculum** (**Allium siculum**) is the species in the catalogues — height 4 ft (1.2 m), 1 in. (2.5 cm) long pink- and green-tinted cream flowers, flowering period May-June. These bell-shaped pendent flowers are borne in loose clusters. The variety **'Bulgaricum'** bears green-shaded white flowers. Nectaroscordum is mainly grown by flower arrangers who dry the seed heads for their displays.

SITE & SOIL: Any well-drained soil will do — thrives best in full sun.

PROPAGATION: Divide mature clumps in autumn when overcrowding becomes a problem.

Nectaroscordum siculum

Bedding plant: half-hardy annual

N. strumosa

NEMESIA Nemesia

Nemesias are easy to grow, they flower quickly after bedding out and the blooms are multicoloured. Their major drawback is that flowering quickly comes to an end when the summer is hot and dry — keep the plants well watered during periods of drought. Pinch out the tips after bedding out and cut back the stems once the first flush is over.

VARIETIES: **N. strumosa** has given rise to many garden varieties — height 9 in.-1 ft (22.5-30 cm), spacing 6 in. (15 cm), 1 in. (2.5 cm) wide funnel-shaped lipped flowers, flowering period June-September. Single colours include **'Blue Gem'** (pale blue) and **'Fire King'** (red) — there are also half white/half coloured varieties such as **'KLM'** (white/blue). Mixtures include **'Carnival'**, **'Funfair'** and **'Sparklers'** (many bicolours and tricolours).

SITE & SOIL: Any reasonable soil will do — thrives best in sun or light shade.

PROPAGATION: Sow seeds in March-April in gentle heat. Plant out in late May.

Nemesia strumosa 'Carnival'

Hardy annual

N. menziesii

NEMOPHILA Nemophila

Nemophila is a low-growing carpeting plant which will flourish at the edge of the border or in the rockery if the conditions are moist and cool. The leaves are feathery and the saucer-shaped flowers are borne from early summer to the first frosts if the conditions are right. Dig in organic matter before sowing and water copiously in dry weather.

VARIETIES: You will find two species in the catalogues. The Californian Bluebell or Baby Blue Eyes is **N. menziesii** — height 9 in. (22.5 cm), 1½ in. (3.5 cm) wide white-eyed blue flowers, flowering period June-October. The other Nemophila is Five Spot (**N. maculata**) which is a small plant growing 6 in. (15 cm) high — each of the white petals on the 1 in. (2.5 cm) wide flowers bears a large violet spot at the edge.

SITE & SOIL: Any moisture-retaining soil will do — thrives in sun or partial shade.

PROPAGATION: Dislikes root disturbance. Sow seeds in September or April where they are to flower.

Nemophila maculata

Border perennial

NEPETA Catmint

Catmint is popular with gardeners as a ground-covering plant — it is even more popular with cats who love to roll in its aromatic grey-green foliage. It will flourish in sandy, stony or chalky soils but it dies out rapidly in ground which remains sodden in winter. The flowers are borne on upright spikes — dead-heading will encourage further flushes. Remove old growth when new shoots appear in spring.

VARIETIES: **N. mussinii** (**N. racemosa**) is one of the popular species — height 1 ft (30 cm), ½ in. (1 cm) long pale purple flowers, flowering period May-September. **'Little Titch'** is a 6 in. (15 cm) dwarf variety — **'Snowflake'** is a white-flowered one. Taller species and varieties in blue or lavender include **N. sibirica** (1½ ft/45 cm, large flowers), **N. 'Six Hills Giant'** (3 ft/90 cm), and **N. 'Souvenir d'Andre Chaudron'** (1½ ft/45 cm, large flowers).

SITE & SOIL: Any well-drained soil will do — thrives best in full sun.

PROPAGATION: Divide clumps in spring.

N. mussinii

Nepeta 'Six Hills Giant'

Bulb

NERINE Nerine

Nerines are sometimes considered to be too tender to grow outdoors. The Guernsey Lily (N. sarniensis) produces a group of attractive white, orange or red blooms on 1½ ft (45 cm) stems, but it is an indoor plant. There is, however, one species which can be relied upon to produce its eye-catching blooms in the garden in autumn. Protect the crowns with peat or bracken in winter.

VARIETIES: **N. bowdenii** is the species to grow — height 2 ft (60 cm), 3 in. (7.5 cm) wide pink flowers, flowering period September-October. The long-lasting blooms are clustered at the top of a leafless stalk — each flower is funnel-shaped with wavy narrow petals which curl backwards. The leaves appear in late summer, grow until spring and then die down in summer. **'Pink Triumph'** is a silvery-pink variety.

SITE & SOIL: Well-drained soil, a sheltered spot and full sun are necessary.

PROPAGATION: Divide overcrowded clumps in spring — replant at once.

N. bowdenii

Nerine bowdenii

Bedding plant: half-hardy annual

NICOTIANA Tobacco Plant

Nicotiana alata has been grown as a garden flower for generations — its evening fragrance is intense but it is not particularly decorative. The tall stems need staking and the flowers close during the day. Nowadays the usual choice is one of the dwarf varieties and with many of the modern hybrids the blooms remain open all day. Unfortunately much of the fragrance has gone.

VARIETIES: You will find several dwarf hybrids listed in the catalogues — height 9 in.-1½ ft (22.5-45 cm), flowering period June-October. The **N. 'Domino'** series leads the field of F_1 hybrids — others include **N. 'Havana Apple Blossom'** and the **N. 'Starship'** series. Non-F_1 types include **N. 'Nikki'** and **N. 'Roulette'**. Examples of tall modern hybrids are **N. 'Sensation'** (3 ft/90 cm) and **N. 'Lime Green'** (2½ ft/75 cm).

SITE & SOIL: Any well-drained soil will do — thrives in sun or light shade.

PROPAGATION: Sow seeds in March in gentle heat. Plant out in late May.

N. 'Lime Green'

Nicotiana 'Sensation'

Bedding plant: half-hardy annual

N. caerulea 'Mont Blanc'

NIEREMBERGIA Cup Flower

It is hard to see why a plant with so many advantages is not more popular. It is easy to grow and the compact mounds of foliage are covered with masses of flowers throughout the summer. You can use Nierembergia in a number of ways — it is recommended as an edging plant and also as ground cover in open ground between shrubs. It can also be grown in pots, hanging baskets and as a house plant.

VARIETIES: **N. caerulea** is the basic species — height 9 in. (22.5 cm), ³/₄ in. (1.5 cm) wide cup-shaped lavender flowers, flowering period June-September. Seeds of two varieties appear in the catalogues. **'Mont Blanc'** is a low, spreading plant growing about 4 in. (10 cm) high and bearing yellow-eyed white flowers. **'Purple Robe'** is taller (9 in./22.5 cm) with yellow-eyed violet flowers. Both may survive the winter in mild areas.

SITE & SOIL: Any reasonable soil in a sunny spot will do.

PROPAGATION: Sow seeds in March in gentle heat. Plant out in late May.

Nierembergia caerulea 'Purple Robe'

Hardy annual

N. damascena 'Miss Jekyll'

NIGELLA Love-in-a-mist

Love-in-a-mist describes the way the flowers lie half-hidden in a mist of finely-cut foliage. It has been a blue-flowered plant in our gardens for hundreds of years, but nowadays multicoloured mixtures are popular. Nigella is easily grown, but the flowering season is a short one. Add compost before sowing and dead-head spent blooms.

VARIETIES: The popular species is **N. damascena** — height 1¹/₂ ft (45 cm), 2 in. (5 cm) wide blue flowers, flowering period June-August. **'Miss Jekyll'** is the favourite blue variety — for 6-9 in. (15-22.5 cm) dwarfs grow **'Blue Midget'** or **'Dwarf Moody Blue'**. **'Persian Pink'** is the best-known pink one and the most popular mixture (pink, blue, mauve, white) is **'Persian Jewels'**. **N. orientalis 'Transformer'** has yellow flowers.

SITE & SOIL: Any well-drained soil will do — thrives in sun or light shade.

PROPAGATION: Sow seeds in autumn or early spring where they are to flower.

Nigella damascena 'Persian Jewels'

Bedding plant: half-hardy annual

N. paradoxa 'Blue Bird'

NOLANA Chilean Bellflower

Nolana appeared in the 1980s as an exciting new bedding plant. The trumpet-shaped flowers were large and the neat mounds of foliage were compact — an excellent choice for edging, ground cover and hanging baskets. In the photographs the frilly-edged blooms cover the foliage, but it has not quite lived up to its promise. In some situations the floral display has been disappointing.

VARIETIES: **N. paradoxa 'Blue Bird'** is the variety you are likely to find in the seed catalogues — height 6-9 in. (15-22.5 cm), spacing 9 in. (22.5 cm), yellow-eyed, white-throated blue flowers, flowering period June-September. Plant it in a dry sunny site to see it at its best. Less easy to find is the white variety **'Snow Bird'**. **N. 'Shooting Star'** is a pale blue, semi-trailing variety.

SITE & SOIL: A well-drained soil in full sun is necessary.

PROPAGATION: Sow seeds in March in gentle heat. Plant out in late May.

Nolana paradoxa 'Blue Bird'

Bulb

N. saluenensis

NOMOCHARIS Nomocharis

This bulb is only worth the search if you like unusual subjects and you have a moist and shady spot to fill — peaty soil under trees is ideal. The upper half of the stem bears lance-shaped leaves and the nodding flat or saucer-shaped flowers have petals which may be fringed and are often spotted. Plant the bulbs 4 in. (10 cm) deep in November.

VARIETIES: The easiest to grow is **N. saluenensis** — height 3 ft (90 cm), 3 in. (7.5 cm) wide white-centred maroon-spotted pink flowers, flowering period June. **N. aperta** is shorter (1-2 ft/30-60 cm) and bears five or six flowers on top of each stem. **N. mairei** (**N. pardanthina**) grows 3 ft (90 cm) high — the leaves are whorled around the stem and the 3 in. (7.5 cm) wide flowers have a dark purple eye and fringed petals.

SITE & SOIL: Well-drained, humus-rich soil in partial shade is essential.

PROPAGATION: Dislikes disturbance — buy new bulbs.

Nomocharis mairei

Bulb

N. macrophyllum

NOTHOLIRION Notholirion

An unusual plant with an unusual feature — the bulb dies after flowering and it is the offsets which produce next year's growth. The long and narrow leaves appear at the base of the plant from autumn to early spring — choose a spot near low-growing evergreens so that the tufts of foliage can be given some protection in winter. Plant the bulbs 4 in. (10 cm) deep in October-November.

VARIETIES: The easiest one to find is **N. bulbuliferum** — height 3 ft (90 cm), 1½ in. (3.5 cm) long green-tipped lilac bell-shaped flowers, flowering period June-July. **N. thomsonianum** reaches about the same height but differs by producing 2 in. (5 cm) long pale pink blooms in late spring. **N. macrophyllum** is the most colourful — 1 in. (2.5 cm) long trumpets which are mauve outside and purple-spotted pale lavender within.

SITE & SOIL: Well-drained, humus-rich soil in sun or light shade is necessary.

PROPAGATION: Remove and plant offsets in autumn.

Notholirion thomsonianum

Border perennial

O. macrocarpa

OENOTHERA Evening Primrose

The buds usually but not always open in the evening — hence the common name. The blooms are large, saucer-shaped and silky — somewhat similar to poppies, but nothing like primroses. They love sun and sand — choose something else if your soil is heavy and liable to waterlog. Mulch in spring, water during dry spells and cut down the stems in late autumn.

VARIETIES: The largest blooms are borne by the low-growing **O. macrocarpa** — height 6 in. (15 cm), spread 1½ ft (45 cm), 4 in. (10 cm) wide bowl-shaped yellow flowers, flowering period July-September. **O. fruticosa** is a taller plant — yellow-flowering varieties include **'Fireworks'** (2 ft/60 cm) and **'Erica Robin'** (1 ft/30 cm). For a change of colour there are the pink-flowered varieties of **O. speciosa** — **'Siskiyou'** and **'Rosea'**.

SITE & SOIL: Well-drained light or loamy soil in full sun is necessary.

PROPAGATION: Sow seeds under glass in spring — for named varieties divide clumps in spring.

Oenothera fruticosa 'Fireworks'

Rockery perennial

O. cappadocica
'Anthea Bloom'

OMPHALODES   Omphalodes

The flowers are borne in loose sprays above the foliage which remains green almost all year round. The blooms look like blue or white forget-me-nots and appear early in the season. Both of the popular species described below flourish in the shade under shrubs and trees and they require a humus-rich soil, so add peat, compost or leaf mould before planting and mulch around the stems in spring.

VARIETIES: Blue-eyed Mary is **O. verna** — height 6 in. (15 cm), spread 1½ ft (45 cm), ½ in. (1 cm) wide white-eyed blue flowers, flowering period March-May. An all-white variety (**'Alba'**) is available. **O. cappadocica** (Navelwort) is a taller plant (1 ft/30 cm) with smaller flowers. The flowers are long-lasting and the plant is long-lived — look for one of the varieties such as **'Alba'** (white), **'Anthea Bloom'** (sky blue) or **'Starry Eyes'** (blue-striped white).

SITE & SOIL: Any moisture-retentive soil will do — thrives best in shade.

PROPAGATION: Divide clumps in autumn.

Omphalodes verna

Hardy biennial

O. acanthium

ONOPORDUM   Giant Thistle

This imposing plant is only suitable for a border which is large and deep — plant it at the back for a dramatic effect. It is a biennial — in the first year there is a flat rosette of leaves and in the second season the tall stems with silvery leaves appear — all parts are spiny. It self-seeds readily so that it often appears to be a perennial. Dead-head to prevent it becoming invasive.

VARIETIES: The popular species is the Scotch Thistle **O. acanthium** — height 8 ft (2.4 m), spread 3 ft (90 cm), 2 in. (5 cm) wide pink-purple flower heads, flowering period July-August. The Heraldic Thistle **O. nervosum** grows to the same height and has flower heads which are similar in shape but are darker than the Scotch Thistle. The leaves are spineless above and prominently veined beneath.

SITE & SOIL: Any reasonable soil will do — thrives in sun or light shade.

PROPAGATION: Sow seeds in late summer where they are to grow. Thin as necessary.

Onopordum nervosum

Rockery perennial

O. vulgare
'Aureum'

ORIGANUM   Marjoram

Ordinary marjoram (O. vulgare) is grown as a herb rather than as a flowering ornamental, although one colourful form is grown for its foliage display. There are several other species, however, which are grown in the rockery for their flowers rather than their leaves — the pink or purple small flowers are surrounded by bracts which may add to the display. All are sun-lovers but they are only moderately hardy.

VARIETIES: The best rockery species is **O. amanum** — height 3 in. (7.5 cm), spread 6 in. (15 cm), 1½ in. (3.5 cm) long tubular pink flowers, flowering period July-September. The flowers are surrounded by leaf-like bracts which turn pale purple with age. **O. dictamnus** is different — the pink flowers are borne in hop-like heads of purple bracts. **O. vulgare 'Aureum'** has yellow foliage and in midsummer clusters of tiny pale pink flowers.

SITE & SOIL: Well-drained soil in full sun is necessary.

PROPAGATION: Plant cuttings in a cold frame in summer.

Origanum amanum

ORNITHOGALUM
Ornithogalum

Bulb

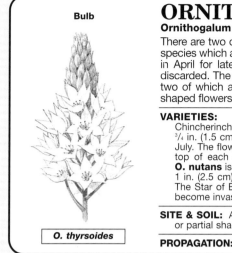

O. thyrsoides

There are two distinct groups. The first one contains the species which are not hardy and so are planted outdoors in April for late summer flowers after which they are discarded. The second group consists of hardy species, two of which are listed in many catalogues. Their star-shaped flowers are a combination of white and green.

VARIETIES: The best known tender species is Chincherinchee (**O. thyrsoides**) — height 1½ ft (45 cm), ¾ in. (1.5 cm) wide white flowers, flowering period June-July. The flowers are clustered to form a conical spike on top of each stem. The hardy species bloom in spring. **O. nutans** is the best one to buy — height 1½ ft (45 cm), 1 in. (2.5 cm) wide green-backed pendent white flowers. The Star of Bethlehem **O. umbellatum** (1 ft/30 cm) can become invasive.

SITE & SOIL: Any well-drained soil will do — thrives in sun or partial shade.

PROPAGATION: Divide clumps in summer — replant at once.

Ornithogalum umbellatum

OSTEOSPERMUM   Osteospermum

Not long ago these South African daisies were an unusual feature but now you will find them offered as bedding plants at every garden centre in spring. They are related to and sometimes confused with Dimorphotheca — like them the flowers close in dull weather but when open offer a bright display of large petals and central discs which are often in a contrasting colour. Some have blooms in the standard daisy pattern but the most eye-catching ones have spoon-shaped petals. This is not a grow-anywhere plant — it needs good drainage and a sheltered site in full sun. The popular hybrids are grown as half-hardy annuals although they will survive the winter in mild areas if given some form of protection. There is one species which is hardy.

VARIETIES: Many Osteospermum hybrids are now offered for sale as bedding plants with blooms which almost cover the plant all summer long when soil and light conditions are right — height 1-2 ft (30-60 cm), 2-3 in. (5-7.5 cm) wide flowers, flowering period June-October. The first star of the show was **O. 'Whirligig'** with blue-backed white spoon-shaped petals — now there are other spooned types such as **'Pink Whirls'** and **'Cannington John'**. Among the plain-petalled types you will find the dark-centred **'Ink Spot'** and the pink **'Langtrees'**. **'Starshine'** and **'Potpourri'** grow only 1 ft (30 cm) high and **'Silver Sparkler'** has variegated foliage. Purple ones include **'Port Wine'** and **'Tresco Purple'** — **'Buttermilk'** is yellow. The hardy variety for the border is **O. jucundum** — height 1 ft (30 cm), gold-centred pink or purple flowers, flowering period June-September. **'Compactum'** and **'Compactum Blackthorn'** (dark purple) are 6 in. (15 cm) dwarfs for the rockery.

SITE & SOIL: Well-drained soil in full sun is necessary.

PROPAGATION: Sow seeds in March in gentle heat. Plant out in late May.

Osteospermum 'Whirligig'

Bedding plant:
half-hardy annual
•
Border perennial
•
Rockery perennial

Osteospermum 'Buttermilk'

O. 'Starshine'

Osteospermum jucundum

Rockery perennial

OURISIA Ourisia

An evergreen perennial for the rock garden. A good choice if the site is shady and moist, but don't expect to find it at your local garden centre — you will have to order it from an alpine plant nursery. It is a mat-forming plant which produces tubular lipped flowers — these flowers may be borne singly, in small groups or massed in whorls on leafless stems. Frost is not a problem but slugs and snails can be destructive.

VARIETIES: The most popular Ourisia is **O. 'Snowflake'** — height 4 in. (10 cm), spread 8 in. (20 cm), ½ in. (1 cm) wide white flowers borne singly or in small groups, flowering period June-July. **O. coccinea** is taller (8 in./20 cm) and spreads more widely — the pendent red flowers are long tubes and are borne in loose racemes. **O. macrophylla** (height 1 ft/30 cm) is quite different — the yellow-throated white blooms are tightly packed in whorls.

SITE & SOIL: Any lime-free, humus-rich soil will do — thrives in partial shade.

PROPAGATION: Divide clumps in spring.

O. macrophylla

Ourisia macrophylla

Rockery perennial

OXALIS Oxalis

Oxalis grows as a rounded clump of clover-like leaves with five-petalled flowers which open when the sun shines. Make sure you choose a hardy non-invasive variety — some can spread rapidly and ruin a rockery. They are undemanding plants — simply dig in some peat or compost before planting. It is usual to buy plants in pots but many can be grown from bulbs planted 3 in. (7.5 cm) deep in autumn.

VARIETIES: **O. adenophylla** is a popular species — height 3 in. (7.5 cm), spread 6 in. (15 cm), 1 in. (2.5 cm) wide silvery-pink flowers, flowering period June-July. **O. enneaphylla** in white, pink or red has similar-shaped flowers above silvery partially-folded leaves. **O. 'Ione Hecker'** (veined violet flowers) and **O. laciniata** (blue-purple) are even more restrained. **O. magellanica 'Nelson'** (double white) can be invasive.

SITE & SOIL: Any well-drained soil will do — thrives best in full sun.

PROPAGATION: Divide clumps in autumn.

O. adenophylla

Oxalis laciniata

Border perennial

OZOTHAMNUS Ozothamnus

An unusual plant — you will find this evergreen in some catalogues but not at the garden centre. The problem is that it is usually described as a rather tender plant suitable only for mild areas, but there are two species which are reasonably hardy. It needs good drainage and full sun to produce its 'everlasting' flowers which are white with red or brown bracts below. These blooms can be cut and dried for flower arranging.

VARIETIES: **O. ledifolius** is the Kerosene Bush — height 3 ft (90 cm), 2 in. (5 cm) wide flower clusters, flowering period June-July. Both the leaves and stems are inflammable — hence the common name. **O. rosmarinifolius** is taller and more shrub-like than the Kerosene Bush — the leaves look like rosemary and the flowers are fragrant.

SITE & SOIL: Requires well-drained sandy soil and a sunny site.

PROPAGATION: Plant cuttings in a cold frame in summer.

O. rosmarinifolius

Ozothamnus ledifolius

PAEONIA Peony

Peonies are one of the glories of the flower border. In spring or summer the buds on top of the stalks open to produce blooms which put the neighbouring plants to shame. Vast bowls of petals up to 8 in. (20 cm) across — single, semi-double, double or anemone-flowered in a wide array of colours. Some are fragrant, and the bronzy spring foliage is attractive — it is not surprising that peonies are regarded as the aristocrats of the herbaceous border. When making your choice remember that doubles last longer than singles. Regard peonies as a long-term investment and learn the rules before you start. Early autumn is the best time for planting and the soil should be enriched with compost or leaf mould. Choose an open sunny spot but try to avoid a site where the early morning sun shines on the plants. Set the crown no lower than 1 in. (2.5 cm) below the surface. Remember to leave the plant alone — it may not flower in the first year and will not be fully established for three years. Do not transplant and do not divide clumps to increase your stock. The cultural rules are straightforward — mulch in spring, stake the stems, water in dry weather, dead-head faded blooms, feed with a general fertilizer in late summer and cut down the stems in autumn.

P. officinalis 'Rosea Plena'
Common Peony

P. lactiflora
Chinese Peony

VARIETIES: The *Common* or *May-flowering Peony* (**P. officinalis**) is an old cottage garden favourite — height 2 ft (60 cm), spacing 1¹/₂ ft (45 cm), 5 in. (12.5 cm) wide single red flowers, flowering period May-June. Named double varieties are available — **'Alba Plena'** (white), **'Rosea Plena'** (pink) etc.

The most popular peonies are the varieties of the *Chinese* or *June-flowering Peony* (**P. lactiflora**) — height 2¹/₂-3 ft (75- 90 cm), spacing 2 ft (60 cm), 3-8 in. (7.5-20 cm) wide fragrant flowers, flowering period June-July. There are fine doubles such as **'Duchesse de Nemours'** (white), **'Lady Alexandra Duff'** (pink), **'Inspector Lavergne'** (red), **'Sarah Bernhardt'** (pink), **'M. Jules Elie'** (silvery-rose) and **'Festiva Maxima'** (white). All these doubles are eye-catching, but they do hang their heads after heavy rain. There are singles such as **'William Cranfield'** (red) and the anemone-flowered **'Bowl of Beauty'** (cream-centred pink).

For an early display grow the *April-flowering Peony* (**P. mlokosewitschii**) — height 1¹/₂ ft (45 cm), spacing 1¹/₂ ft (45 cm), 4 in. (10 cm) wide single yellow flowers, flowering period April-May.

SITE & SOIL: Any well-drained soil in a sunny site will do.

PROPAGATION: Buy from a reputable supplier — do not divide clumps.

P. mlokosewitschii
April-flowering Peony

Paeonia officinalis

Paeonia lactiflora 'Bowl of Beauty'

Paeonia lactiflora 'Letitia'

PAPAVER Poppy

The short-lived papery blooms have a special charm and few plants are easier to grow — they will thrive in dry weather when so many other plants have wilted. The Oriental Poppy is the perennial grown in the herbaceous border — a fine sight when the large bowl-shaped flowers are open in early summer. Unfortunately it loses its appeal when flowering is over — the untidy foliage is cut down when the blooms have gone and large bare gaps are left until the bristly, deeply-cut leaves reappear in spring. Stake the flower stems and divide the plants every three years. Annual poppies have a much daintier appearance — the buds bow their heads on top of long stalks and the petals of the open flowers flutter in the breeze. The single ones are cup-shaped and the doubles are ball-like — staking is not necessary but dead-heading is required to prolong the flowering season. Between the robust perennial and the dainty annuals are species such as the Iceland Poppy and Alpine Poppy which are grown either as biennials or short-lived perennials.

VARIETIES: The popular perennial species is the Oriental Poppy **P. orientale** — height 1¹/₂ -3 ft (45-90 cm), 4-6 in. (10-15 cm) wide bowl-shaped flowers, flowering period May-July. The petals usually have a black-blotched base and they enclose a boss of black anthers. Varieties include **'Goliath'** (red), **'Mrs. Perry'** (salmon-pink), **'Turkish Delight'** (salmon-pink), **'Black and White'** (white) and **'Picotee'** (orange-edged white). A few such as **'Allegro'** and **'Pizzicato'** can be raised from seed. The most popular annual poppies are the ones descended from the Corn Poppy **P. rhoeas**. The **'Shirley'** series belongs here — height 2 ft (60 cm), 2-3 in. (5-7.5 cm) wide silky-petalled single or double flowers, flowering period June-September. **'Fairy Wings'** (1 ft/30 cm) is noted for its unusual colour combinations. **P. commutatum 'Ladybird'** grows to the same height and bears black-blotched red blooms. **P. somniferum** (Opium Poppy) is much taller and showier — choose **'Paeony-flowered Mixture'** (4 ft/1.2 m) for its 4 in. (10 cm) wide double blooms. The Iceland Poppy **P. nudicaule** (2 ft/60 cm) is grown as a biennial or short-lived perennial — look for **'Champagne Bubbles'** or **'San Remo'** for mixed colours. The small Alpine Poppy (**P. alpinum**) is also treated as a biennial or short-lived perennial for the rockery — white, yellow and orange flowers are borne on hairless stems.

SITE & SOIL: Any reasonable soil will do — thrives in sun or light shade.

PROPAGATION: Perennials: Divide clumps in autumn. Annuals: Sow seeds in April where they are to flower. Biennials: Sow seeds in August — thin to required spacing in April.

Border perennial
•
Hardy annual
•
Hardy biennial
•
Rockery perennial

P. orientale
'Mrs. Perry'

P. rhoeas
'Shirley Poppy'

P. commutatum
'Ladybird'

P. somniferum
'Paeony-flowered Mixture'

P. nudicaule
'Champagne Bubbles'

Papaver orientale 'Goliath'

Papaver rhoeas 'Shirley Mixed'

Papaver nudicaule

PARADISEA   St. Bruno's Lily

Border perennial

Lily-like flowers are borne above grassy leaves — a good choice for open woodland, naturalising in grassland or for growing at the front of the border. It is not difficult to grow but it is surprisingly difficult to find. The rhizomes cannot be dried and stored, so Paradisea is usually bought as a growing plant. Fleshy rhizomes are sometimes available — plant 3 in. (7.5 cm) deep immediately after purchase.

VARIETIES: Two species are grown as garden plants. **P. liliastrum** is the one you are more likely to see in the catalogues — height 1-2 ft (30-60 cm), 2 in. (5 cm) long funnel-shaped flowers, flowering period June. Each fragrant white bloom has green-tipped petals. **P. lusitanica** is rather taller (2½ ft/75 cm) with white bell-shaped flowers borne in loose clusters. Do not disturb clumps of Paradisea unless it is really necessary.

SITE & SOIL: Well-drained, humus-rich soil is required — thrives in partial shade.

PROPAGATION: Divide overcrowded clumps in early autumn.

P. liliastrum

Paradisea liliastrum

PARAHEBE   Parahebe

Rockery perennial

Some time ago the genus Veronica was split into the woody Hebes and the herbaceous Veronicas. A few, the Parahebes, didn't fit into either group. They are semi-woody plants which grow less than 1 ft (30 cm) high and produce small white, blue or pink speedwell-like flowers. These blooms are borne in loose clusters and appear in late summer and autumn.

VARIETIES: **P. catarractae** is an upright bushy plant — height 10 in. (25 cm), ½ in. (1 cm) wide red-eyed white flowers, flowering period August-October. **P. lyallii** is easier to grow — height 8 in. (20 cm), pink-veined white flowers, flowering period July-August. **P. bidwillii** is more difficult to find — you will see it in some catalogues but not at the garden centre. It is a 6 in. (15 cm) rounded plant with pink-veined white blooms.

SITE & SOIL: Requires well-drained soil and a sunny site.

PROPAGATION: Plant cuttings in a cold frame in early summer.

P. catarractae

Parahebe lyallii

Winter bedding in pots or window boxes usually relies upon plants with colourful foliage such as Variegated Ivy, Euonymus and Ornamental Brassica together with winter-flowering bedding plants such as Universal Pansy, Crescendo Polyanthus and Winter Heather. If you live in a mild district you can be more adventurous by incorporating hardened-off house plants such as Cyclamen and Solanum (Winter Cherry) which can withstand cold but not prolonged frosty conditions. The winter bedding scheme shown here was photographed in January.

PELARGONIUM Geranium

This plant with its bright heads of white, pink, orange, red or purple flowers is found in gardens, greenhouses, window boxes, balconies and window sills everywhere. The most popular type is one of our favourite summer bedding plants, but it is not really a Geranium at all — it is the Zonal Pelargonium. Look at one of the leaves of a typical variety and you will usually find a horseshoe marking or 'zone' — that is where the name comes from. These Zonal Pelargoniums are divided into three groups with somewhat indistinct dividing lines. The most popular ones belong to the Bedding Geranium group which flourish outdoors and bloom from June to October. The second group, the Greenhouse Geraniums, have a similar range of flowers and leaf markings but are disappointing outdoors and so are outside the scope of this book. The Fancy-leaved Geraniums make up the final group — here the leaf marking and colouring are often more decorative than the blooms.

Once it was quite simple. In spring we bought pot-grown geraniums for bedding out in late spring. These had been raised from cuttings by the nurseryman and we in turn took cuttings in late summer for new plants for next year — bushy 1 ft (30 cm) specimens with red, pink or white blooms. Things have now changed. There are 6 in. (15 cm) dwarfs and wide-spreading types, there are orange, salmon and speckled flowers and there is also a large array of F_1 and F_2 hybrids which can be raised from seed at home or bought as plugs in spring for growing on before bedding out.

The universally popular Bedding Geraniums have an aristocratic relation — the Regal Pelargonium, also known as the Martha Washington or Show Geranium. They have saw-edged leaves and large flowers which are bicoloured and ruffled. Unfortunately they require a warm and sheltered locality to succeed outdoors and are best grown as indoor plants. Another relative of the Bedding Geranium is the Ivy-leaved Pelargonium, bearing fleshy leaves or trailing stems which is used for hanging baskets, tubs and window boxes. At the garden centre in spring you may find pots of a variety of Angel Geranium — these are dwarfs with small crinkled leaves and bicoloured flowers. Finally there is the Scented-leaved Geranium — rose-, lemon- and apple-scented foliage much loved by our Victorian ancestors but with flowers which are usually insignificant and so these plants are not dealt with here.

You don't need green fingers to succeed with Bedding Geraniums. They have few diseases and pests and even fewer fussy demands. Whether home-grown or shop-bought the pots should be watered a few hours before planting — make sure that the plants have been properly hardened-off. Plant firmly and pinch out the growing tips occasionally to increase bushiness. Geraniums can withstand dry conditions better than most plants. Constant watering is an easy way to kill them, so water only if dry weather is prolonged and feed occasionally with a potash-rich fertilizer. You must remove the flower stalks once the blooms have faded in order to prolong the flowering season — this is especially important with some of the newer varieties. Before the first frosts arrive carefully dig up the plants and shake off the soil around the roots. Pot them up singly in compost using pots which are no larger than necessary to house the roots. Keep in an unheated room and only water if the leaves begin to flag. In spring move to a well-lit spot and increase the amount of water. Harden off and then plant outdoors in late May.

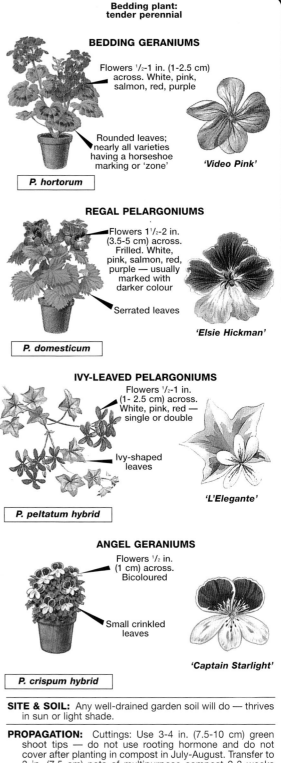

Bedding plant: tender perennial

BEDDING GERANIUMS

Flowers ¹/₂-1 in. (1-2.5 cm) across. White, pink, salmon, red, purple

Rounded leaves; nearly all varieties having a horseshoe marking or 'zone'

P. hortorum

'Video Pink'

REGAL PELARGONIUMS

Flowers 1¹/₂-2 in. (3.5-5 cm) across. Frilled. White, pink, salmon, red, purple — usually marked with darker colour

Serrated leaves

P. domesticum

'Elsie Hickman'

IVY-LEAVED PELARGONIUMS

Flowers ¹/₂-1 in. (1- 2.5 cm) across. White, pink, red — single or double

Ivy-shaped leaves

P. peltatum hybrid

'L'Elegante'

ANGEL GERANIUMS

Flowers ¹/₂ in. (1 cm) across. Bicoloured

Small crinkled leaves

P. crispum hybrid

'Captain Starlight'

SITE & SOIL: Any well-drained garden soil will do — thrives in sun or light shade.

PROPAGATION: Cuttings: Use 3-4 in. (7.5-10 cm) green shoot tips — do not use rooting hormone and do not cover after planting in compost in July-August. Transfer to 3 in. (7.5 cm) pots of multipurpose compost 2-3 weeks after rooting. Water sparingly in winter, and in early April move to a cold frame. Plant out in late May. Seeds: Sow seeds in January-February at 70°-75°F (21°-24°C). Plant out in late May.

PELARGONIUM continued

VARIETIES: The *Bedding Geraniums* are hybrids listed under **P. hortorum**. Old-fashioned single varieties are still available as rooted cuttings — examples include **'Paul Crampel'** (red), **'Elaine'** (pink) and **'Vera Dillon'** (purple). All the doubles are raised from cuttings — look for **'Mrs. Lawrence'** (pink), **'Hermione'** (white) and **'Gustav Emich'** (red). In addition to these standard varieties there are the Deacons with masses of small flower heads (e.g **'Deacon Bonanza'**, double pink) and the Irenes with large semi-double flowers (e.g **'Electra'**, blue-tinted red). More unusual are the Rosebud varieties with flowers like miniature roses (e.g **'Red Rambler'**, double red) and the Cactus ones with narrow and twisted petals (e.g **'Noel'**, white). Miniatures (8 in./20 cm or less) include **'Fantasia'** (white), **'Grace Wells'** (lilac) and **'Red Black Vesuvius'** (red). Nowadays many spring-bought plants are raised from seed and you will find a large selection of varieties in the catalogues and at the garden centre. There are some excellent reds such as **'Ringo Deep Scarlet'**, **'Red Elite'** and **'Cheerio Scarlet'**. **'Orange Appeal'** was the first true orange, **'Cherie'** is salmon and **'Hollywood White'** is pure white. For a white-eyed geranium choose the pink **'Hollywood Star'** or the red **'Bright Eyes'**. The **'Century'** series is noted for sturdy growth and large flower heads — even more compact (8 in./20 cm) is the dark-leaved **'Video'** series. **'Raspberry Ripple'** has red-flecked pink petals. The Multibloom/Floribundas are very early and have an unusually large number of flower heads — look for the **'Multibloom'** and **'Sensation'** series. For decorative foliage as well as flowers there are **'Happy Thoughts'**, **'Mrs. Henry Cox'** and **'Caroline Schmidt'**. The Spreading Geraniums (Balcony Geraniums) branch from the base so that the stems spread out, making them useful for window boxes and hanging baskets — look for the **'Breakaway'** series.

The *Regal Pelargoniums* (**P. domesticum**) provide an eye-catching display, but only if the site is mild and the soil is suitable. If you want to try your luck there are many varieties on offer, such as **'Aztec'** (white/pink), **'Elsie Hickman'** (vermilion/pink/white) and **'Carisbrooke'** (red/pink).

The true trailing types are the *Ivy-leaved Pelargoniums* which are hybrids of **P. peltatum**. Examples include **'L'Elegante'**, **'Crocodile'**, **'Super Rose'**, **'Snow Queen'** and **'La France'**. **'Summer Showers'** can be raised from seed.

The *Angel Geraniums* are hybrids of **P. crispum**. They are bushy small-leaved plants with flowers which look like miniature Regals — examples include **'Tip Top Duet'**, **'Catford Belle'** and **'Captain Starlight'**.

Pelargonium hortorum **'Red Elite'**

Pelargonium hortorum **'Multibloom Mixed'**

Pelargonium hortorum **'Caroline Schmidt'**

Pelargonium domesticum **'Carisbrooke'**

Pelargonium **'Crocodile'**

Pelargonium **'Catford Belle'**

Bog plant

PELTIPHYLLUM Umbrella Plant

The usual giant-leaved plants we see at the pool edge are Rheum, Gunnera and Rodgersia, but this one is worth considering for both its flowers and its leaves. The white or pink flowers are clustered on top of leafless stalks — these are on display in spring before the leaves. In summer the foliage appears — large rounded leaves borne on tall stalks giving the plant an umbrella-like appearance.

VARIETIES: **P. (Darmera) peltatum** needs space — height 3-5 ft (90 cm-1.5 m), 1-2 ft (30-60 cm) wide leaves, ½ in. (1 cm) wide flowers in globular heads on top of 4 ft (1.2 m) stalks, flowering period April-May. During the growing season the foliage has a bronzy-green colour but this changes to reds and browns in autumn. Choose the variety **'Nanum'** (1½ ft/45 cm) where space is limited.

SITE & SOIL: Boggy or moist soil in sun or partial shade is essential.

PROPAGATION: Divide clumps in spring.

P. peltatum

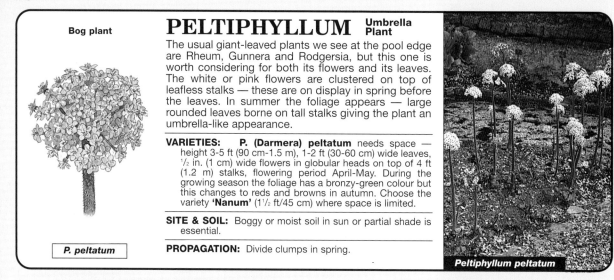

Peltiphyllum peltatum

PENSTEMON Penstemon

Penstemons may be herbaceous or shrubby and some but not all are evergreen. A few are rather tender but the general warning against frost is not deserved — the popular types can be left in the garden over winter provided the soil is free-draining and a mulch is placed over the crowns in frost-prone areas. Several hardy dwarf species are grown as rockery perennials and a few taller species are used as herbaceous border plants, but most are hybrids. Seed is available for the production of bedding plants. Dead-head faded summer blooms to ensure an autumn flush.

VARIETIES: **P. barbatus** is a tall species for the herbaceous border — height 3 ft (90 cm), 1½ in. (3.5 cm) long tubular red flowers, flowering period June-July and September-October. Much more popular are the antirrhinum-like hybrids — height 1-2½ ft (30-75 cm), bell- or tubular-shaped flowers, flowering period June-September. Popular ones include **P. 'Firebird'** (red), **P. 'Garnet'** (dark red), **P. 'Evelyn'** (pink), **P. 'Thorn'** (pink-edged white) and **P. 'Hidcote Pink'** (pink). **P. 'Sour Grapes'** is slate blue and **P. 'Blackbird'** is a tall purple variety. The dwarfs used in rockeries grow 6-9 in. (15-22.5 cm) high and flower between June and September. Look for **P. pinifolius** (orange), **P. newberryi** (pink), **P. menziesii** (violet) and **P. roezlii** (red). The most popular variety available as seed for bedding is **P. 'Hyacinth-flowered'** (1½ ft/45 cm) — **P. 'Bouquet'** is a mixture of flowers in white, pink, blue, purple and red. **P. 'Scarlet Queen'** has white-throated red flowers and **P. 'Monarch'** is a 2½ ft (75 cm) penstemon used as a dot plant in bedding plant schemes.

SITE & SOIL: Well-drained soil is essential — thrives best in full sun.

PROPAGATION: Plant cuttings in a cold frame in late summer or sow seeds in gentle heat in February. Plant out in May.

Penstemon 'Garnet'

Border perennial
•
Rockery perennial
•
Bedding plant:
half-hardy annual

Penstemon roezlii

P. 'Evelyn'	P. 'Scarlet Queen'

Penstemon 'Hyacinth-flowered'

PETUNIA Petunia

Petunias have changed. Once all you could buy were straggly plants with dull pink flowers. Now you can choose from a wide range of colours and flower sizes on plants with an upright, spreading or trailing growth habit. Because of these improvements petunias have become one of the most popular bedding plants — the spreading and trailing types are now favourite subjects for tubs, window boxes and hanging baskets. Nearly all of the modern varieties are F_1 hybrids bearing single or double flowers with smooth or ruffled petal edges. They may be self-coloured, bicoloured, multicoloured, picoteed with a broad white edge or striped to give a star-like effect. Petunias thrive best in hot and dry conditions — the display may be disappointing in a cool and wet summer. Starting from seed is possible but difficult — it is a much better plan to buy small seedlings or plugs and grow them on under glass for planting out when the danger of frost has passed. Pinch out the tips when the stems are 4-6 in. (10-15 cm) high. When buying plants which are ready for bedding out try to get ones which have not yet started to flower. Cut back stems which have become straggly — dead-head regularly. Protect with slug pellets and when in full flower feed with a potash-rich fertilizer.

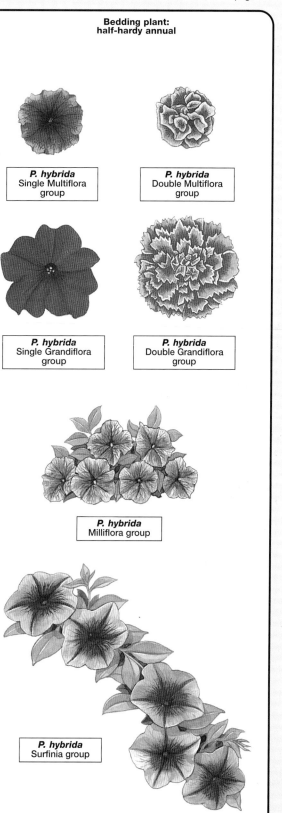

P. hybrida
Single Multiflora
group

P. hybrida
Double Multiflora
group

P. hybrida
Single Grandiflora
group

P. hybrida
Double Grandiflora
group

P. hybrida
Milliflora group

P. hybrida
Surfinia group

VARIETIES: The many varieties of **P. hybrida** can be placed into four groups. The *Multifloras* are the ones which are usually recommended for bedding — height 6 in.-1½ ft (15-45 cm), 2 in. (5 cm) wide flowers, flowering period June-September. The blooms are generally quite small but they are borne in large numbers and stand up to rain better than the larger ones. The **'Resisto'** series fits this description — so do the more modern introductions such as the **'Frenzy'**, **'Carpet'** and **'Primetime'** series which bear rather larger blooms. The largest-flowered Multifloras are sometimes referred to as 'Floribundas' — the **'Celebrity'** and **'Mirage'** series are examples. Some Multifloras have a wide-spreading habit with stems up to 2 ft (60 cm) long — look for **'Purple Wave'** and the **'Cascadia'** series. Double Multifloras (**'Delight'**, **'Duo Mixed'** etc) with carnation-like blooms are available — these double varieties are not as reliable as single ones.

The *Grandifloras* bear larger flowers than the Multifloras, reaching a width of 4-5 in. (10-12.5 cm). These blooms, however, are borne less freely and growth is less compact. **'Express'**, **'Cloud'**, **'Falcon'** and **'Daddy'** are series with veined flowers in many colours. For white-edged flowers look for **'Ice'** — **'Picotee Mixed'** has the added advantage of attractively-waved petals. The best ones to choose for maximum rain resistance are the prize-winning **'Lavender Storm'** (lavender) and **'Prism Sunshine'** (yellow). **'Super Cascade'** has wide-spreading stems but it is not a true trailer. The names to look for if you want a large and frilly double-flowered Grandiflora are **'Giant Victorious'**, **'Harmony'**, **'Pirouette'** and **'Bouquet'**.

The *Millifloras* are an outstanding introduction with masses of blooms measuring 1 in. (2.5 cm) or less. The **'Fantasy'** (**'Junior Petunia'**) series produces 6 in. (15 cm) high domes covered with small open-faced flowers all summer long. Rain resistance is good — a property shared with the **'Million Bells'** series. These plants have spreading stems and yellow-throated pink or blue flowers.

The *Surfinias* are the only true trailing petunias with 4 ft (1.2 m) long stems. Rooted cuttings (not seeds) are available in spring — a wide variety of colours (**'Blue Vein'**, **'Purple Mini'**, **'Hot Pink'** etc) are available. This large-flowered group has become a firm favourite for planting in hanging baskets.

SITE & SOIL: Any well-drained soil will do, but sandy soil is preferred. Choose a sunny site.

PROPAGATION: Sow seeds in January-March. Not easy — germination temperature of 70°-75°F (21°-24°C) is required. Plant out in late May.

PETUNIA continued

Petunia hybrida 'Resisto Rose'

Petunia hybrida 'Frenzy Mixed'

Petunia hybrida 'Purple Wave'

Petunia hybrida 'Express Mixed'

Petunia hybrida 'Red Picotee'

Petunia hybrida 'Bouquet Mixed'

Petunia hybrida 'Fantasy Mixed'

Petunia hybrida 'Million Bells'

Petunia hybrida 'Surfinia White'

Hardy annual

PHACELIA Phacelia

Most plants have at least one characteristic which sets them apart from the other specimens which surround them in the bed or border — with the popular types of phacelia it is the intense blue of the flower. The upturned bells appear in midsummer above the greyish foliage — the bright yellow stamens stand out clearly against the gentian-coloured petals.

VARIETIES: The favourite type is **P. campanularia** (Californian Bluebell) — height 9 in. (22.5 cm), spacing 9 in. (22.5 cm), 1 in. (2.5 cm) wide flowers, flowering period June-September. The hybrid **P. 'Blue Bonnet'** grows about twice as tall and has the same bright blue flowers. Not all species have this intense colour — **P. tanacetifolia** (2¹/₂ ft/75 cm) bears lavender-blue bell-shaped flowers in curved racemes.

SITE & SOIL: Any well-drained soil will do — thrives in sun or light shade.

PROPAGATION: Sow seeds in April where they are to flower — thin to required spacing.

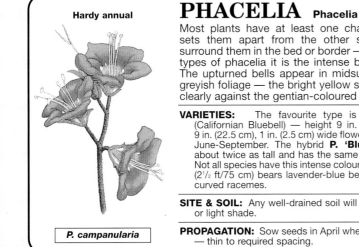

P. campanularia

Phacelia 'Blue Bonnet'

PHLOX Phlox

Prolific flowering is the hallmark of the border phlox and there are numerous dwarf varieties to provide carpets of white, pink, blue, lavender or red flowers in the rockery during early summer. In addition to these perennial types there are the annual varieties which are used as bedding plants.

VARIETIES: The popular border species is **P. paniculata** — height 2-4 ft (60 cm-1.2 m), 1 in. (2.5 cm) wide flowers, flowering period July-September. You will find many varieties on offer at the garden centre and in the catalogues — favourites include **'Brigadier'** (orange-red), **'Balmoral'** (rose-lavender), **'White Admiral'** (white), **'Starfire'** (red), **'Prince of Orange'** (orange) and **'Border Gem'** (violet). For extra colour there are **'Harlequin'** (purple plus variegated leaves) and **'Graf Zeppelin'** (red-eyed white). All these varieties bear their blooms in rounded clusters — for blooms in long columns grow **P. maculata** or one of its varieties such as **'Alpha'** (pink) or **'Omega'** (pink-eyed white). There are two popular dwarf species for the rockery — both **P. subulata** and **P. douglasii** have many named varieties (height 4-8 in./10-20 cm, spread 1¹/₂ ft/45 cm, ¹/₂ in./1 cm wide flowers). The annuals are varieties of **P. drummondii** — height 6 in.-1¹/₂ ft (15-45 cm), 4 in. (10 cm) wide tightly-packed flower heads, flowering period July-September. For a tall old-fashioned type look for **'Brilliant'** or **'Old Fashioned Mix'** — **'Tapestry'** is a modern tall variety with multicoloured blooms. Dwarfs (6-8 in./15-20 cm) are the usual choice — popular ones include **'Star Twinkles'** (star-shaped flowers), **'Beauty Mixed'** (large flowers) and **'Palona'** (rain-resistant flowers).

SITE & SOIL: Any well-drained, humus-rich soil will do — thrives best in full sun.

PROPAGATION: Perennials: Divide clumps in autumn or spring. Annuals: Sow seeds in February-March in gentle heat. Plant out in late May.

Phlox paniculata 'Harlequin'

Border perennial
•
Rockery perennial
•
Bedding plant:
half-hardy annual

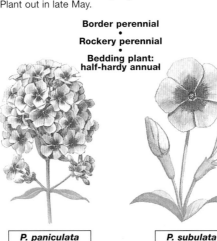

Phlox maculata

P. paniculata

P. subulata

Phlox drummondii 'Tapestry Mixed'

Border perennial

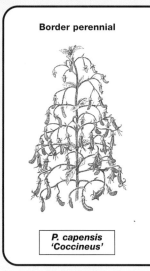

P. capensis
'Coccineus'

PHYGELIUS   Phygelius

In a mild area and against a south-facing wall this plant may be grown as an evergreen flowering shrub, but it is much more usual to treat it as a perennial, pruning it to ground level each April. The panicles of pendent tubular flowers provide an eye-catching feature in a mixed or herbaceous border.

VARIETIES: **P. capensis 'Coccineus'** (Cape Figwort) is the one to choose if you want a tall plant — height 3-5 ft (90 cm-1.5 m), 2 in. (5 cm) long yellow-throated red flowers, flowering period July-September. The blooms are borne all round the flower stalk — with **P. aequalis 'Yellow Trumpet'** (2-3 ft/60-90 cm) the all-yellow flowers are borne on one side of the stalk. The hybrid of the two species (**P. rectus**) has several varieties, such as **'Winchester Fanfare'** (pink) and **'Moonraker'** (yellow).

SITE & SOIL: Any well-drained soil will do — thrives in sun or light shade.

PROPAGATION: Plant cuttings in a cold frame in summer.

*Phygelius aequalis
'Yellow Trumpet'*

Border perennial

P. alkekengi
'Franchetii'

PHYSALIS   Chinese Lantern

The small white flowers have little decorative value, but the picture changes when autumn arrives and the leaves start to turn yellow. Large papery structures expand around the fruits, producing golden or red Chinese lanterns hanging from the stems. A novelty in the garden but much more useful as dried plant material. Cut the stems in September, tie in small bunches and hang upside down in a cool place away from direct sunlight.

VARIETIES: The usual one is **P. alkekengi 'Franchetii'** — height 2 ft (60 cm), 2 in. (5 cm) long inflated calyces (lanterns), flowering period July-August, fruiting period September-October. Varieties include **'Gigantea'** (large lanterns) and **'Variegata'** (yellow-marked foliage). Creeping underground stems make this plant invasive.

SITE & SOIL: Any reasonable soil will do — thrives in sun or partial shade.

PROPAGATION: Divide clumps in autumn or spring.

*Physalis alkekengi
'Franchetii'*

Border perennial

P. virginiana
'Vivid'

PHYSOSTEGIA   Obedient Plant

When the tubular flowers on the upright spikes are moved away from their natural position they stay in the position to which they have been pushed rather than springing back like other flowers — hence the common name. An easy plant to grow — add compost or peat when planting, water in dry weather and cut the stems down in autumn. Tall plants may require staking on an exposed site.

VARIETIES: **P. virginiana** is the only species you are likely to find — height 2-4 ft (60 cm-1.2 m), 1 in. (2.5 cm) long flowers, flowering period July-September. The white, pink or purple flowers are borne in vertical rows on each spike. Lift, divide and replant every three years. Popular varieties include **'Vivid'** (2 ft/60 cm, pink), **'Summer Snow'** (2 ft/60 cm, white) and **'Bouquet Rose'** (4 ft/1.2 m, lilac).

SITE & SOIL: Any well-drained soil will do — thrives in sun or partial shade.

PROPAGATION: Divide clumps in spring.

*Physostegia virginiana
'Summer Snow'*

PHYTOLACCA Pokeweed

Border perennial

This plant comes with a warning. It is grown for its foliage which turns red in autumn and its heads of shiny dark berries. These berries may look attractive to children, but they are extremely poisonous. The appearance of the plant is certainly not worth the risk — it is a coarse shrubby perennial which is more suited to the wild or woodland garden than the herbaceous border.

VARIETIES: **P. americana** is the usual pokeweed — height 4-8 ft (1.2-2.4 m), small white or pink flowers followed by purple-black berries, flowering period July-September. The fruit heads are up to 1 ft (30 cm) high — staking is necessary if the site is exposed. In some catalogues you will find a more compact alternative — **P. clavigera** grows 4 ft (1.2 m) high with red stems and yellow autumn leaves.

SITE & SOIL: Any moisture-retentive soil will do — thrives in sun or partial shade.

PROPAGATION: Divide clumps in spring.

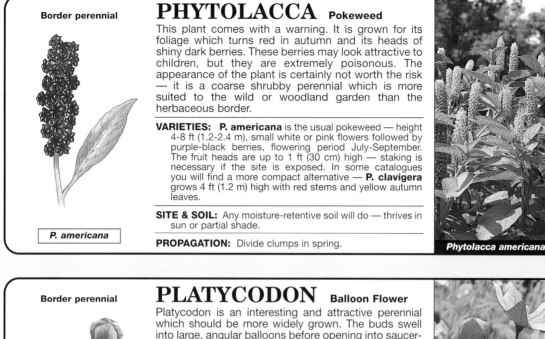

P. americana

Phytolacca americana

PLATYCODON Balloon Flower

Border perennial

Platycodon is an interesting and attractive perennial which should be more widely grown. The buds swell into large, angular balloons before opening into saucer-shaped flowers. It is not a difficult plant — light shade is tolerated and it will flourish in a wide range of soil types. Mulch around the young shoots in early summer and cut back in autumn. There is one problem — the top growth disappears in winter and does not reappear until late spring. Mark the position in late autumn.

VARIETIES: **P. grandiflorus** is the only species — height 1-2 ft (30-60 cm), 2 in. (5 cm) wide flowers, flowering period June-September. White and pink varieties are available but the favourite one is the compact blue **'Mariesii'** (1 ft/30 cm). Others include **'Mother of Pearl'** (pink), **'Albus'** (white) and **'Fuji Pink'** (pink).

SITE & SOIL: Any well-drained soil will do — thrives in sun or light shade.

PROPAGATION: Do not divide — sow seeds under glass in spring. Some varieties flower in the first year.

P. grandiflorus
'Mariesii'

*Platycodon grandiflorus
'Mariesii'*

PLUMBAGO Cape Leadwort

**Bedding plant:
tender perennial**

You would expect to find this tender climber in a book about conservatory plants and not in one dealing with outdoor flowers. It can, however, be used in the garden as an unusual dot plant in a summer bedding scheme or as a temporary specimen plant in a container. The straggly stems need support — the star-faced flowers are borne in large clusters.

VARIETIES: **P. capensis** is the garden species — height 4 ft (1.2 m), 1½ in. (3.5 cm) wide sky blue flowers, flowering period August-September. You can try growing it as an annual, sowing seeds under glass for planting out in June, but it is a much better plan to buy a plant in flower and harden off before planting outdoors. Lift and bring back indoors before the first frosts — trim shoots in spring before bedding out in June. **'Alba'** is a white variety.

SITE & SOIL: Any well-drained soil will do — full sun is essential.

PROPAGATION: Buy as a pot-grown specimen — plant out in June or July.

P. capensis

Plumbago capensis

Border perennial

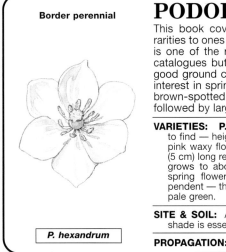

P. hexandrum

PODOPHYLLUM Podophyllum

This book covers the span of garden flowers from rarities to ones you will find in any street. Podophyllum is one of the rare plants — you will find it in some catalogues but not at the garden centre. It provides good ground cover in a shady site and also provides interest in spring and summer. The usual species has brown-spotted leaves and the spring flowers are followed by large fruits.

VARIETIES: **P. hexandrum** is the one you are most likely to find — height 1½ ft (45 cm), 2 in. (5 cm) wide white or pink waxy flowers, flowering period April-June. The 2 in. (5 cm) long red fruits are edible. **P. peltatum** (May Apple) grows to about the same height and the fragrant late spring flowers are similar to P. hexandrum but semi-pendent — the large leaves are palmate and the fruits are pale green.

SITE & SOIL: Any humus-rich soil will do — partial or full shade is essential.

PROPAGATION: Divide clumps in spring.

Podophyllum hexandrum

Border perennial

P. caeruleum

POLEMONIUM Jacob's Ladder

The bright blue flowers studded with golden stamens first appear in June — dead-head when they have faded to prolong the flowering season. The leaves are divided into a series of rung-like leaflets — hence the common name. It is not a long-lived plant but it presents no problems — add peat or compost at planting time, support if necessary and cut down in autumn.

VARIETIES: The old cottage-garden plant is **P. caeruleum** — height 2 ft (60 cm), ½ in. (1 cm) wide blue flowers, flowering period June-August. **'Album'** is a white variety and **'Brise d'Anjou'** is a variegated form grown for its foliage rather than its flowers. **P. foliosissimum** is taller (3 ft/90 cm) with violet, yellow or white flowers — for yellow tubular flowers choose **P. pauciflorum** (1½ ft/ 45 cm).

SITE & SOIL: Any well-drained moist soil will do — thrives in sun or partial shade.

PROPAGATION: Divide clumps in autumn or spring.

Polemonium foliosissimum

Rockery perennial

P. chamaebuxus
'Grandiflora'

POLYGALA Milkwort

The low-growing spreading plants are covered in late spring and early summer with colourful pea-like flowers. The species described below are hardy, but these plants are more likely to be found in specialist catalogues than the garden centre, despite their attractive appearance and evergreen growth habit. Perhaps the blooms are too small for popular appeal, but they are borne in large numbers.

VARIETIES: **P. calcarea** is a creeping plant which forms a mat of leathery leaves — height 2 in. (5 cm), spread 9 in. (22.5 cm), ¼ in. (0.5 cm) wide blue flowers, flowering period May-June. This species thrives in gritty soil and full sun — for moist soil and partial shade **P. chamaebuxus 'Grandiflora'** is more suitable and more brightly coloured with yellow-lipped purple flowers in late spring and early summer. This 3 in. (7.5 cm) high leafy plant is really a sub-shrub rather than a hardy perennial.

SITE & SOIL: Depends on the species — see above.

PROPAGATION: Plant cuttings in a cold frame in early summer.

Polygala calcarea

Border perennial

| P. hybridum |

POLYGONATUM Solomon's Seal

Finding plants which will grow under trees or in the heavy shade cast by large shrubs can be a problem, but Polygonatum thrives in these situations. The leaves clasp the arching stems, providing a decorative effect even before the bell-like flowers appear in early summer. Add compost or peat at planting time, mulch in spring, water in dry weather and cut down stems in autumn. Watch for sawfly.

VARIETIES: **P. hybridum** is the usual one — height 2-3 ft (60-90 cm), spacing 2 ft (60 cm), 1 in. (2.5 cm) long green-tipped white flowers, flowering period May-June. The variety **'Striatum'** has cream-striped leaves. For tall plants reaching 4 ft (1.2 m) or more look for **P. biflorum** — for compact growth and cream-edged leaves choose **P. odoratum 'Variegatum'**. **P. hookeri** has pink open-faced blooms.

SITE & SOIL: Any moisture-retentive soil will do — thrives best in shade.

PROPAGATION: Divide clumps in autumn or spring.

Polygonatum hybridum

POLYGONUM Knotweed

The knotweeds are a large and varied group containing both weeds and garden plants. The garden varieties are mainly vigorous ground covers which can spread and become a nuisance if not kept in check. There is a place for these types between shrubs in the mixed border and in the bog garden, but they can be a menace in the average-sized rockery. There are restrained low-growing types for this situation and there is also a rather tender species which is used as a bedding plant. Knotweeds bear tiny flowers in white, pink or red on upright stalks which appear in spring, summer or autumn depending on the variety.

VARIETIES: Polygonum is often listed as Persicaria. The best-known species is **P. affine** — height 1 ft (30 cm), spread 2 ft (60 cm) or more, 2-3 in. (5-7.5 cm) long pink flower spikes, flowering period July-September. The leaves turn yellow or bronze as the flowers fade in autumn — the popular varieties are **'Darjeeling Red'** and **'Donald Lowndes'**. **P. amplexicaule** is a taller (3 ft/90 cm) border species with red-flowering varieties such as **'Firetail'** and **'Atrosanguineum'**. Perhaps the most attractive border knotweed is the non-invasive **P. campanulatum** (3 ft/90 cm) which bears pink flowers in loose sprays. The variety which is usually recommended for the bog garden is **P. bistorta 'Superbum'** — height 3 ft (90 cm), tall pokers of pink flowers, flowering period July-September. **P. vaccinifolium** is the common rock garden type — height 4 in. (10 cm), spread 2 ft (60 cm), flowering period September-December. For something less spreading grow the spring-flowering **P. tenuicaule**. The species grown as a bedding plant is **P. capitatum** — height 6 in. (15 cm), spherical pink flower heads, flowering period June-August. Plant out rooted cuttings in May.

SITE & SOIL: Any moisture-retentive soil will do — thrives in sun or partial shade.

PROPAGATION: Divide clumps in autumn or spring.

Polygonum bistorta 'Superbum'

Polygonum vaccinifolium

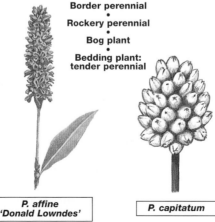

Border perennial
•
Rockery perennial
•
Bog plant
•
Bedding plant: tender perennial

| P. affine 'Donald Lowndes' | | P. capitatum |

Polygonum capitatum

PORTULACA Sun Plant

P. grandiflora

A sandy bank in full sun is not easy to keep clothed in colour all summer long if the weather is dry — Portulaca is one of the few satisfactory plants for such a site. The ground-hugging reddish stems bear fleshy leaves which in summer can be almost totally covered by the saucer-shaped flowers. These blooms are often ruffled and the petals have a silky sheen.

Bedding plant: half-hardy annual

VARIETIES: **P. grandiflora** is the popular species — height 6 in. (15 cm), 1 in. (2.5 cm) wide semi-double flowers, flowering period June-September. **'Double Mixed'** has rose-like blooms — **'Calypso'** is an F_2 hybrid with blooms in many colours on 6-8 in. (15-20 cm) high plants with a 1 ft (30 cm) spread. **'Sundial'** provides many pastel shades and **'Sundance'** claims to stay open when the sun isn't shining.

SITE & SOIL: Well-drained light soil and full sun are essential.

PROPAGATION: Sow seeds in February-March in gentle heat. Plant out in late May.

Portulaca grandiflora 'Double Mixed'

POTENTILLA Cinquefoil

P. 'Gibson's Scarlet'

Border perennial

The border Potentillas are not as popular as the woody ones which are such a common sight in the shrub or mixed border. Both types have small leaves with bright flowers all summer long, but the border varieties do not form neat clumps like their woody relatives — they have weak stems which need support. Water in dry weather and cut down the stems in autumn.

VARIETIES: The garden hybrids have been developed from **P. nepalensis**, **P. atrosanguinea** and **P. argyrophylla** — height 1-2 ft (30-60 cm), 1 in. (2.5 cm) wide saucer-shaped flowers, flowering period June-August. Examples include **'Gibson's Scarlet'** (red), **'William Rollison'** (semi-double, orange) and **'Etna'** (dark red). **P. nepalensis 'Miss Willmott'** (pink) is widely available and so is **P. tonguei** (8 in./20 cm, apricot).

SITE & SOIL: Any well-drained soil will do — thrives best in full sun.

PROPAGATION: Divide clumps in autumn or spring.

Potentilla 'William Rollison'

A bed of Narcissi in full bloom provides a welcome splash of colour, but when the flowers fade the bed can become an eyesore. You cannot cut off the leaves nor lift and store the bulbs at this stage as continued leaf growth is necessary to build up next year's bulbs. The only way to clear the bed is to lift the bulbs with roots and surrounding soil intact and replant in an out-of-the-way spot until the leaves have turned completely brown. Lift the bulbs and store until the autumn.

PRIMULA Primula

Primulas make up a vast genus of garden plants — there are tender ones for indoors, the popular primrose/ polyanthus group, the old-fashioned auriculas, moisture-loving varieties for the bog garden, numerous sorts which are suitable for the border and miniature types for the rockery. Keen collectors divide primulas into more than thirty groups, but only four need concern us here. The *Primrose/Polyanthus Group* have the European Primrose as a parent — crosses with P. juliae have given rise to many named colourful primrose varieties, and crosses with the Cowslip have given rise to the much more popular polyanthus varieties (P. variabilis). The *Auricula Group* are made up of evergreens with fleshy leaves and flowers which usually bear several coloured rings. The foliage may be covered with a mealy deposit. The *Bog/Border Group* contain many larger species with 1-3 ft (30-90 cm) high stems and 4-8 in. (10-20 cm) long leaves — some but not all require boggy soil. Finally there are the *Rockery Group* — clump-forming alpines which grow to 6 in. (15 cm) or less. The dividing line between these groups is not clear-cut — some so-called rockery varieties are suitable for the front of the border and some bog primulas are quite at home in a peaty flower bed. As a general rule all the primulas thrive best in partial shade and in soil which is rich in humus. Some can be grown from seed and all tend to be short-lived. Mulch in spring, water in summer, and dead-head faded blooms.

VARIETIES: The Common Primrose (**P. vulgaris**) has a place in the cottage garden, its yellow flowers appearing on 6 in. (15 cm) stems in March and April. Colourful hybrids include **'Finesse'** (white- or gold-edged mixed colours) and **'Captain Blood'** (double red). **'Husky'** and **'Wanda'** are evergreen but primroses are generally less winter hardy than the taller and showier polyanthus varieties (**P. variabilis**) — height 8 in.-1 ft (20-30 cm), 1-2 in. (2.5-5 cm) wide flowers borne in clusters, flowering period March-May. The **'Pacific Giants'** have the largest flowers but are not fully winter-hardy. For maximum winter reliability and a wide colour range choose either the **'Crescendo'** or **'Rainbow'** strain. **'Gold Lace'** has yellow-edged, golden-eyed red blooms.

The many varieties of **P. auricula** offer a bewildering range of colours on short-stalked plants — height 6 in. (15 cm), spread 6 in. (15 cm), flowering period March-April. Varieties include **'Old Yellow Dusty Miller'** (yellow), **'McWatt's Blue'** (grey-blue) and **'Old Suffolk Bronze'** (red/brown/yellow).

Most of the species and varieties of the Bog/Border Group are Candelabra Primroses — the flowers are borne as a series of whorls up the stem. **P. japonica** is noted for its reliability — height 1¹/₂ ft (45 cm), flowering period May-July. Varieties include **'Miller's Crimson'** and **'Postford White'**. There are other candelabra types which bloom in June-July such as **P. pulverulenta** (2-3 ft/60-90 cm, red), **P. bulleyana** (2-3 ft/60-90 cm, gold) and **P. beesiana** (2 ft/60 cm, yellow-eyed lilac). **P. denticulata** has small lilac or pink flowers crowded into 3 in. (7.5 cm) wide globular heads — hence the common name Drumstick Primrose. **P. florindae** (height 2 ft/ 60 cm, flowering period July-August) is the Giant Yellow Cowslip, each stem bearing a head of pendent yellow flowers. **P. vialii** is an unusual species — the flower spikes are red on top and lavender below. **P. veris** (Cowslip) carries its yellow flowers on one side of the stalk and can be naturalised in grassland.

Finally there are a number of alpine species for the rockery. **P. marginata** is a small plant (height 4 in./15 cm, spread 6 in./15 cm) which blooms in early April — clusters of sweet-smelling blue or lavender flowers above mealy leaves. **P. pubescens** grows 4-6 in. (10-15 cm) high and has numerous spring-flowering varieties including **'Harlow Car'** (cream), **'Faldonside'** (white-eyed pink) and **'Mrs. Wilson'** (white-eyed pink). The baby is **P. minima** — height 2 in. (5 cm), flowering period April-May.

Bedding plant: hardy annual
•
Border perennial
•
Bog plant
•
Rockery perennial

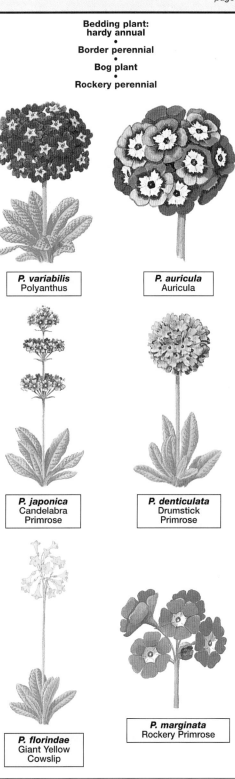

P. variabilis
Polyanthus

P. auricula
Auricula

P. japonica
Candelabra
Primrose

P. denticulata
Drumstick
Primrose

P. florindae
Giant Yellow
Cowslip

P. marginata
Rockery Primrose

SITE & SOIL: Well-drained, humus-rich soil in light shade is the usual requirement, but there are exceptions.

PROPAGATION: Sow seeds in March under glass or divide clumps of named varieties in spring.

PRIMULA continued

Primula vulgaris

Primula 'Wanda'

Primula variabilis 'Pacific Giants'

**Primula auricula
'Old Yellow Dusty Miller'**

Primula japonica

Primula bulleyana

Primula denticulata

Primula vialii

Primula marginata

Border perennial
•
Rockery perennial

P. grandiflora

PRUNELLA   Self-heal

Self-heal is a mat-forming evergreen ground cover for growing between shrubs or over large bare spaces in the rockery. It is not often seen but it does provide an effective way of keeping down weeds. The foliage is dark green and in midsummer the flower spikes appear, each one bearing a cluster of tubular hooded flowers. There are no problems involved in its cultivation but it can be invasive — lift, divide and replant the clumps every two or three years.

VARIETIES: You can buy the wild flower **P. vulgaris** but it is better to grow **P. grandiflora** — height 9 in. (22.5 cm), 1 in. (2.5 cm) long dark-lipped pale purple flowers, flowering period June-July. There are a number of varieties in other colours such as **'Loveliness'** (mauve), **'Pink Loveliness'**, **'White Loveliness'** and **'Rosea'** (rose-pink).

SITE & SOIL: Any reasonable soil will do — thrives best in light shade.

PROPAGATION: Divide clumps in autumn or spring.

Prunella grandiflora

Border perennial

P. angustifolia

PULMONARIA   Lungwort

Lungwort is an old favourite. The white-spotted leaves provide ground cover and the flowers change from pink to blue as they open. Not all varieties follow this pattern — the brightest-flowered ones have all-green foliage and some produce blooms in other colours. It revels in shade and spreads rapidly — if space is restricted you will have to lift and divide every few years. Cut back in autumn.

VARIETIES: The cottage garden lungwort is **P. officinalis** — height 1 ft (30 cm), ³⁄₄ in. (1.5 cm) tubular flowers, flowering period April-May. The leaves are splashed with silver and the flowers are blue when mature — **'Sissinghurst White'** is a white variety. **P. saccharata** is a popular evergreen — look for **'Mrs. Moon'** (pink) and **'Fruhlingshimmel'** (blue). For large red flowers grow **P. rubra 'Redstart'**. **P. angustifolia** has all-green foliage.

SITE & SOIL: Any reasonable soil will do — thrives best in partial shade.

PROPAGATION: Divide clumps in autumn or spring.

Pulmonaria saccharata

Rockery perennial

P. vernalis

PULSATILLA   Pasque Flower

The Pasque Flower is one of the gems of the rockery. In spring the flower stems push up through the earth, each one crowned by a silky bud. The buds open into cup-shaped and later starry flowers. The blooms are followed by the emergence of the ferny foliage and the attractive silky seed heads. It is an easy plant to grow if the site is sunny. Plant Pulsatilla very firmly.

VARIETIES: **P. vulgaris** is the species which is usually seen — height 9 in. (22.5 cm), spread 1 ft (30 cm), 3 in. (7.5 cm) wide pale purple flowers, flowering period April-May. You can buy varieties in other colours such as **'Alba'** (white) and **'Rubra'** (red). **P. vernalis** is even more attractive with pearly white flowers which are flushed purple on the outside, but it needs winter protection. **P. alpina 'Apiifolia'** has yellow bell-shaped flowers.

SITE & SOIL: Well-drained soil and a sunny site are necessary. P. vulgaris and P. vernalis need alkaline soil.

PROPAGATION: Sow seeds in summer under glass.

Pulsatilla vulgaris

Bulb

P. scilloides

PUSCHKINIA Striped Squill

It is surprising that this bulb is not more popular — it remains a poor relation of the bluebells although it is an excellent out-of-the-ordinary alternative. Puschkinia is completely hardy and trouble-free — the attractive starry flowers appear early in the year and the bulbs increase quite quickly to form large clumps. Unlike the bluebell each flower has a small fused tube at the base.

VARIETIES: The species grown as a garden plant is **P. scilloides** (**P. libanotica**) — height 4 in. (10 cm), ½ in. (1 cm) wide flowers, flowering period March-April. Each stem carries 6-12 flowers and each petal is pale silvery blue with a central dark blue stripe. Use it for edging beds or borders, filling small containers or planting in the rock garden — plant 2 in. (5 cm) deep in September-October. **'Alba'** is a white variety.

SITE & SOIL: Any well-drained soil will do — thrives in sun or light shade.

PROPAGATION: Divide clumps in summer — replant at once.

Puschkinia scilloides 'Alba'

Rockery perennial

R. myconi

RAMONDA Ramonda

Ramonda looks appealing in the photographs — large colourful blooms with a central boss of bright orange stamens above a rosette of dark green leaves. Unfortunately it is not an easy plant to grow — it cannot tolerate water standing in the crown in winter and so it is necessary to plant it sideways between stones on the north side of a rockery.

VARIETIES: **R. myconi** is the most popular species — height 5 in. (12.5 cm), spread 9 in. (22.5 cm), 1½ in. (3.5 cm) wide pale purple flowers, flowering period April-May. The oval leaves are rough and crinkled. Varieties such as **'Alba'** (white) and **'Rosea'** (pink) are available but you will have to search to find one. **R. nathaliae** is similar to R. myconi but more compact (4 in. x 4 in./10 cm x 10 cm). The rarest species is **R. serbica** which has purple rather than yellow stamens.

SITE & SOIL: Requires well-drained but damp soil with little or no sun.

PROPAGATION: Divide clumps in autumn.

Ramonda myconi

Many herbaceous borders are spoilt by poor staking — plants are tied too tightly to single canes. The golden rule is to start staking before the need is obvious and to use twigs or brushwood rather than canes wherever possible. Papaver orientalis is a notoriously floppy plant, but it is securely held here by a ring of woody prunings cut from a nearby shrub. For further information on staking see Chapter 4.

RANUNCULUS
Ranunculus, Buttercup

Ranunculus is unique because it is the only genus which you can find in every part of the garden. There are the *Persian Buttercups* which are grown for their bright summer display of semi-double or ball-shaped double blooms. These are grown by planting the tuberous roots claws downwards 1 in. (2.5 cm) deep in a well-drained sunny site in March-April — store the 'tubers' in dry peat over winter. These Persian Buttercups are also available in spring as seed-raised plants ready for bedding out. The *Border Buttercups* are hardy perennials which are taller but with flowers which are smaller and less colourful. They require moist soil and will thrive in sun or partial shade. Bachelor's Buttons is the old favourite — the stems bear masses of small double flowers in summer. There are a number of *Dwarf Buttercups* for the rock garden, but you should choose with care. Some are hard to grow outdoors but at the other end of the scale are the Lesser Celandine varieties which can spread rapidly. These dwarfs need full sun and hate poor drainage, but in contrast there are the *Water Buttercups* which grow in the boggy ground or shallow water around the pool. Finally there are the *Weed Buttercups* which invade the lawn.

Bulb
•
Border perennial
•
Rockery perennial
•
Bog plant

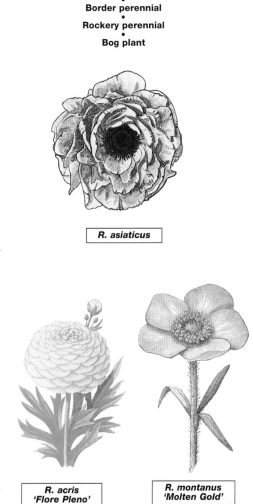

R. asiaticus

VARIETIES: The Persian Buttercups are varieties of **R. asiaticus** — height 9 in.-1 ft (22.5-30 cm), 3-5 in. (7.5-12.5 cm) wide flowers. The plants offered for sale in bloom in April-May are nearly always the **'Accolade'** strain. Plants raised in the garden from spring-planted tuberous roots will bloom in July-August. There are two Border Buttercups to consider. **R. aconitifolius** is commonly called White Bachelor's Buttons — height 2 ft (60 cm), ½ in. (1 cm) wide cup-shaped flowers, flowering period May-July. Look for the variety **'Flore Pleno'** which is taller (3 ft/90 cm) and bears double flowers. The other Border Buttercup is the double-flowered Yellow Bachelor's Buttons **R. acris 'Flore Pleno'** — height 3 ft (90 cm), flowering period June-August. **R. ficaria** (Lesser Celandine) is the most popular Dwarf Ranunculus — height 2-8 in. (5-20 cm), ¾ in. (1.5 cm) wide shiny yellow flowers, flowering period March-April. Varieties to look for include **'Flore Pleno'** (double yellow), **'E.A. Bowles'** (yellow), **'Aurantiacus'** (orange) and **'Brazen Hussy'** (yellow flowers, purple-brown foliage). **R. montanus 'Molten Gold'** (4 in./10 cm) bears yellow flowers in spring — for white flowers in January grow **R. calandrinioides** (6 in./15 cm). **R. crenatus** (3 in./7.5 cm) is white — **R. gramineus** is a 1 ft (30 cm) summer-flowering yellow. For the edge of the pond there is the Great Spearwort **R. lingua 'Grandiflorus'** — height 2½ ft (75 cm), 2 in. (5 cm) wide yellow flowers, flowering period June-September.

**R. acris
'Flore Pleno'**

**R. montanus
'Molten Gold'**

SITE & SOIL: Depends upon the species — see above.

PROPAGATION: Sow seeds under glass in spring or divide clumps in autumn.

**Ranunculus asiaticus
'Accolade Mixed'**

**Ranunculus aconitifolius
'Flore Pleno'**

Ranunculus calandrinioides

Rockery perennial

R. australis

RAOULIA Scabweed

Raoulia is a true carpeting plant with a pile which is no higher than 1/2 in. (1 cm) when in full flower. The tiny leaves and tiny blooms hug the surface over which the living mat has spread — an effective cover for ground in which dwarf bulbs have been planted. Unfortunately this plant from New Zealand is never fully at home in our climate. A very hard winter can be fatal, and if possible a pane of glass should be supported over the plant from late autumn until spring to keep off winter rain.

VARIETIES: The best-known variety is **R. australis** — height 1/2 in. (1 cm), spread 1 ft (30 cm), 1/4 in. (0.5 cm) wide yellow flowers, flowering period May. It is grown mainly for the tiny grey-green leaves. Look for plants sold as **R. lutescens** or **R. australis 'Hooker Group'** for the best floral display — bright yellow flowers cover the surface from April to June.

SITE & SOIL: Requires well-drained gritty soil in full sun.

PROPAGATION: Divide the mats in autumn.

Raoulia lutescens

Hardy annual

R. odorata

RESEDA Mignonette

A great Victorian favourite which has lost its popularity. One reason is that it dislikes transplanting and so requires being sown where it is to flower. Its other drawback is its appearance — untidy stems bearing clusters of tiny greenish flowers. The main appeal, however, remains — grow it under a window or near a door and the evening air will be filled with fragrance. The flowering season is short in a hot and dry summer.

VARIETIES: **R. odorata** is the only species offered — height 1 ft (30 cm), 1/4 in. (0.5 cm) wide flowers borne in cone-like trusses, flowering period July-August. **'Machet'** (red-tinged greenish-yellow) is the traditional favourite — others include **'Goliath'** (red) and **'Red Monarch'** (red and green). It is better to choose a variety for maximum scent rather than its colour — pick **'Sweet Scented'** or **'Giant'**.

SITE & SOIL: Any reasonable non-acid soil will do — thrives in sun or light shade.

PROPAGATION: Sow seeds in April where they are to flower.

Reseda odorata

Bog plant
•
Border perennial

R. palmatum
'Atrosanguineum'

RHEUM Ornamental Rhubarb

Rheum has two basic requirements — moist soil and space. It is a favourite poolside plant where it thrives in the boggy ground, but it will grow under drier conditions than its usual companion Gunnera and it can be planted in a humus-rich border. It also needs plenty of space as the large and wide-spreading leaves can cover 6 ft (1.8 m) or more. In early summer plumes of tiny flowers appear on stout stems.

VARIETIES: **R. palmatum** is the most popular species — height 6 ft (1.8 m), spread 6 ft (1.8 m), tiny greenish or pink flowers, flowering period May-June. The varieties **'Atrosanguineum'** and **'Bowles' Crimson'** are more colourful — the leaves are purplish-red when young and the flowers are crimson. Use it as a specimen plant as little will grow under its leaves — plant **R. 'Ace of Hearts'** (3 ft/90 cm) where space is limited.

SITE & SOIL: Moist soil is essential — thrives in sun or light shade.

PROPAGATION: Divide crowns in spring.

Rheum palmatum

RHODOHYPOXIS
Rhodohypoxis

Rockery perennial

The attractive flower form and the exceptional length of the flowering season make Rhodohypoxis an excellent subject for a pot, sink garden or a tiny pocket in the rockery. Unfortunately this South African alpine has none of the robust hardiness of some plants from the European Alps — it is an alpine for a sheltered spot in a mild area. Top dress around the crown with grit.

VARIETIES: The named plants are varieties or hybrids of **R. baurii**, **R. deflexa** or **R. milloides** — height 2-6 in. (5-15 cm), ³/₄ in. (1.5 cm) wide white, pink, red or purple flowers, flowering period June-September. Examples include **'Ruth'** (white), **'Fred Broome'** (pink) and **'Picta'** (pink-edged white). Plant tubers 2 in. (5 cm) deep in April. The flowers are unusual — there is an outer ring of three petals and an inner ring of three petals.

SITE & SOIL: Requires well-drained, lime-free gritty soil — full sun is essential.

PROPAGATION: Divide clumps in autumn.

R. baurii

Rhodohypoxis milloides 'Picta'

RODGERSIA   Rodgersia

Bog plant
•
Border perennial

Like Rheum this is a plant for the bog garden or moist border where the decorative leaves and plumes of tiny flowers can provide a focal point. The finger-like leaflets radiate from the long stalks and the petal-less flowers form fluffy heads in summer. Add plenty of compost, leaf mould or peat at planting time and mulch around the leaves in spring. Water in dry weather and cut back in autumn.

VARIETIES: The usual choice where space is limited is **R. pinnata 'Superba'** — height 3-4 ft (90 cm-1.2 m), spread 4 ft (1.2 m), ¹/₄ in. (0.5 cm) wide pink flowers, flowering period July-August. **R. aesculifolia** is larger (6 ft x 6 ft/ 1.8 m x 1.8 m) with large Horse Chestnut-like leaves displaying a metallic bronzy sheen and plumes of white flowers. **R. podophylla** needs less moisture than the other species but the floral display is disappointing.

SITE & SOIL: Any moisture-retentive soil will do — thrives best in partial shade.

PROPAGATION: Divide clumps in autumn or spring.

R. aesculifolia

Rodgersia pinnata 'Superba'

ROMULEA   Romulea

Bulb

This crocus-like plant is a rarity — searching the catalogues for it is only worthwhile if you like a challenge and enjoy growing things that your neighbour won't recognise. The yellow-throated pale purple flowers are attractive but can be easily mistaken for an ordinary crocus. Protect the crowns with peat or leaf mould in winter and provide some protection against heavy spring rain.

VARIETIES: The hardy species in the catalogues is **R. bulbocodium** (**Crocus bulbocodium**) — height 3 in. (7.5 cm), 1 in. (2.5 cm) long funnel-shaped flowers, flowering period June-September. The flowers open wide when the sun is shining and close up when it is dull — the backs of the petals are veined and streaked with purple and the leaves are long and narrow. Plant the corms 2 in. (5 cm) deep in autumn.

SITE & SOIL: Well-drained sandy soil in full sun is necessary.

PROPAGATION: Divide overcrowded clumps in late summer.

R. bulbocodium

Romulea bulbocodium

ROSCOEA Roscoea

Bulb

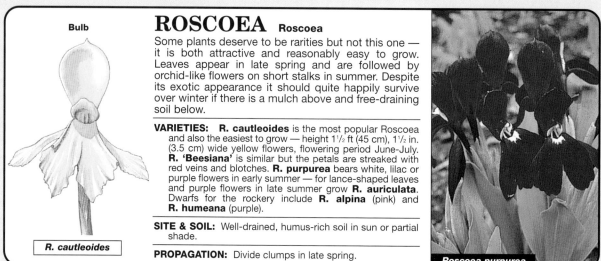

R. cautleoides

Roscoea purpurea

Some plants deserve to be rarities but not this one — it is both attractive and reasonably easy to grow. Leaves appear in late spring and are followed by orchid-like flowers on short stalks in summer. Despite its exotic appearance it should quite happily survive over winter if there is a mulch above and free-draining soil below.

VARIETIES: **R. cautleoides** is the most popular Roscoea and also the easiest to grow — height 1½ ft (45 cm), 1½ in. (3.5 cm) wide yellow flowers, flowering period June-July. **R. 'Beesiana'** is similar but the petals are streaked with red veins and blotches. **R. purpurea** bears white, lilac or purple flowers in early summer — for lance-shaped leaves and purple flowers in late summer grow **R. auriculata**. Dwarfs for the rockery include **R. alpina** (pink) and **R. humeana** (purple).

SITE & SOIL: Well-drained, humus-rich soil in sun or partial shade.

PROPAGATION: Divide clumps in late spring.

RUDBECKIA Cone Flower

There are perennial and annual types — both are valuable for adding colour to beds and borders in late summer and autumn. This colour range is limited to yellow, orange and mahogany red, but the flowers are large and plentiful. The key feature of these blooms is the prominent cone-shaped disc at the centre —usually but not always brown or near black. The range of varieties has been greatly extended in recent years — there are now dwarfs and double-flowered ones as well as the old-fashioned tall single-flowered varieties.

VARIETIES: The favourite border species is **R. fulgida** — height 2-3 ft (60-90 cm), spacing 2 ft (60 cm), dark-centred yellow flowers, flowering period July-October. **'Goldsturm'** (2 ft/60 cm, 5 in./12.5 cm wide flowers) has taken over from **'Speciosa'** as the most popular variety — other perennial Rudbeckias to look out for include **R. 'Herbstsonne'** (6 ft/1.8 m, single flowers) and **R. laciniata 'Hortensia'** (6 ft/1.8 m, double flowers) for the back of the border. For the middle of the border there is the more compact **R. 'Goldquelle'** (2½ ft/75 cm, double flowers). Curiosities include **R. occidentalis 'Green Wizard'** which has green sepals instead of yellow petals around the black cone. The annuals are varieties or hybrids of **R. hirta** — flowering period August-October. The giant variety is **'Gloriosa Daisy'** — height 2½-3 ft (75-90 cm), 6-7 in. (15-17.5 cm) wide flowers. **'Marmalade'** (2 ft/60 cm) has orange petals and a purple-black cone — **'Irish Eyes'** has a green cone. **'Rustic Dwarfs'** is a multicoloured mixture of single blooms — **'Goldilocks'** bears semi-double and double flowers. The dwarfs (8 in.-1 ft/20-30 cm) include **'Becky'**, **'Sonora'** and **'Toto'**.

SITE & SOIL: Any well-drained soil will do — thrives in sun or light shade.

PROPAGATION: Perennials: Divide clumps in autumn or spring. Annuals: Sow seeds in February-March in gentle heat — plant out in mid-late May.

Rudbeckia fulgida 'Goldsturm'

Border perennial
•
Bedding plant:
half-hardy annual

Rudbeckia 'Goldquelle'

R. fulgida

R. 'Marmalade'

Rudbeckia 'Gloriosa Daisy'

Border perennial

R. graveolens

RUTA Rue

This woody-based herbaceous perennial grows as a rounded bush. It was once widely cultivated for its medicinal properties but now its place in the garden is in the border or planted as a low hedge. It is grown for its evergreen foliage rather than its floral display. If you decide to grow rue in your garden then wear gloves when handling the leaves — the sap can cause a severe and long-lasting rash.

VARIETIES: **R. graveolens** is the only species you are likely to find — height 2-3 ft (60-90 cm), ³/₄ in. (1.5 cm) wide greenish-yellow flowers, flowering period June-July. The aromatic leaves are deeply divided which gives a filigree effect of small blue-green lobes. A variety is usually chosen rather than the species — there are **'Jackman's Blue'** (steely blue leaves) and **'Variegata'** (cream-blotched leaves).

SITE & SOIL: Any well-drained soil will do — thrives in sun or partial shade.

PROPAGATION: Plant cuttings in a cold frame in summer.

Ruta graveolens 'Jackman's Blue'

Rockery perennial

S. subulata 'Aurea'

SAGINA Pearlwort

Pearlwort is well known as a lawn weed but its cultivated cousins are much less familiar. None of these lowly rockery perennials is easy to find in the catalogues — the only one you are likely to obtain is Golden Pearlwort and even this one has a restricted use in the garden. It is sometimes planted as a lawn substitute in small areas where grass will not grow, but its more usual role is as a space filler between paving stones. Here it provides an evergreen strip between the stones plus a mass of tiny white flowers in summer.

VARIETIES: The only cultivated pearlwort with a worthwhile floral display is the Golden Pearlwort **S. subulata 'Aurea'** — height ¹/₂ in. (1 cm), spread 1 ft (30 cm), white flowers, flowering period June-July. The prostrate stems bear ¹/₂ in. (1 cm) long linear yellowish-green leaves.

SITE & SOIL: Any well-drained, non-alkaline soil will do — thrives in partial shade.

PROPAGATION: Divide mats in spring.

Sagina subulata 'Aurea'

**Bedding plant:
half-hardy annual**

S. sinuata

SALPIGLOSSIS Painted Tongue

Eye-catching is the word. The velvety, funnel-shaped flowers are prominently veined — yellow on red, red on yellow, gold on purple etc, which makes this plant one of the most exotic of all annuals. Pinch out the tips of young plants to induce bushiness — support stems with twigs. Salpiglossis is rather tender — do not grow on an exposed site.

VARIETIES: **S. sinuata** is the garden species and the recommended variety is **'Casino'** — height 1¹/₂ ft (45 cm), 2 in. (5 cm) wide flowers, flowering period July-September. The bushy plants bear a host of flowers — **'Bolero'** is rather taller (2 ft/60 cm) but produces fewer flowers. The tallest plants and the widest flowers are produced by **'Grandiflora'** — for 1 ft (30 cm) dwarfs choose **'Festival'** or **'Flamenco'**.

SITE & SOIL: Well-drained soil and a sunny, sheltered site are essential.

PROPAGATION: Sow seeds in January-February in gentle heat. Plant out in late May.

Salpiglossis sinuata

SALVIA Sage

There are several types of Salvia — looking at the garden next door you may find annuals in the beds, both evergreen and deciduous hardy perennials in the border and leafy herbs in the vegetable garden. The most popular annual is the Scarlet Sage which can be seen in any street during the summer months. Its favourite use has been to provide the red in red, white and blue bedding schemes where the cost of geraniums is felt to be prohibitive. The fiery red of the upright spikes is regarded as too vivid by some purists, but it is in the top ten list of bedding plants. Pinch out the tips of seedlings to induce bushiness and plant out when the buds have started to colour. Red is not the only colour and there are other species. S. coccinea is grown for its pink or red flowers — S. horminum is grown for its coloured bracts and is treated as a hardy annual or raised by the half-hardy annual technique like Scarlet Sage. There is also a blue annual Salvia which should be more widely grown — S. farinacea produces long-lasting displays of whorled flowers on erect spikes.

The herbaceous perennial Salvias are less well known than the annuals but are no less valuable in the garden. The hooded tubular flowers which are usually blue or lavender are borne on slender spikes above the grey-green leaves — both butterflies and bees find these blooms particularly attractive. They are easy to grow provided the soil is well-drained, and there is no need to lift and divide the clumps every few years. The spikes of the taller varieties may need staking on exposed sites and after flowering the faded heads should be removed.

The evergreen types with aromatic leaves (Common Sage and its varieties) are not dealt with here as they are grown for the ornamental or culinary value of their foliage and not for the lilac flowers which appear in summer.

VARIETIES: **S. splendens** is the popular Scarlet Sage — height 1-1½ ft (30-45 cm), 1 in. (2.5 cm) long tubular bright red flowers with red bracts, flowering period June-October. The bright red **'Blaze of Fire'** was once the only variety you could find, but not any more. The types with dark green leaves and red flowers have become popular — look for **'Red Arrow'**, **'Vanguard'**, **'Red Riches'**, **'Rambo'** and **'Maestro'**. **'Tom Thumb'** is a 6 in. (15 cm) dwarf. Red is not the only colour — you can buy **'Laser Purple'** or a salmon, pink, cream, lilac and red mixture such as **'Phoenix'**, **'Dress Parade'** and **'Sizzler'**. The red shades need full sun but partial shade is better for the pastel mixtures. **S. coccinea** has two excellent varieties — **'Coral Nymph'** (1½ ft/45 cm, coral pink) and **'Lady in Red'** (1 ft/30 cm, scarlet). **S. horminum** (Annual Clary) is a bushy plant (1½ ft/ 45 cm) grown for its stalks of colourful bracts which can be dried for flower arranging — varieties include **'Pink Lady'** (pink) and **'Blue Beard'** (purple) but for the largest, most colourful bracts grow **'Claryssa'**. **S. farinacea** grows about 2 ft (60 cm) tall — some catalogues list **'Victoria'** which bears spikes of blue-purple flowers on blue stalks, but the eye-catching one is **'Strata'** with deep blue petals and silvery sepals. The biennial Clary (**S. sclarea**) is a cottage garden plant (3 ft/90 cm) with tall spikes and pale flowers.

The species of border perennial you are most likely to find is **S. nemorosa 'East Friesland'** — height 1½ ft (45 cm), ½ in. (1 cm) long blue-violet flowers, flowering period July-August. **S. sylvestris** is taller (2½ ft/75 cm) and blooms earlier — look for the variety **'May Night'** which flowers in May and June. **S. pratensis** (Meadow Clary) is another Salvia worth looking for — tall spikes of 1 in. (2.5 cm) long lavender flowers appear on branched stalks in June-September. **S. patens** (Gentian Sage) grows about 2 ft (60 cm) high — the 2 in. (5 cm) long deep blue flowers appear from July to September. **'Cambridge Blue'** is a pale blue variety — like the species it is not long-lived. **S. uliginosa** (Bog Sage) is sometimes recommended for the back of a moist border — the 5 ft (1.5 m) stems bear short spikes of blue flowers from September to late autumn. Unfortunately it is not fully hardy and will be killed by heavy frosts.

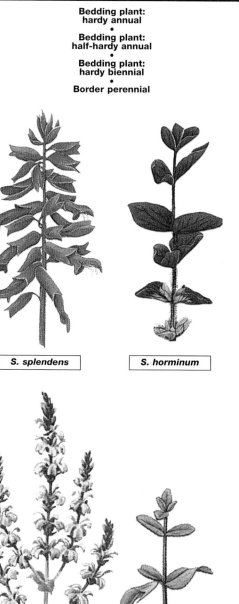

- Bedding plant: hardy annual
- Bedding plant: half-hardy annual
- Bedding plant: hardy biennial
- Border perennial

S. splendens

S. horminum

S. nemorosa

S. patens

SITE & SOIL: For most species and varieties any well-drained soil will do — thrives in sun or light shade.

PROPAGATION: Annuals: Sow seeds in February-March — germination temperature 70°-75°F (21°-24°C). Plant out in late May. Biennials: Sow seeds in the open in May or June. Plant out in autumn. Perennials: Divide clumps in autumn or spring.

SALVIA continued

Salvia splendens 'Blaze of Fire'

Salvia splendens 'Phoenix'

Salvia coccinea 'Lady in Red'

Salvia horminum 'Pink Lady'

Salvia farinacea 'Strata'

Salvia nemorosa 'East Friesland'

Salvia sylvestris 'May Night'

Salvia pratensis

Salvia uliginosa

Rockery perennial

S. canadensis

SANGUINARIA Bloodroot

As you would expect from the common name, the root of this N. American plant oozes red sap if it is severed. Sanguinaria is a spreading perennial which belongs to the poppy family, and it has unfortunately inherited the drawback of having flowers with a very brief life span. Although fleeting the large blooms nestling in the greyish lobed leaves are extremely attractive. It is an easy plant to grow if you can supply its basic needs — peaty, acid soil and some shade.

VARIETIES: S. canadensis is the only species — height 6 in. (15 cm), spread 1½ ft (45 cm), 2-3 in. (5-7.5 cm) wide white flowers, flowering period April-May. The single blooms with a central boss of golden stamens last for less than a day. Choose instead the double variety **'Flore Pleno'** — the blooms last longer. Do not disturb after planting.

SITE & SOIL: Acid, humus-rich soil is necessary — thrives best in light or partial shade.

PROPAGATION: Not easy — buy new plants.

Sanguinaria canadensis 'Flore Pleno'

Border perennial

S. obtusa

SANGUISORBA Burnet

An out-of-the-ordinary plant for the border or wild garden. Slender stems bear tiny flowers in bottlebrush-like heads above the ferny foliage — it is fully hardy, vigorous and can be invasive. There are several decorative species which are closely related to the Salad Burnet (Sanguisorba minor) of the herb garden where it is grown for its cucumber-flavoured leaves. Tall varieties may need support.

VARIETIES: S. obtusa (Japanese Burnet) is the easiest one to find in the catalogues — height 2 ft (60 cm), spread 2 ft (60 cm), 1½ ft (45 cm) long greyish-green pinnate leaves, 3 in. (7.5 cm) long pink flower heads, flowering period July-August. **S. canadensis** (Canadian Burnet) is much taller (6 ft/1.8 m) with 6 in. (15 cm) white flower heads in July-September. **S. officinalis** (4 ft/1.2 m) has 1 in. (2.5 cm) dark red flower heads.

SITE & SOIL: Any well-drained, humus-rich soil will do — thrives in sun or partial shade.

PROPAGATION: Divide clumps in spring or autumn.

Sanguisorba canadensis

Bedding plant: half-hardy annual

S. procumbens

SANVITALIA Creeping Zinnia

You will find this low-growing annual in some but not all the seed catalogues — it is worth growing if you like unusual plants. The common name describes its spreading growth habit and the form of the flowers. Sanvitalia will grow quite happily in both wet and dry seasons, and is recommended for both hanging baskets and as ground cover in beds and borders.

VARIETIES: S. procumbens is the basic species — height 6 in. (15 cm), spread 1½ ft (45 cm), ¾ in. (1.5 cm) wide black-centred yellow flowers, flowering period July-October. The flowers appear continually above the dense foliage. There are several varieties which are similar in growth habit but differ in flower colour. **'Mandarin Orange'** has black-centred orange flowers and **'Irish Eyes'** has green-centred golden ones.

SITE & SOIL: Any well-drained soil will do — thrives best in full sun.

PROPAGATION: Sow seeds in March in gentle heat. Plant out in late May.

Sanvitalia procumbens 'Irish Eyes'

Rockery perennial
•
Border perennial

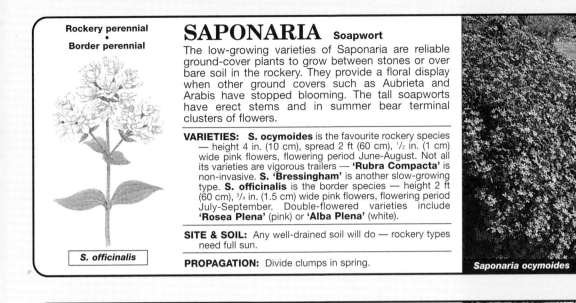

S. officinalis

SAPONARIA Soapwort

The low-growing varieties of Saponaria are reliable ground-cover plants to grow between stones or over bare soil in the rockery. They provide a floral display when other ground covers such as Aubrieta and Arabis have stopped blooming. The tall soapworts have erect stems and in summer bear terminal clusters of flowers.

VARIETIES: **S. ocymoides** is the favourite rockery species — height 4 in. (10 cm), spread 2 ft (60 cm), ½ in. (1 cm) wide pink flowers, flowering period June-August. Not all its varieties are vigorous trailers — **'Rubra Compacta'** is non-invasive. **S. 'Bressingham'** is another slow-growing type. **S. officinalis** is the border species — height 2 ft (60 cm), ¾ in. (1.5 cm) wide pink flowers, flowering period July-September. Double-flowered varieties include **'Rosea Plena'** (pink) or **'Alba Plena'** (white).

SITE & SOIL: Any well-drained soil will do — rockery types need full sun.

PROPAGATION: Divide clumps in spring.

Saponaria ocymoides

SAXIFRAGA Saxifrage

Most saxifrages come from mountainous regions and are usually low-growing and wide-spreading. A group of leafy rosettes or a mossy mat is formed and from this arise upright flower stalks bearing loose clusters of starry flowers. Spring or early summer is the usual flowering season and the blooms may be white, pink, red, yellow or purple. But these are generalisations and all sorts of variations occur.

VARIETIES: The *Border* group consists of large and invasive types which are more suited to the flower border than a modest rockery. **S. urbium** (London Pride) is the best-known example — height 1 ft (30 cm), spread 1½ ft (45 cm), flowering period May-July. The *Encrusted* or *Silver* group contains plants which have rosettes of lime-encrusted leaves and star-shaped flowers in May-July. Examples are **S. aizoon** (**S. paniculata**) with its sprays of white flowers and **S. cochlearis** (height 8 in./20 cm, spread 9 in./22.5 cm) with clusters of white flowers on red stalks. **S. cotyledon** is very tall — choose instead one of the compact Encrusted hybrids such as **S. 'Whitehill'** (white) or **S. 'Esther'** (cream). The *Mossy* group contains plants which form moss-like hummocks and flower in April-May. Popular ones include **S. 'Hi-Ace'** (pink), **S. 'Pixie'** (rose red), **S. 'Cloth of Gold'** (white, leaves golden) and **S. 'Peter Pan'** (pink). Finally, there is the *Cushion* group with a low mound of lime-encrusted leaves and early flowers in February-April. **S. burseriana** (2 in./5 cm, white) is a popular beauty which blooms in late winter — **S. apiculata** (4 in./10 cm, yellow) blooms a little later. Other popular Cushion Saxifrages include **S. 'Jenkinsiae'** (pale pink) and **S. 'Cranbourne'** (pink).

SITE & SOIL: All require well-drained soil. Provide a moist spot with some shade from the midday sun — only the Encrusted group will thrive in full sun.

PROPAGATION: Detach part of a clump and plant in a cold frame in early summer.

Saxifraga urbium

Rockery perennial
•
Border perennial

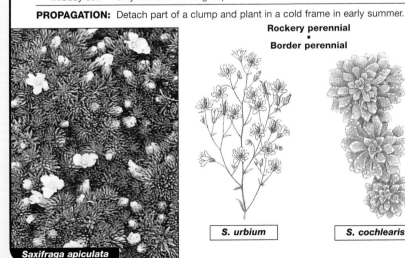

S. urbium

S. cochlearis

Saxifraga apiculata

Saxifraga 'Cloth of Gold'

SCABIOSA Scabious

The annual varieties (Sweet Scabious) have never become popular like their perennial cousins. The colour range is wide — white right through to deepest red. The domed fragrant heads are borne on wiry stems and are excellent for cutting. Sweet Scabious is an easy plant to grow but it is distinctly unhappy in prolonged wet weather. The hardy perennial varieties are favourite subjects for the herbaceous border even though they do not produce an abundance of blooms at any one time.

VARIETIES: **S. atropurpurea** is the annual species grown for bedding — height 1½-2½ ft (45-75 cm), 2 in. (5 cm) wide flower heads, flowering period August-October. Occasionally you may find single-colour varieties such as **'Blue Moon'** or **'Rose Cockade'** but it is more usual to buy a mixture. There are **'Dwarf Double Mixed'** (1½ ft/45 cm) with flowers in an assortment of colours and **'Double Large-Flowered Mixed'** (2½ ft/75 cm) with flowers which require staking. All these varieties can be dried for indoor use — for something unusual grow **S. stellata 'Paper Moon'** which produces 3 in. (7.5 cm) wide papery bronze globular heads when dried. The basic perennial species for the border is **S. caucasica** — height 2-3 ft (60-90 cm), 3 in. (7.5 cm) wide lavender flowers, flowering period June-October. The species has now been largely replaced by its named varieties. The one you are most likely to be offered is **'Clive Greaves'** — mid-blue, large-flowered and long-stemmed. There are a few whites such as **'Miss Willmott'** and some deep violet types like **'Moerheim Blue'**. Where space is limited choose one of the compact varieties — **S. 'Butterfly Blue'** and **S. 'Pink Mist'** grow about 1 ft (30 cm) high and **S. lucida** reaches 8 in. (20 cm).

SITE & SOIL: Any well-drained, non-acid soil will do — thrives best in full sun.

PROPAGATION: Annuals: Sow seeds under glass in March — plant out in May. Perennials: Divide clumps in spring.

Scabiosa atropurpurea
'Dwarf Double Mixed'

Border perennial
•
Bedding plant:
hardy annual

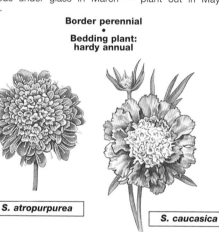

S. atropurpurea

S. caucasica

Scabiosa stellata
'Paper Moon'

Scabiosa caucasica
'Clive Greaves'

Bedding plant:
tender perennial

SCAEVOLA Fairy Fan Flower

It was in the 1990s that this conservatory plant was first widely offered as a summer-flowering bedding plant. Its thick trailing stems bear dandelion-like leaves and in the axils of these leaves the floral spikes appear. It is the shape of the blooms which caught the public fancy — the petals are borne on one side only, giving the flower a fan-like appearance. Use it in hanging baskets and other containers.

VARIETIES: Several varieties of **S. aemula** are offered — length 1 ft (30 cm), 1 in. (2.5 cm) wide blue or lilac flowers, flowering period June-September. The most popular one is **'Blue Fan'** — there is a white eye at the base of the lilac petals. **'Blue Wonder'** is another variety you should be able to find at the garden centre in spring, but the white **'Alba'** is hard to find.

SITE & SOIL: Any well-drained, humus-rich soil will do — thrives best in full sun.

PROPAGATION: Take cuttings under glass in summer — plant out in late May.

S. aemula
'Blue Fan'

Scaevola aemula
'Blue Fan'

SCHIZANTHUS Poor Man's Orchid

S. pinnatus
'Hit Parade'

Each bloom of Poor Man's Orchid or Butterfly Flower looks like a miniature orchid, streaked and spotted in a wide variety of colours — only Salpiglossis can challenge it for the most exotic bedding plant title. The flowers are borne in large numbers above pale green ferny foliage. Pick a sheltered spot and pinch out the tips to induce bushiness.

VARIETIES: Named varieties of **S. pinnatus** are available — height 9 in.-3 ft (22.5-90 cm), 3 in. (7.5 cm) wide two-lipped flowers, flowering period July-August. Avoid the tall ones such as **'Giant Hybrids'** (3 ft/90 cm) which are more suited to the conservatory. Choose instead one of the compact ones such as **'Hit Parade'** (1 ft/30 cm) or **'Angel Wings'** (1½ ft/45 cm). Even shorter (9 in./22.5 cm) are **'Bouquet'** and **'Star Parade'**.

SITE & SOIL: Any well-drained soil will do — thrives best in full sun.

PROPAGATION: Sow seeds in March in gentle heat. Plant out in late May.

Schizanthus pinnatus 'Bouquet'

SCHIZOSTYLIS Kaffir Lily

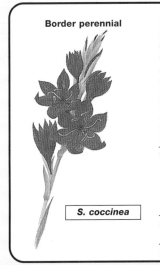

S. coccinea

Despite its common name this bulbous plant belongs to the iris and not the lily family. Use it in the middle of the border where its miniature gladiolus-like flowers will add colour at the end of the season. Schizostylis cannot tolerate dryness at the roots, so it is a plant for humus-rich soil and thorough watering during prolonged dry spells. Plant the rhizomes 1 in. (2.5 cm) deep in spring. It is an evergreen, but the usual practice is to cut down the stems when flowering is over and to cover the crowns with leaf mould or peat.

VARIETIES: **S. coccinea** (height 2 ft/60 cm, flowers 1½ in./3.5 cm wide, flowering period September-November) has numerous varieties. **'Mrs. Hegarty'** is a pink one which blooms earlier than the others but **'Viscountess Byng'** (pink) does not bloom until November. Look for **'Sunrise'** (salmon-pink), **'Alba'** (white) and **'Major'** (large, deep red).

SITE & SOIL: Well-drained but moist soil is necessary — thrives in sun or light shade.

PROPAGATION: Divide clumps in spring.

Schizostylis coccinea 'Mrs. Hegarty'

The usual spring bedding procedure is to plant biennials. When the blooms fade they are dug up and thrown away. Some such as Bellis and Polyanthus can be treated as perennials. Lift in spring and plant in an out-of-the-way spot — in autumn lift once again and plant in bed, border or container for a spring display. A number of spring-flowering perennials can be treated in the same way — examples include Aubrieta, Arabis, Dicentra and Doronicum (illustrated).

SCILLA Bluebell, Squill

Bluebells are a common springtime sight in both woodlands and gardens. Upright stems above strap-like leaves bear drooping flowers — bells or stars in shades of blue or violet. But not all Scillas are the same — there are winter-flowering dwarfs for the rockery and traditional bluebells under trees, under shrubs or naturalised in grassland as well as tall squills with tight heads of blue stars in early summer. Flower colour as well as height and flowering season covers a wide range — there are white, pink, purple and mauve as well as the familiar blue. Most are easy to grow and can be left in the ground to spread into large clumps.

VARIETIES: The earliest and smallest species is **S. tubergeniana** — height 3 in. (7.5 cm), $^3/_4$ in. (1.5 cm) wide dark-striped pale blue flowers, flowering period February-March. **S. bifolia** (deep blue starry flowers) is another early dwarf but the favourite early-flowering species is the Siberian or Spring Squill **S. siberica** — height 6 in. (15 cm), $^1/_2$ in. (1 cm) wide blue cup-shaped flowers in loose clusters, flowering period March-April. Varieties include **'Alba'** (white) and **'Spring Beauty'** (dark blue). The best-known Scilla is the English Bluebell or Wild Hyacinth which has a host of Latin names — **S. non-scripta, S. nutans, Hyacinthoides non-scripta** and **Endymion nonscriptus** (height 10 in./25 cm, $^1/_2$ in./1 cm long blue bell-shaped flowers, flowering period April-May). Plant the bulbs 2 in. (5 cm) deep in August-September. Flowering at the same time is the Giant or Spanish Bluebell (1-1$^1/_2$ ft/30-45 cm) **S. campanulata** (**Hyacinthoides hispanica**) — blue, pink and white varieties are available. Last to bloom is the Cuban Lily **S. peruviana** — height 1 ft (30 cm), blue flowers in rounded clusters, flowering period May-June.

SITE & SOIL: Any well-drained, humus-rich soil will do — thrives in sun or light shade.

PROPAGATION: Divide overcrowded clumps in August-September — replant at once.

Scilla tubergeniana

Bulb

Scilla non-scripta

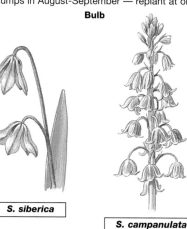
S. siberica

S. campanulata

Scilla peruviana

SCUTELLARIA Skullcap

The common name is derived from the shape of the bloom — each two-lipped erect flower is hooded. Most types are suitable for a modest-sized rockery and are useful as they bloom in mid to late summer when so many alpines have ceased to flower. Another virtue in many situations is their ability to flourish in shade. Taller skullcaps can be grown in the front of the border.

VARIETIES: **S. alpina** is a mat-forming species for the rockery — height 6 in. (15 cm), spread 1 ft (30 cm), 1 in. (2.5 cm) long cream-lipped pale purple flowers, flowering period July-August. **S. indica parvifolia** is a much laxer species (height 6 in./15 cm) with lilac flowers in 4 in. (10 cm) high flower heads. **S. baicalensis** is a blue-flowered taller plant (1$^1/_2$ ft/45 cm) which is suitable for the border.

SITE & SOIL: Any well-drained, non-acid soil will do — thrives in sun or partial shade.

PROPAGATION: Divide clumps in autumn or spring.

Rockery perennial
•
Border perennial

S. indica parvifolia

Scutellaria alpina

SEDUM Ice Plant, Stonecrop

Sedum is a large genus of fleshy-leaved plants. A few grow to 1-2 ft (30-60 cm) and bear large plates of tiny flowers in late summer which act like a magnet for butterflies. These are the *Ice Plants* which belong in the herbaceous border and they lose their leaves in winter. The *Stonecrops* are a much larger group — like the Ice Plants they thrive in hot and dry conditions but they are low-growing plants which belong in the rockery and are usually evergreen. The basic characteristics of this group are starry flowers in early summer which are usually yellow and are borne singly or in flat heads. They sprawl or form a mat and are generally easy to grow — they are also easy to propagate and deserve their popularity as carpeters for growing between rocks and stones. Infertile soil is no problem, but you must choose with care if your rockery is a small and choice one. As noted below there are rampant ones you should avoid — heading the list is the Common Stonecrop which can easily become a weed.

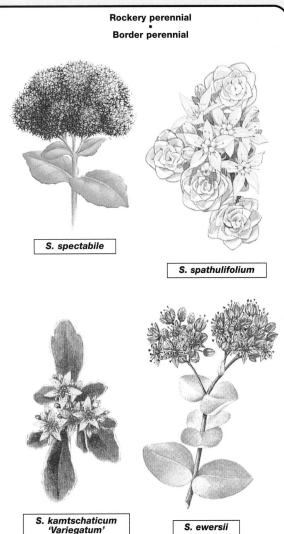

S. spectabile

S. spathulifolium

VARIETIES: The basic Ice Plant is **S. spectabile** — height 1-2 ft (30-60 cm), 4-6 in. (10-15 cm) wide pink or purple flower heads, flowering period August-October. Varieties include **'Brilliant'** (dark pink), **'Meteor'** (red) and **'Iceberg'** (white). The hybrids are more popular — widely available ones include **'Ruby Glow'** (red), **'Bertram Anderson'** (dark pink) and **'Autumn Joy'** (salmon pink maturing to rusty brown).

The best-known stonecrop is **S. acre** (Common Stonecrop) — height 2 in. (5 cm), 1 in. (2.5 cm) wide yellow flower heads, flowering period June-July. This species is useful if you have a large area of bare ground to cover, but in a rockery it is better to choose a plant which is less invasive. **S. album 'Coral Carpet'** (4 in./10 cm) has red leaves and pink flowers — **'Murale'** is a purple-leaved variety of the species. The old favourite **S. spathulifolium** has small rosettes of silver-grey leaves and heads of yellow flowers — the popular varieties are **'Purpureum'** (purple leaves) and **'Cape Blanco'** (powdery white inner leaves). For white, red or purple flowers choose a variety of **S. spurium** (4 in./10 cm) — look for **'Dragon's Blood'** (purple-tinted leaves, dark pink flowers) and **'Variegatum'** (cream-edged leaves). **S. kamtschaticum 'Variegatum'** is one of the most colourful of all stonecrops — yellow and orange flowers above cream- and red-edged leaves. Unusual stonecrops include **S. cauticola** (red flowers, deciduous) and **S. humifusum** (solitary yellow flowers). **S. ewersii** is a pink-flowered trailer.

S. kamtschaticum 'Variegatum'

S. ewersii

SITE & SOIL: Any well-drained soil will do — thrives best in full sun.

PROPAGATION: Divide clumps in autumn or spring.

Sedum 'Autumn Joy'

Sedum spathulifolium 'Purpureum'

Sedum spurium

Rockery perennial

S. tectorum

SEMPERVIVUM Houseleek

This succulent is a popular rockery resident where it grows in the crannies between stones. Thick flower stalks appear in summer or autumn bearing yellow, red or purple multi-petalled flowers, but houseleeks are usually grown for their foliage. The leaves are grouped into a ball-like rosette — there is a wide variation in colour, texture, hairiness etc. The rosette at the base of the flower stalk dies when flowering comes to an end.

VARIETIES: The Common Houseleek **S. tectorum** is the best known — height 3 in. (7.5 cm), spread 1 ft (30 cm), deep pink or purple flowers on 1 ft (30 cm) flower stalks, flowering period July. For a smaller plant with hairy leaves but similar flowers choose **S. montanum**. For more decorative foliage look for **S. arachnoideum** (dense white webbing), **S. 'Commander Hay'** (green-tipped purple) or **S. 'Rubin'** (reddish-bronze).

SITE & SOIL: Any well-drained soil will do — full sun is necessary.

PROPAGATION: Remove and plant offsets in spring.

Sempervivum arachnoideum

Border perennial
•
Bog plant

S. pulcher

SENECIO Senecio

Senecio is a popular genus in both the house and garden. You will find Cineraria in The House Plant Expert, the Shrubby Ragwort in The Tree & Shrub Expert and Dusty Miller in The Bedding Plant Expert. Surprisingly flowering hardy perennial species are few in number and hard to find — you will have to look through the catalogues to find one.

VARIETIES: **S. smithii** is a plant for the bog garden or moist border — height 4 ft (1.2 m), 6 in. (15 cm) wide flower heads, flowering period June-July. The yellow-centred white daisies are followed by fluffy seed heads. The leathery 1 ft (30 cm) long leaves are borne on stout stems. **S. tanguticus** (Chinese Groundsel) is another tall moisture-loving species which is grown for its decorative seed heads — **S. pulcher** is a rather tender border plant (1½ ft/45 cm) with 2 in. (5 cm) wide reddish-purple flowers.

SITE & SOIL: Moisture-retentive soil in a sunny spot is necessary.

PROPAGATION: Divide clumps in spring.

Senecio smithii

Rockery perennial

S. uniflora

SHORTIA Shortia

This rockery evergreen has nothing in common with Sempervivum above or Sedum on the previous page. It is hard to find, loves shade and detests the presence of lime in the soil. It needs cool peaty ground where it can display its decorative blooms. The shiny leaves are usually tinged with brown or red, and in winter the foliage may turn completely bronze or crimson.

VARIETIES: **S. galacifolia** is in one or two catalogues — height 6 in. (15 cm), 1 in. (2.5 cm) wide white fading to pink flowers, flowering period April-May. The trumpet-shaped blooms are borne singly on top of the flower stems. **S. uniflora** has 1½ in. (3.5 cm) wide white fringed flowers and is more eye-catching — the variety **'Grandiflora'** is pink.

SITE & SOIL: Well-drained, humus-rich soil in partial shade is necessary.

PROPAGATION: Divide clumps in early spring.

Shortia uniflora

Border perennial

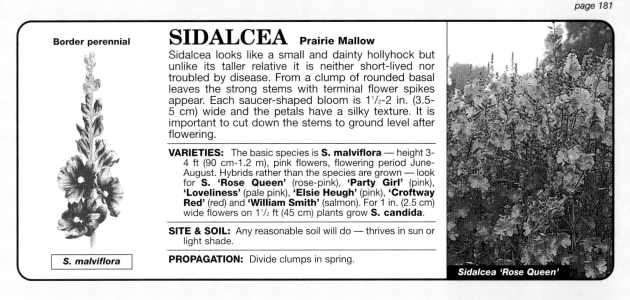

SIDALCEA Prairie Mallow

Sidalcea looks like a small and dainty hollyhock but unlike its taller relative it is neither short-lived nor troubled by disease. From a clump of rounded basal leaves the strong stems with terminal flower spikes appear. Each saucer-shaped bloom is 1½-2 in. (3.5-5 cm) wide and the petals have a silky texture. It is important to cut down the stems to ground level after flowering.

VARIETIES: The basic species is **S. malviflora** — height 3-4 ft (90 cm-1.2 m), pink flowers, flowering period June-August. Hybrids rather than the species are grown — look for **S. 'Rose Queen'** (rose-pink), **'Party Girl'** (pink), **'Loveliness'** (pale pink), **'Elsie Heugh'** (pink), **'Croftway Red'** (red) and **'William Smith'** (salmon). For 1 in. (2.5 cm) wide flowers on 1½ ft (45 cm) plants grow **S. candida**.

SITE & SOIL: Any reasonable soil will do — thrives in sun or light shade.

PROPAGATION: Divide clumps in spring.

S. malviflora

Sidalcea 'Rose Queen'

SILENE Campion, Catchfly

The perennial species (the campions) are more popular than the annual ones. Most of these perennials bear soft, hairy leaves and have stems which spread slowly to form a low carpet. They relish dry, sandy soil and will grow in the cracks and crevices between rocks or in walls. In summer or autumn the flat-faced tubular flowers appear — the petals are blunt-ended and often notched. These mat-forming campions are useful in the rockery as they keep their leaves in winter and some bloom when most alpines are no longer in flower.

VARIETIES: **S. acaulis** is the popular Moss Campion — height 2 in. (5 cm), spread 1 ft (30 cm), ½ in. (1 cm) wide white or pink flowers, flowering period May-June. The sheet of mossy green foliage is attractive but the number of flowers is often disappointing. **S. uniflora (S. maritima)** is a better choice — the variety **'Flore Pleno'** has 1 in. (2.5 cm) wide double flowers in July-October. Best of all carpeters is **S. schafta** — height 6 in. (15 cm), spread 1½ ft (45 cm), 1 in. (2.5 cm) wide pink flowers, flowering period June-October. The varieties **'Abbotswood'** (deep pink) and **'Shell Pink'** (pale pink) bloom profusely. Campions for the border include **S. asterias** (1 ft/30 cm, red) and **S. dioica** (2½ ft/75 cm, pink). You can buy seeds of single-colour varieties of the hardy annual Viscaria (**S. coeli-rosa**) — height 1 ft (30 cm), 1 in. (2.5 cm) wide flowers, flowering period June-August. The two you are most likely to find are **'Blue Angel'** (azure blue) and **'Love'** (rose-pink), but the usual choice is a mixture such as **'Brilliant Mixed'**. The Nodding Catchfly (**S. pendula**) is another hardy annual which grows 6 in. (15 cm) high and bears drooping pink flowers in June-August.

SITE & SOIL: Well-drained soil in full sun is necessary.

PROPAGATION: Perennials: Plant cuttings in a cold frame in summer. Annuals: Sow seeds in September-April where they are to flower.

Silene acaulis

Rockery perennial
•
Border perennial
•
Hardy annual

S. schafta

S. coeli-rosa

Silene dioica

Silene coeli-rosa 'Brilliant Mixed'

Hardy biennial

S. marianum

SILYBUM   Holy Thistle

The flower heads of this striking plant are made up of masses of tiny pale purple flowers surrounded by long green spines. It is the foliage rather than the flowers which makes this biennial so distinctive. The leaves are about 9 in. (22.5 cm) wide and 1½ ft (45 cm) long — they form a basal rosette which always attracts attention. Each leaf is glossy, spiny and heavily marbled with white veins.

VARIETIES: **S. marianum** is the species you will find — height 4 ft (1.2 m), spread 3 ft (90 cm), 2 in. (5 cm) wide flower heads, flowering period July-September. This is a plant for the back of the border or the wild garden. Protect young growth from slugs and snails and do not feed as it does best in poor soil. Self-sown seedlings can be a problem so remove flower heads when blooms fade.

SITE & SOIL: Any well-drained soil will do — thrives best in full sun.

PROPAGATION: Sow seeds in the open in May or June. Plant out in autumn.

Silybum marianum

Border perennial
•
Rockery perennial

S. angustifolium

SISYRINCHIUM   Sisyrinchium

You should be able to find one or two types of this member of the iris family in pots at the garden centre and some specialist bulb nurseries offer tubers. Like other members of its family it produces erect fans of sword-like leaves but the blooms are simple six-petalled stars or bells. The blooms are not long-lived but they appear over a long period.

VARIETIES: The usual border Sisyrinchium is **S. striatum** — height 2 ft (60 cm), pale yellow flowers, flowering period June-July. The blooms are borne in whorls on upright spikes — **'Aunt May'** has cream-striped leaves. Dwarfs (6 in./15 cm) for the rockery include **S. brachypus** (yellow) and **S. 'Pole Star'** (white) — both bloom between June and September. Blue varieties include **S. angustifolium** (9 in./22.5 cm).

SITE & SOIL: Requires well-drained, humus-rich soil in full sun.

PROPAGATION: Divide clumps in autumn or spring.

Sisyrinchium striatum

Border perennial

S. stellata

SMILACINA   Smilacina

This woodland plant produces arching leafy stems like Solomon's Seal but the flowers which are borne at the stem tips are tiny fluffy blooms in clusters and are not solitary pendent bells. The scented starry blooms are often followed by red berries. Make sure the conditions are right before buying this one — it needs moisture-retentive and rich lime-free soil in shade. Mulch in spring.

VARIETIES: The species you are most likely to see is **S. racemosa** (False Spikenard) — height 3 ft (90 cm), ¼ in. (0.5 cm) wide creamy-white flowers, flowering period May-June. The leaves are bright green and the flower clusters are 6 in. (15 cm) long. **S. stellata** (Star-flowered Lily of the Valley) is smaller (2 ft/60 cm) with white flowers — this species can be invasive.

SITE & SOIL: Humus-rich acid soil in light or partial shade is necessary.

PROPAGATION: Divide clumps in spring.

Smilacina racemosa

Rockery perennial

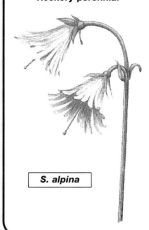

S. alpina

SOLDANELLA Snowbell

Deeply fringed bell-like flowers droop gracefully from the top of the upright flower stalks. Lavender-blue is the usual colour but varieties in other shades are available. They are not plants which can be left to look after themselves — most types require some form of protection against winter rains and you will need to keep slugs at bay in late winter and spring.

VARIETIES: **S. alpina** is a typical snowbell — height 4 in. (10 cm), spread 9 in. (22.5 cm), ½ in. (1 cm) long pale purple flowers, flowering period March-April. An attractive alpine but it is not easy to grow outdoors. You will have more success with **S. montana** (8 in./20 cm) or **S. carpatica** (6 in./15 cm), but the most floriferous and the easiest to grow is **S. villosa** (6 in./15 cm). It flowers later than the others (May-June) and is more robust.

SITE & SOIL: Requires well-drained, humus-rich soil in light shade.

PROPAGATION: Divide clumps in summer.

Soldanella montana

Border perennial

S. 'Golden Wings'

SOLIDAGO Golden Rod

The bright yellow heads of Golden Rod are a common sight in herbaceous borders in late summer, but the plants are often tall, weedy and badly staked. S. canadensis is the plant which is so often seen, but these days there are many compact hybrids which are more attractive. All are easy to grow — mulch in spring, provide unobtrusive support and water in dry weather.

VARIETIES: The hybrids have been derived from such species as **S. canadensis**, **S. virgaurea** and **S. brachystachys** — height 1-6 ft (30 cm-1.8 m), yellow flowers, flowering period July-September. There are giants such as **S. 'Golden Wings'** and a number in the 2-3 ft (60-90 cm) range like **'Crown of Rays'** and **'Goldenmosa'**. Best of all perhaps are the 1-1½ ft (30-45 cm) dwarfs (e.g **'Queenie'** and **'Cloth of Gold'**).

SITE & SOIL: Any well-drained soil will do — thrives in sun or light shade.

PROPAGATION: Divide clumps in autumn or spring.

Solidago 'Goldenmosa'

Border perennial

S. luteus

SOLIDASTER Solidaster

As noted above you will see Solidago in herbaceous borders everywhere and Aster (Michaelmas Daisy) is even more popular as an autumn-flowering border perennial. It is therefore surprising that the hybrid of these two is not popular apart from one exception. The massed heads of small yellow daisies are sought after for indoor decoration and so Solidaster is often seen in the flower arranger's garden.

VARIETIES: The only species is **S. luteus (S. hybridus)** — height 3 ft (90 cm), spread 1 ft (30 cm), ½ in. (1 cm) wide yellow daisy-like flowers, flowering period July-September. The blooms are borne in large domed clusters, each flower bearing a central golden disc and canary yellow petals. **'Lemore'** is the favourite variety — it is shorter (2-2½ ft/60-75 cm) and the petals are lemon yellow.

SITE & SOIL: Any well-drained soil will do — thrives in full sun.

PROPAGATION: Divide clumps in autumn or spring.

Solidaster luteus 'Lemore'

Bulb

S. tricolor

SPARAXIS Harlequin Flower

Sparaxis is not for you if you want a bulb you can plant in the rockery or front of the border and then leave it to look after itself. It can only be grown in a sheltered, south-facing site in a mild district, and even then you will have to follow an unusual routine. The corms are lifted in midsummer once the foliage has died down and are then kept dry until planting time in November.

VARIETIES: **S. tricolor** is bought as a mixture — height 8 in.-1½ ft (20-45 cm), 2 in. (5 cm) wide star-shaped flowers, flowering period May-June. Plant the corms 3 in. (7.5 cm) deep in November. Some of the flowers will be plain — all-orange, all-yellow etc. Others will be bicolours with a distinct black ring separating the petals and throat colours. **S. elegans** is a 6 in. (15 cm) dwarf.

SITE & SOIL: Well-drained soil and full sun are essential.

PROPAGATION: Remove cormlets when plants are lifted in summer — plant in November.

Sparaxis tricolor

Border perennial
•
Rockery perennial

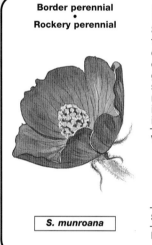

S. munroana

SPHAERALCEA Sphaeralcea

Sphaeralcea is a sprawling plant which can be used in the border or large rock garden but it is at its best in a container growing among taller upright plants. It is not often seen so you cannot expect to find it at your local garden centre — look for it in the catalogues. It is sometimes recommended that this plant should be moved indoors in winter — this is usually because of its dislike of prolonged cold rain rather than frost intolerance.

VARIETIES: **S. munroana** is the usual one in the catalogues — height 2 ft (60 cm), spread 3 ft (90 cm), 1 in. (2.5 cm) wide red saucer-shaped flowers, flowering period June-September. The blooms are borne in clusters above the grey-green lobed leaves — pink-flowered varieties are available. **S. fendleri** is a taller and less hardy plant which bears orange-red flowers in summer.

SITE & SOIL: Well-drained soil and full sun are necessary.

PROPAGATION: Divide clumps in spring.

Sphaeralcea munroana

Bulb

S. formosissima

SPREKELIA Jacobean Lily

You will need a sunny, sheltered spot for this exotic flower — it is one of several showy tender bulbs in this book which can be grown outdoors if you have free-draining soil in a mild area. The large blooms have an orchid-like appearance. The velvety petals are borne in two groups — the upper three are erect and the lower three are pendent, forming a flared green-throated tube.

VARIETIES: **S. formosissima** is the only species and there are no varieties from which to make your choice — height 1-1½ ft (30-45 cm), 5 in. (12.5 cm) wide crimson flowers, flowering period June. The blooms are carried singly on top of the flower stalk. Plant the bulbs 2 in. (5 cm) deep in April. Lift once the foliage has withered and store in dry peat at about 60°F (15°C) — replant in spring.

SITE & SOIL: Well-drained soil in a sheltered sunny spot is necessary.

PROPAGATION: Remove bulblets when plants are lifted — plant in spring.

Sprekelia formosissima

Border perennial

S. macrantha

STACHYS Stachys

The popular Stachys is a grey-leaved ground cover commonly known as Lamb's Ears. Flowers are borne in whorls on upright spikes but these blooms are usually insignificant — this perennial is generally grown for its attractive evergreen foliage. The usual flowering Stachys is Big Betony — a deciduous plant which produces spikes of showy hooded flowers above all-green leaves.

VARIETIES: Lamb's Ears is **S. byzantina (S. lanata)** — height 1½ ft (45 cm), ½ in. (1 cm) long pale purple flowers, flowering period July-August. **'Silver Carpet'** has the best foliage but there are no flowers — **'Cotton Boll'** has white bobble-like blooms on the stems. **S. macrantha** (Big Betony) is in many catalogues — height 2 ft (60 cm), 1½ in. (3.5 cm) long pale purple tubular flowers, flowering period May-July.

SITE & SOIL: Any well-drained soil will do — thrives in sun or partial shade.

PROPAGATION: Divide clumps in autumn or spring.

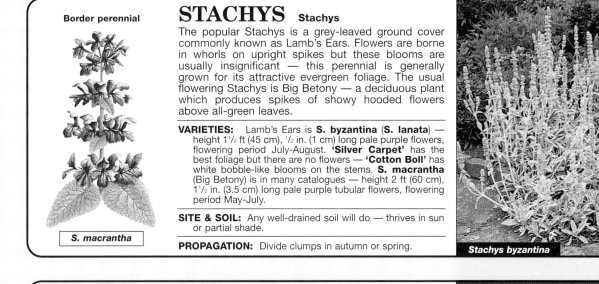

Stachys byzantina

Bulb

S. lutea

STERNBERGIA Autumn Daffodil

Despite its common name this autumn-flowering bulb looks much more like a crocus than a daffodil — the leaves are grass-like and the blooms are wineglass-shaped. These blooms, however, are borne on a stalk and not an extension of the petal tube and there are six rather than three stamens. A difficult plant — it needs near-perfect drainage, protection from strong winds and warm, dry weather in summer if it is to flourish.

VARIETIES: The most reliable species is **S. lutea** — height 6 in. (15 cm), 1½ in. (3.5 cm) wide yellow flowers, flowering period September-October. Plant the bulbs 5 in. (12.5 cm) deep in July-August. **S. clusiana** has larger flowers — the goblet-shaped blooms are up to 3 in. (7.5 cm) long. The dwarf (3 in./7.5 cm) species is **S. sicula**.

SITE & SOIL: Well-drained alkaline soil and full sun are essential.

PROPAGATION: Buy new bulbs — Sternbergia hates disturbance.

Sternbergia sicula

In recent years we have become much more aware that a few plants should be treated with care as they can be harmful. Some berries can cause stomach upsets or even worse problems — examples include Lathyrus, Digitalis, Arum and Phytolacca. Much less has been written about plant allergies than plant poisoning, but they are much more common. If you have ever developed a rash after gardening it is a good idea to wear gloves when handling the leaves of Pelargonium, Chrysanthemum, Helleborus or Primula obconica (illustrated).

Border perennial

STOKESIA Stokes' Aster

Here is something different for the front of the border. The flowers look like Callistephus or Centaurea but in fact Stokesia is an evergreen perennial with blooms which first appear in midsummer and continue to open until the first frosts arrive. Mulch in spring and provide support if necessary. Water during dry spells, dead-head faded blooms and cut down the stems to ground level in early winter.

VARIETIES: **S. laevis** is the only species — height 1-1½ ft (30-45 cm), 3 in. (7.5 cm) wide lilac saucer-shaped flowers, flowering period July-October. The leaves are long and narrow, and the flowers have deeply notched petals. Varieties in shades of white, pink and blue are available, including **'Alba'** (white), **'Blue Star'** (pale blue), **'Blue Moon'** (mid blue) and **'Superba'** (lavender).

SITE & SOIL: Any well-drained soil will do — thrives best in full sun.

PROPAGATION: Divide clumps in spring.

S. laevis

Stokesia laevis

Border perennial

STYLOPHORUM Stylophorum

An unusual member of the poppy family which can be recognised by its large, deeply-lobed leaves on stout stalks and its papery-petalled flowers which have large styles. It can be grown in the border but as it relishes peaty soil and needs some shade it is more suited to the woodland garden. The four-petalled flowers are borne singly or in small clusters and are followed by silvery seed pods.

VARIETIES: **S. diphyllum** (Wood or Celandine Poppy) is the species you are more likely to find — height 1½ ft (45 cm), spread 1 ft (30 cm), 2 in. (5 cm) wide bright yellow saucer-shaped flowers, flowering period May-June. The 6 in. (15 cm) wide leaves are borne on 1½ ft (45 cm) high stalks. **S. lasiocarpum** bears 1½ in. (3.5 cm) wide pale yellow flowers on branched stems — it is a short-lived plant.

SITE & SOIL: Well-drained, humus-rich soil in partial shade is necessary.

PROPAGATION: Sow seeds in spring where they are to flower.

S. diphyllum

Stylophorum diphyllum

Border perennial

SYMPHYTUM Comfrey

These days comfrey is grown as a vigorous ground cover in woodland or other shady sites rather than as a medicinal herb. Drooping heads of tubular flowers appear in spring or summer and this tough and hardy plant can be expected to succeed under a wide range of conditions. Two words of warning — some varieties are invasive and contact with the leaves can result in a rash.

VARIETIES: **S. ibericum** is one of the popular species — height 1 ft (30 cm), spread 2 ft (60 cm), ½ in. (1 cm) long creamy-yellow flowers, flowering period May-June. **S. 'Hidcote Pink'** and **S. 'Hidcote Blue'** offer other colours. For a compact plant with gold-edged leaves grow **S. 'Goldsmith'** and for a much larger variegated plant choose **S. uplandicum 'Variegatum'** (3 ft/90 cm, purplish-pink flowers).

SITE & SOIL: Any reasonable soil will do — thrives in sun or partial shade.

PROPAGATION: Divide clumps in spring.

S. ibericum

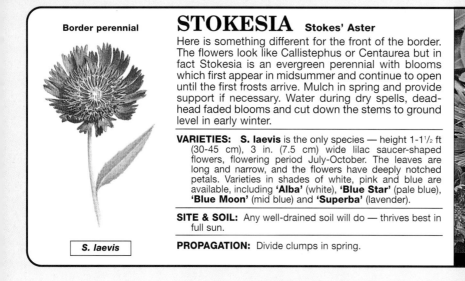

Symphytum 'Hidcote Pink'

TAGETES **Marigold, Tagetes**

Marigolds are the most popular source of yellows and oranges in bedding schemes. They are easy to raise from seed, reliable under all sorts of conditions, long-flowering from June until the first frosts arrive and are inexpensive to buy as seedlings for planting out in spring. Love them or hate them, they are a basic feature of summer-flowering beds and containers. At the start it is necessary to clear up any confusion over naming. The half-hardy marigolds described here (not to be confused with the hardy Pot Marigold described on page 39) are species or varieties of Tagetes.

The smallest ones are varieties of T. signata which are listed as Tagetes or Signet Marigolds. These ferny-leaved plants are 6-9 in. (15-22.5 cm) high with masses of $^1/_2$-1 in. (1-2.5 cm) single flowers. The favourite marigold is the French Marigold (T. patula). The varieties bear lots of 2 in. (5 cm) wide single, semi-double or double blooms on bushy plants which are 6 in.-1 ft (15-30 cm) high. T. erecta is the African Marigold — taller (1-3 ft/30-90 cm), more upright and with fewer but larger (3-5 in./7.5-12.5 cm) flowers than the French Marigolds. Between the two are the Afro-French Marigolds, which are hybrids of the African and French Marigold. These plants have larger blooms than the French ones but are more free-flowering and compact than the African Marigolds.

Plant out before the flowers open — avoid plants in full flower. Water when the weather is dry and keep watch for slugs. Stake tall-growing varieties and dead-head to prolong the display.

VARIETIES: The *Tagetes* varieties (**T. signata**) have been dominated by the **'Gem'** series for many years. The favourite one is **'Golden Gem'** (6 in./15 cm, small golden-yellow flowers) — you will also find **'Lemon Gem'**, **'Yellow Gem'** and the taller (9 in./22.5 cm) **'Tangerine Gem'**. For bicolours look for **'Paprika'** (gold-edged red) and **'Ursula'** (orange-marked yellow). The mixture to buy is **'Starfire'** (yellows, oranges and browns with many bicolours).

You will find many *French Marigold* varieties (**T. patula**) in the catalogues and at the garden centre with colours ranging from white to deepest red. The double ones are now more popular than the single types which used to dominate the range. Among the doubles there are the large-flowered **'Aurora'** series, the dwarf (6 in./15 cm) **'Boy'** series and the **'Boy O' Boy'** mixture. The **'Sophia'** and **'Safari'** series have large blooms with fluted overlapping petals on 8-10 in. (20-25 cm) bushy plants. The single types include the old favourite **'Naughty Marietta'** (1 ft/30 cm, yellow and maroon), the smaller **'Dainty Marietta'**, **'Disco'** (6 in./15 cm) and the **'Mischief'** series. The crested varieties have inner petals which are crowded and tightly rolled. Look for **'Tiger Eyes'** (orange and red), **'Honeycomb'** (orange and red), **'Queen Bee'** (yellow and red) and **'Orange Jacket'** (orange).

The *African Marigold* varieties (**T. erecta**) have double ball-like blooms and are classified by their height. The tall types reach 2-3 ft (60-90 cm) — in the catalogues you will find **'Doubloon'** (5 in./12.5 cm yellow flowers) and the **'Jubilee'** series in yellow and orange. The intermediate types (1$^1/_2$-2 ft/45-60 cm) include **'First Lady'** and the **'Perfection'** series, and the low types (1 ft/30 cm) are represented by **'Discovery'**, **'Vanilla'** (white), **'Antigua'** and the **'Inca'** series.

The *Afro-French Marigold* varieties grow 1-1$^1/_2$ ft (30-45 cm) high and the blooms measure about 3 in. (7.5 cm) across. The popular single ones are **'Nell Gwynn'** and **'Little Nell'**. Doubles include **'Sunrise'** (orange), **'Red Seven Star'** (red-brown), the early-flowering **'Zenith'** and the **'Solar'** series.

SITE & SOIL: Any reasonable soil will do — thrives best in full sun.

PROPAGATION: Sow seeds in February-March. Plant out in late May.

Bedding plant: half-hardy annual

T. signata

T. signata **'Lemon Gem'** Tagetes

T. patula

T. patula **'Naughty Marietta'** French Marigold: Single group

T. patula **'Scarlet Sophia'** French Marigold: Double group

T. patula **'Tiger Eyes'** French Marigold: Crested group

T. erecta **'Doubloon'** African Marigold

T. **'Nell Gwynn'** Afro-French Marigold: Single group

T. **'Sunrise'** Afro-French Marigold: Double group

TAGETES continued

Tagetes signata 'Lemon Gem'

Tagetes signata 'Starfire'

Tagetes patula 'Aurora Mixed'

Tagetes patula 'Disco Gold'

Tagetes patula 'Honeycomb'

Tagetes erecta 'First Lady'

Tagetes erecta 'Perfection Gold'

Tagetes 'Red Seven Star'

Tagetes 'Solar Sulphur'

TANACETUM Pyrethrum, Feverfew

The genus Tanacetum now houses the garden plants which were formerly listed as Pyrethrum and Matricaria — in common name terms this means that the feverfews have joined tansy as species of Tanacetum. There are perennial types for both the border and the rockery, and there are also short-lived perennials which are usually grown as half-hardy annuals. The most popular perennial is T. coccineum which is usually sold under its old Pyrethrum name. It is a plant for the herbaceous or mixed border and is a favourite among flower arrangers. The large daisy-like blooms are borne singly on long stalks above the feathery foliage. The single blooms bear a prominent central disc and the doubles are usually smaller with a mass of miniature petals within an outer ring of large ones. Always remove the flower stalks once the blooms have faded so as to induce a second flush. The smaller perennials are generally grown for their silvery foliage rather than their button-like white or yellow flowers. T. parthenium is the species grown as an annual — the compact leafy mound is covered with masses of cushion-like flowers in late summer and looks like a miniature chrysanthemum.

Border perennial
•
Rockery perennial
•
Bedding plant: half-hardy annual

T. coccineum 'Vanessa'

T. coccineum 'Eileen May Robinson'

T. parthenium 'Golden Ball'

VARIETIES: The Pyrethrum of the garden border is **T. coccineum** — height 1½-2½ ft (45-75 cm), 2 in. (5 cm) wide white, pink or red flowers, flowering period May-June. There are several good singles including **'Brenda'** (dark pink), **'Eileen May Robinson'** (pink), **'Robinson's Red'** (red), **'Snow Cloud'** (white) and **'James Kelway'** (dark pink). For double flowers look for **'Aphrodite'** (white) or **'Vanessa'** (yellow-centred pink). Provide support for the stems and water when the weather is dry. **T. vulgare** is the Common Tansy and is a plant for the wild garden rather than the border — masses of tiny yellow button-like flowers are borne on 3 ft (90 cm) stems above the feathery leaves in late summer and autumn. **T. haradjanii** and **T. densum** are the two dwarf rockery species you are most likely to find. They form 6 in. (15 cm) high dense mounds of feathery silver-grey leaves with small yellow flower heads in summer. The blooms of T. haradjanii are smaller (⅛ in./0.25 cm) than those of T. densum (½ in./1 cm). **T. parthenium (Matricaria eximia)** is the species grown as a half-hardy annual — height 4 in.-1 ft (10-30 cm), 1 in. (2.5 cm) wide white or yellow flowers, flowering period July-September. The single **'White Star'** is no longer easy to find, but the double forms appear in most seed catalogues. The ball-like **'Golden Ball'** is popular but the more usual pattern is a double flower with an outer ring of larger petals — examples include **'Snow Ball'**, **'Snow Puffs'**, **'Butterball'** and **'Lemon Santana'**.

SITE & SOIL: Well-drained soil is essential — thrives best in full sun.

PROPAGATION: Perennials: Divide clumps in spring. Annuals: Sow seeds in February-March in gentle heat — plant out in late May.

Tanacetum coccineum 'Brenda'

Tanacetum vulgare 'Crispum'

Tanacetum parthenium 'Snow Puffs'

Bulb

T. cyanocrocus

TECOPHILAEA Chilean Blue Crocus

The Chilean Blue Crocus is extremely uncommon, yet it is not particularly hard to grow and it has been described as one of the most eye-catching of all small bulbs. The problems are that it is only suitable for outdoor cultivation in free-draining sandy soil in a mild area, and it is the most expensive bulb you will find in the few catalogues in which it is listed.

VARIETIES: The only species you will find is **T. cyanocrocus** — height 6 in. (15 cm), 1 in. (2.5 cm) wide funnel-shaped flowers, flowering period March-April. Plant 2 in. (5 cm) deep in September-October. There is nothing special about the size or shape of the blooms which are borne singly on the flower stalks — it is the intense blue colour which makes them unique. Varieties on offer are **'Leichtlinii'** (white-throated blue) and **'Violacea'** (deep purple).

SITE & SOIL: Well-drained light soil in full sun is necessary.

PROPAGATION: Remove and plant offsets in late summer.

Tecophilaea cyanocrocus 'Leichtlinii'

Border perennial

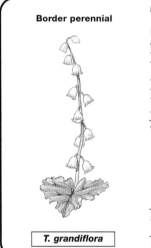

T. grandiflora

TELLIMA Fringecup

Like its close relative Tiarella this semi-evergreen ground cover has lobed leaves which are prominently veined. They may look similar at first glance but Tellima has bell-shaped flowers which are pale green and not white frothy stars like Tiarella. This plant is a good choice if you are looking for ground cover or a front of border item for a dry area — it withstands drought much better than most other border plants.

VARIETIES: **T. grandiflora** is the only species you can buy — height 1½ ft (45 cm), spread 1½-2 ft (45-60 cm), ½ in. (1 cm) wide fringed flowers, flowering period May-June. The heart- or kidney-shaped leaves are lobed and scalloped, and the flowers on the upright spikes turn pink with age. The variety **'Purpurea'** has purplish leaves and pink-edged flowers and the **'Odorata'** group are sweetly scented.

SITE & SOIL: Any well-drained soil will do — thrives in sun or partial shade.

PROPAGATION: Divide clumps in autumn or spring.

Tellima grandiflora

Rockery perennial
•
Border perennial

T. chamaedrys

TEUCRIUM Germander

The germanders are evergreen shrubs or shrub-like perennials which bear two-lipped flowers throughout the summer. The stems are square in cross-section and all need sun and free-draining soil. The tall woody ones are outside the scope of this book but there are low-growing ones which form leafy mounds and are suitable for the rockery or the front of the border.

VARIETIES: **T. chamaedrys** is the Wall Germander — height 1 ft (30 cm), ½ in. (1 cm) long rosy-purple flowers, flowering period June-August. Its leaves are dark green above and grey below — for silvery-grey leaves and purplish-blue flowers grow the dwarf (4 in./10 cm) **T. aroanium**. For lilac and cream flowers on trailing stems look for **T. pyrenaicum** — the spiny Teucrium with tiny pink flowers is **T. subspinosum**. The white-flowered **T. scorodonia** is not reliably hardy.

SITE & SOIL: Requires well-drained soil in full sun.

PROPAGATION: Plant cuttings in a cold frame in summer.

Teucrium pyrenaicum

Border perennial
•
Rockery perennial

T. delavayi

THALICTRUM   Meadow Rue

A light and airy plant for the back of the border which makes a change from the heavy-leaved and large-flowered types which usually dominate this space. The stems are slender and the dainty leaflets have the appearance of Maidenhair Fern. The foliage and the large heads of tiny flowers are used for flower arranging. Provide support for the stems and cut down in autumn.

VARIETIES: **T. delavayi** is a widely available species — height 5 ft (1.5 m), 6 in. (15 cm) wide heads of lavender flowers, flowering period June-September. **'Hewitt's Double'** (3 ft/90 cm) is a popular variety. **T. aquilegiifolium** produces masses of fluffy flowers in white, mauve, pink or purple in late spring. **T. flavum 'Glaucum'** is yellow — **T. kiusianum** is a 6 in. (15 cm) dwarf.

SITE & SOIL: Any humus-rich soil will do — thrives in sun or partial shade.

PROPAGATION: Divide clumps in autumn or spring.

Thalictrum aquilegiifolium 'Album'

Border perennial

T. villosa

THERMOPSIS   False Lupin

One for the collector of unusual plants. The spikes of yellow pea-like blooms have a lupin-like appearance although the plants are usually taller than their well-known cousin and the leaves are made up of only three leaflets. There are several species which you will find in the catalogues — they are fully hardy and easy to grow, but the rhizomes spread quickly and can be invasive.

VARIETIES: **T. villosa** is the tallest species — height 5 ft (1.5 m), 1 in. (2.5 cm) flowers on 10 in. (25 cm) long spikes, flowering period May-June. **T. montana** is smaller (3 ft/90 cm) and more invasive. Another False Lupin in the 2½-3 ft (75-90 cm) range is **T. lanceolata** which bears dense spikes of clear yellow flowers which are followed by curved hairy pods. **T. lupinoides** is similar but has straight pods.

SITE & SOIL: Any well-drained soil will do — thrives best in full sun.

PROPAGATION: Divide clumps in spring.

Thermopsis montana

**Bedding plant:
half-hardy annual**

T. alata

THUNBERGIA   Black-eyed Susan

One or two of the Thunbergia species which are grown as woody climbers in the conservatory can be raised from seed and the young plants bedded out in a sunny and sheltered bed or border. These annual types can be used for climbing up posts and trelliswork or left to trail over banks and walls or down the sides of hanging baskets. Thunbergia grows rapidly, the showy flowers standing out above the arrow-shaped leaves.

VARIETIES: **T. alata** is the main species grown as an annual — height 4-10 ft (1.2-3 m), 2 in. (5 cm) wide funnel-shaped flowers, flowering period July-September. The petals are cream, yellow, pale brown or orange and the throat is dark purple, giving a black-eye effect. The only one you are likely to find is the variety **'Susie'** (4 ft/1.2 m). **T. fragrans 'Angel Wings'** has yellow-eyed white flowers.

SITE & SOIL: Any well-drained soil will do — full sun is essential.

PROPAGATION: Sow seeds in pots in March in gentle heat. Plant out in late May.

Thunbergia alata 'Susie'

**Bedding plant:
half-hardy annual**

THYMOPHYLLA   Dahlberg Daisy

You will have to raise this annual from seed because you cannot expect to find it among the bedding plants for sale at the garden centre in spring. It is listed in numerous seed catalogues and is worth considering if the idea of masses of small golden daisies amid ferny foliage appeals to you. It can be used in beds or rockeries but the Dahlberg Daisy is seen at its best in tubs and hanging baskets.

VARIETIES: **T. tenuiloba** is the only species available — height 9 in.-1 ft (22.5-30 cm), ½ in. (1 cm) wide starry flowers, flowering period July-October. Varieties offered include **'Golden Cascade'** and **'Shooting Star'**. The much branched stems have a trailing growth habit and the finely divided foliage is pungent when crushed. Where winters are mild Thymophylla may survive as a perennial.

SITE & SOIL: Any well-drained soil in full sun will do.

PROPAGATION: Sow seeds in February-April in gentle heat. Plant out in late May.

T. tenuiloba

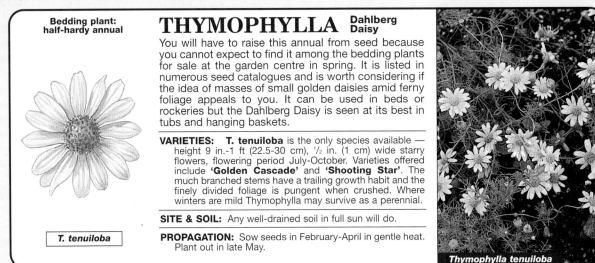

Thymophylla tenuiloba

THYMUS   Thyme

Thyme is a basic feature of most herb gardens but is much less widely used as a decorative garden plant. It should be more widely grown as there is a profusion of flowers in early summer on an easy-to-grow plant. The carpeting varieties can be used to provide sheets of colour in the rock garden or to fill cracks between paving stones. It has few rivals in this latter function — thyme can happily withstand foot traffic and has the bonus of being fragrant when crushed in this way. In addition to the carpeters there are dwarf bushy varieties which can be grown in the border or the rock garden. There are a couple of cultural points — thyme will not succeed if your soil is acid or heavy, and remember to cut back the stems of bushy types in spring.

VARIETIES: The major carpeting species is **T. serpyllum** — height 1-3 in. (2.5-7.5 cm), spread 2 ft (60 cm), ½ in. (1 cm) wide heads of tiny pink flowers, flowering period May-July. The trailing stems bear small oval leaves. There are numerous varieties from which to make your choice. **'Pink Chintz'** (flesh pink flowers) is the most popular one, but you will also find **'Snowdrift'** (white), **'Albus'** (white), **'Annie Hall'** (pink), **'Minor'** (pink), **'Minimus'** (pink), **'Goldstream'** (mauve) and **'Coccineus'** (red). **T. 'Bressingham'** is a widely available pink-flowered carpeter — another popular carpeting hybrid is **T. 'Doone Valley'**. Most popular dwarf bushy thymes are varieties of **T. citriodorus**, the Lemon-scented Thyme. It grows about 1 ft (30 cm) high with lance-shaped leaves and oval flower heads — there are several variegated varieties including **'Silver Queen'** (silver/green leaves), **'Golden King'** (gold-edged green) and **'Bertram Anderson'** (yellow-splashed green).

SITE & SOIL: Requires well-drained light soil in full sun.

PROPAGATION: Divide clumps in autumn or spring, or plant cuttings in a cold frame in summer.

Thymus serpyllum 'Albus'

Rockery perennial
•
Border perennial

Thymus citriodorus 'Golden King'

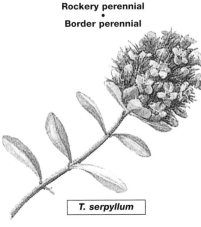

T. serpyllum

Thymus 'Bressingham'

Border perennial

T. cordifolia

TIARELLA Foam Flower

Evergreen perennials with foliage which turns bronze or red in winter are useful in the herbaceous border as they provide colour when everything around them is lifeless. Tiarella fulfils this role — mounds of prominently-veined leaves which are bronze or red cover the ground in winter and in early summer spikes of small frothy flowers appear. Tiarella will grow quite happily under trees and the flowers last for many weeks.

VARIETIES: The most popular species is **T. cordifolia** — height 8 in. (20 cm), tiny white star-shaped flowers, flowering period May-July. A dense leafy carpet is produced and this can be invasive — for a non-invasive species choose **T. wherryi** which is taller (1 ft/30 cm) and has a longer flowering season (June-September). **T. polyphylla** is the tallest species with 1½-2 ft (45-60 cm) flower spikes.

SITE & SOIL: Any moisture-retentive soil will do — thrives best in partial shade.

PROPAGATION: Divide clumps in autumn or spring.

Tiarella wherryi

Bulb

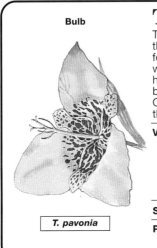

T. pavonia

TIGRIDIA Tiger Flower

Tigridia comes into bloom at the end of summer and the flower is a thing of exotic beauty. Each one lasts for only a day but a succession appears over several weeks. Unfortunately this plant is only moderately hardy so in most districts it is necessary to set the bulbs 4 in. (10 cm) deep in late April and then lift in October when the leaves have withered. Overwinter the bulbs in dry peat.

VARIETIES: **T. pavonia** is the only species for growing outdoors — height 1½ ft (45 cm), 4 in. (10 cm) wide flowers, flowering period July-September. The three outer petals are large and single-coloured — the three inner ones are small and are usually splashed with dark red and purple. The throat is also blotched. Tigridia is sold as a mixture rather than as single-coloured varieties.

SITE & SOIL: Well-drained soil in full sun is essential.

PROPAGATION: Remove offsets when bulbs are lifted in autumn — plant in spring.

Tigridia pavonia

**Bedding plant:
half-hardy annual**

**T. rotundifolia
'Goldfinger'**

TITHONIA Mexican Sunflower

Consider Tithonia if you are looking for a large plant for the centre of the bed or the back of the border. The blooms look like a large dahlia but the foliage is different and the flowers are slightly fragrant. You will need a sunny site and the tall varieties will require staking. The flowers last well in water and should be cut when they are beginning to open. Protect young growth from slugs.

VARIETIES: The basic species is **T. rotundifolia** — height 5 ft (1.5 m), 3 in. (7.5 cm) wide flowers, flowering period July-September. The orange-red petals are yellow underneath and there is a central yellow disc. **'Torch'** is a less vigorous variety — look for **'Yellow Torch'** if you want all-yellow flowers. **'Sundance'** is orange and so is the most popular and most compact variety **'Goldfinger'** (2½ ft/75 cm).

SITE & SOIL: Any well-drained soil will do — full sun is essential.

PROPAGATION: Sow seeds in pots in March in gentle heat. Plant out in early June.

*Tithonia rotundifolia
'Yellow Torch'*

Bedding plant: half-hardy annual

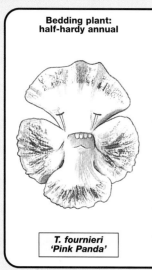

T. fournieri 'Pink Panda'

TORENIA Wishbone Flower

The Wishbone Flower has weak stems which are staked or are left to trail over the sides of containers. Torenia fournieri is quite easy to raise from seed and will flower abundantly in both sunny and partially shady situations. There are now several varieties which are more colourful than the species and can be grown as bushy plants by pinching out the stem tips.

VARIETIES: The basic species is **T. fournieri** — height 1 ft (30 cm), 1 in. (2.5 cm) wide tubular flowers, flowering period July-September. The blooms are pale violet with a dark purple lower lip and yellow blotch. You are more likely to find the variety **'Clown Mixed'** — the velvety flowers are larger than the species. **'Pink Panda'** is a 5 in. (12.5 cm) dwarf and **'Susie Wong'** has chocolate-eyed yellow flowers.

SITE & SOIL: Any well-drained soil will do — thrives in sun or partial shade.

PROPAGATION: Sow seeds in February-March in gentle heat. Plant out in late May.

Torenia fournieri 'Susie Wong'

Border perennial

T. andersoniana

TRADESCANTIA Spiderwort

Spiderwort is a grow-anywhere plant — in wet or dry soil, in sun or partial shade, the three-petalled flowers begin to appear in early summer and the display continues until early autumn. The silky petals surrounding the showy stamens last only a day, but the clusters of buds in each flower head ensure a continuous succession of flowers. Support the stems if necessary and cut back in late autumn.

VARIETIES: **T. andersoniana** is sometimes listed as **T. virginiana** — height 1½-2 ft (45-60 cm), 1 in. (2.5 cm) wide purple flowers, flowering period June-September. The leaves are sword-shaped, 1 ft (30 cm) long and attractive to slugs in spring. Purple is not the only colour — popular varieties include **'Osprey'** (white), **'Isis'** (deep violet-blue), **'Purewell Giant'** (red) and **'Pauline'** (lilac).

SITE & SOIL: Any reasonable soil will do — thrives in sun or partial shade.

PROPAGATION: Divide clumps in autumn or spring.

Tradescantia andersoniana 'Isis'

Border perennial

T. hirta

TRICYRTIS Toad Lily

The Toad Lily is an attractive but fussy plant for the border or woodland garden. It needs acid humus-rich soil and some shade together with shelter from strong winds. If you can provide these conditions you will be rewarded with a display of boldly spotted orchid-like flowers. These blooms are good for cutting. Slugs are the main enemy so protect the young growth in spring.

VARIETIES: **T. formosana** is the most popular species — height 2 ft (60 cm), 1½ in. (3.5 cm) wide funnel-shaped flowers, flowering period August-October. The blooms are white or pale mauve and are spotted with dark purple. **T. hirta** grows to about the same height but the white or mauve flowers have paler spots than T. formosana — the variety **'Alba'** has no spots.

SITE & SOIL: Acid moisture-retentive soil in partial shade is necessary.

PROPAGATION: Divide clumps in spring.

Tricyrtis formosana

Bulb

T. erectum

TRILLIUM Wood Lily

Trillium is not a common plant as it demands a special environment — it only flourishes in woodland where it can have leafy shade above and leaf mould below. A thick underground rhizome produces several fleshy stems which bear the foliage and flower parts in threes — three broad leaves on each stalk and flowers with three sepals and three petals around the stamens.

VARIETIES: **T. grandiflorum** (Wake Robin) is the favourite species — height 1 ft (30 cm), spread 1 ft (30 cm), 3 in. (7.5 cm) wide white flowers which turn pink with age, flowering period April-June. A double-flowered variety **'Flore Pleno'** is available. White and pink are not the only colours — **T. cuneatum** is dark red and **T. erectum** bears wine-coloured blooms. **T. luteum** (8 in./20 cm) has yellow flowers.

SITE & SOIL: A well-drained, humus-rich soil is essential — thrives in partial shade.

PROPAGATION: Divide mature clumps in autumn — replant at once.

Trillium grandiflorum

Bulb

T. rosea

TRITONIA Blazing Star

Tritonia produces strap-like leaves and wiry stems bearing starry blooms in bright colours — features it shares with its close relatives Crocosmia and Ixia. Unfortunately it is even less hardy than Crocosmia and so it should only be grown outdoors if you live in a mild area. Plant the corms 2 in. (5 cm) deep in September. Mulch the crowns in winter and remove this cover once the danger of severe frost has passed.

VARIETIES: **T. rosea** (**T. disticha 'Rubrolucens'**) is the only species which can be expected to survive over winter — height 2 ft (60 cm), 1 in. (2.5 cm) wide pink funnel-shaped flowers, flowering period August-September. The blooms are borne on one-sided spikes — remove faded flower heads and withered leaves in late autumn. Varieties include **'Orange Delight'**.

SITE & SOIL: A well-drained sheltered spot in full sun is essential.

PROPAGATION: Remove cormlets after lifting overcrowded clumps. Plant in autumn.

Tritonia rosea

Bog plant
•
Border perennial

T. cultorum

TROLLIUS Globe Flower

In early summer globular flowers which look like giant buttercups appear on erect stems. This plant will flourish only where its basic requirement can be satisfied — adequate moisture. It is a popular choice for the bog garden — for the border add a plentiful supply of compost or well-rotted manure before planting. Mulch in spring and water in dry weather. Cut the stems down to ground level in autumn.

VARIETIES: The usual choice is a variety of **T. cultorum** — height 1$\frac{1}{2}$-2$\frac{1}{2}$ ft (45-75 cm), 1-2$\frac{1}{2}$ in. (2.5-6 cm) wide yellow or orange flowers, flowering period May-June. **'Alabaster'** is pale cream — yellows include **'Earliest of All'**, **'Lemon Queen'**, **'Superbus'** and **'Canary Bird'**. For orange flowers look for **'Orange Princess'** and **'Fireball'**. **T. chinensis** is taller (3 ft/90 cm) — **'Golden Queen'** is the popular variety.

SITE & SOIL: Moisture-retentive soil is essential — thrives in sun or partial shade.

PROPAGATION: Divide clumps in autumn or spring.

Trollius chinensis

TROPAEOLUM Nasturtium

Grouped here are a number of annuals including the popular nasturtium varieties and the Canary Creeper together with the much less well known perennial species. There are nasturtiums for all sorts of purposes — climbers for clothing walls or scrambling over banks, semi-trailers for window boxes and dwarfs for bedding and edging. The perennial Tropaeolum species are climbers or trailers which do not have the grow-anywhere constitution of the hardy annual nasturtiums — they need a fertile light soil in a sunny spot. Plant the rhizomes horizontally 1 in. (2.5 cm) deep in April.

VARIETIES: Nasturtiums are hybrids of **T. majus** — height 6 in.-8 ft (15 cm-2.4 m), 2 in. (5 cm) wide spurred flowers, flowering period June-October. Climbers grow up to 8 ft (2.4 m) and include **'Tall Mixed Hybrids'** and **'Spitfire'** (red-speckled orange). The semi-trailers (1-1½ ft/30-45 cm) are dominated by the **'Gleam'** hybrids and the dwarfs (6-10 in./15-25 cm) are represented by **'Tom Thumb'** and **'Whirlybird'** mixtures. Other nasturtiums to look for are **'Alaska'** (white-speckled foliage), **'Jewel Mixed'** (semi-double), **'Empress of India'** (dark red) and **'Peach Melba'** (red-blotched yellow). **T. peregrinum** (Canary Creeper) is an annual climber with small yellow flowers. The perennial Tropaeolum you are most likely to find is **T. speciosum** (Flame Creeper) — height 10-15 ft (3-4.5 m), 1 in. (2.5 cm) wide red flowers, flowering period July-September. **T. tuberosum 'Ken Aslet'** blooms at the same time but the flowers are orange-backed yellow. **T. polyphyllum** is a tender plant which should be lifted in autumn and replanted in spring every year — height 5 ft (1.5 m), flowering period June-July.

SITE & SOIL: Well-drained soil is necessary — thrives best in full sun.

PROPAGATION: Annuals: Sow seeds in April where they are to flower or in February in gentle heat for planting out in May. Perennials: Divide rhizomes in autumn.

Tropaeolum 'Alaska Mixed'

**Bedding plant:
hardy annual**
•
**Bedding plant:
tender perennial**
•
Bulb

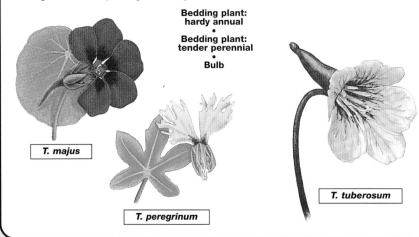

T. majus

T. peregrinum

T. tuberosum

Tropaeolum polyphyllum

TULBAGHIA Wild Garlic

Bulb

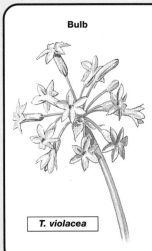

T. violacea

It is not surprising that Tulbaghia is offered in only a few catalogues — most species of this semi-evergreen are not really hardy which means that they need a warm sheltered situation during the growing season and a protective mulch of bark or peat in winter. Not easy, but it does have two desirable features — the flowers appear all summer long and it has good drought resistance.

VARIETIES: **T. violacea** is the only species you are likely to find — height 2 ft (60 cm), ¾ in. (1.5 cm) long fragrant pale purple flowers, flowering period June-August. The tubular blooms are borne in round clusters on top of the stalks — the variegated variety **'Silver Lace'** is usually chosen rather than the species. The white-flowered dwarf (6 in./15 cm) **T. natalensis** is frost-hardy.

SITE & SOIL: Well-drained light soil in full sun is essential.

PROPAGATION: Remove and plant cormlets in April when overcrowded corms are lifted.

Tulbaghia natalensis

TULIPA Tulip

There are more narcissi than tulips in our gardens and in the countryside in spring, but tulips are unsurpassed in the bulb world as a source of both subdued and brilliant colours from early to late spring. Hundreds of different varieties are available and the range they cover is remarkable. There are dwarf Botanical Tulips which open their small flowers on 4 in. (10 cm) stalks in early March and Rembrandts growing 2½ ft (75 cm) high with blooms in mid May. The colour range is also extensive covering nearly every shade from pure white to near black. Tulip colour is a fascinating subject — most varieties are single- (self-) coloured or simple blends, but there are 'broken' tulips where second or third colours appear as complex streaks, splashes or feathery lines. This is caused by a virus and at one time such bizarre varieties commanded astronomically high prices, but they are no longer popular.

The basic tulip pattern is a bell-, bowl- or star-shaped flower made up of shiny petals on top of a leafless stalk. These blooms are generally borne singly, but in a few cases the flower head bears several blooms. There are generally just a few wide leaves but there are varieties with grassy foliage. Most tulips are used either in formal bedding schemes or in containers, but there are other places for them in the garden. Tall varieties can be planted as informal colourful groups in a mixed border and the dwarf varieties are excellent subjects for a rockery.

This genus has been split into 15 Divisions and the numbers appear in the rest of this section and in many catalogues. Divisions 1-11 are known as *Garden Tulips* and their ancestry is usually not known. Divisions 12-15 are the *Botanical Tulips* which are either species or hybrids of known species. It is from this Botanical group that you should choose varieties for the rockery — they are generally left in the ground over winter.

Select your bulbs from a catalogue or at your local garden centre. Make your selection early if you are after choice varieties which may run out but don't be in a hurry to plant them. November is the best month and you can carry on until Christmas — planting too early can result in frost damage to the shoot tips. The recommended planting depth is 6-8 in. (15-20 cm) for Garden Tulips and 4 in. (10 cm) for Botanical Tulips. Remove dead flower heads if practical. The problem with Garden Tulips is that unlike Narcissi they tend to deteriorate if not lifted every year and so the usual practice is to lift them when the foliage turns yellow and then store the bulbs in a frost-free place until replanting time — avoid planting in the same bed year after year. Not everyone lifts them — if you plant at the recommended depth and lime the soil if it is acid or neutral then you should be able to leave Garden Tulips undisturbed for about three years. For containers choose one of the low-growing Botanical Tulips such as T. kaufmanii or T.greigii.

SITE & SOIL: Well-drained soil is necessary — thrives best in full sun.

PROPAGATION: Remove bulblets at lifting time. Dry, store and replant in late autumn or early winter.

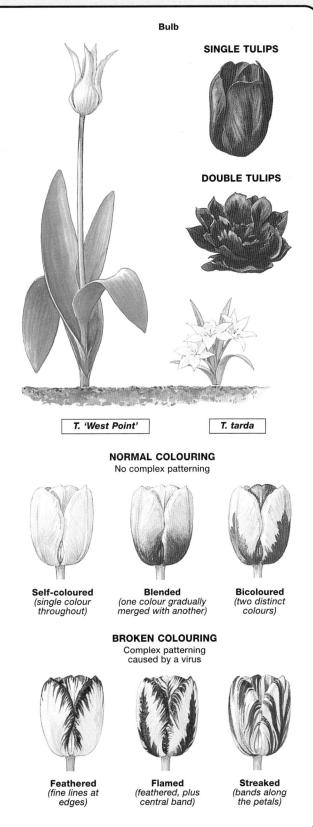

Bulb

SINGLE TULIPS

DOUBLE TULIPS

T. 'West Point'   T. tarda

NORMAL COLOURING
No complex patterning

Self-coloured
(single colour throughout)

Blended
(one colour gradually merged with another)

Bicoloured
(two distinct colours)

BROKEN COLOURING
Complex patterning caused by a virus

Feathered
(fine lines at edges)

Flamed
(feathered, plus central band)

Streaked
(bands along the petals)

TULIPA continued

Division 1:
SINGLE EARLY TULIPS

Cup-shaped single flowers, smaller than the late-flowering varieties. Flowers early-mid April. Height 9 in.-1½ ft (22.5-45 cm).

Strong stems — blooms open flat. Examples include **'Apricot Beauty'** (orange-tinged salmon) and **'Bellona'** (yellow, fragrant). Red is a popular colour — look for **'Brilliant Star'**, **'Couleur Cardinal'**, **'Charles'** and **'Dr. Plesman'**. Some of the other colours are white (**'Diana'**), orange (**'General de Wet'**) and yellow/red (**'Keizerskroon'** and **'Flair'**).

Division 2:
DOUBLE EARLY TULIPS

Fully double flowers which are long-lasting and good for cutting. Flowers mid April. Height 9 in.-1½ ft (22.5-45 cm).

Strong stems, but many-petalled heads bend over after heavy rain. Short — 10 in. (25 cm) is the usual height. Favourites include **'Peach Blossom'** (dark pink), **'Orange Nassau'** (red-flushed orange) and **'Carlton'** (red). There are other reds (**'Electra'**, **'Stockholm'** etc) and whites such as **'Snowstorm'**. **'Monte Carlo'** is a tall yellow — for an attractive bicolour look for **'Fringed Beauty'** (yellow-edged red).

Division 3:
TRIUMPH TULIPS

Single flowers — conical then rounded. Large, but smaller than Darwins. Flowers late April-early May. Height 1½ ft (45 cm).

Strong stems — useful for beds which will have to be cleared for summer bedding plants. Triumphs grow well in light shade. All-reds include **'Ajax'** and **'Cassini'** — examples of other single-coloured Triumphs are white (**'White Virgin'**), pink (**'Don Quixote'**) and purple (**'Attila'**). The showiest ones are the bicolours such as **'Kees Nelis'** (red-edged yellow) and **'Garden Party'** (red-edged white).

Tulipa 'General de Wet'

Tulipa 'Monte Carlo'

Tulipa 'Ballade'

Division 4:
DARWIN HYBRID TULIPS

Single flowers — usually rounded. Very large on tall stems. Flowers late April-early May. Height 2 ft (60 cm).

Very popular for massed bedding — blooms measure up to 4 in. (10 cm) across. The Apeldoorn varieties dominate this Division — **'Apeldoorn'** is yellow-based red and among its relatives are **'Apeldoorn Elite'** (yellow-edged red) and **'Golden Apeldoorn'** (black-based yellow). There are many non-Apeldoorns — **'Golden Oxford'** (yellow), **'Gordon Cooper'** (red-edged pink) etc.

Division 5:
SINGLE LATE TULIPS

Square or oval single flowers. Large on tall stems. Flowers early-mid May. Height 2-2½ ft (60-75 cm).

This Division is made up of the old-fashioned Cottage Tulips and the non-hybrid Darwins. They are traditionally planted to follow the early varieties. Colours range from white (**'Maureen'**) to near-black (**'Queen of the Night'**). Between them are **'Golden Harvest'** (yellow), **'Clara Butt'** (salmon-pink) etc. Bicolours include **'Shirley'** (purple-edged white).

Division 6:
LILY-FLOWERED TULIPS

Single flowers with long pointed petals reflexed at the tips. Flowers early-mid May. Height 1½-2 ft (45-60 cm).

Strong stems — useful for formal beds, containers and flower arranging. **'West Point'** (yellow) is a popular variety — **'Ballerina'** (orange) is fragrant. Tall ones include **'Red Shine'** (red), **'Mariette'** (pink) and **'White Triumphator'** (white). Among the bicolours are **'Ballade'** (white-edged dark pink), **'Aladdin'** (yellow-edged red) and **'Queen of Sheba'** (orange-edged red).

TULIPA continued

Division 7:
FRINGED TULIPS

Single flowers with finely-fringed petals. Flowers early-mid May. Height 1¹/₂-2 ft (45-60 cm).

Blooms look like Single Late Tulips but there is a mass of hair-like fringes. Examples are **'Burgundy Lace'** (red), **'Maja'** (yellow), **'Blue Heron'** (lilac) and **'Bellflower'** (pink).

Division 8:
VIRIDIFLORA TULIPS

Single flowers with petals which are partly green. Flowers early-late May. Height 1-1¹/₂ ft (30-45 cm).

Strong stems — grown mainly for cutting. Blooms have green bands, stripes or blotches. Examples are **'Humming Bird'** (green-feathered yellow) and **'Spring Green'** (green-striped white).

Division 9:
REMBRANDT TULIPS

Large single flowers which are 'broken'. Flowers early-mid May. Height 1¹/₂-2¹/₂ ft (45-75 cm).

Stems need support. Petals are feathered, flamed or streaked — see page 197. Hard to find — examples are **'Cordell Hull'** (red/white) and **'San Marino'** (red/yellow).

Division 10:
PARROT TULIPS

Single flowers with frilled, wavy petals. Very large. Flowers mid-late May. Height 1¹/₂-2 ft (45-60 cm).

Stems may need support. The most spectacular of all tulips — flowers are up to 8 in. (20 cm) across and petals are cut and twisted. The Parrot series is extensive — **'White Parrot'**, **'Flaming Parrot'** etc. Others include **'Estella Rijnveld'** (white/red) and **'Texas Flame'** (red/yellow).

Tulipa 'Humming Bird'

Tulipa 'Texas Flame'

Tulipa clusiana

Division 11:
DOUBLE LATE TULIPS

Fully double flowers which are large and long-lasting. Flowers mid-late May. Height 1¹/₂-2 ft (45-60 cm).

Weak stems — plant close together but some support may still be needed for the cup-shaped blooms. Much less popular than Double Earlies — you will find **'Angelique'** (pale pink) and **'Mount Tacoma'** (white) in several catalogues but the bicolours are harder to find. Look for **'Bonanza'** (yellow-edged red), **'Orange Triumph'** (yellow-edged orange) and **'Allegretto'** (yellow-edged red).

Divisions 12-15:
BOTANICAL TULIPS

Species or varieties, plus hybrids of species in which some or all of the original features are present. There is a wide range of flowering periods (March-May), flower shape and height (4 in.-1¹/₂ ft /10-45 cm). They can be left in the ground to spread.

T. kaufmanniana hybrids are low-growing (6-10 in./15-25 cm) and early-flowering (March). These Water-lily Tulips are used in rockeries, beds and containers. Flowers open into colourful stars — greyish foliage is often mottled. Popular ones include **'Heart's Delight'** (white-edged red), **'Stresa'** (red/yellow) and **'Giuseppi Verdi'** (yellow-edged red).

T. fosteriana hybrids grow to 1-1¹/₂ ft (30-45 cm) and bloom in April. The blooms are extremely wide and the foliage is often striped or spotted. **'Madame Lefeber'** (red) is the best known — others include **'Hit Parade'** (red/yellow), **'Princeps'** (red) and **'Orange Emperor'** (orange).

T. greigii hybrids are low-growing (9 in.-1 ft/22.5-30 cm) and bloom in April-May. The blooms are long-lasting and the leaves are often streaked with purple. Look for **'Red Riding Hood'** (black-centred red), **'Zampa'** (yellow), **'Oratorio'** (pink) and **'Cape Cod'** (yellow-edged apricot).

Species Tulips are mainly dwarfs with small flowers. **T. aucheriana** (pink, April) grows only 4 in. (10 cm) high — **T. batalinii 'Bright Eyes'** (yellow, May) is equally small. **T. biflora** (yellow-centred white, March) has about five blooms on each stem — other multi-headed species include **T. tarda** (yellow-centred white stars, April), **T. praestans** (red, April) and **T. turkestanica** (orange-centred white, March). **T. clusiana** (pink-streaked white, April) has grassy foliage. For bright red flowers on tiny stems grow **T. linifolia**.

Bedding plant: half-hardy annual

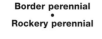
U. anethoides

URSINIA   Ursinia

Ursinia is a colourful S. African daisy which will brighten up a sunny bed or border in midsummer. The flowers are large and do not close up as readily as Arctotis or Mesembryanthemum in dull weather, but it has never become popular. The reason may be the limited colour range or the short flowering season — in addition it needs warm and dry conditions to flourish.

VARIETIES: In the catalogues you will find **U. anethoides** or a **'Special Hybrids'** mixture — height 1-1½ ft (30-45 cm), 2 in. (5 cm) wide yellow or orange flowers, flowering period July-August. The plants are bushy and the pale green leaves are finely divided. At the base of each petal there is a red or maroon band and the central disc turns purple as the flower matures.

SITE & SOIL: Any well-drained light soil will do — full sun is essential.

PROPAGATION: Sow seeds in March in gentle heat. Plant out in late May.

Ursinia anethoides

Border perennial
•
Rockery perennial

U. grandiflora

UVULARIA   Merrybells

This woodland plant is not often seen, but it is a good choice for a shady humus-rich border or rockery if the soil is acid. Uvularia is a member of the lily family, spreading underground by means of rhizomes. The upright stems bear glossy clasping leaves and in spring these branching stems bear long pendent bells with narrow and twisted petals.

VARIETIES: The usual species is **U. grandiflora** (Large Merrybells) — height 1½ ft (45 cm), 2 in. (5 cm) long yellow tubular flowers, flowering period April-May. The flowers and later the fruits hang down on slender stalks — the variety **'Pallida'** has pale yellow flowers. **U. perfoliata** is similar to U. grandiflora but both the leaves and flowers are rather smaller, and the stem appears to pass through the leaves. **U. sessilifolia** bears 1 in. (2.5 cm) cream flowers.

SITE & SOIL: Well-drained but moist soil is necessary — thrives in partial shade.

PROPAGATION: Divide clumps in summer.

Uvularia grandiflora

Border perennial
•
Rockery perennial

V. officinalis

VALERIANA   Valerian

Common Valerian was once widely grown as a medicinal herb but is now planted for its flowers in informal borders, cottage gardens and wild flower gardens. Dwarf species of Valeriana are available for growing in a rock garden. In summer clusters of small flowers are borne above the leaves — the plants spread by means of underground rhizomes.

VARIETIES: **V. officinalis** is Common Valerian — height 3 ft (90 cm), ¼ in. (0.5 cm) white or pink flowers in 2 in. (5 cm) wide heads, flowering period June-July. **V. phu 'Aurea'** (4 ft/1.2 m) is more widely available — it is grown for its yellow spring foliage rather than its midsummer heads of tiny flowers. These tall valerians may require staking. The rockery dwarfs (6 in./15 cm) bloom in early summer and include **V. arizonica**, **V. montana** and **V. saxatilis**.

SITE & SOIL: Any well-drained, humus-rich soil will do — thrives in full sun or light shade.

PROPAGATION: Divide clumps in spring.

Valeriana officinalis

Border perennial

VERATRUM Veratrum

Veratrum is an eye-catching perennial which should be grown as a specimen plant in order to display its numerous floral spikes radiating from the stems. There are purple, white and green species to choose from, but it has never become popular. One of the difficulties is that veratrum may not flower for several years after planting — in addition its flowers have an unpleasant smell.

VARIETIES: The usual species is **V. nigrum** — height 4 ft (1.2 m), small purple starry flowers in 3 ft (90 cm) long flower heads, flowering period August. The pleated leaves have a fan-like appearance. **V. album** grows to the same height but its flower heads are white and shorter — the giant is **V. viride** (Indian Poke) which grows to 7 ft (2.1 m) with yellow-green flowers.

SITE & SOIL: Humus-rich soil and partial shade are necessary.

PROPAGATION: Divide clumps in autumn.

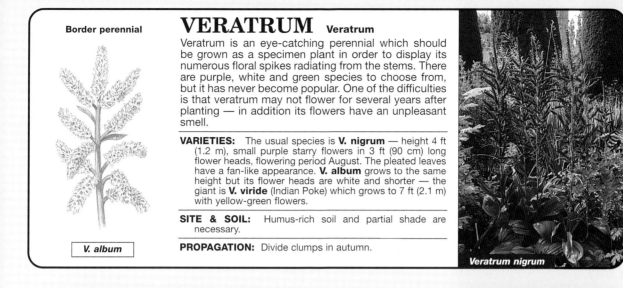

V. album

Veratrum nigrum

VERBASCUM Mullein

Verbascums are best known as back of the border plants with tall spikes of showy saucer-shaped flowers above a rosette of woolly leaves. A wide range of colours and heights is available — tall ones need staking. Keep watch for caterpillars and remove the spikes once the flowers have faded. Not all mulleins are 3-6 ft (90 cm-1.8 m) border perennials — there are three species which are small enough for the rock garden and are worth growing in a sunny spot. These dwarfs have most of the familiar features — hairy leaves, a profusion of flat flowers and a dislike of heavy and rich soil, but only one produces spire-like flower heads. Many mulleins are evergreen or semi-evergreen and some are short-lived. This lack of permanence is less of a problem than you would expect as most species readily self-seed.

VARIETIES: **V. olympicum** is a typical tall mullein — height 6 ft (1.8 m), 1 in. (2.5 cm) wide yellow flowers on 2½ ft (75 cm) high spikes, flowering period July-August. Other yellow-flowered giants include **V. bombyciferum** and **V. 'C.L. Adams'**. There is a larger selection in the 3-4 ft (90 cm-1.2 m) range and this group is dominated by the named hybrids of **V. chaixii** which bloom from June to August. Popular ones include **'Gainsborough'** (pale yellow), **'Pink Domino'** (rose-pink), **'Royal Highland'** (yellow/apricot), **'Cotswold Queen'** (apricot) and **'Mont Blanc'** (white). Other plants in this medium height range are the easy to grow **V. phoeniceum** (purple) and **V. densiflorum** (yellow). The rockery species which is closest in growth habit to the border mulleins is **V. dumulosum** — height 9 in. (22.5 cm), ½ in. (1 cm) wide yellow flowers, flowering period July-August. **V. spinosum** is different — the leaves are tiny and the yellow flowers are borne in loose clusters. The most popular dwarf is **V. 'Letitia'**, a hybrid of these two rockery mulleins.

SITE & SOIL: Well-drained infertile soil in full sun is necessary.

PROPAGATION: Divide clumps in spring or sow seeds in a cold frame in early summer.

Verbascum 'C.L. Adams'

Border perennial
•
Rockery perennial

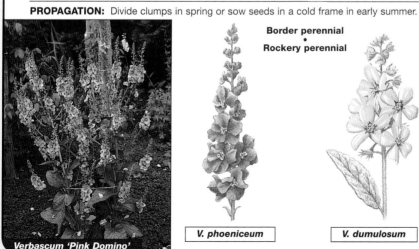

Verbascum 'Pink Domino'

V. phoeniceum

V. dumulosum

Verbascum 'Letitia'

VERBENA Verbena

The only Verbena known by most gardeners is the popular bedding plant seen growing in beds and containers in summer. Much less well known are the border perennials. Most of them, such as V. corymbosa and V. peruviana are not hardy, but the three described below can be grown outdoors.

VARIETIES: Nearly all the seed packets of Verbena you will find at the garden centre or in the catalogues are named varieties of **V. hybrida** — height 6 in.-1 ft (15-30 cm), ¹/₂-1 in. (1-2.5 cm) flowers in 2-3 in. (5-7.5 cm) wide clusters, flowering period July-October. For bushy upright plants in a wide range of colours look for the **'Novalis'**, **'Derby'** and **'Showtime'** series. There are several types with a spreading growth habit which are useful for containers as well as bedding — look for **'Romance Mixed'** and the highly recommended **'Imagination'** (violet-blue). For trailing growth with stems up to 2 ft (60 cm) long **'Tapien'** is the one to buy — there are more flower heads than are found on ordinary Verbenas. For single colours rather than a mixture there are **'Adonis Blue'** (blue), **'Peaches and Cream'** (pink ageing to cream), **'Silver Anne'** (pink ageing to white), **'Sissinghurst'** (pink), **'Lawrence Johnston'** (red), **'Blue Lagoon'** (blue) etc. Some of these are raised from cuttings rather than seed. There are two perennial Verbenas which can be regarded as truly hardy — **V. hastata** (5 ft/1.5 m) and **V. 'Homestead Purple'** (1 ft/30 cm). **V. bonariensis** (5 ft/1.5 m) needs a winter mulch to protect the crowns from frost — all these perennials have blue or purple flowers from June to October.

SITE & SOIL: Any well-drained soil will do — thrives best in full sun.

PROPAGATION: Annuals: Sow seeds in March in gentle heat — plant out in late May. Alternatively plant cuttings in late summer under glass. Perennials: Plant cuttings in late summer under glass.

Verbena 'Showtime'

Verbena 'Tapien'

Bedding plant:
half-hardy annual
•
Border perennial

V. hybrida

Verbena hastata

Beds and borders can provide the flower arranger with abundant material for drying. Tying the flower stems in bunches and hanging them upside-down in a dark and dry place is by far the most popular method, and many types can be preserved in this way. All the 'everlasting' flowers, of course, such as Helichrysum and Limonium, but many others such as Achillea, Calendula, Nigella and Salvia will dry perfectly well. Roses, however, need a different technique — try the microwave method described in The Flower Arranging Expert.

VERONICA **Speedwell**

The speedwells are a large genus of plants with small flat-faced flowers in white, blue, purple or pink. These blooms are usually borne on tall and narrow spikes — heights range from 3 in. (7.5 cm) to 4 ft (1.2 m). Most border speedwells grow 1-1½ ft (30-45 cm) high and will thrive in chalky soil. They are generally trouble-free but they do need soil which drains freely — waterlogging in winter is the usual cause of death. Mulch in spring and water when the weather is dry. Tall-growing species may require support — cut stems back once the flowers have faded. There are several dwarf species which can be used in the rockery to provide midsummer colour — the popular ones are spreading plants which form a leafy mat. A word of caution — some can be invasive.

Veronica gentianoides

VARIETIES: The earliest border speedwell is **V. gentianoides** — height 1½ ft (45 cm), pale blue flowers, flowering period May-June. **V. incana** flowers a little later — height 1-1½ ft (30-45 cm), blue flowers, silvery semi-evergreen leaves, flowering period June-July. **V. spicata** grows to the same height as V. incana and blooms at the same time, but the leaves are green and there are flowers in other colours than blue such as the varieties **'Icicle'** (white) and **'Rotfuchs'** (dark pink). For the brightest blue flowers grow **V. teucrium** — for the tallest plants (3-4 ft/90 cm-1.2 m) look for **V. exaltata** and **V. longifolia**. Rockery speedwells grow to 6 in. (15 cm) or less. The most popular of these dwarf varieties is **V. peduncularis 'Georgia Blue'** (blue flowers, bronzy leaves), but you should have no difficulty in finding the rapid-spreading **V. prostrata** or one of its varieties such as **'Mrs. Holt'** (pink) or **'Spode Blue'** (pale blue). Other dwarfs include the non-invasive **V. pectinata** and the grey-leaved **V. cinerea**.

SITE & SOIL: Any well-drained soil will do — thrives in sun or light shade.

PROPAGATION: Divide clumps in autumn or spring.

Border perennial
•
Rockery perennial

Veronica pectinata

V. spicata

V. prostrata

Veronica cinerea

Border perennial
•
Bog plant

V. virginicum 'Album'

VERONICASTRUM **Culver's Root**

This stately plant is not often seen and you will have to search for a supplier, unlike its close relative described above which you will find at any garden centre. Veronicastrum is at home at the back of the border or in boggy ground around the pond — it cannot tolerate dry conditions. Frost and shade do not pose a problem, but mildew can be a nuisance.

VARIETIES: The only species on offer is **V. virginicum** which is sometimes sold as **Veronica virginica** — height 5 ft (1.5 m), spread 2 ft (60 cm), ¼ in. (0.5 cm) long tubular purplish-blue flowers, flowering period July-September. The stems bear whorls of toothed lance-shaped leaves and are crowned by the tall and narrow flower heads. There are numerous varieties including **'Album'** (white) and **'Roseum'** (pink).

SITE & SOIL: Humus-rich moist soil is essential — thrives in sun or partial shade.

PROPAGATION: Divide clumps in spring.

Veronicastrum virginicum

VIOLA   Pansy, Viola, Violet

Violas make up a large genus of low-growing plants which bear flat-faced flowers in the axils of their leaves. These flowers have two upper petals, two side petals and a lower spurred petal. By far the most popular ones are the pansies and violas which are short-lived perennials but are generally grown as annuals or biennials. With care and the proper choice of varieties it is quite possible to have *Pansies* in flower during every month of the year. The flowering period extends for four or five months and no other flower exceeds the wide colour span ranging from pure white to almost jet black — only green is missing. Faced varieties have a large dark marking ('face' or 'mask') at the centre of the bloom. The dividing line between *Violas* and pansies is not a clear one, but you will generally find them on different pages of the catalogue. Violas are usually shorter and more compact than pansies and the flowers are smaller and less rounded. These blooms are often single-coloured and the life span of the plant is longer when grown as a perennial.

Do not expect the *Border Violets* to produce the large and colourful blooms associated with the pansies and violas described above. These violets are perennials with 1-1½ in. (2.5-3.5 cm) wide flowers and are used as ground cover or edging — some shade is necessary. These border types are small and can be grown in the rock garden, but there are several varieties of *Rockery Violets* which are associated with alpine plants rather than herbaceous border ones.

VARIETIES: Pansies may have an old fashioned look, but they are the result of 19th century hybridisation which produced **V. wittrockiana** — height 6-9 in. (15-22.5 cm), 1½-4 in. (3.5-10 cm) wide flowers. The Winter-flowering group is sown as a biennial in summer for flowering in November-May — the major display is usually in the spring. The **'Universal'** series dominates this group — buy as a mixture or as a faced, plain or bicoloured variety. The **'Ultima'** series contains varieties in many colours and **'Delta'** pansies are larger than other Winter-flowering ones. The Summer-flowering group is sown in spring for flowering in summer and autumn. Mixtures are popular — for the largest flowers grow **'Majestic Giants'** and for a range of single colours choose **'Clear Crystals Mixed'**. The faced variety **'Swiss Giants'** remains popular but some people prefer single colours. Look for **'Padparadja'** (orange), **'Black Beauty'** (near-black) and **'Azure Blue'** (mid blue). **'Rippling Waters'** has white-edged purple flowers and **'Joker'** is pale blue with a dark blue face. **'Jolly Joker'** is a purple and orange bicolour and **'Rococo'** has ruffled petals. **'Romeo and Juliet'** has many pastel shades and the **'Turbo'** series can be sown under glass in September for spring/early summer flowers. Mini-pansies are compact dwarfs which flower from spring to autumn — look for **'Velour Mixed'**.

Violas have a complex parentage, including **V. williamsii**, **V. tricolor** and **V. cornuta** — height 4-6 in. (10-15 cm), 1½-2 in. (3.5-5 cm) wide flowers, flowering period March-July or June-October depending on the time of sowing (see below). **'Johnny Jump-up'** is an old favourite and the **'Sorbet'** range is a modern series noted for its winter hardiness. **'Sorbet Yesterday, Today and Tomorrow'** bears flowers which change from white to deep blue. The **'Princess'** series is chosen for its long flowering season and **'Bambini'** for its cat-like face. Single colours include **'Chantreyland'** (apricot), **'Prince Henry'** (deep purple), **'Blue Heaven'** (blue), **'Sunbeam'** (yellow) and **'Blackjack'** (yellow-eyed black).

There are two Border Violets which are widely available. **V. odorata** (Sweet Violet) is the smaller one and blooms earlier — height 4-6 in. (10-15 cm), 1 in. (2.5 cm) wide white or blue scented flowers, flowering period February-April. Varieties include **'Alba'** (white) and **'Rosea'** (pink). **V. cornuta** is the Horned Violet — height 6-9 in. (15-22.5 cm), 1½ in. (3.5 cm) wide lilac-blue flowers, flowering period May-August — the variety **'Minor'** is a smaller version. The easiest Rockery Violet to grow is **V. lutea** and the smallest is **V. jooi**. **V. labradorica 'Purpurea'** is a popular spring-flowering variety and **V. biflora** bears yellow flowers in summer.

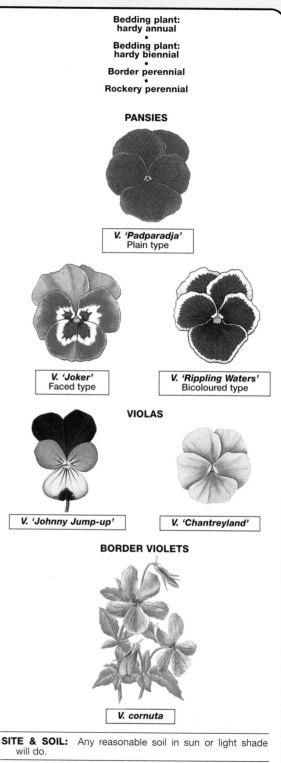

- Bedding plant: hardy annual
- Bedding plant: hardy biennial
- Border perennial
- Rockery perennial

PANSIES

V. 'Padparadja'
Plain type

V. 'Joker'
Faced type

V. 'Rippling Waters'
Bicoloured type

VIOLAS

V. 'Johnny Jump-up'

V. 'Chantreyland'

BORDER VIOLETS

V. cornuta

SITE & SOIL: Any reasonable soil in sun or light shade will do.

PROPAGATION: Annuals for summer/autumn flowers: Sow seeds in February-April under glass — plant out in May. Biennials for winter/spring flowers: Sow seeds in June-July under glass or in open ground — plant out in autumn. Perennials: Divide clumps in autumn or plant cuttings in a cold frame in summer.

VIOLA continued

Viola 'Universal Mixed'

Viola 'Turbo Mixed'

Viola 'Velour Blue'

Viola 'Sorbet'

Viola 'Bambini'

Viola 'Blue Heaven'

Viola odorata

Viola labradorica 'Purpurea'

Viola lutea

Rockery perennial

VITALIANA Vitaliana

This is one for the alpine enthusiast who wants a yellow spring-flowering plant which visitors are unlikely to have seen before. The ground-hugging mat of tiny leaves is suitable for rockeries, scree gardens and troughs, but it is not easy to grow. Good drainage is essential and non-alkaline gritty soil is required — it will also be necessary to provide some protection against rain in winter.

VARIETIES: **V. primuliflora** is the only species — height 1 in. (2.5 cm), spread 10 in. (25 cm), ³/₄ in. (1.5 cm) wide tubular yellow flowers, flowering period April-May. The star-faced flowers are borne above the leafy rosettes — the leaves have variety silvery margins and the **'Praetutiana'** has foliage which is white below. The flowers are borne singly and not in groups. Vitaliana may be listed under Androsace or Douglasia in the catalogues.

SITE & SOIL: Well-drained soil in full sun is essential.

PROPAGATION: Plant offsets in summer.

V. primuliflora

Vitaliana primuliflora

Rockery perennial

WAHLENBERGIA Wahlenbergia

Like the plant described above this is an unusual alpine for the rock garden enthusiast. It is once again low-growing and spreading, but it differs from Vitaliana in many ways. The leaves are lance-shaped or oval and the flowers are upturned bells. Some are not fully hardy and they flower in summer and not spring. Wahlenbergia tolerates more winter rain and less sun than Vitaliana.

VARIETIES: There are just two species you are likely to find in the catalogues. **W. albomarginata** is the New Zealand Bluebell — height 3 in. (7.5 cm), spread 10 in. (25 cm), 1 in. (2.5 cm) wide white or blue flowers, flowering period June-July. The flowers are bell-shaped — for open star-faced bells choose instead **W. gloriosa** which grows to about the same size and has lilac or violet blooms.

SITE & SOIL: Requires well-drained soil — thrives in sun or partial shade.

PROPAGATION: Sow seeds in gentle heat in early spring or divide clumps in spring.

W. gloriosa

Wahlenbergia gloriosa

Border perennial
•
Rockery perennial

WALDSTEINIA Waldsteinia

This semi-evergreen is a low-growing spreading plant for the woodland garden, front of the border or the rockery. The surface-rooting stems produce a mass of lobed leaves which turn golden in autumn. It is a member of the rose family with five-petalled flowers which are similar to Potentilla and are borne in loose clusters. It can be invasive so do not plant close to small or delicate alpines.

VARIETIES: The only species you are likely to find is **W. ternata** — height 4 in. (10 cm), spread 2 ft (60 cm), ¹/₂ in. (1 cm) wide yellow flowers, flowering period April-June. It is an easy plant which will grow in nearly all soil types and in shade. **W. geoides** is listed in a few catalogues — the flowers are larger and it has five- rather than three-lobed leaves. The strawberry-leaved **W. fragarioides** is even harder to find.

SITE & SOIL: Any well-drained soil will do — thrives best in partial shade.

PROPAGATION: Divide clumps in late summer.

W. ternata

Waldsteinia ternata

WATSONIA Bugle Lily

Bulb

W. borbonica

This uncommon plant has the sword-like leaves you would expect from a relative of Gladiolus but the flowers are quite different — they are star-faced tubes borne on either side of the flower stem. You will find a few species listed in specialist bulb catalogues — none of them can withstand frost so it is necessary to plant the corms in April-May and then lift in autumn. Store in a dry, frost-free place.

VARIETIES: **W. pillansii** (**W. beatricis**) is the species you are most likely to find — height 3 ft (90 cm), 2 in. (5 cm) long orange flowers, flowering period June-July. **W. borbonica** (**W. pyramidata**) is a taller plant (5 ft/1.5 m) with 1 in. (2.5 cm) long pink flowers — staking is necessary. There is a dwarf but there are only two or three suppliers — **W. humilis** grows 1 ft (30 cm) high and produces 1½ in. (3.5 cm) long pink flowers.

SITE & SOIL: Any well-drained soil in full sun will do.

PROPAGATION: Remove and store cormlets at lifting time. Plant in spring.

Watsonia pillansii

XERANTHEMUM Common Immortelle

Hardy annual

X. annuum

The Common Immortelle is grown for its 'everlasting' flowers. The petals are strawy and crisp with an outstanding reputation for keeping their colour after drying. Support the plants with small twigs — the blooms appear in midsummer on the top of wiry stems. Cut just before the flowers are fully open and remove the leaves. Tie in bunches and hang upside down in a cool place away from sunlight.

VARIETIES: **X. annuum** is bought as a mixture of single, semi-double and double varieties — height 2 ft (60 cm), 2 in. (5 cm) wide white, pink, purple, red or lilac flowers, flowering period July-September. The silvery leaves are lance-shaped. The ordinary seed mixtures tend to produce plants which look thin and weedy — for bed or border display it is better to grow **'Lumina Mixed'** which produces bushier plants.

SITE & SOIL: Any well-drained soil in full sun will do.

PROPAGATION: Sow seeds in March-April where they are to flower. Thin to required spacing.

Xeranthemum annuum

ZANTEDESCHIA Arum Lily, Calla Lily

Bog plant
•
Border perennial

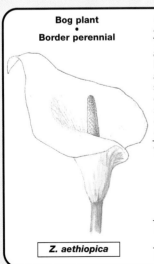

Z. aethiopica

The eye-catching flower of the Arum Lily is made up of a trumpet-shaped spathe and a yellow central spadix. Many attractive types are available but only Z. aethiopica and its varieties are hardy enough to survive over winter. Other Arum Lilies have to be grown in a greenhouse or set out in bloom for an early summer display in the garden. Moist or wet ground is essential and so is a thick winter mulch to protect the crowns from frost damage.

VARIETIES: **Z. aethiopica** is the species for the moist border or the boggy ground around the pool — height 3 ft (90 cm), spread 2 ft (60 cm), 6-9 in. (15-22.5 cm) long white flowers, flowering period April-June. **'Crowborough'** is the most reliable variety — others include **'Green Goddess'** with cream-centred green flowers and the 1½ ft (45 cm) dwarf **'Apple Court Babe'**.

SITE & SOIL: Moist humus-rich soil is essential. Thrives best in full sun.

PROPAGATION: Divide clumps in late summer.

Zantedeschia aethiopica **'Crowborough'**

Rockery perennial
•
Border perennial

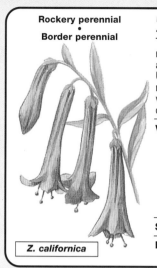

Z. californica

ZAUSCHNERIA Californian Fuchsia

This uncommon plant provides a welcome feature in a rock garden or at the front of the border as it provides a showy display of bright flowers late in the year. Unfortunately it is not a grow-anywhere plant — it needs a warm and sheltered spot. It is hardy and well worth looking for in the catalogues or at larger garden centres.

VARIETIES: The only species you are likely to find is **Z. californica**, sometimes listed as **Epilobium californicum** — height 1 ft (30 cm), 1 in. (2.5 cm) long tubular scarlet flowers, flowering period August-October. The grey-green leaves are hairy and the flowers are borne in clusters at the tips of the stems. Several varieties are available — **'Glasnevin'** is orange-red and so is **'Dublin'** which is the most reliable variety. **'Cana'** is scarlet and **'Solidarity Pink'** is pale pink.

SITE & SOIL: Requires well-drained gritty soil in full sun.

PROPAGATION: Plant cuttings in a cold frame in summer.

Zauschneria californica 'Solidarity Pink'

Bulb

Z. candida

ZEPHYRANTHES Zephyr Lily

This dainty plant produces crocus-like flowers in summer or autumn, but like Zantedeschia on the previous page there is only one species which is hardy enough to be grown outdoors. The other Zephyr Lilies are grown as conservatory plants. April is the time to plant the bulbs — set them 2 in. (5 cm) deep and 4 in. (10 cm) apart. In autumn place a mulch of peat or leaf mould over the crowns when the leaves have died down.

VARIETIES: **Z. candida** is the Zephyr Lily to grow outdoors — height 6 in. (15 cm), 1½ in. (3.5 cm) wide white flowers, flowering period September-October. The flower stalks appear in large numbers above the grassy foliage at the end of summer — the stalks bear buds which open wide to form star-shaped blooms. It is a good subject for a sheltered pocket in a sunny rockery.

SITE & SOIL: Well-drained, sandy soil is essential. Thrives best in full sun.

PROPAGATION: Divide overcrowded clumps in the spring — remove and plant up bulblets.

Zephyranthes candida

Bedding plant: half-hardy annual

Z. elegans 'Ruffles'

ZINNIA Zinnia

Few annuals look as appealing as Zinnia in the seed catalogues, but to get similar results you will need fertile soil and a fine summer. All colours apart from blue are available, and the daisy-like heads are single, semi-double or double. The strong stems do not need staking and the cut blooms last well in water.

VARIETIES: The named Zinnias are varieties of **Z. elegans** or **Z. haageana** — height 6 in.-2½ ft (15-75 cm), 1-5 in. (2.5-12.5 cm) wide flowers, flowering period July-October. For maximum display choose **'Dahlia-flowered Mix'** (5 in./ 12.5 cm wide flowers on 2½ ft/75 cm stems). At the other end of the scale are the 6-10 in. (15-25 cm) dwarfs such as **'Hobgoblin'**, **'Peter Pan'**, **'Short Stuff'** and **'Thumbelina'**. **'Persian Carpet'** is a mixture of bicolours, **'Ruffles'** has a multitude of petals and **'Envy'** is the green one.

SITE & SOIL: Any humus-rich soil will do — thrives best in full sun.

PROPAGATION: Sow seeds in March in gentle heat. Plant out in early June.

Zinnia elegans 'Envy'

CHAPTER 3

BUYING PLANTS

WHERE TO BUY

As a general rule you get what you pay for. It is not an absolute rule — there are times when you may be sold rubbish by a garden centre and many gardeners have obtained excellent plants as a bargain offer from a newspaper advertisement. But the general rule still applies — you get what you pay for. There are many places where plants are sold, but there are just five major sources of supply with the garden centre (which buys in its stock) and the nursery (which raises some or all of its plants) dominating the scene.

BARGAIN OFFER NURSERY
The 'bargain offers' advertised in newspapers and magazines are sometimes good value, but don't expect too much. Caution is needed with the 'wonder offers' — phrases such as 'everlasting blooms' etc should not be taken too literally.
Advantage: An inexpensive way to obtain old favourites which are known for their reliability.
Drawbacks: If the plants are truly cheap, there must be a reason. Perennials may be only rooted cuttings which will take time to establish or they may be substandard or damaged stock.
If something goes wrong: Write and complain if the plants are dead or diseased, but not if they are smaller than expected.

GARDEN CENTRE
The garden centre or nursery is the only place to go if you want to choose from a large selection for immediate planting. A visit is one of the joys of gardening, but a few words of advice — go at the start of the planting season, avoid weekends if you can and do not buy on impulse. Always check the suitability of a plant before you buy, and that may mean looking in a book such as this one.
Advantages: You can see exactly what you are buying and you can take it home with you. At larger garden centres there is advice on hand, but do check the advice in the A-Z guide.
Drawbacks: The varieties on offer are usually the more popular sorts and the number of any one variety may be limited — for a massed planting you may have to order from a nursery. Garden centres are generally out of town — you will need a car.
If something goes wrong: Take the plant back and explain what happened if you are sure it was not your fault. You will need proof of purchase.

MAIL ORDER NURSERY
Mail order nurseries remain an important source of supply. Try to choose one with a good reputation, one you have used before or one which has been recommended to you. Order early in the season and
Advantages: There is often an excellent catalogue from which you can choose your requirements in the peace and comfort of your own home. Rarities as well as popular ones can be obtained from the larger nurseries and there are specialist suppliers of particular groups such as alpines and bulbs.
Drawbacks: Obviously you cannot see what you are buying and you cannot take your order home with you. This means that the perennials may arrive when planting is inconvenient. Some of the plants on your order may be out of stock and the delivery charge on container-grown plants may be high.
If something goes wrong: Write to the company and explain what happened if you are sure it was not your fault. Some nurseries will return your money.

MARKET STALL
In many street and indoor markets there is a stall which sells plants — in autumn there are border perennials and bulbs, and in spring you will find bedding plants.
Advantages: Plants are inexpensive — the market stall is often the cheapest source of supply. It is also usually conveniently sited and some stallholders are quite knowledgeable.
Drawbacks: The selection is very limited — only fast-moving lines can be stocked and this means that only the most popular varieties are offered. In addition some of the stock may have travelled back and forth to the stall — try to buy at the beginning of the planting season.
If something goes wrong: You can try complaining — stallholders have to maintain trading standards.

HIGH STREET SHOP
In autumn and spring many popular varieties are sold at greengrocers, department stores, supermarkets etc — they are usually available as bare-rooted plants in labelled polythene bags.
Advantages: You can pick up a few items while doing your everyday shopping — only a virtue if your plot is small and a trip to a garden centre is a chore. A more important advantage is that pre-packaged perennials tend to be cheaper than pot-grown ones.
Drawbacks: The selection is limited as only fast-moving lines can be stocked, and warm conditions in store can lead to drying-out.
If something goes wrong: You can try complaining to the shop, but the response will depend on the policy of the store.

WHAT TO BUY

Buy good quality plant material rather than unnamed, poor grade stock — plants may not fully recover from a poor start in life. Where possible check over the plants or bulbs you propose to buy, using the notes below as your guide. One of the most profound changes in the gardening world during the second half of the 20th century has been the change in the way plants are offered for sale. Shrubs and trees are now generally container-grown rather than ball-rooted in sacking or bare-rooted in straw. Bedding plants are now usually bought in strips or packs rather than in large wooden trays. Until recently buying bedding plants in this form for a large area meant that it was an expensive business, but things have changed. Nowadays you can buy plugs or seedlings in small trays which you can pot on, harden off and then plant out in the ordinary way. These grow-on seedlings are much cheaper than ready-to-plant ones.

CONTAINER-GROWN PLANTS

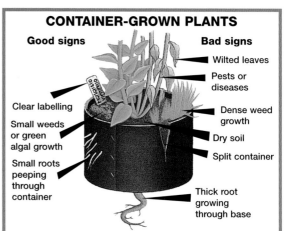

Good signs

- Clear labelling
- Small weeds or green algal growth
- Small roots peeping through container

Bad signs

- Wilted leaves
- Pests or diseases
- Dense weed growth
- Dry soil
- Split container
- Thick root growing through base

Containers are much more likely to hold trees or shrubs than perennials, although large specimens such as Cortaderia, Rheum and Gunnera are sold in this way. A container-grown perennial is a plant which has been raised as a seedling or cutting and has then been potted on until it is housed in the whalehide or plastic container on display. It should *not* have been lifted from the open ground and its roots plus surrounding soil stuffed into the container. Such lifted plants are sold and can give successful results, but they should neither be called nor be priced as container-grown plants. The true container-grown hardy perennial can be planted at any time of the year as long as the ground is neither frosty nor waterlogged. The most convenient of all the planting types for large specimen plants, but also the most expensive.

POT-GROWN PLANTS

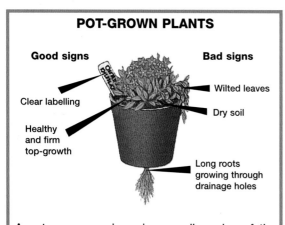

Good signs

- Clear labelling
- Healthy and firm top-growth

Bad signs

- Wilted leaves
- Dry soil
- Long roots growing through drainage holes

A pot-grown specimen is a small version of the container-grown plant — it is the usual way in which both border and rockery perennials are sold. The pots are usually made of plastic these days, but clay ones are still used and so are peat ones which can be planted directly into the soil. Rigid plastic and clay pots are reusable. The plant in the pot may be mature as in the case of an alpine or it may be the juvenile form (seedling or rooted cutting) of a border perennial. There are two points to watch for. If the plant is housed in a small pot it will be necessary to water regularly in dry weather until the plant is established, and if the soil ball is covered with matted roots the surface ones should be teased out before planting. Individual pots are the most expensive way to buy bedding plants, but this is the way to buy dot plants and also mature bedding plants in full flower. Plants are available over a long period and not just during the traditional bedding-out season, and there is no check to growth after planting out.

PRE-PACKAGED PLANTS

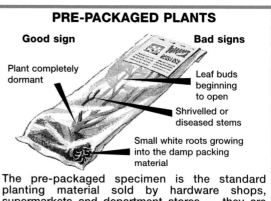

Good sign

- Plant completely dormant

Bad signs

- Leaf buds beginning to open
- Shrivelled or diseased stems
- Small white roots growing into the damp packing material

The pre-packaged specimen is the standard planting material sold by hardware shops, supermarkets and department stores — they are also available at garden centres. The usual plants are shrubs and roses, but some popular perennials are offered in this way — you will find lupins, delphiniums, poppies etc. The bare-rooted perennial has moist peat, sphagnum moss or compost around the roots and the whole plant is housed inside a labelled polythene bag — this bag may be contained within an attractive cardboard carton. Such plants are cheaper than their pot-grown counterparts but there are drawbacks. You can't see what you are buying and premature growth may begin in the warm conditions which occur in the shop. Planting time is the dormant season between autumn and spring.

PACKS

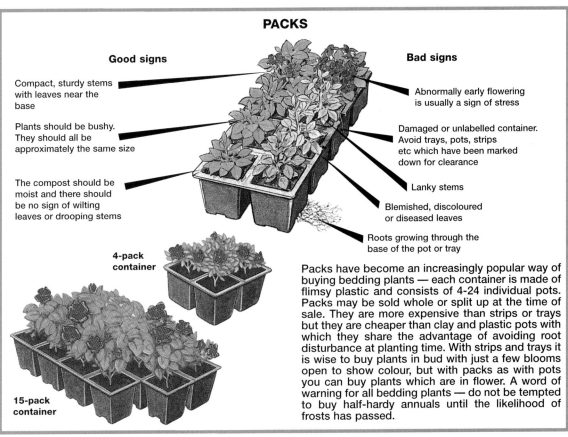

Good signs

Compact, sturdy stems with leaves near the base

Plants should be bushy. They should all be approximately the same size

The compost should be moist and there should be no sign of wilting leaves or drooping stems

Bad signs

Abnormally early flowering is usually a sign of stress

Damaged or unlabelled container. Avoid trays, pots, strips etc which have been marked down for clearance

Lanky stems

Blemished, discoloured or diseased leaves

Roots growing through the base of the pot or tray

4-pack container

15-pack container

Packs have become an increasingly popular way of buying bedding plants — each container is made of flimsy plastic and consists of 4-24 individual pots. Packs may be sold whole or split up at the time of sale. They are more expensive than strips or trays but they are cheaper than clay and plastic pots with which they share the advantage of avoiding root disturbance at planting time. With strips and trays it is wise to buy plants in bud with just a few blooms open to show colour, but with packs as with pots you can buy plants which are in flower. A word of warning for all bedding plants — do not be tempted to buy half-hardy annuals until the likelihood of frosts has passed.

BULBS

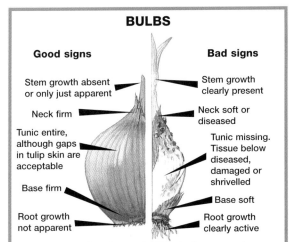

Good signs

Stem growth absent or only just apparent

Neck firm

Tunic entire, although gaps in tulip skin are acceptable

Base firm

Root growth not apparent

Bad signs

Stem growth clearly present

Neck soft or diseased

Tunic missing. Tissue below diseased, damaged or shrivelled

Base soft

Root growth clearly active

Always examine loose bulbs before you buy — reject any rogue ones which may have been accidentally introduced from another box. Look for the bad signs — a poor quality bulb will never produce a good quality plant. This is especially important with 'bargain' offers, although it is quite acceptable to buy very low-priced stock if it is good quality undersized material which can be grown on to produce flowers in the second season. Large-sized bulbs are usually the best choice, but hyacinths for outdoors should be the medium and not the large grade. The outer scales of lily bulbs should be firm and succulent — do not buy the bulbs if they are covered with withered scales.

LIFTED PLANTS
Small clumps and divisions of large clumps of perennials are sometimes lifted and placed in polythene bags for sale. The problem here is that some roots will have been broken during the transfer and so tap-rooted varieties may take a long time to become established in their new home.

SEEDS

Raising annuals and biennials from seed at home offers two distinct advantages compared with buying seedlings or young plants. It is less expensive which is important if you require a large number of bedding plants, and the choice of varieties is much wider which is important if you are a keen gardener and like to grow out-of-the-ordinary plants. Look for types marked F_1 hybrid — this means that the variety has been carefully bred to have more uniformity and more vigour than the standard types. Remember that some perennials can also be raised from seed. Growing your own plants from scratch is one of the joys of gardening, but it is not for everyone. With many seeds both time and some skill are necessary.

TRAYS

Flimsy plastic tray

Half tray

The tray is the traditional method of buying bedding plants. It is the cheapest way, but roots are damaged when the plants are torn apart at planting time. Wooden trays holding 40-60 plants have been largely replaced by flimsy plastic ones — even more popular is the plastic half tray holding about 20 plants. Trays are recommended when you require a large number of tough grow-anywhere plants such as Alyssum and French Marigolds.

SEEDLINGS

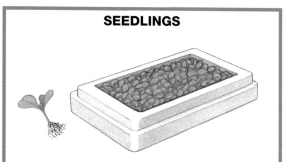

This is the smallest stage at which you can buy plants for growing on, and they are the least expensive. The seedlings are despatched in a rigid polystyrene pack — 100 is the usual count but some seed houses offer 250 and 400 seedling packs. The tiny plants are at the expanded seed leaf stage and need to be pricked out shortly after arrival into trays or cellular trays filled with compost.

STRIPS

Flimsy plastic strip

The strip has become a popular way to buy bedding plants for transplanting into beds or containers. The plants are grown in a series of snap-off strips which are made of rigid white polystyrene or flimsy plastic. Each strip contains from 3 large plants such as Pelargoniums to 10-12 ordinary half-hardy annuals such as Antirrhinums. Roots may be damaged as you prise the plants apart but this is less likely than with tray-grown ones.

PLUGS

Trade names include 'Speedplugs', 'Easiplants', 'Starter Plants' and 'Plantlets'. Plugs are larger and more advanced than seedlings — they are small but well-rooted plants which are raised in cellular trays by the grower. A great advantage here is that there is no root disturbance when the plug is potted on into 3 in. (7.5 cm) pots. Plugs can be planted directly into hanging baskets but of course cannot be put outdoors until the danger of frost has passed.

CELLULAR TRAYS

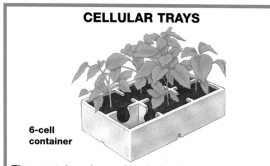

6-cell container

The container is made of rigid polystyrene, and each cell contains a single plant. The number of cells may be as few as 4 or as many as 40, but the standard one is the 6-cell container. Root disturbance is avoided at planting out time — an advantage shared with packs and pots. Cellular trays are an excellent way of buying and also raising seedlings — containers bearing a large number of mini-cells are used to raise plugs.

JIFFY PLANTS

A 'Jiffy 7' is a block of compressed peat which expands when soaked in water — the plastic netting around it provides support. The Jiffy 7 is a popular method ('Jiffy Plants', 'Pot-ready Plants' etc) of selling Pelargonium and Fuchsia rooted cuttings by mail order. Young seed-raised plants of Impatiens and Begonia are also sold in this way. Jiffy Plants are sold in 5s or 10s in a polystyrene pack — transfer into compost-filled 3¹/₂-4 in. (8.5-10 cm) pots and grow on before moving the plants outdoors.

CHAPTER 4

PLANT CARE

DIGGING

The first step in preparing a new bed or border is to get the soil ready for planting. Digging is the age-old method — as the books will tell you the upper layer is broken up, clods are exposed to the weather and annual weeds are buried. The basic problem is sometimes omitted — apart from the hard work there is a real danger of burying the fertile top few inches and bringing up infertile clay or sand.

Dedicated gardeners will continue to dig over their flower beds every year, but this is not essential for the ordinary weekend gardener. The no-dig programme will give perfectly acceptable results in most soils. By this technique the plot is dug only once, and then only if the ground has not been cultivated before or if it has become badly compacted. Follow the routine shown below — remember that the incorporation of humus-making material such as compost or manure is vital. In subsequent years an organic dressing is placed between the plants or over the bare bed when the soil is moist and reasonably warm. The soil should be cleared of weeds and lightly pricked over before this annual mulch of compost or well-rotted manure is applied.

(1) Choose the right season — early winter for most soils and early spring for light land. Choose a day when the ground is moist but not waterlogged nor frozen

(2) Wear clothes that are warm — you should not be uncomfortably hot nor cold when digging. Make sure your back is fully covered and wear stout shoes

(3) Use the right equipment — a spade for general work or a fork if the soil is very heavy or stony. Carry a scraper and use it to keep the blade or prongs clean

(4) When digging it is essential to put a layer of organic matter at the bottom of the trench before turning over the soil to fill it as shown below

(5)
Drive in the spade vertically. Press (do not kick) down on the blade. This should be at right angles to the trench

(6)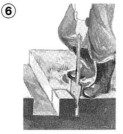
The next cut should be parallel to the trench, 6-8 in. (15-20 cm) behind the face. Do not take larger slices

(7)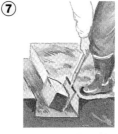
Pull steadily (do not jerk) on the handle so as to lever the soil on to the blade. Lift up the block of soil

(8)
With a flick of the wrist turn the earth into the trench in front — turn the spadeful right over to bury the weeds

(9) Work for 10 minutes if you are reasonably fit but out of condition, then sit down or do a non-strenuous job until you feel rested. Work for 20 minutes between rests if you are fit and used to physical exercise. For most people 30 minutes digging is quite enough for the first day

Large Areas
Think twice before lifting a spade if you have a large area of hard and compacted earth to turn over. A typical example is the ground left by the builders. Hire a cultivator which can work to a depth of 8 in. (20 cm) or call in a contractor.

PLANTING

You will never finish stocking your garden as long as you are a gardener, so it is important to learn the right way to plant. The recommended method depends on the type of planting material you have bought or have grown, and the time to do the work depends on the recommended planting season for the specimen in question — there may be just a few restrictions as with hardy perennials or there may be a much more limited time of planting as with bulbs and bedding plants. Within this recommended planting season it is necessary to choose a time when the ground is in the right condition. Choose a day when the soil is moist. Squeeze a handful of soil — it should be wet enough to form a ball but dry enough to shatter when dropped on to a hard surface.

With small lifted plants and ones grown in small pots the hole is generally filled with the soil removed during the planting process. With pre-packaged plants with bare roots, large lifted plants and container-grown plants it is better to use a planting mixture. Make up the mixture in a wheelbarrow on a day when the soil is reasonably dry and friable — 1 part topsoil, 1 part moist peat and 3 handfuls of Bone Meal per barrow load. Keep this mixture in a shed until you are ready to start planting.

SMALL LIFTED PLANTS • BEDDING PLANTS FROM TRAYS AND STRIPS

④ Plant properly. For small plants, fill around the soil ball with loose soil and firm with the fingers or the trowel handle. With larger plants, fine soil should be added, each layer being gently compressed with the fists until the hole is full. Handle non-woody plants by the soil ball or the leaves — never by the stem. Water in after planting

③ Plant at the right depth. Set all bedding plants, seedlings and rooted cuttings so that the top of the soil ball is just below ground level. With lifted mature plants use the old soil mark on the stem as your guide

② Use the right tool. A trowel is generally the best thing to use

① Dig the hole to fit the roots. The hole should be much wider than it is deep — the roots at the base and at the sides should never have to be bent to fit into the hole

PRE-PACKAGED BARE-ROOTED PLANTS
•
LIFTED PLANTS WITH LARGE ROOTS BEYOND THE SOIL BALL

Planting time is the dormant season between autumn and spring — choose mid October-late November if you can, but delay planting until March if the soil is heavy and wet. Cut off leaves, dead flowers, weak stems and damaged roots. If the stem of a bare-rooted plant is shrivelled plunge the roots in a bucket of water for two hours before planting

③ Work a couple of trowelfuls of the planting mixture around the roots. Shake the plant gently up and down — add a little more planting mixture. Firm this around the roots with the fists — do not press too hard. Half-fill the hole with more planting mixture and firm it down

② The old soil mark should be level with the soil surface — set a board across the top of the hole to ensure correct planting depth

④ Add more planting mixture until the hole is full. Firm by pressing with the fists or gentle treading — on no account tread heavily. Loosen the surface once the hole has been filled. Water in after planting

① The hole should be wide enough to allow the roots to be spread evenly. Put a layer of planting mixture (see introduction) at the bottom of the hole — important if soil condition is poor

CONTAINER-, POT- and PACK-GROWN PLANTS
•
LIFTED PLANTS WITH COMPACT SOIL BALL

A large container-grown plant should not have been lifted from the open ground and its roots and surrounding soil stuffed into the container prior to sale. The test is to pull the plant gently and see if the soil ball comes up easily. If it does, the plant should be rejected. Planting can take place at any time of the year, but the soil must be neither frozen nor waterlogged

(2) Water the pot or container thoroughly at least an hour before planting. Remove the plant very carefully — do not disturb the soil ball. With a pot-grown plant place your hand around the crown of the plant and turn the pot over. Gently remove — tap the sides with a trowel if necessary

(4) After planting there should be a shallow water-holding basin. Water in after planting

(3) Examine the exposed surface — cut away circling or tangled roots but do not break up the soil ball. Fill the space between the soil ball and the sides of the hole with planting mixture. Firm down the planting mixture with your hands

(1) The hole should be deep enough to ensure that the top of the soil ball will be about 1 in. (2.5 cm) below the soil surface after planting. The hole should be wide enough for the soil ball to be surrounded by a layer of planting mixture. Put a 1 in. (2.5 cm) layer of planting mixture (see introduction) at the bottom of the hole

BULBS

As a general rule the bulbs should be planted as soon as possible after purchase, but the big four (tulip, narcissus, hyacinth and crocus) will come to no harm if stored in a cool, dry place before planting. However, they must go in the ground while they are still firm and without prominent sprouts. Bulbs with roots and without a protective tunic can be stored in moist peat for a little time but planting should not be long delayed

(6) Bulbs leave no above-ground indication of their presence after planting. It is therefore sometimes necessary to put in a label to remind you that there are bulbs below

(3) It is vital that there should not be an air space between the bottom of the bulb and the soil at the base of the hole. If the soil is heavy it is useful to put in a shallow layer of grit or moist peat

(4) Push the bulb down to the base of the hole and twist gently. Make sure the bulb is the right way up

(5) Put the earth back and press it down gently. Use the dug-out soil for this job, but it is a good idea to mix it with peat, coarse sand, well-rotted compost or leaf mould if the ground is heavy. Rake over the surface if a large area has been planted and water in if the weather is dry

(2) The width of the hole should be about twice the diameter of the bulb. The depth will depend upon the variety you are planting — check in the A-Z guide. As a general rule, the common large bulbs such as tulip, narcissus and hyacinth will need to be covered by twice their own height — most small bulbs are covered to about their own height. The bottom should be reasonably flat and the sides reasonably vertical — avoid making 'ice cream cone' holes

(1) Nearly all bulbs require free-draining soil. Dig about a week before the planting date if the soil is compacted — adding coarse sand or grit will help if the ground is heavy. Free drainage is equally or even more important when planting up containers — make sure that the drainage holes are large enough and not blocked

WATERING

The way most people treat their plants during a prolonged dry spell is wrong. The usual sequence is to wait until the plants have started to droop and then to go round the garden with a watering can or a hose and dampen the surface every day or two. Not only does this involve a lot of effort but it can do more harm than good.

There are two basic errors. We try to water everything including the lawn instead of concentrating on the high-risk plants, and we apply too little water too frequently. To avoid these errors learn how to water properly. First of all get to know the plants which must be kept watered when the weather turns dry. There are some flowering perennials which tolerate dryness remarkably well. Included here are Acanthus, Achillea, Bergenia, Centaurea, Euphorbia, Geranium, Kniphofia, Nepeta, Phlox, Salvia and Sedum. In addition there are some annuals with better than average tolerance to dry conditions — examples include Alyssum, Arctotis, Calendula, Cosmos, Dimorphotheca, Helichrysum, Nasturtium, Portulaca, Tagetes and Zinnia. Note carefully, however, that this ability to withstand dry conditions better than other plants only applies when these perennials and annuals are established — high-risk plants include *all* bedding plants for at least six weeks after planting and *all* perennials for the first year after planting. In times of drought you must concentrate your watering on these high-risk types if you cannot get round to everything. All container plants are at high risk — see The Container Expert for details.

So the first rule is to concentrate your watering activity on the plants most in need, and the next rule is to water properly. Soil with an average plant cover will lose at least 2 gallons of water per sq. yd (11 litres per sq. m) each week in summer, which is equivalent to ½ in. (1 cm) of rain or applied water. If there is no rain and you have not watered then this must come from the soil reserves. Once these reserves are depleted the plants will begin to suffer — to avoid problems follow the instructions on the right. The basic principles laid down here are to begin early, to apply an adequate amount of water and then to water again in about seven days time if rain has not fallen.

FOUR STEPS TO SUCCESS

1 **DON'T WAIT** Begin before the plants have started to wilt. The time to begin watering is when the soil is dry to a depth of 2 in. (5 cm) or more and the foliage has a dullish tinge. When this occurs depends on the weather and the soil type. A sandy soil dries out much more rapidly than a heavy one, and low-humus soils hold less water than organic-rich earth

2 **WATER THOROUGHLY** Once you decide to water then do the job thoroughly. Applying a small amount every few days may well do more harm than good as it encourages surface rooting and weed seed germination

3 **USE THE RIGHT TECHNIQUE** Decide which method to use. **Point watering** is the simpler method — this calls for holding the spout of a watering can close to the base of each plant and then adding water gently to soak the ground around the root zone. Troughs, small beds, pots, window boxes and hanging baskets can be tackled in this way, but it is extremely time consuming if the area to be covered is extensive as you may need to apply 2-3 gallons per sq. yd (11-16.5 litres per sq. m). For large beds and borders with many plants of various sizes the obvious choice is **Overall watering**. This involves applying water to the whole area rather than treating each plant. You can try watering over the top of them with a watering can which is filled from a hose pipe but the usual procedure is to walk slowly along the border or around the bed with a hand-held hose and a suitable nozzle. This is a boring job and a common error is to move too quickly so that the plants receive too little water. A sprinkler which can be moved along the border at regular intervals is usually more satisfactory — always carry out this task in the evening and never in hot sunshine. Trickle irrigation through a perforated hose laid close to the plants is perhaps the best method of watering

4 **REPEAT IF NECESSARY** Water again if rain does not fall but do not try to keep the land constantly soaked. There must be a period of drying-out between waterings. As a general rule you will need to water every seven days if rain does not fall. The precise interval depends on many factors — to check if water is needed the best plan is to examine the soil 2 in. (5 cm) below the surface. Water immediately if it is dry

MULCHING

A mulch is a layer of bulky organic matter which is placed on the soil around the stems. It is generally not used around bedding plants, but around border perennials it provides five positive benefits:

● The soil is kept moist in summer, reducing the need to water. It is also kept cooler than soil without a mulch — this cool and moist root zone promotes active growth.

● The soil is kept warmer than uncovered ground in winter — a definite benefit for many plants.

● Soil structure is improved as humus is added, worm activity is increased and surface capping by rain is eliminated.

● Some mulches provide a small amount of plant food but this is insufficient to meet the needs of most plants.

● Growth of annual weeds is suppressed — weeds which break through are easily removed by hand pulling.

The standard time for applying a humus mulch is May when the soil is warm and moist. Before you put down organic matter it is necessary to prepare the soil surface. Remove debris and hand pull or hoe annual weeds — dig out perennial weeds or treat with glyphosate. The final job is to apply a general fertilizer and rake in lightly.

The soil is moist, warm and free from weeds — it is now time to spread a 2-3 in. (5-7.5 cm) layer of the chosen mulching material over the ground around the stems. If mulching material is plentiful you can cover the whole bed or border, but with partial and all-over cover make sure that the mulch does not come right up to the stems. Do not disturb this layer during the summer months. If weeds do appear pull out by hand or paint with glyphosate. Some people fork in the mulch in October but it is more usual to leave the mulch in place and top up as necessary in May.

MULCHING MATERIALS

Peat
Peat is widely available and reasonably inexpensive for small areas. It has a natural look, but when dry it tends to blow about or forms a cake which is difficult to wet. Sphagnum peat helps to maintain acid conditions around lime-haters

Bark or Cocoa shell
Bark is a better choice than peat. The chips should be 1/2-2 in. (1-5 cm) long. Cocoa shell is a good alternative but can be smelly when wet. Use them in the same way as peat — both provide an attractive cover and will last on the surface for two to three years

Well-rotted manure
Manure is less attractive than peat or bark as a surface cover, but it is available very cheaply and is the best soil improver of all. It must be well-rotted and quality from an unknown source can be a problem. Annual topping up is necessary

Garden compost
Garden compost is not only free — it also gets rid of grass clippings, stem prunings etc. Like manure it provides some nutrients and improves soil structure as well as acting as an insulator, but is usually less effective. It must be good quality

Straw
Straw is easy and cheap to obtain in rural areas and was widely used in past times. It is rather unsightly around the plants in beds and borders, and it poses two problems. Weed seeds are often present and it is necessary to apply a nitrogen-rich fertilizer at the same time

Old growing compost
Spent peat compost has the virtues and limitations of peat with the added value of having some nutrients present. Examples include the contents of old growing bags, spent potting compost, and spent mushroom compost (for non lime-haters only)

Grass clippings
Short grass clippings from the lawn can be used as a shallow mulch (not more than 1 in./2.5 cm) around plants. Top up as necessary in summer. Do not use if a weedkiller has been applied or if it contains weeds and/or grass in flower

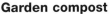

WEEDING

Surveys reveal that there are several gardening tasks which are disliked by most gardeners. Digging is hard but for most people it is a once a year job or it is avoided altogether by using a no-digging technique (see page 213). Watering can be tedious, but outdoors it is generally a dry-weather task. It is weeding which is regarded as the most unpleasant task of all — a season-long round of stooping, pulling and hoe-pushing.

In most gardens the task is tackled badly. Little is done to prevent an infestation around growing plants and little is done while the weeds are small. We wait until the weeds are an eyesore and then spend hours hoeing, forking out and hand pulling each bed and border in turn — only to find that the first bed is again full of weeds before the last bed or border is reached!

There is no way of completely protecting your border unless you grow everything through plastic sheeting, but you can do much better than the sorry tale above. The first task is to get to know a little about weeds. They are not the outlaws of the plant world — they are simply wild flowers, grasses and sometimes garden plants (e.g self-sown Alchemilla, Calendula etc) growing where you don't want them to be. They give the garden a neglected look and compete with the garden plants for space, light, water and nutrients. As you will see below there are annual weeds and perennial weeds — the perennials generally pose a more serious problem and are tackled in a different way.

It is necessary to use a few simple techniques in order to keep your beds and borders weed-free. As described on the next page the first step is to keep them away as far as possible — prevention is better than cure. Secondly it is necessary to deal with the weeds which do appear as soon as possible — annual weeds should always be eradicated before they have produced seed and perennial ones should be tackled before they have started to spread. Chemicals have a part to play, but they must be used with care as they cannot distinguish between friend and foe. One day there may be a complete chemical answer, but until then the mainstays of weed control must remain hoeing, mulching and hand pulling.

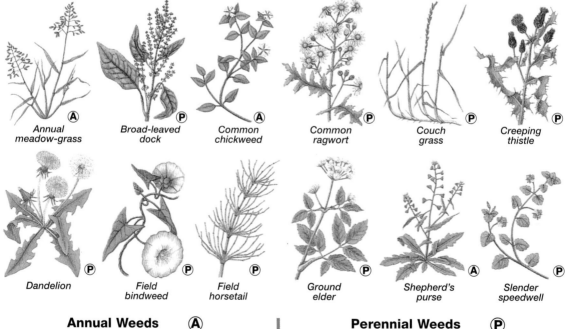

| Annual meadow-grass Ⓐ | Broad-leaved dock Ⓟ | Common chickweed Ⓐ | Common ragwort Ⓟ | Couch grass Ⓟ | Creeping thistle Ⓟ |
| Dandelion Ⓟ | Field bindweed Ⓟ | Field horsetail Ⓟ | Ground elder Ⓟ | Shepherd's purse Ⓐ | Slender speedwell Ⓟ |

Annual Weeds Ⓐ

Annual weeds complete at least one life cycle from seed to seed during the season. They spread by seeding, and all fertile soils contain a large reservoir of annual weed seeds. The golden rule is that emerged annual weeds must be killed before they produce seeds — kill them by hand pulling, hoeing or burning off with a contact weedkiller.

Perennial Weeds Ⓟ

Perennial weeds survive by means of underground stems or roots which act as storage organs over winter. Dig out the whole plant including the root if you can. Otherwise the leaves must be regularly removed to starve out the underground storage organs or else use a translocated weedkiller which will travel to the underground parts.

WEEDKILLERS

You will find a large range of weedkillers (other name: herbicides) on the shelves of garden centres and DIY stores in spring and summer. Unfortunately there is no single product which is safe on all plants and lethal to all weeds, so you will have to pick and apply with care.

Residual weedkillers

Residual weedkillers enter the plant through the roots. These products remain in the soil for weeks or even years — the basic ingredient for path weedkillers but cannot be used on weeds around plants. Example: simazine.

Contact weedkillers

Contact weedkillers kill only those parts of the plant which are touched, so complete leaf cover is required. These products are fast-acting and are excellent for dealing with annual weeds, acting as a chemical hoe. But movement within the plant is very limited or absent, so there is no long-lasting action against perennial weeds. Example: paraquat/diquat.

Translocated (Systemic) weedkillers

Translocated weedkillers move in the sap stream, so roots as well as leaves are affected after spraying. Complete leaf cover is not required. These products are effective against many weeds including perennial ones, but action is often slow and results depend on growth stage, weather etc. Example: glyphosate.

The usual procedure is to use a non-persistent contact weedkiller to get rid of annual weeds and to burn off the tops of perennial ones. The translocated weedkiller glyphosate is used to kill perennial weeds. Apply when the weeds are growing actively — a repeat treatment may be necessary. For difficult weeds such as ground elder and bindweed try painting the leaves with glyphosate gel. A few products which combine both contact and translocated weedkillers are available.

TWO STEPS TO SUCCESS

① **TRY TO PREVENT WEEDS FROM APPEARING** The basic reason why you have a weed problem is bare ground. You can hoe or hand pull the weeds around growing plants and in some cases they can be safely sprayed, but if the soil is uncovered then the problem will return as weed seeds on or near the surface and pieces of perennial weeds start to grow. Digging is often an ineffectual way of controlling weeds on a long term basis. The annual types on the surface are buried, but a host of seeds are brought to the surface. With care some perennial weed roots and bulbs can be removed, but all too often the roots of dandelions, thistles etc and the bulbs of ground elder are spread around. The real answer is to try to cover the surface around plants in beds and borders. You can use a non-living cover (a mulch) or a living one (ground-cover plants). Use one of the following techniques:

Apply a mulch One of the purposes of a humus mulch (see page 217) is to suppress the germination of weed seeds and to make easier the hand pulling of the ones which may appear. Using peat, bark etc in this way reduces but does not eliminate the problem.

Plant ground cover Creeping evergreens with leafy stems provide an excellent way of suppressing weed growth around clumps of perennials. With bedding plants you can solve the ground cover problem by planting them closer together than the usually recommended distance.

② **GET RID OF WEEDS PROMPTLY WHEN THEY APPEAR** Weeds will appear around your plants in beds or borders unless you have put some form of weed-proof blanket such as plastic sheeting around them. These weeds should be kept in check while they are still small. Hand pulling may be sufficient, especially if you have put down a humus mulch. If there are a lot of weeds, however, you will have to use one of the alternative techniques listed below:

Pull by hand The simplest method for the removal of well-established but easily-uprooted annual weeds in beds and borders and the removal of all types of weeds in the rockery. Use a small fork to uproot perennial weeds — don't pull up by the stems.

Use a hoe The hoe is the traditional enemy of the emerged weed and still remains the most popular control method around growing plants. It will kill large numbers of annual weeds if the surface is dry, the blade is sharp and the cut is kept shallow. Hoeing at regular intervals is needed to starve out the roots of perennial weeds.

Use a weedkiller Numerous contact and translocated weedkillers are available for use around growing plants. Make sure you use the right type — see the notes on this page.

FEEDING

Flowers, like all other living things, require food. The production of stems, leaves, roots and flowers is a drain on the soil's reserves of nitrogen, phosphate, potash and numerous trace elements. If one or more of these vital elements runs short then hunger signs may appear on the leaves or flowers and both vigour and display are affected. The answer is to apply a fertilizer at some stage or stages of the plant's life.

The golden rule is that no fertilizer is ideal for all plants at all stages of growth. Nitrogen-rich fertilizers stimulate leaf growth whereas potash-rich feeds promote flower and fruit production. During the preparation of the soil prior to planting work a powder or granular fertilizer into the soil. The nitrogen content of this basic fertilizer should not be higher than the phosphate or potash content — use Bone Meal for rockery perennials and either Growmore or Bone Meal for other flowering plants. Check with the A-Z guide before taking this step — a few plants grow best under starvation or infertile conditions and should therefore not be fed.

Most growing plants will need feeding — with border perennials sprinkle Growmore around the stems in spring and feed large and leafy plants such as Dahlia, Florist Chrysanthemum, Fuchsia etc with a liquid fertilizer at regular intervals. Most bulbs also respond to liquid feeding as the below-ground storage organs have to be built up for next year's display. Most but not all bedding plants benefit from in-season feeding. Apply a liquid feed in midsummer and then repeat at monthly intervals if you are a keen gardener — annuals do not need to be fed to the same extent as perennials as they do not have to build up a storage root system to tide them over the winter. Rockery perennials need little or no in-season feeding — once a year with a potash-rich feed is ample.

A few rules. The soil should be moist before feeding — water first if the soil is dry. Make sure that you use no more than the amount recommended on the package. Finally, keep solid fertilizers off leaves and flowers — water in after application.

The rules for containers are different to those for plants in the open garden. The nutrients incorporated into most soilless composts are designed to last for about eight weeks, after which regular feeding with a liquid fertilizer is essential — follow the label instructions.

FERTILIZER TYPES

Soluble or Liquid fertilizer

The most popular feeding method these days — a watering can is a suitable applicator if you have a small area to feed but a hose-end dilutor is much more satisfactory if a large number of plants have to be fed. These products are quick-acting and effective but they are not long-lasting — containers will need feeding approximately every 14 days

Powder or Granular fertilizer

Powders and granules are applied to the soil by hand or occasionally by applicator if a large area of bare ground has to be treated. Powders are dustier than granules but generally act more quickly. All types of solid fertilizer last longer than their liquid counterparts but take more time to work

Fertilizer stick

Pellets or sticks of compressed fertilizer are pushed into the soil or compost in containers. The feeding effect lasts for two to three months

Steady-release fertilizer

Coated fertilizer which has been formulated into granules, blocks or cones is sprinkled over or pushed into the soil. The fertilizer steadily breaks down and provides a prolonged supply of nutrients for about six months

Foliar fertilizer

Suitable soluble or liquid fertilizer is diluted and then sprayed on to the foliage — nutrient quickly enters the sap stream. A useful method where root feeding is impaired and also for applying some trace elements where deficiencies are seen. Follow the instructions carefully

RENOVATING

If a border perennial has formed a large clump and the central area is bare then the plant requires treatment. Other conditions calling for renovation are overcrowding and flower deterioration where leaf growth has taken over from bloom development.

Lift the plant and divide the clump. If active growth has become restricted to the outer ring, remove pieces of shoots with their attached roots and discard the old central section. Do this work in late autumn, but if your soil is heavy it should be delayed until early spring. Replant the pieces at the same depth as the original clump.

A word of caution. Look up the plant in the A-Z guide before attempting renovation work. The correct time may be different from the general rule given above and for some plants lifting is not recommended.

CUTTING FOR INDOORS

Cutting flowers and decorative leaves to take indoors for arranging is, of course, one of the pleasures of gardening. This form of spring or summer pruning generally does no harm but there are pitfalls. Obviously the garden display is diminished and in the case of newly-planted perennials the loss of stems and green leaves can affect next year's growth.

If you have the space and are a keen flower arranger it is worthwhile having a separate bed where plants for cutting can be grown. Here you can cultivate varieties which are not particularly decorative as garden flowers but are much admired as dried flowers for indoor arrangements. Examples are Scabiosa stellata and Limonium sinuatum.

FEEDING

The removal of dead flowers has several advantages — it helps to give the bed or border a well-maintained appearance, it prolongs the floral display and in several cases (Lupin, Delphinium etc) it induces a second flush of flowers later in the season. Obviously dead-heading is not a practical proposition in all cases.

CUTTING BACK

Dead-heading is a form of cutting back, but with a few bedding plants more drastic action is needed during the growing season. Some have a straggly growth habit and cutting back the ends of the stems will encourage new shoots and flowers. In a container vigorous varieties can threaten to swamp more delicate types — cut back when growth starts to get out of hand.

The rock garden is another area where cutting back will be necessary. Some of the more popular spring-flowering types will have formed long and straggly stems during summer, and these should be cut back to make the plant look neater and to ensure that there will be a cushion of blooms rather than a hollow-centred ring of flowers next season. Cutting back can sometimes induce a second flush of flowers.

HARDENING OFF

Bedding plants raised indoors or in a greenhouse have tender tissues — suddenly moving them outdoors in spring means a transition to colder conditions and drying winds for which they are not prepared. The result of this shock is a severe check to growth or even the death of the specimen.

To avoid this problem there must be a gradual acclimatisation to the harsher conditions to be faced outdoors. Ventilation is increased during the day after which the plants are moved to a cold frame. The lights are kept closed for a week or two and the ventilation is steadily increased until the plants are continually exposed to the outside air for about seven days before planting out.

Most bedding plants are bought rather than being home-raised so you must take it on trust that they have been properly hardened off. If in doubt keep the plants in a sheltered and protected spot for a few days before planting out.

STAKING

Weak-stemmed plants, tall varieties on exposed sites, large-headed flowers and climbers all need some form of support, and care has to be taken to ensure that an attractive display is not ruined by ugly staking. The golden rule is to put the stake in position when the plant is quite small so that the stems can cover it. For many plants brushwood is the best idea — twiggy branches pushed into the soil when the stems are about 6 in. (15 cm) high.

This will not do for tall plants which often require staking at planting time. Stout canes are the usual answer, the stems being tied to the support as growth proceeds. This single-pole method is suitable for plants with a main stem such as a standard Fuchsia, but it should be avoided with bushy plants as an ugly 'drumstick' effect can be produced. A better plan is to insert three or four canes around the stems and enclose them with twine tied around the canes at 6-9 in. (15-22.5 cm) intervals.

Climbing plants are generally happier growing up netting, trellis etc rather than up a single pole. It is essential to ensure that the framework is strong and well-anchored. It should be put in position at an early stage and new growth trained into it regularly.

With both free-standing and wall supports it is generally necessary to tie the stems to them. Soft twine and raffia are the traditional and still recommended materials and avoid tying too tightly. When training a climber on to a trellis, wires etc you should not tie the stems vertically — spread them at an angle to form a fan so as to increase the display.

WINTER CARE

For the annuals there is no winter care — their life span is over. The half-hardy perennials must also leave the garden, but for them there is a stay indoors before being reintroduced into the garden with the return of frost-free weather in the spring. It is unwise to generalise about the proper conditions for half-hardy perennials and bulbs which must overwinter indoors. It is a period of rest during which bulbs are kept dry and cool whilst varieties overwintered as green plants are given just enough water to keep them alive.

Outdoors the border perennials, rockery perennials and hardy bulbs await the return of spring in the open ground. Most of them have nothing to fear. The snow and frost will do them no harm provided the soil does not become waterlogged — drowned roots kill more plants than frozen ones.

Late autumn is the usual time for cutting back the dead stems of border perennials. Do not cut down evergreens and winter-flowering plants, of course, and perennials which are not fully hardy should be cut down in spring.

Forking over is a traditional autumn technique but if you have put down a mulch in late spring you can leave it undisturbed until next year — see page 217. Use a fork to break up the surface crust, turning over the top couple of inches of soil between the plants. Forking over is an enjoyable job to do on a sunny day in autumn, but it probably does you more good than the plants unless your soil is prone to severe crusting and mossing over.

Perennials which are not completely hardy present a problem. You can cover them with glass cloches but it is more usual to put a blanket of straw, bracken, leaf mould or peat over the crowns.

Delicate but hardy alpines need protection from winter rains rather than from frosts. The standard method is to cover the plants with a pane of glass supported by bricks.

CHAPTER 5
INCREASING YOUR STOCK

There are several ways of raising new plants, but there is no 'best' way. Sowing seeds is a relatively inexpensive method of producing large numbers of flowers for the garden — it is the standard way for annuals and biennials but can be beset with difficulties for most perennials. Border and rockery perennials are generally propagated by vegetative (non-seed) means, especially where a named variety is involved. Dividing up a mature clump is, of course, the easiest method of vegetative propagation, but not all perennials can be split in this way and even when practical you have to disturb an established plant. Cuttings are a much more practical proposition in most cases if you want lots of new plants — the cuttings are usually taken from non-flowering shoot tips but roots, leaves and small basal shoots are also used. Don't try to guess the way to increase your stock _ look up the plant in the A-Z guide and employ the recommended technique.

DIVIDING PLANTS

BORDER and ROCKERY PERENNIALS

Division is a form of propagation which is often forced upon you — spreading border perennials will often deteriorate after a few years if not lifted and divided.

Choose a mild day in spring or autumn when the soil is moist. Dig up the clump with a fork, taking care not to damage the roots more than necessary. Shake off the excess soil and study where the basic divisions should be. You might be able to break the clump with your hands — if the clump is too tough for this technique then use two hand forks or garden forks. Push the forks back-to-back into the centre and prise gently apart. Treat the resulting divisions in a similar fashion or tear apart with the fingers.

Select the divisions which came from the outer region of the clump — discard the central dead region of an old plant. Replant the divisions as soon as possible and water in thoroughly. Always check in the A-Z guide before lifting a perennial. Some dislike disturbance and some which can be moved may have a distinct preference for either autumn or spring.

RHIZOMES

Carefully dig up the clumps of rhizomes — retain the roots. Divide up each rhizome into sections so that each piece bears leaves or buds above and roots below. Replant the sections at the same depth as the original plant. Summer is the usual time.

BULBS and CORMS

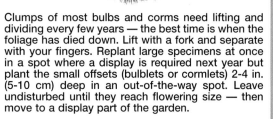

Clumps of most bulbs and corms need lifting and dividing every few years — the best time is when the foliage has died down. Lift with a fork and separate with your fingers. Replant large specimens at once in a spot where a display is required next year but plant the small offsets (bulblets or cormlets) 2-4 in. (5-10 cm) deep in an out-of-the-way spot. Leave undisturbed until they reach flowering size — then move to a display part of the garden.

SOWING SEEDS

Looking through the seed catalogues is one of the joys of gardening, and each year about 50 million packets of flower seeds are bought from mail order companies, garden centres, High Street shops and DIY stores. Many gardeners begin their growing experience with a packet of Stocks or Nasturtiums, and perhaps we forget too quickly the thrill of starting from scratch. Growing bedding plants and some perennials from seed is usually a straightforward matter if you follow a few basic rules. The first decision is whether to raise the seeds indoors (half-hardy annuals, hardy annuals and some perennials) or outdoors (hardy annuals, hardy biennials and some perennials).

SOWING SEEDS INDOORS

Most bedding plants are sensitive to frost. Waiting until the danger of frost has passed before sowing outdoors would seriously shorten the flowering season — for this reason seeds of half-hardy annuals are sown in compost in spring and the trays or pots are kept in a greenhouse, propagator or on the windowsill. For most types mid March to early April is the best time to sow seeds but there are variations — see the A-Z guide for the recommended timing for individual plants. The seedlings are set out in the garden in late May or early June. Indoor sowing is not restricted to half-hardy subjects. It is also used for raising hardy annuals when early blooms are required or when the site is in a cold or wet area. Sow the seeds in March and plant out in April or May when the soil condition is suitable. A few border perennials can be raised under glass in the same way.

To ensure success you need a greenhouse — this will provide the all-round light and warmth needed by young seedlings. The problem is to provide enough heat to make sure that the seeds will germinate properly — as you will see from the table below a minimum temperature of at least 60°-70°F (15°-21°C) is required for many popular annuals. This means that seed sowing in March or April calls for additional warmth — you can heat part of the greenhouse for the seed trays or you can install a heated propagator.

A modern way to solve the problem is to buy seedlings or plugs (page 212) by mail order or from the garden centre and so cut in at stage 7 of the Steps to Success on page 225. Note that the temperature required at this late stage is much lower than the warmth required for germination.

Germination Facts

Plant	Germination Temperature	Germination Time (Days)
Ageratum	65°-70°F (18°-21°C)	10-14
Alyssum	60°-65°F (15°-18°C)	14
Antirrhinum	60°-65°F (15°-18°C)	10-21
Begonia, Fibrous-rooted	65°-70°F (18°-21°C)	14-21
Callistephus	65°-70°F (18°-21°C)	10-14
Dahlia, Bedding	65°-70°F (18°-21°C)	14-21
Dianthus	60°-65°F (15°-18°C)	14-21
Impatiens	70°-75°F (21°-24°C)	21
Lobelia	65°-70°F (18°-21°C)	21
Marigold & Tagetes	65°-70°F (18°-21°C)	7-14

Plant	Germination Temperature	Germination Time (Days)
Matthiola	65° (18°C)	10-14
Mesembryanthemum	65°-70°F (18°-21°C)	14-21
Mimulus	65°-70°F (18°-21°C)	14-21
Nemesia	65°-70°F (18°-21°C)	14-21
Pelargonium	70°-75°F (21°-24°C)	7-21
Petunia	70°-75°F (21°-24°C)	7-14
Phlox	60°F (15°C)	14-21
Salvia	70°-75°F (21°-24°C)	14-21
Verbena	65°-70°F (18°-21°C)	21-28
Zinnia	65°-70°F (18°-21°C)	7-14

EIGHT STEPS TO SUCCESS

1 **SEED** You must start with good quality seed. Buy from a reputable supplier and do not open the packet until you are ready to sow. Hard-coated seed should be shaken in a jar with coarse sand and then soaked overnight before sowing — chipping them is a risky business. The traditional technique of mixing very fine seed with dry silver sand before sowing is best avoided.

2 **CONTAINER** Many types of container are suitable provided they have holes or cracks at the base for drainage. Avoid old wooden trays — disease organisms are difficult to remove by washing. Choose plastic — full trays are usually too large and a better choice is a 3^1/$_2$-5 in. (8.5-12.5 cm) half pot or a half tray. Large seeds can be sown into the cells of cellular trays, peat pots filled with compost or into Jiffy 7s (see page 212).

3 **COMPOST** A peat-based seed or multipurpose compost is ideal — sterile, light and consistent. Fill the container with compost and firm gently with a piece of board — the surface should be about ^{1}/$_2$ in. (1 cm) below the top of the pot or tray. Sprinkle the surface with water the day before seed sowing — it should be moist but not wet when you scatter the seeds thinly over the surface. Larger seeds can be sown in rows.

4 **COVER** Do not cover very fine seed with compost — examples include Begonia, Lobelia, Petunia and Mimulus. Other seeds should be covered with compost or vermiculite to a depth which is twice the diameter of the seed. Compost should be applied through a sieve to form a fine and even layer. Firm gently with a board after sowing. Put brown paper over the tray or pot and place a sheet of glass on top. Condensation is absorbed by the paper and so does not drip on to the compost below. Change the paper if necessary. It is not true that seeds always germinate better in darkness — do not use brown paper for seeds which need light in order to germinate. Examples are Antirrhinum, Alyssum, Mimulus, Impatiens, Nicotiana and Begonia.

5 **WARMTH** Most seeds require a fairly warm temperature (65°-70°F/18°-21°C) for satisfactory germination. Heating a whole greenhouse in March or April can be wasteful — a thermostatically-controlled heated propagator is a better idea. Make sure you buy one which is large enough for your future needs. For windowsill propagation you will need a centrally-heated room where the temperature can be kept in the 60°-70°F (15°-21°C) range. Raise pots or trays from the sill so that they are level with the glass.

6 **LIGHT & WATER** As soon as the seedlings break through the surface, remove the paper and prop up the sheet of glass. After a few days the glass should be removed and the container moved to a bright but sunless spot. Windowsill pots or trays should be turned every couple of days. Never let the compost dry out. The safest way to water is to use a fine sprayer — watering with a fine-rosed watering can or soaking the container in a basin of water can dislodge tiny plants. Overwatering can cause the stems and roots to rot or become infected by damping off.

7 **PRICK OUT** As soon as the first set of true leaves has opened the seedlings should be pricked out into trays, small pots or 24-cell cellular trays filled with compost. Set the seedlings so that the seed leaves are just above the surface — handle the plants by the seed leaves and not the stems. The seedlings should be set 1-1^1/$_2$ in. (2.5-3.5 cm) apart in pots or trays. Large seedlings such as Dahlia and Pelargonium should be pricked out into individual 3 in. (7.5 cm) pots. Keep containers in the shade for a day or two after pricking out. High temperatures are not required — 50°-55°F (10°-13°C) is satisfactory. Water as necessary.

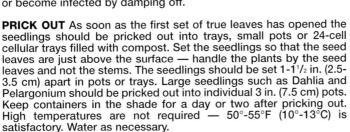

Correct stage for pricking out ►

8 **HARDEN OFF** When the seedlings have recovered from the pricking out move, they must be hardened off to prepare them for the life outdoors. This calls for steadily increasing the ventilation and lowering the temperature — see page 221 for details.

SOWING SEEDS continued

SOWING SEEDS OUTDOORS

Hardy biennials are raised by sowing seeds outdoors. Germination takes place in a nursery bed and when the seedlings are large enough they are transferred to the place where they are to flower. Some hardy perennials can be raised in the same way, but they are transplanted into pots in the autumn. The problem with some but not all of these perennials is that you might have to wait several years before they reach flowering size.

Annuals can be sown outdoors in two ways. Firstly hardy annuals can be sown in a nursery bed and then lifted as bedding plants for transfer to bed, border or container — half-hardy annuals can be sown after the danger of frost has passed if late flowering is acceptable.

The other way to grow hardy annuals from seed outdoors is to sow them in the bed or border where they are to flower. This may be to save the time, trouble and expense of raising seedlings under glass or it may be because the plants concerned hate root disturbance.

SIX STEPS TO SUCCESS

 1   **TIMING** Hardy biennials are sown between May and July — June is usually the best month. Hardy annuals are generally sown in March or April, but the weather is more important than the calendar — the soil should be warm enough to permit germination and dry enough to make a seed bed. A good guide that sowing time has arrived is the appearance of annual weeds. Some hardy annuals (e.g Centaurea, Calendula, Iberis and Gypsophila) can be sown in September — these autumn-sown annuals bloom earlier than their spring-sown counterparts.

2   **PREPARE A NURSERY BED** Choose an open site away from trees — fork over, add peat but not fertilizer, tread over with your heels and then rake to produce an even and crumbly surface. Rotate the site of the nursery bed each year if possible — a spot in the vegetable garden is ideal.

or

PREPARE A FLOWER BED You can scatter seed over the allotted area but this will make thinning and weeding difficult. It is much better to sow the seeds in drills at the recommended distance apart

Mark out a zone for each variety with a pointed stick

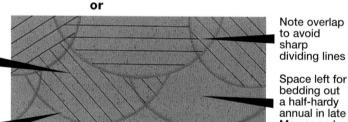

Note overlap to avoid sharp dividing lines

Space left for bedding out a half-hardy annual in late May or early June

3   **PREPARE SEED DRILLS** The depth of the drill depends upon the size of the seeds. A general rule is to ensure that the seeds will be covered with soil to about twice their size. Remember that you should never water the seed bed after sowing — if the soil is dry then gently water the drills before sowing.

For small seeds

For large seeds

4   **SOW** Seed must be sown thinly. Do not sow directly from the packet — place some seed in the palm of your hand and gently sprinkle between thumb and forefinger. Aim to sow at $1/4$ in. (0.5 cm) intervals. After sowing, carefully rake the soil back into the drill and then firm with the back of the rake or your fingers. Do not water — if the weather is dry then cover the surface with newspaper. Some seeds need protection from birds — cover the surface with wire guards or twigs.

5   **THIN OUT** When the first true leaves have appeared, it is time to start thinning. Reduce the stand to one seedling every 2 in. (5 cm) — do not disturb the seedlings you wish to retain. Repeat this thinning ten days later, leaving small varieties about 4 in. (10 cm) apart and larger ones at 6 in. (15 cm) intervals.

6   **PLANT OUT** Lift biennials in autumn with a trowel and transfer to the bed, border or container where they are to flower. Spring-sown hardy annuals grown as bedding plants should be planted in May when the weather and soil are suitable — autumn-sown hardy annuals should be set out in their permanent site in April or May. Hardy perennials should be transferred to small pots filled with compost.

TAKING CUTTINGS

Stem-tip cuttings are by far the most popular type — 2-4 in. (5-10 cm) long pieces of non-flowering shoot tips which are ideally soft and green at the top and rather firm at the base. Some border perennials (e.g Lupin, Delphinium, Peony) produce young shoots around the base of the main stem in spring — these can be pulled away or cut off at ground level to provide **basal cuttings**.

The A-Z guide will tell you the best time to take cuttings — spring or summer is the usual time. Use a sterile rooting medium such as a soilless compost recommended for cuttings. Many experienced gardeners mix this compost with an equal amount of a fertilizer-free medium such as vermiculite or perlite. Plant the cuttings as soon as possible after severance from the parent plant. Some form of cover will be required to ensure that the cuttings are kept in a humid atmosphere — the exception is Pelargonium. For most hardy perennials a cold frame is the usual place, but for difficult subjects and half-hardy perennials it is necessary to raise cuttings by the polythene bag or propagator method.

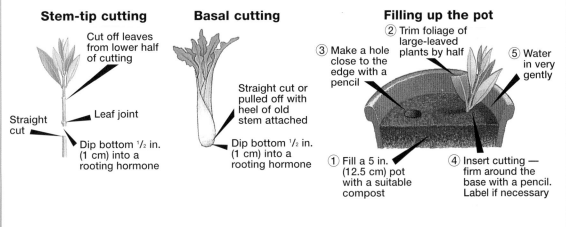

Stem-tip cutting

Cut off leaves from lower half of cutting

Straight cut

Leaf joint

Dip bottom ½ in. (1 cm) into a rooting hormone

Basal cutting

Straight cut or pulled off with heel of old stem attached

Dip bottom ½ in. (1 cm) into a rooting hormone

Filling up the pot

② Trim foliage of large-leaved plants by half

③ Make a hole close to the edge with a pencil

⑤ Water in very gently

① Fill a 5 in. (12.5 cm) pot with a suitable compost

④ Insert cutting — firm around the base with a pencil. Label if necessary

Polythene bag method

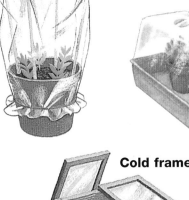

① Place four canes in the pot and drape a polythene bag over them. Secure with a rubber band. Stand pot in a bright spot, away from direct sunlight

② Leave undisturbed until new growth appears. Harden off by giving more ventilation and then lift out each rooted cutting after watering — transfer into a compost-filled 3 in. (7.5 cm) pot

Propagator method

① Place pots in the propagator. Keep at 65°-75°F (18°-24°C). Shade and ventilate on hot days

② Leave undisturbed until new growth appears. Harden off by giving more ventilation and then lift out each rooted cutting after watering — transfer into a compost-filled 3 in. (7.5 cm) pot

Cold frame method

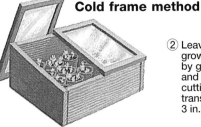

① Place pots in a cold frame — shade glass and ventilate on hot days. Water gently when necessary. In frosty weather cover glass with sacking

② Leave undisturbed until new growth appears. Harden off by giving more ventilation and then lift out each rooted cutting after watering — transfer into a compost-filled 3 in. (7.5 cm) pot

CHAPTER 6
PLANT SELECTOR

GROUND COVER PLANTS

Ground cover plants are reasonably or highly ornamental species or varieties with a spread of leafy growth which is sufficiently dense to partly or completely inhibit weed development. Most but not all are low-growing and most but not all are evergreen.

Acaena	RP. E	Lamium	BP. SE
Acanthus	BP. D	Lysimachia	RP. E (some)
Ajuga	BP. E	Nepeta	BP. SE
Alchemilla	BP. D	Polygonum	BP. D
Alyssum	RP. E	Prunella	BP. E
Anaphalis	BP. D	Pulmonaria	BP. D
Aubrieta	RP. E	Saponaria	RP. D
Bergenia	BP. E	Saxifraga	RP. E
Brunnera	BP. E	Sedum	RP. E (some)
Epimedium	BP. E (some)	Sempervivum	RP. E
Euphorbia	BP. E (some)	Senecio	BP. E
Geranium	BP. E (some)	Stachys	BP. E
Gypsophila	BP. D	Symphytum	BP. E
Helianthemum	RP. E	Tellima	BP. SE
Heuchera	BP. E	Thymus	RP. E
Hosta	BP. D	Waldsteinia	BP. SE

**KEY: BP – Border perennial • RP – Rockery perennial •
E – Evergreen • SE – Semi-evergreen • D – Deciduous**

Geranium 'Russell Pritchard'

PLANTS FOR HANGING BASKETS

The big six for summer display are Pelargonium, Fuchsia, Lobelia, Petunia, Impatiens and Begonia, but the list of flowering bedding plants which will grow in a hanging basket is much larger. Do not forget the non-flowering ones such as Hedera, Helichrysum and Glechoma. For a winter display there are Universal Pansies and Bellis together with a few plants outside the scope of this book such as Erica and Hedera.

Asarina	Dianthus	Osteospermum
Bacopa	Diascia	Pelargonium
Begonia	Felicia	Petunia
Bellis	Fuchsia	Phlox
Bidens	Gazania	Portulaca
Brachycome	Heliotropium	Scaevola
Calceolaria	Impatiens	Tagetes
Calendula	Lobelia	Thunbergia
Campanula	Mimulus	Tropaeolum
Convolvulus	Nemesia	Verbena
Cyclamen	Nierembergia	Viola

BULBS ALL ROUND THE YEAR

The outdoor bulb season is much more extended than the late winter-late spring show of Crocuses, Daffodils and Tulips followed by the summer display of Lilies. As shown below you can have flowers all year round, but do remember that not all will be suitable for your conditions. Some genera have a remarkably extended flowering season — Anemone (February-April and June-October) is a good example. The reason is that the genus contains a number of species with differing flowering seasons.

JANUARY
Crocus
Cyclamen
Eranthis
Galanthus

FEBRUARY
Anemone
Bulbocodium
Chionodoxa
Crocus
Cyclamen
Eranthis
Galanthus
Iris
Leucojum
Narcissus
Scilla
Tulipa

MARCH
Anemone
Bulbocodium
Chionodoxa
Crocus
Cyclamen
Eranthis
Galanthus
Hyacinthus
Iris
Leucojum
Muscari azureum
Narcissus
Puschkinia
Scilla
Tulipa

APRIL
Anemone
Arum
Bulbocodium
Chionodoxa
Convallaria
Crocus
Cyclamen
Erythronium
Fritillaria
Hyacinthus
Ipheion
Iris
Leucojum
Muscari
Narcissus
Ornithogalum
Puschkinia
Scilla

Sisyrinchium
Trillium
Tulipa

MAY
Allium
Arum
Asphodelus
Brodiaea
Camassia
Convallaria
Corydalis
Erythronium
Fritillaria
Gladiolus
Hyacinthus
Ipheion
Iris
Leucojum
Muscari
Narcissus
Ornithogalum
Scilla
Sisyrinchium
Sparaxis
Trillium
Tulipa

JUNE
Allium
Alstroemeria
Anemone
Asphodelus
Begonia
Camassia
Gladiolus
Iris
Lilium
Nomocharis
Oxalis
Ranunculus
Scilla peruviana
Sisyrinchium
Sparaxis
Trillium
Tropaeolum

JULY
Agapanthus
Allium
Alstroemeria
Anemone
Begonia
Canna
Cardiocrinum
Crocosmia

Cyclamen
Gladiolus
Iris
Lilium
Oxalis
Ranunculus
Sisyrinchium
Tropaeolum

AUGUST
Acidanthera
Agapanthus
Alstroemeria
Anemone
Begonia
Canna
Cardiocrinum
Colchicum
Crinum
Crocosmia
Cyclamen
Dierama
Freesia
Galtonia
Gladiolus
Lilium
Ranunculus
Sisyrinchium
Tigridia
Tropaeolum

SEPTEMBER
Acidanthera
Agapanthus
Amaryllis
Anemone
Begonia
Canna
Colchicum
Crinum

Crocosmia
Crocus
Cyclamen
Dierama
Freesia
Galtonia
Gladiolus
Leucojum
Lilium
Nerine
Schizostylis
Sisyrinchium
Sternbergia
Tigridia
Tropaeolum
Zephyranthes

OCTOBER
Amaryllis
Anemone
Canna
Colchicum
Crocus
Cyclamen
Dierama
Freesia
Lilium
Nerine
Schizostylis
Sisyrinchium
Zephyranthes

NOVEMBER
Colchicum
Crocus
Cyclamen
Schizostylis

DECEMBER
Crocus
Cyclamen

BORDER PERENNIALS FOR SHADY SITES

Shade is a problem in many gardens, especially in small plots where boundary fences and neighbouring houses may cast a shadow over beds or borders for much of the day. In such situations always make sure that the plants you choose are tolerant of some shade — avoid types which demand full sun. For moist shady borders there are numerous woodland plants which will thrive, but the dry shade under trees is a difficult area and the choice of plants which will flourish there is distinctly limited.

DRY SHADE

Alchemilla mollis
Anaphalis species
Anemone japonica
Bergenia species
Brunnera macrophylla
Cortaderia selloana
Doronicum excelsum
Epimedium species
Euphorbia species
Iris foetidissima
Lamium species
Liriope muscari
Physalis alkekengi
Pulmonaria species
Waldsteinia ternata

MOIST SHADE

Aconitum species
Ajuga species
Alchemilla mollis
Aquilegia hybrids
Astilbe arendsii
Astrantia major
Bergenia species
Caltha palustris
Cimicifuga racemosa
Dicentra spectabilis
Digitalis species
Filipendula species
Helleborus species
Hosta species
Ligularia species

Lysimachia clethroides
Lythrum salicaria
Monarda hybrids
Omphalodes species
Physostegia virginiana
Polygonum affine
Pulmonaria species
Ranunculus species
Rodgersia species
Saxifraga urbium
Thalictrum species
Tiarella cordifolia
Tradescantia andersoniana
Trollius cultorum
Viola species

Doronicum excelsum

Bergenia cordifolia

Tradescantia andersoniana

BEDDING PLANTS FOR SUNNY, DRY SITES

No plant can survive for too long in completely dry soil, which means that watering is always necessary during periods of prolonged drought in summer. However, there are some sun-lovers which revel in sandy soil and do not require watering in the bed or border except under prolonged dry conditions.

Helichrysum 'Hot Bikini'

Alyssum
Arctotis
Calandrinia
Calendula
Celosia
Coreopsis
Cosmos
Dimorphotheca
Eschscholzia
Felicia
Gazania

Gomphrena
Helichrysum
Mesembryanthemum
Petunia
Phlox
Portulaca
Salvia
Tagetes
Tropaeolum
Ursinia
Zinnia

Felicia amelloides 'Variegata'

BORDER PERENNIALS ALL ROUND THE YEAR

It is usual for a herbaceous border to be devoid of flowers from late autumn until mid spring, but by careful selection you can have hardy perennials in bloom in your mixed border during every month of the year. In the list below there are perennials which can be expected to be in full flower for each month of the year. Remember that some of these plants may come into bloom earlier and may continue to flower for weeks later.

JANUARY
Helleborus niger
Iris unguicularis

FEBRUARY
Helleborus niger
Helleborus orientalis
Iris unguicularis
Viola odorata

MARCH
Bergenia cordifolia
Helleborus niger
Helleborus orientalis
Primula japonica
Primula variabilis
Primula vulgaris
Ranunculus ficaria
Viola odorata

APRIL
Bergenia cordifolia
Brunnera macrophylla
Caltha palustris
Doronicum excelsum
Epimedium species
Euphorbia polychroma
Iris (Dwarf Bearded)
Paeonia
   mlokosewitschii
Primula japonica
Primula variabilis
Primula vulgaris
Pulmonaria officinalis
Ranunculus ficaria
Viola odorata

MAY
Ajuga reptans
Aquilegia vulgaris
Dicentra spectabilis
Doronicum excelsum
Epimedium species
Euphorbia polychroma
Incarvillea delavayi
Iris (Intermediate
   Bearded)
Iris pseudacorus
Nepeta mussinii
Omphalodes
   cappadocica
Paeonia officinalis
Papaver orientale
Polygonatum hybridum
Tanacetum coccineum
Tiarella cordifolia
Trollius cultorum
Veronica
   gentianoides

JUNE
Ajuga reptans
Anchusa azurea
Aquilegia vulgaris
Astrantia major
Centaurea dealbata
Delphinium hybrids
Dianthus plumarius
Eremurus robustus
Filipendula
   hexapetala
Geranium
   'A. T. Johnson'
Geum chiloense
Iris (Tall Bearded)
Iris kaempferi
Leucanthemum
   superbum
Lupinus hybrids
Meconopsis
   betonicifolia
Nepeta mussinii
Paeonia lactiflora
Primula florindae
Prunella grandiflora
Ranunculus
   aconitifolius
Saxifraga urbium
Stachys macrantha
Veronica incana

JULY
Achillea filipendulina
Aconitum
   carmichaelii
Alchemilla mollis
Alstroemeria aurea
Anchusa azurea
Astilbe arendsii
Campanula species
Catananche caerulea
Centranthus ruber
Coreopsis grandiflora
Delphinium hybrids
Dianthus allwoodii
Dictamnus albus
Erigeron speciosus
Gaillardia grandiflora
Gypsophila paniculata
Hemerocallis hybrids
Heuchera hybrids
Linum narbonense
Lychnis chalcedonica
Lythrum salicaria
Meconopsis cambrica
Monarda didyma
Nepeta mussinii
Penstemon hybrids
Platycodon
   grandiflorus
Polemonium
   caeruleum
Potentilla hybrids
Scabiosa caucasica
Sidalcea malviflora
Thalictrum delavayi
Tradescantia
   andersoniana
Trollius chinensis
Verbascum hybridum

AUGUST
Acanthus spinosus
Achillea filipendulina
Agapanthus africanus
Anchusa azurea
Campanula species
Dianthus caryophyllus
Echinacea purpurea
Echinops ritro
Eryngium species
Gaillardia grandiflora
Helenium autumnale
Helianthus decapetalus
Heliopsis scabra
Hosta species
Kniphofia uvaria
Ligularia dentata
Limonium latifolium
Lysimachia clethroides
Macleaya cordata
Oenothera macrocarpa
Phlox species
Physostegia
   virginiana
Polygonum affine
Potentilla hybrids
Rudbeckia fulgida
Salvia nemorosa
Saponaria officinalis
Sidalcea malviflora
Solidago hybrids
Stachys byzantina
Stokesia laevis
Thalictrum delavayi
Tradescantia
   andersoniana
Verbascum hybrids

SEPTEMBER
Acanthus spinosus
Achillea filipendulina
Agapanthus africanus
Anaphalis species
Anemone japonica
Aster novi-belgii
Cimicifuga racemosa
Clematis heracleifolia
Cortaderia selloana
Dendranthema
   hybrids
Echinacea purpurea
Eryngium species
Inula hookeri
Kniphofia uvaria
Liatris spicata
Ligularia dentata
Liriope muscari
Lysimachia clethroides
Lythrum salicaria
Oenothera macrocarpa
Phlox species
Physalis alkekengi
Physostegia virginiana
Polygonum affine
Potentilla hybrids
Rudbeckia fulgida
Salvia nemorosa
Saponaria officinalis
Schizostylis coccinea
Sedum spectabile
Solidago hybrids
Stokesia laevis
Tradescantia
   andersoniana
Viola odorata

OCTOBER
Anemone japonica
Aster novi-belgii
Centranthus ruber
Cimicifuga foetida
Cortaderia selloana
Dendranthema
   hybrids
Echinacea purpurea
Liriope muscari
Phlox paniculata
Physalis alkekengi
Polygonum affine
Rudbeckia fulgida
Scabiosa caucasica
Schizostylis coccinea
Sedum spectabile
Viola odorata

NOVEMBER
Iris unguicularis
Liriope muscari
Nerine bowdenii
Viola odorata

DECEMBER
Iris unguicularis

FLOWERS FOR CUTTING

There is no fundamental reason why any flower may not be cut and used for floral decoration indoors, but some are recommended and others are not. The ones listed below have a reasonable or long vase life and/or they are suitable for drying. For detailed information on conditioning and preserving see The Flower Arranging Expert.

Alchemilla

Antirrhinum

Achillea	R. D1, D2	Iberis	O. D1, G, S
Alcaea	O. D1, S	Iris	O. X
Alchemilla	O. D1, G	Kniphofia	O. X
Allium	O. D1, D3, G	Lathyrus	O. S
Alstroemeria	O. D1	Lavatera	B or O. S
Amaranthus	R. D1, D2, G	Leucanthemum	O. S
Ammobium	O. D1	Liatris	O. D1
Anemone	O. S	Lilium	O. S
Antirrhinum	O. X	Limonium	O or R. D1, D2
Argyranthemum	O. S	Lunaria	O. D2
Aster	O. X	Lupinus	O. X
Astilbe	O. D1	Matthiola	O. S
Astrantia	O. D1	Molucella	O or R. D2, G
Calendula	O. D1, S	Monarda	O. D1
Callistephus	O. S	Muscari	O. S
Campanula	O. X	Narcissus	B, O or R. S
Cheiranthus	O. S	Nepeta	O. D1
Chrysanthemum	O. S	Nerine	O. S
Clarkia	O. D1, S	Nigella	O. D1
Convallaria	O. S	Oenothera	O. X
Coreopsis	R. S	Ornithogalum	O. S
Cosmos	O. S	Pelargonium	O. X
Crocosmia	O. D1, S	Penstemon	O. S
Dahlia	O. D1, D2, S	Phlox	O. X
Delphinium	O. D1, D2, S	Physalis	R. D1
Dendranthema	O. S	Primula	O. S
Dianthus	O. X	Pulmonaria	O. X
Dicentra	O. S	Ranunculus	O. D1, S
Digitalis	O. D1	Reseda	O or R. D1, G
Doronicum	O. X	Rudbeckia	O. S
Echinacea	O. X	Salvia	O. D1
Echinops	O or R. D1, G	Scabiosa	O. D1, S
Eremurus	O. X	Scilla	O. S
Eryngium	O or R. D1, G	Sedum	O. X
Freesia	O. S	Solidago	O. D1
Fuchsia	O. S	Tagetes	O. S
Gaillardia	O. D1	Tanacetum	O. D1, S
Gladiolus	O. S	Tropaeolum	O. X
Godetia	O. X	Tulipa	B or O. S
Helichrysum	O. D1	Verbascum	O. D1
Helipterum	O. D1	Verbena	O. X
Helleborus	O. G, S	Veronica	O. S
Hemerocallis	O. X	Viola	O. S
Heuchera	O. S	Xeranthemum	O or R. D1
Hyacinthus	O. X	Zinnia	O or R. S

Callistephus

Delphinium

Eremurus

Gladiolus

Lathyrus

Solidago

KEY: Time to cut: B – Bud stage • O – Open stage, some flowers fully open • R – Ripe stage, all flowers fully open
Preserving method: D1 – Upside-down drying • D2 – Upright drying • D3 – Flat drying • S – Silica gel • G – Glycerine • X – Not suitable for preserving

ROCKERY PERENNIALS ALL ROUND THE YEAR

By careful selection you can ensure that your rockery will have flowers almost all year round. For each month there is a list of perennials which can be expected to be in full bloom — remember that some of these plants may come into flower earlier and can continue to bloom for weeks later.

FEBRUARY
Hepatica nobilis
Primula edgeworthii

MARCH
Arabis albida
Arenaria balearica
Aubrieta deltoidea
Hepatica nobilis
Polygonum tenuicaule
Primula auricula
Primula variabilis
Ranunculus
    calandrinioides
Saxifraga (Cushion)
Soldanella alpina

APRIL
Aethionema 'Warley
    Rose'
Alyssum saxatile
Androsace
    sarmentosa
Arabis albida
Arenaria balearica
Armeria juniperifolia
Aubrieta deltoidea
Draba aizoides
Erinus alpinus
Erysimum alpinum
Hepatica nobilis
Morisia monanthos
Phlox subulata
Polygonum
    tenuicaule
Primula auricula
Primula variabilis
Pulsatilla vulgaris
Ramonda myconi
Sanguinaria
    canadensis
Saxifraga (Mossy)
Shortia galacifolia
Soldanella villosa
Viola biflora
Waldsteinia ternata

MAY
Alyssum saxatile
Androsace
    sarmentosa
Antennaria dioica
Arenaria balearica
Armeria juniperifolia
Armeria maritima
Aubrieta deltoidea
Cerastium
    tomentosum
Dianthus caesius
Dryas octopetala

Erinus alpinus
Gentiana acaulis
Gentiana verna
Haberlea rhodopensis
Iberis sempervirens
Iris species
Lewisia cotyledon
Phlox subulata
Raoulia australis
Saxifraga (Encrusted)
Silene acaulis
Uvularia grandiflora
Viola cornuta
Viola biflora

JUNE
Arenaria balearica
Armeria maritima
Campanula species
Cerastium
    tomentosum
Dianthus species
Dodecatheon meadia
Dryas octopetala
Erigeron
    karvinskianus
Erinus alpinus
Gentiana acaulis
Gentiana verna
Geranium cinereum
Geum montanum
Helianthemum
    nummularium
Iberis sempervirens
Iris species
Leontopodium
    alpinum
Linnaea borealis
Lychnis alpina
Oxalis adenophylla
Primula vialii
Ranunculus
    gramineus
Sedum species
Sisyrinchium
    angustifolium
Veronica prostrata

JULY
Anacyclus depressus
Androsace lanuginosa
Aster alpinus
Campanula species
Cerastium
    tomentosum
Dianthus species
Dodecatheon meadia
Erigeron
    karvinskianus
Erinus alpinus

Geranium cinereum
Geum reptans
Gypsophila repens
Helianthemum
    species
Helichrysum
    bellidioides
Leontopodium
    alpinum
Linnaea borealis
Lithospermum
    diffusum
Lychnis alpina
Lysimachia
    nummularia
Mazus reptans
Mimulus burnetii
Penstemon pinifolius
Sedum species
Sempervivum
    tectorum
Sisyrinchium species
Thymus serpyllum
Verbascum species

AUGUST
Acaena microphylla
Achillea tomentosa
Anacyclus depressus
Androsace lanuginosa
Astilbe chinensis
Campanula species
Cyananthus
    microphyllus
Dianthus deltoides
Erigeron
    karvinskianus
Gentiana septemfida
Geranium cinereum
Gypsophila repens
Helichrysum
    bellidioides
Lithospermum
    diffusum
Mazus reptans
Mimulus burnetii
Origanum amanum

Penstemon pinifolius
Potentilla hybrids
Saponaria ocymoides
Silene uniflora
Sisyrinchium species
Verbascum 'Letitia'

SEPTEMBER
Acaena microphylla
Achillea tomentosa
Androsace lanuginosa
Astilbe chinensis
Campanula species
Cyananthus
    microphyllus
Dianthus deltoides
Erigeron
    karvinskianus
Gentiana sino-ornata
Geranium cinereum
Lithospermum
    diffusum
Origanum amanum
Penstemon pinifolius
Polygonum
    vaccinifolium
Potentilla hybrids
Saponaria ocymoides
Silene uniflora
Sisyrinchium species

OCTOBER
Androsace lanuginosa
Astilbe chinensis
Gentiana sino-ornata
Polygonum
    vaccinifolium
Silene uniflora
Sisyrinchium species

NOVEMBER
Gentiana sino-ornata
Polygonum
    vaccinifolium

DECEMBER
Polygonum
    vaccinifolium

FLOWERS TO ATTRACT WILDLIFE

For many people the wildlife which some flowers attract is an important bonus. Butterflies are attracted by the nectar — small plants should be grown in clumps and not singly as masses of flowers are required. Birds are attracted by berries, seeds, insects etc on the plants — to attract winter birds do not cut off the seed heads on border perennials in autumn.

Ajuga	Bu	Helichrysum	Bu
Alyssum	Bu	Heliotropium	Bu
Aster	Bi, Bu	Iberis	Bu
Aubrieta	Bu	Lunaria	Bi, Bu
Calendula	Bu	Monarda	Bu
Centaurea	Bi	Muscari	Bu
Chrysanthemum	Bu	Myosotis	Bi, Bu
Dianthus	Bu	Papaver	Bi
Echinacea	Bu	Scabiosa	Bu
Echinops	Bi	Sedum	Bu
Helianthus	Bi	Solidago	Bi

KEY: Bi – Birds • Bu – Butterflies

EVERGREEN PLANTS

Some of the plants in the A-Z guide are evergreen or semi-evergreen, retaining all or most of their foliage during the winter months. They are useful as a way of providing a mixed border or rockery with patches of living green during the dead season, but having a few isolated evergreens in the herbaceous border will do little to brighten this area of the garden during the winter period.

Epimedium	E (some)	Parahebe	E
Eryngium	E	Penstemon	E or SE (some)
Erysimum	E		
Euphorbia	E (some)	Polygala	E
Frankenia	E	Prunella	E
Geranium	E or SE (some)	Pulmonaria	E
		Ruta	E
Helianthemum	E	Salvia	E (some)
Helichrysum	E	Saxifraga	E
Helleborus	E or SE	Sedum	E (some)
Heuchera	E	Sempervivum	E
Iberis	E	Senecio	E
Iris	E (some)	Silene	E or SE
Kniphofia	E	Sisyrinchium	E or SE
Lamium	E or SE	Stachys	E
Lavatera	E or SE	Symphytum	E
Lewisia	E	Tellima	SE
Libertia	E	Teucrium	E (some)
Limonium	E	Thymus	E
Liriope	E or SE	Tiarella	E or SE
Lysimachia	E or SE (some)	Verbascum	E or SE (some)
Morina	E	Veronica	E or SE (some)
Nepeta	SE		
Osteospermum	E (some)	Viola	E or SE (some)
		Waldsteinia	SE

Acaena	E	Bergenia	SE
Achillea	SE	Brunnera	E
Aethionema	E or SE	Campanula	E or SE (some)
Ajuga	E		
Alyssum	E	Cerastium	E
Antennaria	E	Cortaderia	E
Arabis	E	Dianthus	E or SE
Arenaria	E	Dierama	SE
Armeria	E	Digitalis	E (some)
Aubrieta	E	Dryas	E

KEY: E - Evergreen • SE - Semi-evergreen

CHAPTER 7

PLANT TROUBLES

Things occasionally go wrong in even the best cared-for gardens — it is utter nonsense to believe that pests and diseases will only attack sickly plants. However good the beds and borders may appear, you must be on your guard against outside invaders — the insects and fungal diseases which can attack your plants and spoil all your efforts. This chapter contains a frighteningly large rogues' gallery but you are unlikely to see more than a few in your own garden. It is much more likely that your plants will be harmed by an enemy from within rather than by an outside marauder — these inside causes may be the poor nature of your soil, lack of water, starvation, shade, frost, or you for choosing the wrong plants or doing the wrong things. The golden rule for having healthy flowers is to prevent trouble before it starts and to deal with it quickly once it is seen.

Prevent trouble before it starts

● **Choose wisely.** Do not buy soft bulbs, lanky bedding plants nor disease-ridden perennials — read the rules on pages 210-212. Even if you buy good stock it will not succeed in the wrong location. Use the A-Z guide and avoid types which are too tender for your garden. Do not plant sun-loving annuals under trees — the display is bound to disappoint.

● **Prepare the ground thoroughly.** A strong-growing plant is more likely to recover from a pest or disease attack than a weak specimen. Waterlogging is one of the worst problems in clayey soils. Read the section on digging (page 213). If you plan to dig then remember to incorporate organic matter below the surface. Get rid of all weed roots if you propose to plant perennials.

● **Plant or sow properly.** You have chosen the right plants or seeds and the soil is in a fit state to receive them, but trouble lies ahead if you do not bother to follow the rules for good planting laid down in this book. Pages 214-215 tell you how to ensure that there will be no air pockets and that the roots will spread out into the garden soil in the minimum possible time. Seed sowing (pages 224-226) calls for doing the right thing at the right time — sow too early outdoors and the seeds may rot, sow too late and the display may be short-lived. When sowing seed indoors, remember that hardening off will be essential before moving the seedlings outdoors.

● **Never leave rubbish lying about.** Boxes, old flower pots etc are a breeding ground for slugs and woodlice. Rotting plants can be a source of infection and may actually attract pests to the garden.

● **Feed the plants properly.** Shortage of nutrients can lead to many problems — poor growth, undersized blooms, lowered disease resistance and discoloured leaves. Read the instructions on the box or bottle — overfeeding can cause scorch and using an unbalanced fertilizer with too much nitrogen will give you lots of leaves and very few flowers.

● **Inspect plants regularly.** Keep watch for trouble and look up the cause in the following pages. Once you have put a name to the problem, act quickly — most pests and diseases can be checked quite easily if treated promptly, but may be difficult or impossible to control if left to get out of hand due to ignorance or neglect.

Deal with trouble as soon as you can

● **Remove occasional problems by hand.** Minor attacks by caterpillar or leaf miner can often be controlled by hand picking. If a plant suddenly dies, dig it up and examine it closely to find the cause. Examine the roots and the earth for soil pests — take remedial action if they are found. Do not replace the dead specimen with a similar plant if the description of the trouble in this chapter calls for a period of quarantine.

● **Keep a small plant-aid kit.** It may be several days before you are able to go to the shops, but a sudden attack by greenfly, caterpillars or slugs calls for immediate action. It is therefore a good idea to keep a small selection of pesticides in the garden shed for emergency use. You will need a bottle of a general insecticide for leaf pests, a box of slug pellets and a carton of general purpose fungicide. Do not buy more than you will need — it is better to buy a new small container each year rather than keep packs from one season to another.

● **Spray properly.** Once pests or diseases have started to take hold it will be necessary to act promptly. Read the label carefully and make sure that the product is recommended for the plant you wish to spray. Follow the instructions — do not make the solution stronger than recommended and never use equipment which has contained a weedkiller.

Pick a time when the weather is neither sunny nor windy and in the flowering season apply the spray in the evening when the bees have stopped working. Use a fine forceful spray and continue until the leaves are covered and the liquid has just started to run off. Do not direct the spray on to delicate open blooms.

After spraying, wash out equipment and wash hands and face. Store packs in a safe place and do not keep unlabelled or illegible packs. Never store pesticides or weedkillers in a beer bottle or similar container.

● **Speed recovery with a foliar feed.** Plants, like humans, can be invalids. The cause may have been a pest or disease attack, and the best way to get things moving again is to use a fertilizer which is recommended for spraying on the leaves.

ROOT TROUBLES

The major problem with soil pests is that they work unseen. Most of the ones shown below eat away at roots and by the time the damage becomes obvious the plant may be beyond recovery. There are no all-purpose soil-pest killers — the biological ones based on beneficial nematodes will help to control some pests including vine weevil, chafer grubs and cutworm, but others such as wireworm need a specific insecticide.

LEATHERJACKET

Grey or greyish-brown grubs which can be a serious nuisance in herbaceous borders on poorly-drained soil. Leatherjacket attacks are always worst after a wet winter — they are rarely a nuisance in sandy areas. If found at the roots of plants which have failed, sprinkle methiocarb over the ground and lightly rake in.

1 in. (2.5 cm) grub

WIREWORM

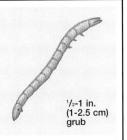

These hard shiny insects are a problem in new gardens and in plots adjoining grassland. They are slow-moving — not active like the friendly centipede. They eat the roots of most flowering plants and may burrow up the stems of Chrysanthemums. Water the soil with pirimiphos-methyl where they are a problem.

¹/₂-1 in. (1-2.5 cm) grub

MILLEPEDE

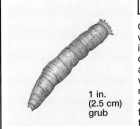

Various types, both black and spotted, occur in the soil. They tend to curl up when disturbed, and should always be destroyed when found as they damage the underground parts of many plants. Damaged or diseased areas are prime targets. Methiocarb can be used to keep this pest under control.

CUTWORM

These 2 in. (5 cm) long green, grey or brown soil-living caterpillars gnaw roots and stems, but their tell-tale effect is to sever seedlings at ground level. Look for and destroy the cutworms near the attacked plants. Always remove the grubs exposed when digging. Use a biological soil-pest killer.

VINE WEEVIL

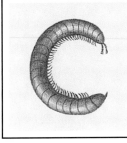

These wrinkled white grubs are extremely destructive underground both outdoors and under glass, eating the roots of many plants, especially alpines and pot plants. If a plant suddenly dies, look in the soil for this rolled-up grub. If present pick out and destroy. Use a biological soil-pest killer.

CHAFER GRUB

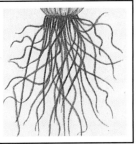

The fat curved grubs of the chafer beetle feed throughout the year on the roots of garden plants. Bedding plants are occasionally attacked — badly affected plants are killed. If these grubs are found in the soil, or if you intend to plant into newly broken-up grassland, use a biological soil-pest killer for prevention or control.

CLUB ROOT

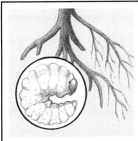

This serious disease of the vegetable garden can affect Wallflowers and Stocks. Below ground the roots are swollen and distorted — above ground the plants are small and die off earlier than normal. Apply lime to the soil before planting and avoid growing Wallflowers on the same site year after year.

BLACK ROOT ROT

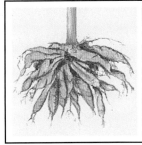

A common disease affecting Antirrhinum, Begonia, Sweet Pea, Geranium etc. Above ground the leaves turn yellow and wilt. Below ground the roots are blackened. There is no cure, so avoid the causes — unsterilized compost indoors, uncomposted leaf mould outdoors and replanting the same type of plant in infected soil.

CATS

Cats can be a serious pest of annual flowers. Seed beds and newly transplanted bedding plants are disturbed by their scratching. The resulting root damage can lead to the death of the seedlings. Protection is not easy if cats have chosen your flower bed for their toilet — one of the cat deterrent sprays may help.

MOLES

An invasion by moles can cause havoc. The hills are unsightly and tunnelling causes root damage. Small plants may be uprooted. Eradication is not easy. Smokes or sonic deterrents should be tried first, it may be necessary to set traps or to gas them. This work should be done by a professional exterminator.

TUBER, CORM & BULB TROUBLES

Many plants are raised from bulbs, corms, rhizomes and tubers. These fleshy organs are at risk throughout their life cycle. They may be attacked in the soil by swift moth caterpillar, bulb aphid, narcissus fly and eelworm (see below) and by animals searching for food. Root pests such as wireworm, chafer grub and vine weevil (see page 237) will also attack bulbs and corms.

TUBER ROT

Dahlia tubers can be destroyed in store by fungal rots. To prevent this from happening, stand the tubers upside down after lifting and allow them to dry. Remove any remaining soil. Leave them to dry before storing in boxes in a dry frost-free place. Inspect tubers from time to time — cut away any diseased parts.

RHIZOME ROT

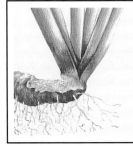

A destructive disease of Flag Iris, especially in badly drained soil. Leaf tips yellow and wither — later the fan of leaves collapses. A yellowish slimy rot affects the rhizomes. Plants can be saved if the soft diseased areas on the rhizome are cut away as soon as they are seen and the rhizome and soil are treated with a copper dust.

BULB ROTS

Several serious storage rots affect Tulips and Daffodils. **Narcissus smoulder** causes the bulbs to decay, small fungal growths appearing on the outer scales. **Basal rot** begins at the base of the bulbs of Daffodils and Lilies, the brown rot spreading upwards through the inner scales. **Tulip fire** is the most serious disease of this bulb — small fungal growths appear on outer scales and both shoots and flowers are damaged. In all cases the procedure is the same — dig up affected plants and never plant soft or mouldy bulbs. Remove rotten bulbs from store.

Narcissus smoulder   Basal rot   Tulip fire

NARCISSUS FLY

Affected Daffodil bulbs are soft and rotten, producing a few leaves but no flowers if planted or left in the soil. The maggots are $1/2$-$3/4$ in. (1-1.5 cm) long. Control is not easy — always discard bulbs at lifting or planting time if they are found to be soft. Hoe around the plants as the foliage dies down.

STEM & BULB EELWORM

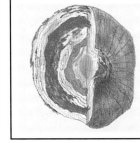

Affected bulbs of Daffodil, Tulip, Hyacinth etc are soft and rotten. Tell-tale dark rings can be seen in a cut bulb. Daffodil leaves are pale, twisted and bear characteristic small yellow swellings on the surface. Throw away all soft bulbs. Do not plant bulbous plants on affected land for at least three years.

CORM ROTS

Several serious storage rots occur on Crocus and Gladiolus corms. **Dry rot** causes many black spots to appear on the corm, which later merge and the tissue completely decays. With **hard rot** the spots are brown and the affected corm becomes shrivelled. The spots of **scab** are round, brown and shiny. **Core rot** is quite different from the other corm diseases — it starts at the central core of Gladiolus corms and then spreads outwards as a moist rot. In all cases the procedure is the same — dig up affected plants and never plant soft or mouldy corms. Remove rotten corms from store.

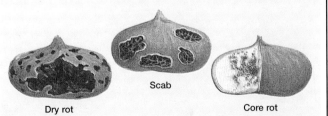

Dry rot   Scab   Core rot

SWIFT MOTH

These soil-living caterpillars attack Gladiolus corms, Iris rhizomes and all types of bulbs. Unlike cutworms (page 237) they move backwards when disturbed. If swift moth is known to be a serious problem, rake in a soil insecticide before planting. Otherwise keep the pest under control by hoeing regularly.

BULB APHID

Colonies of greenfly may develop on Tulip and Lily bulbs and on Crocus and Gladiolus corms in store, sheltering and feeding under the outer scales. Young growth is severely affected when infested bulbs are planted. Rub off aphids before planting — chemical treatment is not necessary.

PEA & BEAN WEEVIL

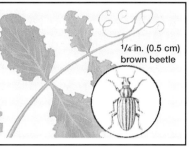

1/4 in. (0.5 cm)
brown beetle

A common pest of the vegetable garden which can be damaging to flowers belonging to the Pea family (Sweet Pea, Lupin etc). Seedlings are most at risk, and should be protected by spraying with pirimiphos-methyl or derris if the characteristic U-shaped notches appear on the leaves. Leaves of older plants may be damaged, but spraying here is not usually necessary.

Holes and tears in tender leaves are sometimes caused by frost or severe weather, but the usual culprit is an insect pest. Seedlings, small plants and the lower leaves of tall perennials can all be seriously damaged by pests such as slugs, snails, woodlice and vine weevils which feed on the foliage at night and hide under stones, debris etc during the day. Above-ground pests can attack leaves growing at all levels — capsid bugs produce small, brown-edged holes and caterpillars form large holes or even completely skeletonise the foliage. Many types of caterpillar may be found — the angle shades moth attacks the widest range of plants and the vapourer moth can be a nuisance in town gardens. Note that these garden caterpillars are the larval stage of moths rather than butterflies — the abundant cabbage white is the only exception.

CATERPILLAR

Many different leaf-eating caterpillars attack annuals and perennials in the flower garden. Some are uncommon — a few such as the angle shades moth and the cabbage white butterfly can be serious pests. Pick off the caterpillars if this is practical — if damage is widespread spray with an insecticide such as fenitrothion, derris or heptenophos.

ANGLE SHADES MOTH

Smooth caterpillar, about 2 in. (5 cm) long, which can be a serious nuisance on Dahlia, Gladiolus and many perennials.

CABBAGE MOTH

Smooth caterpillar, about 1 1/4 in. (3 cm) long, which attacks several annuals and perennials. Leaves may be skeletonised.

CABBAGE WHITE BUTTERFLY

Slightly hairy caterpillar, about 1 1/2 in. (3.5 cm) long, which attacks several annuals and perennials. Leaves may be skeletonised.

VAPOURER MOTH

Colourful caterpillar, about 1 in. (2.5 cm) long, which feeds on the leaves of many perennials from May until August.

WOODLICE

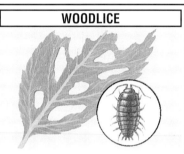

An abundant pest in shady town gardens, hiding under stones or leaves during the day and devouring young leaves of a wide range of flowering plants during the night. Woodlice favour plants which have already been damaged by a previous pest. Control is not easy — do not leave rubbish in the garden and scatter methiocarb around the plants.

SLUGS & SNAILS

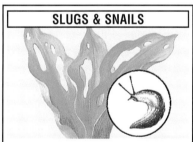

Serious pests, especially on Tulip, Iris, Delphinium, annuals and rock plants. Irregular holes are formed and tell-tale slime trails can be seen. Damage is worst on a shady, poorly drained site. These pests generally hide under garden rubbish during the day, so keeping the area clean and cultivated is the first control measure. Scatter methiocarb or metaldehyde pellets around damaged plants.

EARWIG

A familiar pest which attacks Chrysanthemums, Dahlias and several other garden plants during summer and autumn. Females bear straight pincers. They are night feeders, hiding in the petals during the day. Shake the stems and then spray the plants and ground thoroughly with pirimiphos-methyl.

Leaf not distorted

Leaf distorted

FLEA BEETLE

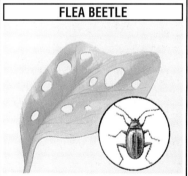

Tiny black or black and yellow beetles attack seedlings of the Crucifer family (Stock, Wallflower, Aubrieta, Alyssum etc). Numerous, small round holes appear in the leaves. Growth is slowed down and seedlings may be killed. The beetles jump when disturbed. Spray or dust the young plants with derris or pirimiphos-methyl as soon as the first signs of damage are noticed.

CAPSID BUG

These little bugs are a serious pest of Dahlias, Chrysanthemums and Salvias. At first the leaves are spotted — as the foliage enlarges small ragged holes with brown edges are formed. The leaves are distorted and puckered. Spray both the plants and soil with fenitrothion or heptenophos.

LEAF & STEM TROUBLES

Aphids and powdery mildew are serious problems in a dry summer, and grey mould can be destructive when the weather is wet. Starvation leads to poor leaf and stem development, and traces of lawn weedkiller can lead to severe distortion. The major leaf and stem problems are shown on these two pages — other insects or moulds may occasionally appear but they seldom, if ever, call for treatment.

DAMPING OFF

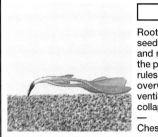

Roots and stem bases of seedlings are attacked. Shrinkage and rot occur at ground level and the plants topple over. The golden rules are to sow thinly and never overwater. Ensure adequate ventilation under glass. Remove collapsed seedlings immediately — water remainder with Cheshunt Compound.

LEAFHOPPER

Pale mottled patches or flecks appear on the leaves — common on Pelargonium and Primula during the summer months. Small yellowish insects or their empty white skins will be found on the underside. Direct damage is usually slight but they can transmit viruses. Spray with fenitrothion or heptenophos.

CHRYSANTHEMUM EELWORM

The leaves develop brown areas between the veins — the plants may be killed if the infestation is severe. Aster and Peony as well as Chrysanthemum may be attacked. The closely-related leaf blotch eelworm produces similar symptoms on Begonia and ferns. Pick off and burn affected leaves — destroy severely infested plants.

STEM ROT

Several types of stem rot attack garden flowers — all are serious. Part or all of the stem decays and the leaves wilt. Sclerotinia disease is a common cause in herbaceous border plants — Sunflower, Campanula, Chrysanthemum etc. Hard black bodies occur in the pith. There is no cure — lift badly diseased plants and burn.

COLD DAMAGE

A sudden cold snap in spring can affect developing leaves and leaf buds by destroying chlorophyll. The affected leaf, when it expands, may be yellow-edged (Anemone, Sweet Pea etc), almost white (many bedding plants) or white-banded (Daffodils). Pick off badly affected leaves — spray with a foliar fertilizer to speed recovery.

LEAFY GALL

A mass of shortened shoots with thickened, distorted leaves sometimes develops at the base of the plant. This disease is spread by tools or by taking cuttings from diseased stock, so affected plants should be destroyed and not used for propagation. Susceptible plants are Sweet Pea, Chrysanthemum, Dahlia and Pelargonium.

FROGHOPPER

The frothy white masses ('cuckoo spit') which occur on the stems of Geum, Solidago, Chrysanthemum and many other flowering plants, are familiar to everyone. Less well known is the cause — pinkish 1/8 in. (0.25 cm) froghoppers which suck the sap and distort young growth. Hose with water, then spray with heptenophos if attack is severe.

PHLOX EELWORM

The young leaves of infested plants are strap-like and die off prematurely. Older leaves are distorted. Several perennials, such as Phlox, Gypsophila and Aubrieta may be attacked. The crowns of Polyanthus are killed. Dig up and burn infested specimens — do not replant with susceptible perennials for at least three years.

FOOT ROT

The tell-tale sign is the blackening and rotting of the base of the stem. The name depends on the plant affected — geranium blackleg, pansy sickness, campanula crown rot etc. Use sterile compost in seed boxes or pots. Avoid waterlogging. Destroy infected plants and water remainder with mancozeb if there are many plants to save.

TULIP FIRE

A serious disease of Tulips, causing scorched areas on the leaves and spots on the flowers. Young shoots may become covered with a grey, velvety mould. Rotting of bulbs occurs (see page 238). Cut off diseased emerging shoots below ground level — spray the remaining plants with carbendazim. Repeat at 14-day intervals.

APHID

Several species of aphids infest annual and perennial flowers in warm, settled weather. The commonest are the black bean aphid and the peach-potato aphid. Young growth is distorted and weakened — leaves are covered with sticky honeydew which later becomes covered with sooty mould. Keep plants well-watered in dry weather. Spray with derris or a systemic insecticide as soon as colonies start to appear.

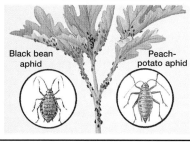

Black bean aphid

Peach-potato aphid

RED SPIDER MITE

If leaves develop an unhealthy bronze colour, look for tiny spider-like mites on the underside of the leaves. The presence of fine silky webbing is a tell-tale sign. In hot settled weather spraying may be necessary — spray with derris.

LEAF MINER

Long winding tunnels are eaten in the leaf tissue by small grubs. At first the tunnels appear white, later they turn brown. Chrysanthemum foliage is commonly attacked in this way. The carnation fly behaves rather differently, producing blotches on the leaves and sometimes killing the plant. Pick and destroy mined leaves. Spray with heptenophos.

WILT

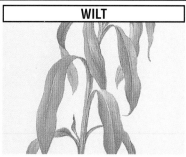

Leaves and shoots sometimes wilt badly even though the soil is moist. If the plant is an Antirrhinum, Aster, Sweet Pea, Carnation, Chrysanthemum, Lupin or Poppy then the likely cause is a soil-borne fungus. Tissue inside stem will probably be stained brown. There is no cure. Remove diseased plants — do not grow susceptible plants on the same spot.

VIRUS

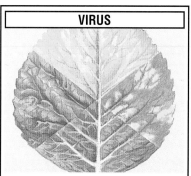

Viruses may be carried by insects, tools or fingers. There are many different symptoms of virus infection — leaves may be yellow, covered with yellow spots or patches (**mosaic**), crinkled and distorted or white-veined. Stems may be covered with brown stripes (**streak**) or stunted and distorted. There is no cure — if you are sure of your diagnosis, lift and burn. Buy healthy stock — keep aphids under control.

GREY MOULD (Botrytis)

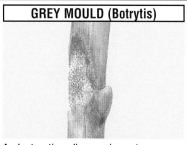

A destructive disease in wet seasons. Fluffy grey mould appears on the leaves — with many bedding plants (Godetia, Clarkia, Petunia, Zinnia etc) stems are attacked. Remove mouldy leaves and badly infected plants immediately. Spray with carbendazim.

RUST

Look for the tell-tale sign of coloured swellings on the leaves and stems. These raised spots may be yellow, orange or brown. It is a common disease of Antirrhinum, Hollyhock, Pelargonium, Carnation, Chrysanthemum and Sweet William. Pick off and burn diseased leaves — spray with mancozeb every two weeks.

LEAF SPOT

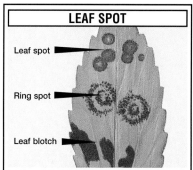

Leaf spot

Ring spot

Leaf blotch

Leaf spot is a family name for a wide group of diseases which appear on many types of flowering plants. **Leaf spot** (round or oval coloured spots) is an important disease of Pansy, Phlox, Polyanthus, Poppy, Iris and Sweet William. **Ring spot** (dark concentric rings of spores) is common on Carnation, and **leaf blotch** (irregular-shaped spots) affects Delphinium. Pick off diseased leaves. Spray with mancozeb, but control may be difficult.

POWDERY MILDEW

The main symptom is a white mealy growth on the leaf surface. It is encouraged by overcrowding and lack of soil moisture. This is the disease commonly seen on Michaelmas Daisy, Delphinium and Chrysanthemum. Spray with carbendazim at the first sign of disease and again one week later. Repeat if disease reappears.

DOWNY MILDEW

Less likely to be troublesome than powdery mildew, although Antirrhinum, Sweet Pea, Poppy and Wallflower are often affected in damp weather. Upper leaf surface shows yellow or dull patches — greyish mould growth occurs below. Plants are crippled by a severe attack. Spray with mancozeb at the first sign of disease — repeat at 14-day intervals.

BUD & FLOWER TROUBLES

Blooms may be poor in size and quantity. They may also be damaged, distorted or spotted. In addition to the pests and diseases shown here, there are other flower enemies illustrated on previous pages — slugs (page 239), eelworm (pages 238 and 240), tulip fire (page 240) and the angle shades moth (page 239).

BIRDS

Birds are extremely selective in their choice of flowers. Nearly all blooms are ignored but Polyanthus, Primula 'Wanda' and Crocus (especially the yellow-flowering varieties) may be stripped of buds and flowers in spring by sparrows and blackbirds. Surprisingly, plants in one garden may be ruined and similar plants next door completely ignored. Control is difficult because netting is unsightly in the flower garden. A bird repellent spray may be tried.

NO FLOWERS

There are several possible reasons why plants may fail to bloom. Some herbaceous border plants dislike being moved and may not bloom during their first year in the garden. Daffodils suffer from a disorder known as grassiness (grass-like leaves and no flowers) — there is no cure. Tulips sometimes suffer from blindness. But the most likely cause of failure to flower is the effect of one of the factors in the paragraph below.

FEW FLOWERS

A common problem is the failure of plants to produce the normal number of blooms. The two most frequent reasons are too much shade and too much nitrogen. Some bedding and rockery plants will hardly bloom at all in deep shade — always choose carefully for such locations. Too much nitrogen, due to overmanuring, is the cause of too much foliage and too little bloom — use a fertilizer which has more potash than nitrogen in order to redress the balance. There are many other possibilities — failure to pinch out the growing point of bedding plants to induce bushiness, failure to cut off dead blooms in order to induce repeat flowering and failure to water in dry weather. Bud drop can occur if there is a late frost or even a cold night — Sweet Peas frequently suffer in this way. Finally, an attack by some of the pests and diseases described on this page can reduce the number of blooms.

APHID

Aphids, both greenfly and blackfly, can seriously reduce the quantity and quality of the floral display. When the weather is warm and dry, large colonies of these pests build up on the buds of many types of flowering plants, causing the flowers when they are open to be undersized. In a severe attack the buds may fail to open. Spray with derris, bifenthrin or a systemic insecticide when the pests are first seen.

EARWIG

An important pest of Chrysanthemum and Dahlia blooms. At night the petals are eaten, making them ragged and unsightly. During the day the earwigs hide in the heart of the blooms or beneath leaves and other debris on the ground. Clear away rubbish. Shake open blooms, then spray plants and soil with pirimiphos-methyl.

THRIPS

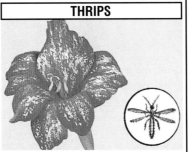

Thrips or thunderflies swarm over leaves and flowers in a hot summer. The usual symptom is silvery flecking of flowers and leaves. Gladioli are particularly susceptible. Flowers may be ruined by a bad attack. Spray at the first sign of attack with heptenophos or fenitrothion.

CAPSID BUG

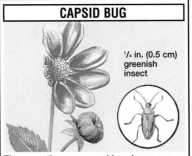

¼ in. (0.5 cm) greenish insect

These active, sap-sucking bugs are a serious pest of Dahlias, Chrysanthemums and many other flowers. Buds may be killed — if they open the flowers are lop-sided. Begin spraying with fenitrothion as soon as damage appears on the leaves (see page 239). Repeat two or three times at 14-day intervals.

PETAL BLIGHT

In a cold and wet summer this Chrysanthemum disease can ruin the flowers. Small water-filled spots appear on the petals, eventually spreading to destroy the bloom. Anemone, Cornflower and Dahlia are affected. Spray with mancozeb when buds begin to show colour. Repeat at weekly intervals. Pick off diseased flowers.

GREY MOULD (Botrytis)

Grey mould is a serious disease of the flower garden which strikes when the weather is humid. It can attack a wide variety of blooms — Chrysanthemum, Dahlia, Peony, Lily and bedding plants are particularly susceptible. Flowers may be spotted at first, but later rot and become covered with a fluffy mould. Badly diseased buds fail to open. Pick off mouldy leaves and flowers as soon as they are seen. Spray with carbendazim.

COLOUR BREAK

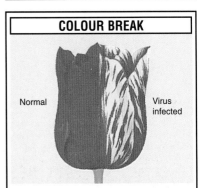

Normal   Virus infected

Petals sometimes possess streaks or patches of an abnormal colour. This colour break is caused by a virus and there is no cure. Tulips are the most likely flowers to be affected — it may also occur in Dahlia, Chrysanthemum, Lily, Viola and Wallflower. The effect may be attractive — multicoloured Tulip varieties are bred in this way. But in a single-colour bed the effect is undesirable and the plants should be destroyed if you wish to keep the stock pure. The removal of diseased plants is essential where **phyllody** occurs — a virus-like condition which causes the flowers to turn green.

CHAPTER 8

GLOSSARY

A

ACID SOIL A soil which contains no free lime and has a *pH* of less than 6.5.

ADVENTITIOUS Term applied to organs produced at a point where such growth would not appear naturally. Roots on an above-ground stem are an example.

AERATION The loosening of soil by digging or other mechanical means to allow air to pass freely.

ALKALINE SOIL A soil which has a *pH* of more than 7.3. Other terms are chalky and limy soil.

ALPINE A rather vague term used to describe low-growing rockery perennials.

ALTERNATE Leaves or buds which arise first on one side of the stem and then on the other. Compare *opposite*.

ANNUAL A plant which flowers and then dies in a single season.

ANTHER The part of the flower which produces *pollen*. It is the upper section of the *stamen*.

ASEXUAL REPRODUCTION See *vegetative reproduction*.

AWL-SHAPED A narrow leaf which tapers to a stiff point.

AXIL The angle between the upper surface of the leaf stalk and the stem that carries it. An axillary bud arises in this angle.

B

BASAL PLATE The disc of tissue to which the *scales* of a *bulb* are attached.

BASAL ROOTING The root system arising from the *basal plate* of a *bulb*.

BASAL SHOOT A shoot arising from the neck or *crown* of the plant.

BASTARD TRENCHING Another term for double digging — see page 213.

BEARDED A petal bearing a tuft or row of long hairs.

BED A planted area designed to be viewed from all sides.

BEDDING PLANT A plant which is 'bedded out' in quantity to provide a temporary display.

BERRY A fleshy fruit in which the *seed* or seeds are buried.

BICOLOUR A flower bearing two distinctly different colours.

BIENNIAL A plant which completes its life cycle in two growing seasons.

BISEXUAL A flower bearing both male and female reproductive organs — compare *dioecious* and *monoecious*.

BLANKET BEDDING The use of a single variety of bedding plant to cover a whole bed or border.

BLEEDING The abundant loss of sap from severed plant tissues.

BLEND A flower bearing two or more colours with one gradually merging into the other.

BLIND Term applied to a mature *bulb* which produces normal foliage but fails to flower.

BLOOM Two meanings — either a fine powdery coating or a flower.

BLOTCHED A flower with petals bearing distinctly coloured patches which are irregularly scattered.

BORDER A planted area designed to be viewed from one, two or three sides but not from all angles.

BOSS A ring of prominent and decorative *stamens*.

BOTTOM HEAT Undersurface heat provided in the soil by organic fermentation, electric cables or hot water pipes.

BRACT A modified leaf at the base of a flower. A cluster of small bracts is a bracteole.

BREAKING BUD A *bud* which has started to open.

BUD A flower bud is the unopened bloom. A growth bud or eye is a condensed shoot.

BULB Botanically an underground organ (true bulb) made up of fleshy or scale-like leaves arising from a *basal plate*. Popular meaning is any plant which produces fleshy *storage organs* at the base and which can be used for propagation.

BULBOUS PLANT See *bulb* above.

C

CALCAREOUS Chalky or limy soil.

CALCIFUGE A plant which will not thrive in *alkaline soil*.

CALLUS The scar tissue which forms at the base of a cutting.

CALYX The ring of *sepals* which protect the unopened flower bud.

CAMPANULATE Bell-shaped.

CAPITULUM A type of flower head — see page 246.

CHELATE An organic chemical which can supply nutrients to plants in a soil which would normally lock up the plant-feeding element or elements in question.

CHIMAERA A *mutation* which produces two kinds of tissue — e.g one or more wild coloured petals in a Chrysanthemum.

CHLOROPHYLL The green pigment found in leaves which is capable of using light-energy to transform carbon dioxide and water into carbohydrates by the process known as photosynthesis.

CHLOROSIS An abnormal yellowing or blanching of the leaves due to lack of *chlorophyll*.

CLIMBER A plant which climbs by clinging to or twining round a support — also loosely applied to some weak-stemmed plants which are tied to trellis, arches etc.

CLOCHE A temporary structure of glass or plastic sheets used to protect and hasten the growth of plants in the open.

CLONE A group of identical plants produced by *vegetative reproduction* from a single parent plant.

COLD FRAME A rigid container for plants in which access is through the roof. This roof is made of one or more transparent and movable *lights* — the sides are brick, wood, metal, concrete, plastic or glass.

COLLARETTE A flower bearing large petals with an inner ring of small and narrow petals.

COLOURED LEAF A leaf with one or more distinct colours apart from green, white or cream. Compare *variegated* leaf.

COMPOSITAE The Daisy family — each flower bears 'petals' which are really *florets*.

COMPOST Two meanings — either decomposed vegetable or animal matter for incorporation in the soil, or a potting/cutting/seed sowing mixture made from peat ('soilless compost') or sterilized soil ('loam compost') plus other materials such as sand, chalk and fertilizers.

COMPOUND FLOWER A flower composed of *florets*.

COMPOUND LEAF A leaf composed of two or more *leaflets*.

CONE A prominent and raised *disc* at the centre of the flower.

CORDATE Heart-shaped.

CORM A *bulbous plant* which is bulb-like but is composed of solid tissue and not *scales*.

COROLLA The ring of *petals* inside the *calyx* of the flower.

CORONA The *trumpet* produced in certain flowers, e.g Narcissus.

CORYMB A type of flower head — see page 246.

COTYLEDON A seed leaf which usually differs in shape from the true leaves which appear later.

CROCK A piece of broken flower pot used at the bottom of a container to improve drainage.

CROSS The offspring arising from cross-pollination.

CROWN The bottom part of a *herbaceous* plant from which the roots grow downwards and the shoots arise.

CRUCIFERAE The Cabbage or Wallflower Family, in which the flower bears four petals in the shape of a cross.

CULTIVAR Short for 'cultivated variety' — it is a *variety* which originated in cultivation and not in the wild. Strictly speaking, virtually all modern varieties are cultivars, but the more familiar term 'variety' is used for them in this book.

CUP A *corona* which is broader than it is long. See *trumpet*.

CUTTING A part of a plant which is removed and used for propagation.

CYME A type of flower head — see page 246.

D

DEAD-HEADING The removal of faded flowers.

DECIDUOUS A plant which loses its leaves at the end of the growing season.

DECUMBENT A prostrate stem with an ascending tip.

DENTATE Toothed margin.

DIBBER A blunt-ended wooden stick used to make holes in the soil for transplants.

DIGITATE LEAF A leaf composed of finger-like radiating leaflets.

DIOECIOUS A plant which bears either male or female flowers. Compare *monoecious*.

DISC (DISK) The flat central part of a *compound flower*. It is made up of short, tubular *florets*.

DORMANT PERIOD The time when a plant has naturally stopped growing due to low temperatures and short day length.

DOT PLANT A bedding plant grown singly or in a small group at the centre of a bedding scheme where it is bold enough to serve as a focal point.

DOUBLE A flower with many more than the normal number of petals. When the whole of the bloom appears to be composed of petals it is called 'fully double' — a 'semi-double' flower is the half-way point between a *single* bloom and a fully double one.

DRAWN Term applied to pale and *lanky* seedlings which have been sown too thickly or grown in shady conditions.

DRILL A straight and shallow furrow in which seeds are sown.

E

EDGING PLANT A low-growing plant grown to line the rim of a bed or border.

ENTIRE LEAF An undivided and unserrated leaf.

EVERGREEN A plant which retains its leaves in a living state during the winter.

EVERLASTING Flowers with papery petals which retain some or all of their colour when dried for winter decoration.

EXOTIC Strictly any plant which is not native to the country in which it is grown, but popular meaning is a plant which is not hardy and has a tropical appearance.

EYE Two meanings — a dormant growth bud, or the centre of a single or semi-double bloom where the colour of this area is distinctly different from the rest of the flower.

F

F$_1$ HYBRID A first generation offspring of two pure-bred closely related plants. An F$_1$ hybrid is generally more vigorous and more uniform than an ordinary *hybrid*. F$_1$ hybrids do not breed true.

F$_2$ HYBRID A plant produced by crossing F$_1$ hybrids. Usually less vigorous than F$_1$ hybrids and like them does not breed true.

FAMILY A group of related *genera*.

FEATHERED A petal on which there are feather-like markings on a ground colour which is distinctly different.

FERTILIZATION The application of *pollen* to the *stigma* to induce the production of seed.

FERTILIZER A material which provides appreciable quantities of one or more major plant nutrients without adding significantly to the *humus* content of the soil.

FIBROUS-ROOTED A root system which contains many thin roots rather than a single tap root.

FILAMENT The supporting column of the *anther*. It is the lower part of the *stamen*.

FIMBRIATE Frilly-edged.

FLAKED A petal bearing broad stripes running inwards from the edges.

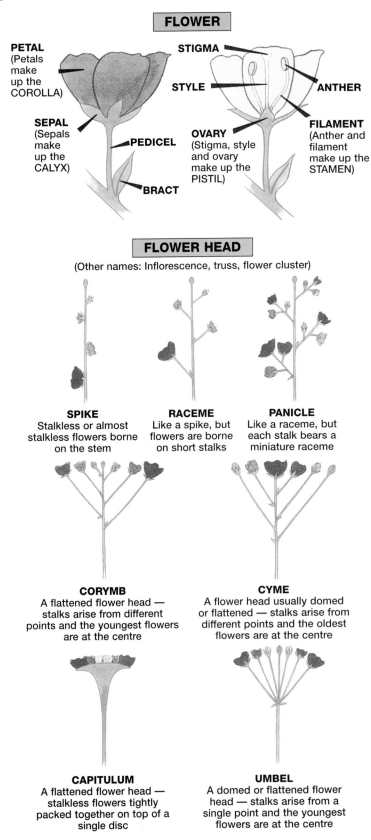

FLOWER

PETAL
(Petals make up the COROLLA)

STIGMA

STYLE

ANTHER

SEPAL
(Sepals make up the CALYX)

PEDICEL

OVARY
(Stigma, style and ovary make up the PISTIL)

FILAMENT
(Anther and filament make up the STAMEN)

BRACT

FLOWER HEAD

(Other names: Inflorescence, truss, flower cluster)

SPIKE
Stalkless or almost stalkless flowers borne on the stem

RACEME
Like a spike, but flowers are borne on short stalks

PANICLE
Like a raceme, but each stalk bears a miniature raceme

CORYMB
A flattened flower head — stalks arise from different points and the youngest flowers are at the centre

CYME
A flower head usually domed or flattened — stalks arise from different points and the oldest flowers are at the centre

CAPITULUM
A flattened flower head — stalkless flowers tightly packed together on top of a single disc

UMBEL
A domed or flattened flower head — stalks arise from a single point and the youngest flowers are at the centre

FLAMED A *feathered* petal which bears a distinct central band.

FLORE PLENO Term applied to *double* flowers.

FLORET The individual flowers of a *compound flower* or dense flower head.

FLOWER The reproductive organ of the plant.

FLUSH The display of flowers when blooming is at its peak. Some *perennials* but not many *annuals* produce flowers in distinct flushes with a non-blooming gap between each one.

FLUTED A long and narrow petal which is loosely rolled. See *quilled*.

FOLIAGE A collective term for the leaves of a plant.

FOLIAR FEED A fertilizer capable of being sprayed on and absorbed by the leaves.

FORCING The inducement of flowering before its natural time.

FORMAL BEDDING A *bed* or *border* in which the plants are arranged in a geometrical pattern.

FRIABLE Term applied to crumbly soil.

FROST POCKET An area where cold air is trapped during winter and in which *half-hardy* plants are in much greater danger.

FRUIT The *seed* together with the structure which bears or contains it.

FUNGICIDE A substance used to control infectious diseases caused by a *fungus* — e.g mildew, damping off and rust.

FUNGUS A primitive form of plant life which is the most common cause of infectious disease — e.g mildews and rusts. Such diseases are controlled or prevented by means of *fungicides*.

G

GENUS (plural **GENERA**) A group of closely-related plants containing one or more *species*.

GERMINATION The emergence of the root and shoot from the seed.

GLABROUS Smooth, hairless.

GLAUCOUS Covered with a *bloom*.

GROUND COLOUR The main or background colour of a petal.

GROUND COVER An ornamental plant which requires little attention and is used to provide a low-growing and partially weed-proof carpet between other plants.

GROUNDWORK PLANT A medium-height bedding plant used to fill most or all of a bedding scheme.

GROWING ON The process of transferring seedlings to larger containers and allowing them to increase in size before planting outdoors.

GROWING POINT The tip of a stem which is responsible for extension growth.

H

HALF-HARDY A plant which will only grow outdoors when the temperature remains above freezing point. The term is not precise — some half-hardy plants can be left outdoors in winter in mild regions.

HARDENING OFF The gradual acclimatisation of a plant raised under warm conditions to the environment it will have to withstand outdoors.

HARDY A plant which will withstand overwintering without protection.

HEAVY LAND Soil in which the clay content is high. Difficult to cultivate.

HEELING-IN The temporary planting of newly-acquired stock pending suitable weather conditions for permanent planting.

HERBACEOUS A plant which does not form permanent woody stems.

HERMAPHRODITE See *bisexual*.

HIRSUTE Covered with stiff or coarse hairs.

HONEYDEW Sticky, sugary secretion deposited on the leaves and stems by such insects as aphids and whitefly.

HOSE-IN-HOSE A flower which gives the appearance of one bloom inside the other — e.g Canterbury Bell.

HUE The 'pure' version of a colour. See *shade* and *tint*.

HUMUS Term popularly (but not correctly) applied to partly decomposed organic matter in the soil. Actually humus is the jelly-like end-product which coats the soil particles.

HYBRID Plants with parents which are genetically distinct. The parent plants may be different *species*, *cultivars*, *varieties* or occasionally *genera*.

I

IMBRICATE Closely overlapping.

INFLORESCENCE The part of the plant bearing the flowers — the flower head.

INFORMAL BEDDING A *bed* or *border* in which the plants are arranged irregularly without any attempt to create straight lines or geometric patterns.

INORGANIC A chemical or fertilizer which is not obtained from a source which is or has been alive.

INSECTICIDE A chemical used to control insects and other small pests.

INTERNODE The part of the stem between one *node* and another.

INVOLUCRE A ring of *bracts* surrounding a flower or cluster of flowers.

J

JOINT See *node*.

K

KEEL Boat-shaped structure formed by the two lower petals of many members of the *Leguminosae*.

L

LANCEOLATE Spear-shaped.

LANKY Spindly growth — a stem with a gaunt and sparse appearance.

LARVA Immature stage of some insects, popularly known as a caterpillar, maggot or grub.

LATERAL SHOOT A shoot which arises from the side of a main stem.

LEACHING The loss of soluble chemicals from the soil due to the downward movement of water.

LEAF MOULD Peat-like material composed of partially-rotted leaves.

LEAFLET One of the parts of a *compound leaf*.

LEGGY See *lanky*.

LEGUMINOSAE The Pea family. Many have papilionaceous (butterfly-like) flowers — e.g Sweet Pea.

LIGHT Movable part of a *cold frame*.

LIGHT LAND Soil in which the sand content is high. Easy to cultivate.

LINEAR Very narrow with parallel sides.

LOAM *Friable* soil which is not obviously clayey nor sandy.

LOBE Rounded segment which protrudes from the rest of the leaf, petal or other plant organ.

M

MEDIUM LAND See *loam*.

MOISTURE-RETENTIVE SOIL A soil which is capable of retaining an appreciable amount of water within its crumbs. The water in the spaces between the crumbs may drain away quite freely after rain — see *well-drained soil*.

MONOCARPIC A plant which dies after flowering and seeding.

MONOCHROMATIC SCHEME A colour scheme in which the various *tints*, *shades* and *hues* of a single colour are used.

MONOECIOUS A plant which bears both male and female flowers. Compare *dioecious*.

MOUTH The open end of a bell-shaped or tubular flower.

MULCH A layer of bulky organic matter placed around the stems — see page 217.

MULTICOLOURED A flower bearing at least three distinctly different colours.

MULTIPURPOSE COMPOST A *soilless compost* which can be used for seed sowing, potting up plants and for filling hanging baskets and other containers.

MUTATION A sudden change in the genetic make-up of a plant, leading to a new feature which can be inherited.

N

N:P:K Shorthand for the nitrogen : phosphate : potash declaration of a *fertilizer*.

NATIVE A species which grows wild in this country and was not introduced by man.

NATURALISING Establishing a group of plants (usually bulbs) in grassland or woodland and then letting them increase without interference.

NECTAR Sweet substance secreted by some flowers to attract insects.

NEUTRAL SOIL A soil which is neither *acid* nor *alkaline* — pH 6.5-7.3.

NODE The point on the stem at which a leaf or bud arises.

FLOWER COLOURS

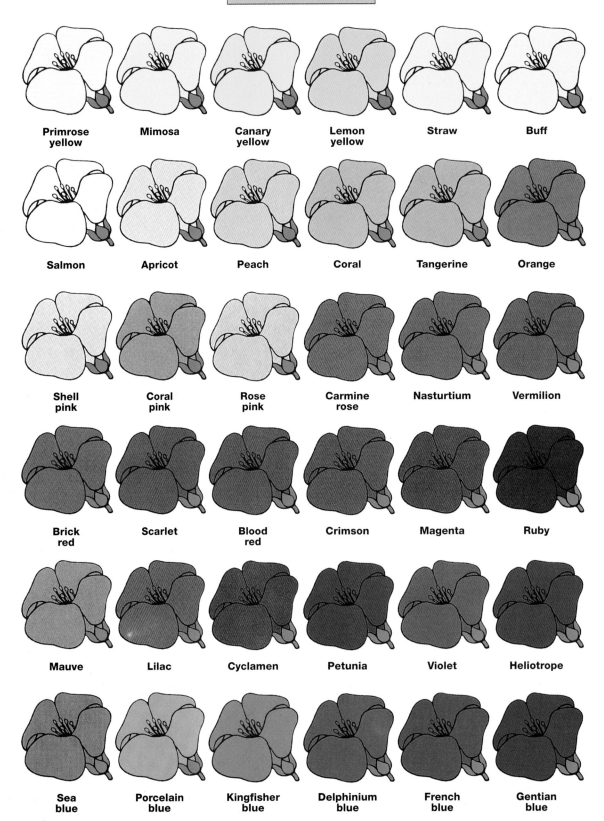

Primrose yellow	Mimosa	Canary yellow	Lemon yellow	Straw	Buff
Salmon	Apricot	Peach	Coral	Tangerine	Orange
Shell pink	Coral pink	Rose pink	Carmine rose	Nasturtium	Vermilion
Brick red	Scarlet	Blood red	Crimson	Magenta	Ruby
Mauve	Lilac	Cyclamen	Petunia	Violet	Heliotrope
Sea blue	Porcelain blue	Kingfisher blue	Delphinium blue	French blue	Gentian blue

NODULE Swelling on the root of a member of the *Leguminosae*.

NOSE The tip of a *bulb*.

NURSERY BED A plot of land on which seedlings are raised for later transfer to their permanent quarters.

O

OBLONG Longer than broad, with parallel sides.

OBOVATE Egg-shaped, with broadest end at the top. Compare *oval* and *ovate*.

OFFSET Young plant which arises naturally on the parent plant and is easily separated — e.g bulblet and cormlet.

OPPOSITE Leaves or buds which are borne in pairs along the stem. Compare *alternate*.

ORGANIC A chemical or fertilizer obtained from a source which is or has been alive.

OVAL Egg-shaped, with broadest part in the middle. Compare *obovate* and *ovate*.

OVARY The part of the female organ of the flower which contains the *ovules*.

OVATE Egg-shaped, with broadest end at the base. Compare *obovate* and *oval*.

OVULE The part of the female organ of the flower which turns into a seed after *fertilization*.

P

PALMATE Five or more lobes arising from one point — hand-like.

PANICLE An *inflorescence* made up of a number of *racemes*.

PEAT Plant matter in an arrested state of decay obtained from bogs or heathland.

PEDICEL The stalk of an individual flower.

PEDUNCLE The stalk of an *inflorescence*.

PELTATE LEAF A leaf in which the stalk is attached to the undersurface and not to an edge — e.g Nasturtium.

PERENNIAL A plant which will live in the garden or pot for years providing the conditions are suitable.

PERIANTH The outer organs of a flower — the *petals* plus the *sepals*.

PETAL One of the divisions of the *corolla* — generally the showy part of the flower.

PETALOID Term applied to organs which assume the form of petals — e.g *stamens* in double flowers.

PETIOLE The leaf stalk.

pH A measure of acidity and alkalinity. Below pH 6.5 is *acid*, above pH 7.3 is *alkaline*.

PICOTEE Term applied to a narrow band of colour on a pale ground at the edge of a petal.

PICTURE BEDDING A *bed* or *border* in which the plants are arranged to form an illustration such as a monogram or message.

PINCHING OUT The removal between the finger and thumb of the growing tip of the stem to induce bushiness or to hasten maturity.

PINNATE LEAF A leaf with a series of *leaflets* borne on either side of a central stalk.

PIPING A cutting obtained by pulling off the tip of a non-flowering shoot — e.g Pinks and Carnations.

PISTIL The female organ of a flower, consisting of the *stigma*, *style* and *ovary*.

PLUG A small but well-rooted seedling raised in a cellular tray and used for *growing on*.

PLUNGE Term applied to the insertion of a potted plant up to its rim in a bed of peat, sand or ashes.

POLLEN The yellow dust produced by the *anthers*. It is the male element which fertilizes the *ovule*.

POLLINATION The application of *pollen* to the *stigma* of the flower.

POLYCHROMATIC SCHEME A colour scheme in which a wide variety of *hues* are used — reds, violets, yellows, blues, oranges etc.

POT BOUND The stage when the roots of a bulbous plant growing in a pot are extensive enough to prevent active growth of the plant. *Potting on* or *repotting* is necessary.

POT-GROWN A bedding plant which is offered for sale in an individual pot rather than in a communal container with other specimens.

POTTING ON The transfer of a plant from its pot into a larger one.

POTTING UP The first planting out of a rooted cutting into a container.

PREVAILING WIND The direction from which the wind usually blows — an important consideration on exposed sites.

PRICKING-OUT The first planting out of a seedling or rooted cutting into another container or *nursery bed.*

PROPAGATION The multiplication of plants.

PROSTRATE Growing flat on the soil surface — procumbent.

Q

QUILLED A long and narrow petal which is tightly rolled. See *fluted*.

R

RACEME An unbranched *inflorescence* which bears flowers on stalks.

RADICAL Term applied to a leaf which arises at soil level.

RAISED BED A bed with its surface above ground level and enclosed by a retaining wall of stone, brick, wood etc.

REFLEXED A *petal* or *tepal* that is bent back.

RENIFORM Kidney-shaped.

REPOTTING The transfer of a plant from its pot into one of a similar size but with fresh compost.

RETICULATE Marked with a branched network of veins or fibres.

REVERSION A *sport* which has gone back to the colour or growth habit of its parent.

RHIZOME A horizontally-creeping underground stem which produces shoots and roots.

ROOTING HORMONE A chemical in powder or liquid form which promotes the formation of roots at the base of a cutting.

ROSETTE Term applied to a *whorl* of leaves arising at the base of a plant.

RUGOSE Rough and wrinkled.

RUNNER A stem which grows along the soil surface, rooting at intervals.

S

SAGITTATE Arrow-shaped.

SCALES The fleshy modified leaves which make up a *bulb*.

SCREE Bed of gravel, peat and soil for growing *alpines*.

SEED The reproductive unit of a flowering plant.

SEED LEAF See *cotyledon*.

SELF-COLOURED Term applied to a flower of a single uniform colour.

SELF-SEED The natural propagation of a plant by the *germination* of its *seeds* around it.

SEMI-DOUBLE A halfway point between a *single* bloom and a *double* one. In most cases there are two rows of petals.

SEPAL One of the divisions of the *calyx*.

SERIES A variety which is available in a number of different colours.

SERRATE Saw-edged.

SESSILE Stalkless.

SHADE A darker version of a *hue*.

SIMPLE LEAF A leaf which is not *compound*.

SINGLE A flower with no more than the normal number of petals.

SOILLESS COMPOST A seed, multipurpose or potting compost with a non-soil base such as *peat*.

SPADIX A fleshy *spike* in which small flowers are embedded.

SPATHE A *bract* surrounding an *inflorescence*.

SPATHULATE Spoon-shaped.

SPECIES Plants which are genetically similar and which breed true to type from seed.

SPIKE A type of flower head — see page 246.

SPIT The depth of the spade blade — about 10 in. (25 cm).

SPLASHED A petal with broken stripes of various sizes.

SPORT A plant which shows a marked and inheritable change from its parent — a *mutation*.

SPUR A tube-like projection from a flower.

STAMEN The male organ of a flower, consisting of the *anther* and *filament*.

STANDARD Two meanings — either the large upper petal of Sweet Pea-like flowers, or a plant with a tall bare stem and a terminal head of leaves and flowers.

STELLATE Star-shaped.

STEM ROOTING A root system from the stem of a *bulb*. See *basal rooting*.

STERILE Two meanings — freedom from harmful pest and disease organisms, or flowers (e.g Afro-French Marigolds) which do not set seed.

STIGMA The part of the female organ of the flower which catches the *pollen*.

STIPULE A small outgrowth at the base of the leaf stalk.

STOLON A runner-like stem which forms roots and produces a new shoot at its tip (not at intervals along its length).

STOOL The *crown* of a border perennial used for *propagation*.

STOPPING See *pinching out*.

STORAGE ORGAN The thickened root, stem or miniature plant which stores nutrients and develops roots and one or more shoots after planting.

STRAIN A selection of a *variety*, *cultivar* or *species* which is raised from seed.

STREAKED A petal with coloured bands.

STRIKE The successful outcome of taking cuttings — cuttings 'strike' whereas grafts 'take'.

STYLE The part of the female organ of the flower which connects the *stigma* to the *ovary*.

SUBSHRUB A *perennial* with stems which are woody at the base but soft and *herbaceous* above — this upper part may die down in winter.

SUBSOIL Soil below the fertile top layer.

SUCCULENT A plant with fleshy leaves and/or stems adapted to growing under dry conditions.

SYNONYM An alternative plant name.

SYSTEMIC A pesticide which goes inside the plant and travels in the sap stream.

T

TENDRIL A modified stem or leaf which can wind around a support.

TEPAL The proper name of the 'petal' when the *petals* and *sepals* of the *perianth* are identical e.g Crocus.

TERMINAL Term applied to organs borne at the tip of a stem.

THROAT The tube formed by the *corolla* of some flowers.

TILTH The crumbly structure of soil at the surface.

TINT A paler version of a *hue*.

TOMENTOSE Densely covered with fine hairs.

TRACE ELEMENT An element such as boron, iron and magnesium which is required in small quantity for healthy growth.

TRANSPIRATION The loss of water from the surface of the leaves and stems.

TRANSPLANTING The movement of a plant from one site to another.

TRUMPET A *corona* which is narrower than it is long. See *cup*.

TRUSS A flower head or tightly packed *inflorescence*.

TUBER A *storage organ* (a fleshy root or underground stem) used for propagation.

TUNIC A dry and often papery covering of corms and some bulbs.

U

UMBEL A type of flower head — see page 246.

UNISEXUAL A flower of one sex only — see *monoecious* and *dioecious*.

V

VARIEGATED Leaves which are spotted, blotched or edged with a colour which is different to the basic one.

VARIETY Strictly speaking, a naturally-occurring variation of a species — see *cultivar*.

VEGETATIVE REPRODUCTION Division, cuttings, grafting and layering as distinct from sexual reproduction by seeds.

VIRUS An organism which is too small to be seen through a microscope and which is capable of causing malformation or discoloration of a plant.

W

WEED A plant growing in the wrong place.

WELL-DRAINED SOIL A soil which is not subject to waterlogging as it allows water to drain downwards after heavy rain. It can still be *moisture-retentive*.

WHORL Leaves, petals or branches arranged in a ring.

CHAPTER 9
PLANT INDEX

Acknowledgements

The author wishes to acknowledge the painstaking work of Gill Jackson, Paul Norris and Angelina Gibbs.
Grateful acknowledgement is also made for the help received from Joan Hessayon, Colin Bailey,
Eric Steele (Colegrave Seeds), David Arnold (Suttons Seeds), David Kerley (Unwins Seeds) and
Barry Highland (Spot On Digital Imaging Ltd). The author is also grateful for the photographs and/or artworks
received from Harry Smith Horticultural Photographic Collection, Pat Brindley, John Dye, Henk Dijkman/GPL,
Steven Wooster/GPL, Lynne Brotchie/GPL, Jerry Pavia/GPL, Lamontagne/GPL, Jane Legate/GPL,
Howard Rice/GPL, Gil Hanly/GPL, Nigel Francis/GPL, Heather Angel and Marie O'Hara/Elizabeth Whiting & Associates.